D0848689

PLEASURES & PASTIMES IN
VICTORIAN BRITAIN

Among the means towards a higher civilization, I unhesitatingly assert that the deliberate cultivation of public amusements is a principal one . . . popular amusements are no trivial matter but one that has great influence on national manners and character.

W.S. Jevons, the economist, in 1878

PLEASURES & PASTIMES IN
VICTORIAN BRITAIN

PAMELA HORN

SUTTON PUBLISHING

First published in the United Kingdom in 1999 by
Sutton Publishing Limited · Phoenix Mill
Thrupp · Stroud · Gloucestershire · GL5 2BU

British Library Cataloguing in Publication Data

A catalogue record for this book is available from the British Library

ISBN 0-7509-1666-4

Jacket illustration: detail from *On the Beach* by Charles Wynne Nicholis
(1831–1903). (Scarborough Borough Council, North Yorkshire, UK/Bridgeman
Art Library, London.)

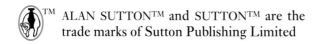
TM ALAN SUTTON™ and SUTTON™ are the
trade marks of Sutton Publishing Limited

Typeset in 11/12pt Ehrhardt.
Typesetting and origination by
Sutton Publishing Limited.
Printed in Great Britain by
Redwood, Trowbridge, Wiltshire.

Contents

Acknowledgements

I should like to thank all those who have assisted me with the preparation of this book by providing information and illustrations, or who have helped in other ways. In particular, my thanks are due to the Thomas Cook Group Ltd for permission to use their archives, and to Jill Lomer, the archivist, and her colleagues for their assistance. I should also like to thank staff at the Tate Gallery; the Rural History Centre, University of Reading; and the Museum of Welsh Life, Cardiff (particularly Mr A. Lloyd Hughes). I am grateful to Mrs I. Moon for permission to use the Sulham House photographs at the Rural History Centre, Reading. I have received much efficient assistance from staff at the various libraries and record offices at which I have worked and I am indebted to them all. These include the Bodleian Library, Oxford; the British Library; the Public Record Office; the local history libraries at Bournemouth, Cardiff, Exeter, Halifax, Liverpool, Margate (where particular thanks are due to the late Penny Ward), Newport, Isle of Wight, Oxford, and Ramsgate; and the record offices and archives centres for Derbyshire and Portsmouth, as well as the London Metropolitan Archives and Library.

Most of all I owe a debt of gratitude to my husband. He has accompanied me on many research 'expeditions' and has helped in countless other ways with comments and advice. Without his help this book could not have been written.

Pamela Horn
October 1998

NOTE ON THE SYSTEM OF REFERENCES

The reference numbers in the text refer the reader to the corresponding entry in the Bibliography at the end of the book. Notes on additional material used have been added at the end of each chapter, as relevant.

NB: When Flora Thompson's *Lark Rise to Candleford* (1963 edn) is quoted, the north Oxfordshire hamlet where she lived is given its correct name of Juniper Hill, rather than the fictional Lark Rise used in the book.

SHILLINGS AND PENCE CONVERSION TABLE

Old money	*Decimal*	*Old money*	*Decimal*
1*d*	½p	1*s* 7*d*	8p
2*d* or 3*d*	1p	1*s* 8*d*	8½p
4*d*	1½p	1*s* 9*d* or 1*s* 10*d*	9p
5*d*	2p	1*s* 11*d*	9½p
6*d*	2½p	2*s*	10p
1*s*	5p	2*s* 6*d*	12½p
1*s* 1*d*	5½p	3*s*	15p
1*s* 2*d* or 1*s* 3*d*	6p	5*s*	25p
1*s* 6*d*	7½p	20*s*	100p, i.e. £1

CHAPTER 1
The Growth of Leisure

The class-consciousness of the Victorians, which showed itself in the segregation by class and sub-class in the social zoning of towns and suburbs, in the refined grading of schools, clubs and societies, and in the differential pew-rents within the churches and chapels, was nowhere more evident than in their pleasure resorts. People of different status might be forced to meet and mingle in factories and markets, city streets and even political meetings; some might still wish to in the surviving deferential society of rural village and country town. But most . . . took their pleasures separately, in the company of their social equals.

> H.J. Perkin, 'The "Social Tone" of Victorian Seaside Resorts in the North-West' in *Northern History*, Vol. II (1976 for 1975), 180

It was a paradox of nineteenth-century Britain that while work was the bedrock upon which the Victorian vision of progress and improvement was constructed, the years between 1837 and 1901 saw the greatest upsurge in leisure pursuits hitherto witnessed. These ranged from music hall entertainment, railway excursions and commercial sporting activities to the effects of technological change in making available cheap books, newspapers and musical instruments, including the piano. The development of suburbs and the greater spending power of most workers at the end of the period similarly created opportunities for new kinds of recreation. There was a strengthening of belief in the 'rural idyll', with many of the more affluent wanting to live in villages or the outer suburbs. Concern for the conservation of the countryside grew, exemplified by the establishment of the Commons Preservation Society in 1865. Initially it sought to protect common land near London but its ideals were soon adopted elsewhere. This also had a wider aspect, as the early exhortations of the National Trust, itself set up in the mid-1890s, made clear. 'It is on the ground of patriotism and the poetry of great ideas that help a nation . . . that we call upon the lovers of Britain to rally round the cause . . . Men are beginning to learn . . . that it is good to have a country to live for as well as a fatherland to die for', declared the Trust's second *Annual Report*.[64]

Improved transport enabled excursionists to go on day trips to the seaside or the country, for picnics, rambles and boating. Already in the 1880s the South Western Railway was advertising cheap excursions from Waterloo to Windsor, while the Great Western offered visits to Henley. On one ordinary summer

Members of the well-to-do Wilder family on a picnic at Sulham, Berkshire, c. 1889. (Sulham Collection, Rural History Centre, University of Reading, and Mrs Iris E. Moon)

Sunday in July 1888, almost a thousand passengers travelled back to the capital from Henley on the last train alone.[100]

However, the spread of these recreational activities was uneven, dependent upon the availability of surplus cash and a measure of free time among consumers, as well as a weakening of the dominant work ethic. This latter particularly affected members of the middle classes, who often possessed what Peter Bailey has called 'an attenuated leisure tradition', and for whom 'the new lifespace they had won for themselves was something of an embarrassment'.[85] Even when shorter working hours and extra holidays were introduced, many felt guilty about taking advantage of them. It was an issue debated in the contemporary press, with readers assured that pastimes and pleasures were beneficial because they reduced stress and enriched the individual's cultural and intellectual life. G.J. Romanes, writing in the *Nineteenth Century* in 1879, was one who justified recreation not as 'a pastime entered upon for the sake of the pleasure which it affords, but an act of duty undertaken for the sake of the subsequent power which it generates, and the subsequent profit which it insures'. This could mean that play was as much about a change *of* work as a change *from* work. In such circumstances a scientist might relax by reading history, while an historian found recreation in the pursuit of science.[66] For some, this uncertainty over the moral justification of leisure led to an interest in gardening or in the collection of botanical and geological specimens – pursuits which engaged both mind and body. Significantly the wealthy Leeds merchant John Sheepshanks, who retired from business when he was in his thirties and settled in London, then spent the rest of his life looking after his art collection and gardening. So keen was his interest in horticulture that guests often mistook their shabbily dressed host for a gardener.[236]

It was the growth of urbanization and industrialization, especially in the north of England, which most altered the character of recreational activities. The more strictly regimented employment pattern imposed in the new machine-powered textile mills led to a lengthening of the traditional working day, from the 6 a.m. to 6 p.m. with two hours for meals, which had been common in the pre-industrial era, to a range of from 6 a.m. to 7 p.m. or 8 p.m. with only one hour for meals, which characterized the new dispensation.

Associated with this were fewer opportunities to enjoy traditional holidays such as the celebration of 'Saint Monday', when workers took a break rather than returning to their employment after their Sabbath day of rest. But the speed with which the new, regulated ways were adopted differed both regionally and between industries. Some, such as farming, domestic service and many handicraft trades, continued to follow irregular work patterns which, in the case of agriculture, were governed by seasonal fluctuations even at the end of the century. Shop assistants, too, in 1900 still had a long working day without statutory regulation, with ninety hours a week not uncommon. 'It was not at all unusual for the shops to be kept open, especially in industrial areas, after the pubs and music halls had shut, so that people could shop on their way home', claimed one man who had been a shop assistant in the late 1890s.[187] Elsewhere – for example, in Portsmouth – shops remained open till 7.30 p.m. from Monday to Thursday, 10 p.m. on Fridays and midnight on Saturdays.[393] Even in Lancashire and the West Riding of Yorkshire, where an early closing movement developed from the mid-nineteenth century to demand shorter hours and a weekly half-day holiday, reform was slow in coming. The movement there followed pressure for reduced hours by factory operatives and the desire of some evangelical churchmen for shop staff to finish work early on Saturdays so that they could better prepare to keep the Sabbath as a day of rest and religious observance.[137] But in Halifax, for example, grocers and butchers stayed open until midnight on Fridays and Saturdays into the twentieth century.[375]

The effect of these conflicting demands on employment patterns could be seen in Birmingham, where the introduction of steam-powered machinery and a greater pressure for work discipline led to a decline in the observance of Saint Monday holidays in many of the town's metal-working trades. Yet in those like gunmaking and pearl-buttonmaking, where small workshops proliferated, so did the old practices, especially when workers were paid by the piece. In the early 1860s a brass founder voiced a common complaint among employers when he declared that Birmingham was 'the idlest' manufacturing centre 'in the country.

As a rule, but little work is done on Monday. It is quite a Saint day. Many of those who do come to work on it, do not come in the morning till 10, and leave by 5 in the afternoon'.[4] It was symptomatic of this situation that Monday weddings were frequent in the city up to the 1870s. Only in that decade did Sunday become more popular – an indication that the family and friends of the bride and groom were finding it more difficult to take time off on a Monday.[286]

On a broader basis, criticisms were levelled at trades like printing and coopering where the survival of traditional production methods similarly encouraged irregular work patterns, as well as boisterous celebrations when an apprentice came out of his time. Will Crooks, who learnt the trade of coopering in London in the mid-1860s, recalled that when a youngster completed his training the greater part of the day was given over to revelry and horse-play:

> The ceremonies began at about eleven o'clock in the morning. . . . First, the apprentice was seized and put into a hot barrel. Round him stood some fifty men and boys checking every attempt he made to get out, tapping him with hammers on the head and fingers and shoulders every time he made an effort to escape. When his clothes – the last he was to wear as an apprentice – had been singed in the barrel out of all further use, he would be dragged out and tossed in the air by about a dozen of the strongest men.[182]

The initiation ceremony over, it was the apprentice's 'privilege' to buy bread, cheese and beer for his fellow workers. In the afternoon the yard was transformed into an impromptu fairground. Flags and bunting were liberally festooned and side-shows improvised. 'One feature was to persuade the fattest men to walk the tight-rope'. These traditional junketings were accompanied by periodic Saint Monday absences when the men went on a drinking spree, with some missing two or three days' work at a stretch.

London outwork trades like tailoring and shoemaking kept up the Monday holiday, too, and the popularity of excursions from the capital on that day was commented upon in the 1860s.[18] Again, in certain heavy trades such as the Sheffield metal industry, the South Wales ironworks and the brickfields and mines of the Potteries, the tradition continued to be observed. 'It appears that the unanimity of the men in upholding the customary ways was sufficient to overcome the opposition of the owners', comments Douglas Reid. In Sheffield and in the mining districts owners made the best of the situation by turning Monday into a repair day.[284]

Traditional holidays were, therefore, preserved tenaciously in some areas, and resistance to phasing them out lasted into the final quarter of the century. In the mining industry, in particular, Saint Monday was observed after the fortnightly pay, and there were unofficial days off taken not merely for drinking sessions but for sporting events, too. From the Warwickshire pits, one witness claimed in 1840 that 'when there is such a matter of universal interest as a prize fight most go to see it, and it is a day's play. Upon the average there may be five or six such occasions in the course of a summer.'[85]

But elsewhere, a new, more commercialized culture began to take hold, with an acceptance by masters and men alike of the need to curtail popular festivals and develop alternative amusements more suited to the environment of the modern industrial town. The rising spending power of working families during the 1870s and 1880s helped the process, at a time when, partly as a result of parliamentary legislation and partly due to trade union pressure in the early 1870s, regional and occupational discrepancies in the pursuit of pleasure were diminishing.[355]

It was in the textile areas that longer working hours and a more tightly regulated employment schedule had been first adopted. In coalmining, too, men whose hours at the end of the eighteenth century had been relatively short, at six to eight a day, were by 1842 almost all working a twelve-hour shift, with only short breaks for refreshment. These extensions became particularly onerous in the 1830s, at a time when workers were under pressure to put in longer hours to meet the relentless demands of new production techniques.[136]

Yet the additional burdens did not weaken the desire for leisure among working people. Consequently the 1830s also saw calls from factory operatives for the introduction of protective legislation to regulate the length of the working day. That found its first success in the 1833 Factory Act, which restricted the employment of children and young persons under eighteen years of age, so as to outlaw night-work and regulate the length of the working day. A maximum of twelve hours was allowed for youngsters between thirteen and eighteen years of age, and eight hours

Liverpool boys engaging in impromptu bathing in the Leeds–Liverpool canal during the 1890s. (Liverpool Libraries and Information Service)

for those between nine and thirteen. In addition certain statutory holidays were awarded. These were Christmas Day and Good Friday, plus eight half-days during the rest of the year. In Scotland 'any other days' could be substituted for the Christmas Day and Good Friday breaks. The provisions were extended to women in 1844 when, in addition, shorter hours on Saturdays were laid down, with 4.30 p.m. fixed as the latest leaving time. That may have been building on an earlier tradition in some textile factories, since even in 1816 there were reports of cotton mills where owners had conceded a 4 p.m. finish on Saturdays, and in 1833 workers in Yorkshire woollen mills also stopped two hours earlier on that day.[136] Then in 1847, after years of struggle, a fresh Act finally granted a ten-hour limit to the working day in textile factories. Three years later these concessions were amended, with 2 p.m. fixed as the latest leaving time on Saturdays and a 'normal' statutory working day established, between 6 a.m. and 6 p.m. Saturday night quickly became accepted as 'the ritual climax to the average workingman's week'.[85]

Meanwhile from the 1830s other industries and trades were pressing for reduced working hours. Both the engineering and building trades had secured a ten-hour day before 1847, albeit mainly through local negotiations. The Saturday half-holiday was also widely adopted – in Sheffield in the 1840s, in St Helens in 1857 and in Nottingham around 1861. In Edinburgh the Trades Council originated in agitation for a Saturday half-holiday in the early 1850s and by the early 1860s it was demanding a nine-hour day as well.[172] In Birmingham, where the acceptance of a Saturday half-holiday began in the 1850s, John Henderson of the London Ironworks, Smethwick, argued in 1853 that it helped workers to be 'steady' and promoted temperance and education by giving them time to take up 'rational' recreations on their afternoon off. In Birmingham, however, the move for the Saturday half-day was associated with the wider use of steampower in industry and the consequent desire of employers to end Saint Monday. Charles Iles, a hook and eye manufacturer, claimed in the early 1860s that the Saturday half-holiday concession had enabled him to insist on stricter discipline during the rest of the week. He could say, 'No; you have had your Saturday, and must be regular now', should they seek to revert to their former habits. The fact that the men gave up a whole working day by ending the Saint Monday holiday in return for a few hours on Saturday doubtless had not escaped him. He argued, too, that the organizing of a yearly 'gipsy' party, or holiday excursion, by his firm had raised the workers' moral standards and broadened their perspectives. 'It induces the people to keep themselves tidy to be fit for it,' he declared, 'and it enlarges their ideas by showing them things which they do not see at other times.'[4] By the mid-nineteenth century, therefore, increasing numbers of employers accepted that short holidays, properly regulated, actually benefited working people rather than becoming mere excuses for drunkenness and violence as some had earlier predicted.

During the 1870s there was further pressure for a reduction in the working day to nine hours. This had started in the building trades in the 1850s, but enjoyed little success before the economic boom of the early 1870s. Then first the engineers and later most other organized trades were able to make the breakthrough to a 54-hour week.[136] Even when economic fortunes declined most were able to retain that improvement. In the 1890s there were attempts to reduce the working day to eight hours, but with limited success. Between 1889 and 1897 it was adopted in around five hundred establishments, including the government dockyards and workshops and the majority of London engineering establishments.[157] But widespread acceptance of the eight-hour principle did not come until well into the twentieth century.

Especially among younger people the changing of jobs might be used as a way of obtaining leisure. At the end of the nineteenth century the social investigator Charles Booth talked to a 32-year-old London carpenter who had held no fewer than seventy-nine different situations. Rarely without a job for any length of time, he nonetheless seized the opportunity to have a holiday whenever he changed posts.[327]

As a result of these developments, by the end of Queen Victoria's reign there was acceptance across much of British industry, as well as in middle-class occupations like banking, insurance and the legal profession, that there were benefits in having regulated work patterns and clear distinctions between the spheres of employment and recreation. That trend was increasingly welcomed not merely for economic reasons but on moral grounds as well. Sidney and Beatrice Webb at the end of the century approvingly quoted the comments of an old Scottish compositor in 1859, that 'those trades which had settled wages, such as masons, wrights, painters, etc., *and who were obliged to attend regularly at stated hours* were not so much addicted to day drinking as printers, bookbinders, tailors, shoemakers, and those tradesmen who generally were on piecework, *and not so much restricted in regard to their attendance* at work except when it was particularly wanted'. In the Webbs' view, 'the more thoughtful workmen' accepted that when operatives had to work regularly they became 'more orderly in their conduct and spent less time at the ale-house, and lived better at home'.[374]

The alterations in the nature of the working week led to a more rigid pattern being applied to the working year as well. The factory legislation of 1833 had begun the process by laying down certain (unpaid) holidays for cotton and woollen textile workers, albeit with localized variations. Hence at Bolton, cotton operatives employed by Henry Ashworth preferred to take New Year's Day as a holiday rather than Christmas Day, and a similar choice was exercised elsewhere in the town. The mills were also idle for about four days in the year 'for the wakes and holidays of that kind, which the people have been accustomed to enjoy'. In 1840 Henry Ashworth described how when the factory had been shut on the morning of Good Friday, and the provisions of the 1833 legislation were read to the workers, pointing out their entitlement to a holiday:

> they immediately began to debate the propriety of taking or not taking the holiday proposed to them; eventually it was concluded, that as Easter Monday was following so soon after, and they could not afford to have a holiday each week . . . they would exercise a choice, and they put it to the vote who were for Good Friday and who were for Easter Monday, and the vote was unanimously carried in favour of Easter Monday . . . the same with regard to Christmas-day; in our part of the country Christmas-day is not esteemed a workman's holiday, but New-Year's day is, and the same process has been gone through . . . and they have . . . expressed a desire to take New-Year's day in lieu of it.[137]

At Whitsuntide the firm's two mills were closed from Thursday evening until Monday morning, with more than a thousand workers joining in a Whit Friday procession accompanied by the Bolton Temperance Band. 'Afterwards they separated into the two factories for tea and danced in the fields in the evening to bands provided by their employers.' The Ashworths also gave their operatives the opportunity of taking a week's unpaid holiday during the summer, and there are examples of workers travelling to London, Ireland or Scotland either individually or in groups. In 1851 parties of employees visited London for ten days to see the Great Exhibition at the Crystal Palace.[104] 'Henry Ashworth', declares the firm's historian, 'firmly believed that a fit, travelled, and educated operative was a better and more reliable employee. He believed in holidays, both for himself and his employees.'[104]

Even in cotton, therefore, some customary practices survived, especially as regards holidays. Operatives in the textile areas clung tenaciously to many traditional breaks associated with local fairs and wakes and late in the century took the lead in pressing for these to be recognized formally as holidays, although without pay.[136]

At Courtauld's silk mills in Essex, too, employees were granted holidays for fair days up to the 1870s.[129] However, as fresh factory and workshop legislation in the 1860s regularized holiday provisions outside the textile districts and as four statutory bank holidays were laid down in legislation passed in 1871 and 1875, a more uniform pattern emerged. Initially the 1871 Act had guaranteed modest annual holidays to bank workers (Easter Monday, Whit Monday, the first Monday in August, and Boxing Day). But this soon spread to other groups, such as Stock Exchange staff, while customs officers, inland revenue staff, and those in bonding warehouses and docks were covered by the Act of 1875. Most other workers joined in during the course of the following decade. As a result of these initiatives and of transport improvements, including the expansion of the railway network during the second half of the century, there was a large increase in day excursions and in attendance at sporting events. In the mid-1870s the factory inspector Robert Baker commented approvingly, 'The working class are moving about on the surface of their own country, visiting in turn exhibition after exhibition, spending the wealth they have acquired "in seeing the world" as the upper classes did in 1800, as the middle class did in 1850, and as they themselves are doing in 1875.'[85]

Not all welcomed these opportunities for the working man to make his 'mass breakout from the urban ghetto and thrust himself in upon the privacy of his betters', as Peter Bailey puts it.[85] In the 1890s some clergymen described bank holidays as a great 'curse' because of their alleged association with 'betting, drinking and extravagant expenditure'. Another critic, the novelist Ouida, remembered with disgust the descent of 'townies' upon the rural Derbyshire of her youth:

The excursion trains used to vomit forth, at Easter and in Whitsun week, throngs of the millhands of the period, cads and their flames, tawdry, blowzy, noisy, drunken; the women with dress that aped 'the fashion', and pyramids of artificial flowers on their heads; the men as grotesque and hideous in their own way; tearing through woods and fields like swarms of devastating locusts, and . . . ending the lovely spring day in pot-houses, drinking gin and bitters, or heavy

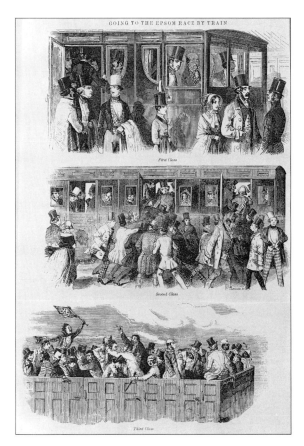

*Travelling by train in the 1840s, from the elegance of the first-class carriages to the 'cattle-truck' standard of third class. The different classes of accommodation mirrored the different ranks in society and encapsulated Victorian social attitudes. The open carriages for third-class passengers meant they were buffeted by smoke, dust, dirt and the elements, but they none the less maintained their exuberance. (*Illustrated London News, *22 May 1847)*

ales by the quart, and tumbling pellmell into the night train, roaring music-hall choruses; sodden, tipsy, yelling, loathsome creatures, such as make a monkey look a king . . . exact semblance and emblem of the vulgarity of the age.[85]

For this reason certain of the newly developing seaside resorts like Bournemouth and Torquay, which sought to attract a 'genteel' clientele, discouraged excursionists. In 1872 a correspondent from Sidmouth in Devon claimed that while it would be 'a great convenience' to have a railway to the resort, 'yet one hardly desires to see its quiet seclusion from the busy world disturbed by ugly rushes of those buoyant spirits, known as "excursionists" . . . What are gilded saloons . . . in comparison with the infinite azure of the sky.'[30] Twenty years later a travel writer was lamenting that Ilfracombe, which had become relatively easy to reach by Bristol pleasure steamers, was now susceptible to tripper invasions. Hence it lacked 'the sad dignity of Torquay and the subdued gentility of Teignmouth'. Nevertheless it could still 'turn up its nose' at the high jinks reported at Weston-super-Mare and other, more boisterous coastal resorts.[347]

This class-conscious approach was reflected in the prices charged by the hotels and boarding houses, with 'exclusive' resorts like Bournemouth having higher rates than mass-market Blackpool, or even Southport, which also aimed at a middle-class clientele. It was shown, too, in the kind of entertainment provided, 'whether classical concerts, expensive indoor baths, art galleries and museums, or brass bands, donkey rides, beach entertainers and catchpenny amusements'.[269] As an 1890 guide loftily observed of Bournemouth, the town was 'not a dull place either in the summer or winter' but there was 'less "fast life" to be seen than in some other well-known resorts'.[50] That mood of refined respectability was reflected in many of the hotel advertisements, as with Newlyn's Royal Exeter Hotel which proudly quoted a recommendation by the *Court Journal*: 'Remarkably quiet and select, with the most refined comforts of a private house.'[50]

Towns like Birmingham which had lost traditional fair day holidays or wakes were particularly enthusiastic in adopting the bank holidays, especially the August break, which became the main focus of their annual migrations. For others, however, as in industrial Lancashire and Yorkshire, traditional Easter or Whitsun junketings remained important, along with the wakes celebrations.

By the late nineteenth century, therefore, employers were increasingly conceding holidays to their workforce, although normally, as in cotton and woollen mills, these were without pay. Railwaymen employed by the Great Northern company in 1872 seem to have been the first working men to receive regular holidays with pay, and in 1897 the Amalgamated Society of Railway Servants negotiated one week's paid holiday after five years' service for workers in their industry.[136] In the state elementary education sector, too, teachers traditionally enjoyed paid holidays at Christmas, Easter and during the summer.

Within the professions generally and in the civil service, white-collar staff fared relatively well as regards working hours and conditions of employment. In 1875 the daily hours of clerks in the civil service were normally from 10 a.m. to 4 p.m. or from 11 a.m. to 5 p.m., although in private firms rather longer hours were required. The London and North-Western Railway Company, for example, expected clerks to work from 9 a.m. to 5 p.m. and the working day for most middle-class employees gradually settled at around those hours. Half-day closing on Saturdays also came relatively early, with 2 p.m. accepted as the finishing time in solicitors' and other law offices by the late 1850s. In the Bank of England Saturday closing hours were cut from 3 p.m. in 1860 to 2 p.m. in 1886.[136]

In the matter of holidays white-collar workers generally fared better than their blue-collar counterparts, although Dickens's characters such as Bob Cratchit and Newman Noggs were certainly not the only clerks given little or no time off.[79] By 1845, however, staff at the Bank of England were awarded six to eighteen days' annual leave, depending on length of service and at the end of the 1860s bank officials in the City could expect up to three weeks off after a certain period of established service. Evidence given to the Civil Service Inquiry Commission of 1875 indicated that clerks in insurance companies, solicitors' offices, railway companies and the civil service itself secured two or three weeks' paid holiday a year.[136] But in smaller firms less generous arrangements applied and in this respect, as in other aspects of employment, the free time obtained by staff depended on employers' attitudes and the bargaining power exerted by the staff themselves, as well as their seniority within the firm. As in Manchester's large warehouses, seasonal fluctuations in demand could cause overtime to be worked and thus leisure time to be curtailed.[79] Even at the Ashworth cotton factory at New Eagley near Bolton, the concessions offered by Henry Ashworth in the early Victorian years had been eroded by 1880, when one of his sons was in control. There is no evidence at this date that a full week's holiday was still given to each operative, and the only improvement was an extra two and a half days' regular holiday for the mill over and above that stipulated by current legislation. This included an annual operatives' day trip in August, which was inaugurated in 1880.[104]

Nonetheless, changes in the occupational structure of the labour force during the Victorian years led to a larger proportion of employees being engaged in professional and clerical activities.[268] As a result, the better working conditions enjoyed by most white-collar staff were being applied to a bigger percentage of the adult population than in the early part of the century, with one estimate suggesting that a quarter of families fell into the 'middle class' category by 1867.[198]

There were differences in the way in which leisure was spent not only on a regional basis but between the classes, while the strength of Sabbatarianism influenced what was deemed 'appropriate' on Sundays. On a broader front distinctions were drawn between 'respectable' and 'non-respectable' recreations. Respectable activities included participation in religious, temperance and educational events, while betting, attendance at the rougher sporting venues and visits to public houses and music halls were considered distinctly dubious.

Overall there was a disturbing ignorance between the classes as to the pastimes and pleasures each enjoyed – a situation which led Charles Dickens to complain in 1850 that the 'upper half of the world' neither knew nor cared how 'the lower half' amused itself.[315] Even within theatres, where there were socially mixed audiences, policies of hierarchical division were applied, with separate entrances for each section of the house, so that affluent 'box holders would not have to rub shoulders at a common entrance with those headed for pit benches or gallery'.[102]

Much the same was true of membership of voluntary organizations like sports clubs, musical societies and self-improvement bodies, with mechanics' institutes intended for the lower orders and literary and philosophical societies for those higher up the social scale. In Edinburgh, while certain of the city's golf clubs drew their membership from professional and superior business groups, others concentrated on those from a humbler background. Likewise 'the university and professional based Grange Cricket Club was clearly of a more exalted social tone than the cricket clubs playing on the Meadows, which on one occasion asked the aid of the Trades Council in preserving their ground'.[171]

Municipal pride and individual philanthropy led to a growing provision of parks, art galleries, libraries and museums, designed to meet the need for 'rational amusement' among members of 'respectable' society. In 1837 William Lovett, a cabinet maker and political reformer, expressed his belief that 'knowledge was the best auxiliary of political power'. He was an early advocate of the Sunday opening of art galleries and museums to provide for study and recreation and in 1841 was involved in forming the National Association for Promoting the Political and

Social Improvement of the People. This had as its aim not only political reform (including universal adult male suffrage) but the erection of public halls or schools for the people which could be used for evening lectures

> on physical, moral, and political science; for *readings, discussions, musical entertainments, dancing* and such other healthful and rational recreations as may serve to instruct and cheer the industrious classes after their hours of toil, and prevent the formation of vicious and intoxicating habits. Such halls to have two commodious play-grounds, and where practicable, a pleasure-garden attached to each; apartments for . . . a small museum, a laboratory and general workshops where the members and their children may be taught experiments in science, as well as the first principles of the most useful trades.[233]

Although no national network of improving institutions was set up in the way Lovett desired, there was greater pressure for the provision of pleasure grounds, free libraries, museums and the like in the second half of the century. This was exemplified in Bolton, where as a result of public and private initiatives the number of parks and meeting places sharply increased. 'A vast new town hall, opened in 1873, looked down upon the Free Library, the Chadwick Museum, a new Co-operative Hall, a second Temperance Hall and a rash of different clubrooms, institutes and coffee taverns', notes Peter Bailey.[85] There was evidence, too, of the widening of recreational activities. From Leeds in 1870 a working men's institute reported provision of cheap concerts, penny readings, church entertainments and public libraries in the town.[85] There were simpler pleasures, too, as Alice Foley remembered of Bolton in the 1890s, when on summer evenings the town's Court and Alley Concert Society arrived in her street with the aim of:

> infusing some sweetness and light into our drab environment. With unconfined joy we hailed the truck bearing the piano and cheered vociferously when it was heaved successfully into position at a convenient gable-end. The conductor, mounted on a borrowed chair, gathered the choristers around him, raised his baton and . . . music and soft airs . . . floated over the odd audience lounging at open doors, and hushed the harsher noises of the day. The street was not particularly musical, but its appreciation was generous and deafening . . . Equally welcome was the weekly visit of the little Italian hurdy-gurdy man who smilingly played his bright, twinkly tunes to our merry capers on the pavement . . .[161]

In many industrial towns there was a strong impetus to increase the amount of open space available. As early as 1833 the Select Committee on Public Walks had stressed the moral benefits which would accrue if the 'humbler classes' had space available where they could amuse themselves instead of engaging in such 'low and debasing pleasures' as visits to public houses or attendance at dog fights and the prize ring.

> It cannot be necessary to point out how requisite some Public Walks or Open Space in the neighbourhood of large Towns must be . . . A man walking out

with his family among his neighbours of different ranks, will naturally be desirous to be properly clothed and that his Wife and Children should be so also; . . . this desire duly directed and controlled, is found by experience to be of the most powerful effect in promoting Civilization, and exciting Industry; and your Committee venture to remark that it is confined to no age, or station, or sex . . .[20]

Thirty years later similar sentiments were expressed by a Birmingham jewellery maker when he attributed the decline in drunkenness in the town to cheap railway excursions and the opening of parks:

People . . . who go to parks and such places, try to appear in as good and neat a dress as they can, which is good for themselves by increasing their self-respect, and also has a good influence on their neighbours in the yards in which many of them live, by shaming them into making themselves respectable too. Many have been reclaimed in this way from spending their money on drink.[4]

Support for public parks thus went through three phases. First they were seen as desirable on moral grounds and as a means of countering the poor hygiene of the larger towns, with their overcrowding and inadequate sanitation. Then they were advocated as centres for rational amusement, providing opportunities for walks, the playing of games and freedom to enjoy the pleasures of nature. However, there was ambivalence with regard to this latter aspect. In certain places, such as Halifax and Bolton, there were restrictions on the activities that could be undertaken in parks. The 12-acre People's Park at Halifax was opened in August 1857, amid great celebrations, as a gift from a local carpet manufacturer.[80] Admission was free but dancing, football and similar amusements were prohibited, as were bathing in the lakes, picking the flowers, holding public meetings and carving names on buildings, seats and trees. Nevertheless it was popular with local people.

The final aspect of support for public parks arose from a broader desire to protect open spaces through the conservation movement. The aim of the Commons Preservation Society, founded in 1865, was to maintain, preserve and improve the commons and open spaces near London.[385] In particular, the society successfully protected a large part of Epping Forest from enclosure and resisted illegal attempts to enclose Berkhamsted Common. Epping Forest was an especially valued resort for London holidaymakers and during the summer months in the mid-1860s it was visited by as many as fifty thousand people in a day. 'They have the run of 1,800 acres of open spaces, where every kind of game, from cricket to "kiss in the ring," is engaged in with "perfect order and decency"', wrote one of the society's supporters in 1867.

So far, attention has been focused on the pastimes and pleasures which appealed to the lower and middle ranks of society. But the upper classes had their own well-established social round, too, much of it linked to the London 'Season', which ran from April or May to the end of July each year. As the Duke of Manchester recalled:

When one came to London for the Season . . . one came prepared for an orgy of parties, and ivory cards fell like snowflakes. One could count on being two or three deep every evening in balls, to say nothing of having a choice of dinner parties beforehand, as well as lunch and even breakfast parties.[158]

Sir Edward Hamilton, too, in May 1887 commented on the way that dinner parties had increased 'of late years. The exception is not to have a dinner provided for one now-a-days.' Although balls were rather less in favour, the time for their commencement was increasingly delayed: 'Nobody now dares to go to a House much before mid-night.' The Prince of Wales was at the centre of this social whirl, and according to Sir Edward there was 'hardly a Ball . . . with any pretentions [sic] to smartness which he not only attends but at which he remains till a very late hour . . . His capacity for amusing himself is extraordinary; he is able to get on with hardly any sleep.'

The Season involved a mixture of urban and rural pleasures, including Drawing-Rooms and *Levées* for those being presented at court, a preview of the Royal Academy's Summer Show, and sporting events like Ascot, the Derby, Henley Regatta and the Eton v Harrow cricket match.

In August, society left London for yachting at Cowes and grouse shooting in Scotland, to be followed by partridge shooting on country estates in the late autumn and then the hunting season during the winter. For these activities a series of country-house parties were held and were an important feature of entertaining among the leading families in the country. August and September were also the months for travelling abroad . . . Fashionable weddings usually took place during May and June and the early summer was considered the best time for other popular events such as garden parties, picnics and river excursions. The season for balls was the winter and into the early spring.[114]

Everyone who was anyone lived near Hyde Park, preferably on Park Lane, and according to the mid-century German visitor Theodor Fontane those with social aspirations would be ashamed to live east of Grosvenor Place and Hyde Park Corner. He also claimed to know of families unable to leave London at the end of the Season who opted to spend September living in the back rooms of their home, while the front was firmly closed up, in order to give neighbours the impression they were out of town, like the rest of the fashionable world.

Even at the end of the century there were still only about four thousand families actively involved in high society during the Season. Early in the century it had probably been nearer four hundred families.[145] The intimate, close-knit nature of these social occasions is shown in diary entries of the period, such as those of Cecilia Harbord, eldest daughter of the 5th Baron Suffield. Her brother Charles was a guards officer and on 14 May 1877 she and her father attended a big field day, involving her brother's regiment, at Wimbledon.

I never liked anything better. They had a battle with a sham enemy, we stood close behind Charlie's men for some time for [I] did not object to the firing.

SOCIAL AGONIES.
(Disadvantage of resembling a Celebrity.)

She. "OH, HOW DO YOU DO, DEAR MR. LYON? HAVE YOU FORGIVEN ME FOR
CUTTING YOU AT MRS. LEO HUNTER'S LAST NIGHT? I WAS ACTUALLY STUPID
ENOUGH TO TAKE YOU FOR THAT HORRID BORE, MR. TETTERBY THOMPSON, WHOM
YOU'RE SAID TO BE SO LIKE. IT'S A HORRID LIBEL—YOU'RE NOT LIKE HIM A BIT."

*The importance of tact when observing
the social niceties in high society is
pinpointed by* Punch *(1887).*

Col. Williams was in command of the Blues . . . They all marched past
beautifully. We went at a foot's pace nearly all the way to London with Charlie's
battalion . . . In the evening we went to the Albert Hall to hear Wagner conduct
his Lohengrin & other things (selections). It was quite beautiful.

  After that went to a drum [i.e. an evening reception or 'kettledrum'] at
Grosvenor House, which ended with a capital dance. The Prince [of Wales] was
there.

Similarly the Countess of Warwick remembered morning drives in the park in
her phaeton, when friends gathered round to chat of 'future meetings, and of
dances, lunches, and dinners within "the Circle." . . . One "booked" friends for
luncheon, and perhaps drove them down Piccadilly prancing on the wide sweep
of pavement, glancing up at the Turf Club window as a possible place to find an
extra man for a dinner-party.'[372] Despite the effects of agricultural depression in
reducing the rental income of some leading landed families during the final
quarter of the nineteenth century, this pattern of aristocratic leisure was little
curtailed before the end of the Victorian era.

  Some contemporaries saw recreation as a way of breaking down class barriers, as
with the social mix of people attending great national sporting events such as the

Derby. In the early 1870s the journalist Blanchard Jerrold praised the role of the Derby in encouraging an intermingling of classes 'for a few hours on the happiest terms . . . It cannot be pretended by the keenest lover of the course and the hunting-field that racing promotes any of the virtues . . . But this Derby-day has its bright – even its useful side, too. It gives all London an airing, an "outing"; makes a break in our over-worked lives; and effects a beneficial commingling of classes.'[56] But others, such as the French observer Hippolyte Taine, were more cynical. Taine was contemptuous of a class familiarity which lasted for a single day.

> Good humour and unreserved merriment; . . . P—, one of our party, has met his usual coachman at table with a gentleman, two ladies, and a child. The gentleman had employed and then invited the coachman; the coachman introduces P—, who is amicably compelled to drink port, sherry, stout, and ale . . . but this lasts for a day only, after the manner of the ancient saturnalia. On the morrow distinctions of rank will be as strong as ever, and the coachman will be as respectful, distant, as is his wont.[137]

Unfortunately, too, most events in Victorian Britain which attracted large crowds easily descended into disorder. Violence occurred at all kinds of mass meetings, from processions of the Salvation Army to public hangings, until these became illegal in 1868. Sporting events were no exception. During the late 1860s there was trouble at a number of horse races in the London area, with welshing a major cause of violence. At Enfield a jockey accused of not trying was saved from lynching by angry punters only through the intervention of armed racecourse officials, while elsewhere pitched battles were fought between welshing bookmakers and those seeking to obtain their winnings. So severe were the disturbances at some race meetings around the capital that in 1879 legislation was passed for their suppression.[355] Such occurrences did little to promote the class conciliation desired by those advocating leisure as a means of securing communal co-operation. The same was true of ritual derby matches in football and rugby in industrial areas, with fights between spectators and attacks on the referee being all too frequent. Rugby in late nineteenth-century South Wales has been described as being 'as coarse and violent as the raw frontier society which nurtured it'.[317]

Furthermore, the fact that most social groups chose to spend their leisure in very different ways made the mediatory influence of pastimes and pleasures difficult to achieve. Even when a wide cross-section of the community attended a given event they were usually segregated by differing admission prices or separate enclosures for members and non-members of the club where the activity was staged.

Similar ambiguities surround the 'social control' aspect of leisure and its association with class hegemony. It has been argued by some that it was the desire of employers to control or mould the leisure pursuits of the lower orders that led them to introduce works outings or to make other provisions for recreational activities, rather than mere benevolence. For example, in Halifax the firm of Akroyd & Son set up a Working Men's College for operatives, with a library, reading room and various educational facilities. Additional organizations established in connection with this included a Mutual Improvement Society; a Young Women's Institute;

Two working-class girls trying on their new hats in readiness for a day out at the Epsom Derby, c. 1900. (The author)

a Musical Society that eventually became a well-respected Choral Society; a Cadet Corps, with a drum and fife band; and a Floral and Horticultural Society in connection with workers' allotment gardens. Annual produce shows were organized with prizes awarded, and encouragement was given to employees to take up outdoor pursuits. Edward Akroyd was president of the whole venture and those attending the Working Men's College were awarded inscribed medals for perseverance, regular attendance and good conduct.[275] Similarly, at Styal in Cheshire the cotton manufacturer Samuel Greg provided a number of pastimes and pleasures for the workers, including music classes, gardens, a playground for games, and tea parties during the winter. Yet the response to this carefully targeted paternalism was not always what the employer intended, as far as making the labour force amenable to his wishes. Greg was much offended when his operatives went on strike in 1847 over the introduction of new manufacturing methods, especially as they had made no attempt to negotiate with him before stopping work.[85]

As Peter Bailey comments, employees might welcome the benefits offered by philanthropic masters but they were prepared to accept them only on their own terms, and were often suspicious of the motives which lay behind such initiatives. One worker expressed typical reservations when recalling his unease at a master attempting to ingratiate himself with his men at the traditional printers' autumn feast:

> Somehow it generally happens that this brief moment of relaxation is immediately followed by a tightening of the reins of government and a rather rough assertion of authority. As if the employer were fearful that his previous sentiments of universal brotherhood with which the hearts of employers expand convulsively and regularly once a year should be mistaken for anything more than they are meant for – mere flowers of rhetoric . . .[85]

Yet despite such cynicism and the persistence of strong class and regional differences in the recreations pursued during the Victorian years, leisure activities overall were both more civilized and more regimented in the late nineteenth century than they had been sixty or seventy years earlier. The blatant abuses

*Rinking (or skating) was particularly popular in the 1870s. It provided ample opportunities for a little harmless flirtation away from the censorious eye of a chaperon. (*Punch, *18 March 1876)*

associated with horse racing, for example, had largely been eradicated by the influence of the Jockey Club, and the brutality and depravity connected with public hangings and prize fights were eliminated as such public spectacles were no longer permitted.[151] By the mid-1880s what Peter Bailey has described as the 'irregular and spasmodic flux of pre-industrial leisure' had been compartmentalized into 'standardised instalments that came with the routine of the modern working week and year'.[85] It was the commercialization of leisure which was to be the most striking feature of the final years of the century rather than its being an excuse for debauchery and disorder, as many of the better-off had feared would be the case when the queen's reign began.

Additional Sources Used

[Anon.], *A Glance at the Commons and Open Spaces near London. Reprinted from the 'Parochial Critic'* (London, 1867) at London Metropolitan Archives and Library.

Commons Preservation Society: Objects of the Society (London, n.d. [1865]), at London Metropolitan Archives and Library.

Devon Weekly Times, 23 August 1872.

Diary of Cecilia Harbord, later Lady Carrington, in Carrington Diaries, MS. Film 1097 at the Bodleian Library, Oxford.

Diary of Sir Edward Hamilton for 1887 at the British Library, Add. MSS. 48,646.

Factory Act for 1833 3 & 4 William IV, cap. 103.

Theodor Fontane, *Ein Sommer in London* (Frankfurt am Main and Leipzig, 1995). (The book was first published in 1854, two years after Fontane's visit.)

CHAPTER 2

Family Amusements and Pastimes

Mr. and Mrs. Veneering were bran-new people in a bran-new house in a bran-new quarter of London . . . All their furniture was new, all their friends were new, all their servants were new, their plate was new, their carriage was new, their harness was new, their horses were new, their pictures were new, they themselves were new . . . This evening the Veneerings give a banquet . . . fourteen in company all told. Four pigeon-breasted retainers in plain clothes stand in line in the hall . . . The great looking-glass above the sideboard reflects the table and the company. Reflects the new Veneering crest, in gold and eke in silver, frosted and also thawed, a camel of all work. The Herald's College found out a Crusading ancestor for Veneering who bore a camel on his shield (or might have done if he had thought of it), and a caravan of camels take charge of the fruits and flowers and candles, and kneel down to be loaded with the salt.

Charles Dickens, *Our Mutual Friend*
(London, 1864–5), Chapter 2

THE DOMESTIC SCENE

The importance attached to family life and domesticity in Victorian Britain made the home a focus for many leisure pursuits, especially in upper- and middle-class circles but extending down the scale as well. Not only were special occasions like birthdays, funerals, weddings and Christmas marked by family get-togethers but there was much visiting between relatives at other times. In the upper ranks of society, where family networks were large and contacts well maintained, this could mean the interchange of hospitality on a major scale for weeks at a time. One child, whose mother was a daughter of the Duke of Abercorn, remembered growing up 'more or less as one gigantic family of thirty-nine with a plurality of residences'. A similar situation existed with Mary Lyttelton, who eventually had twelve children, and her sister, Catherine Gladstone, who had eight. 'Great cavalcades of nurses and children' travelled between Hagley, the Lytteltons' Worcestershire estate, and the Gladstone homes in London and at Hawarden.[195]

Among working-class families links could also be close. Walter Southgate, who was brought up in Bethnal Green, London, in the 1890s, recalled that in his neighbourhood few homes were without a weekly exchange of visits, either on Saturday or Sunday.

Thrown largely upon their own resources for entertainment and amusement, apart from the public house and music halls, relatives met regularly. In my boyhood there seemed never-ending gatherings at each other's houses of uncles, aunts and cousins. Children were relegated to the kitchen until required to say their party piece and given a clap and a piece of cake, for their effort. Beer flowed freely at twopence a pint, providing all the stimulus needed to dance and sing . . . They . . . sang the popular current music hall 'hits' and all the old favourites of which they never tired. The golden rule at all such gatherings was that everyone had to do their best singing solo; no matter if we had heard the darn song a thousand times before no-one ever cribbed at hearing it again . . . Father wore a battered high hat, carried a pail and a sack on his back, did slapstick stuff with old corsets and an assortment of ladies underwear, which never failed to raise a great deal of laughter and applause.[319]

There was family gossip to catch up on, too, and sometimes, especially among Irish families, the old folk would tell the young 'ancient legends and fairy stories'.[106]

These unsophisticated, boisterous pastimes were far removed from the idealized picture of domestic harmony put forward by early Victorian commentators such as the Quaker William Howitt. For Howitt, happiness was 'a fire-side thing . . . a thing of grave and earnest tone; and . . . the more our humble classes come to taste of the pleasures of books and intellect, and the deep fire-side affections which grow out of the growth of heart and mind, the less charms will the outward forms of rejoicing have for them'.[137]

Howitt was writing in 1838 but a similar picture of refined domesticity was being advocated nearly thirty years later by the distinguished art critic and social reformer John Ruskin, when he defined the 'true nature of home' as a 'place of Peace; the shelter, not only from all injury, but from all terror, doubt, and division'. It was the woman's role to achieve this desirable end by providing 'order, comfort and loveliness' within its walls.

But whether seen as a centre of entertainment and conviviality, as in the Southgate family, or as a place of peace and refuge, as with Howitt and Ruskin, the central importance of the home was widely accepted. So was the strong desire of the Victorian middle classes to extend their own vision of domestic life to the lower orders.[253] Nevertheless, even the most optimistic recognized that for families residing in overcrowded urban slums and tenements, that was difficult to attain. As Henry Mayhew commented in the middle of the century, it was 'idle and unfeeling' to suggest that people who had spent their days in heavy labour and whose homes were 'mostly of an uninviting character' should be expected to 'forego *all* amusements, and consent to pass their evenings by their *no* firesides, reading tracts or singing hymns'.[137] The public house and the music hall offered a greater prospect of comfort and pleasure even if these were precisely the venues that middle-class reformers wished to render unappealing.

During the summer, however, working people could enjoy casual companionship with neighbours by gossiping in the street. Angus Bethune Reach, who visited Manchester in 1849, commented on how the families of mill operatives would laugh and talk 'from window to window, and door to door'. The womenfolk sat in groups upon their thresholds, sewing and knitting, with their children sprawling beside them, and there was 'the amount of sweethearting going forward which is naturally to be looked for under such circumstances'.[83] Elsewhere, as in Middleton near Macclesfield in Cheshire, Reach met an elderly silk weaver who told him that when he and his friends had free time they would simply 'turn out' and have 'a great talk' about politics and 'what they're doing in Lunnon, and smoke our pipes. We often have long discussions – we're great chaps for politics, and we just go into each other's houses and talk'.[83] A younger colleague added that they liked 'good company, and a good joke and soom'mut to laugh at'.

Among the better-off, meanwhile, there was a growing desire to move out of the insanitary and over-crowded central areas of the larger towns to new houses on the suburban estates which were springing up. This became increasingly important in the second half of the nineteenth century as better transport and growing wealth among the burgeoning commercial and professional classes enabled them to seek a healthier home environment and the companionship of those of similar social status. One such example was provided by Bedford Park in London, where between 1875 and 1881 the distinguished architect Norman Shaw created what has been called the first garden suburb. The park was planned on community lines, even though the houses were individually designed in the currently fashionable Queen Anne style of red brick, sliding sash windows and white paintwork. A club house, inn, church, shops and art school were provided to emphasize the communal atmosphere and from the start the estate attracted families of a professional or artistic background.[112]

A similar sense of community established itself in Llanishen, built on land belonging to the Bute estate on the outskirts of Cardiff. As prominent businessmen and political leaders from the city moved to this outer suburb, those with social aspirations followed in their wake during the 1880s. The newcomers hastily joined the clubs and societies that the pioneers had set up. Among these was Thomas Ensor, a leading solicitor and Conservative councillor in Cardiff. When he died in 1895 his obituary noted that he had been one of 'the first to build a village residence at Llanishen and his example was soon followed by many others with the result that the district surrounding the pretty little village was quickly dotted with handsome mansions'.[185]

Similar development took place on the roads leading to Manchester, Sheffield, Birmingham and other major cities, with estates laid out and new villas erected. They appealed to artisans as well as to the substantial middle classes, both groups being attracted by properties offering 'flourishes of architectural respectability' and acceptable neighbours.[134] Many also had private gardens, and although these varied according to the size of the property and the affluence of the resident, they offered a refuge from the noise and stress of urban life.[131] There, flowers and vegetables could be grown, a few chickens or rabbits kept, and for the children there was space for 'a mild game of cricket or football'.[106]

On a broader basis, both in town centres and in the suburbs, gas lighting made the streets safer, while in London it transformed the appearance of the city and its night life.

The increasing value attached to the home as a place of refuge and a status symbol led to greater attention being paid to its contents and its comforts. Charles Dickens in *Our Mutual Friend* mocked the pretensions of nouveaux riches families like the Veneerings, with their newly discovered coat of arms and recently acquired house and furnishings.[397] But even among the less ostentatious, greater affluence and the diversification of domestic activities encouraged increased specialization in rooms. Some larger houses emulated the residences of the aristocracy by having smoking, music and billiard rooms as well as a library, dining room, drawing room and perhaps a morning room or boudoir for female members of the family. There they could receive friends, write letters and practise on the pianoforte. But in the average dwelling such lavish use of space was impossible, and the male head of the house probably had to be content with a small study and his wife with the drawing room as their respective special spheres.

The concern with wealth and status led to the acquisition of large quantities of solid furniture, heavy carpets and a variety of ornaments and knicknacks, to say nothing of looking-glasses, silver and brassware. An inventory of the contents of the Kensington home of Linley Sambourne, a *Punch* cartoonist, and his wife Marion in 1877 shows, for example, no fewer than ten chairs in the best bedroom with another ten in the day nursery, while sixty-two photographs hung in the front hall, thirty-five in the rear hall and ninety-four on the staircase. A vast array of photographs was also displayed in the dining room, together with a large quantity of blue-and-white porcelain, and all of the rooms had lampshades made by Mrs Sambourne herself. To modern eyes this might seem impossibly overcrowded, but to the Victorians it signalled comfort and security.[257]

However, in households with several children and a number of servants, the cluttered condition of the rooms proved oppressive and caused tensions and disagreements within the family. Virginia Woolf, writing of her childhood at the end of the century, recalled the house as containing:

> innumerable small oddly shaped rooms . . . There were chests of heavy family plate. There were hoards of china and glass. Eleven people aged between eight and sixty lived there, and were waited upon by seven servants, while various old women and lame men did odd jobs with rakes and pails by day.

In their quest for comfort and display, householders were assisted by technological changes. Developments in textile weaving made possible the mass production of intricate patterns, and there were experiments with artificial aniline dyes which made available a new range of bright colours for furnishings and clothing during the 1860s. In pottery, Parian ware or 'statuary porcelain' was introduced, in imitation of the marble figures owned by the aristocracy, and from the late 1820s in the glass industry a new process made possible the mass manufacture of a handmade cut-glass

A middle-class London family taking tea in their suburban garden, c. 1900. (The author)

effect. In the following decade mechanization led to the cutting of high quality, very thin veneers which could be applied to cheap wood to make inexpensive furniture look costly, while the production of springs gave 'a greater depth, softness and curvature to the upholstery of seat furniture without the skill and expense involved in traditional stuffing'.[90] Wallpaper, too, was cheapened by the repeal in 1836 of a tax on patterned paper and three years later by the patenting of a machine which could print multi-coloured patterns in a single operation on a continuous roll of paper. 'Within a generation the price of wallpaper dropped to ¼d. a yard and what had formerly been a luxury item became a widely available commodity', note the authors of *Victorian Interior Style*.[90] Designers gained inspiration from a variety of sources, including architecture, landscape and flower paintings, while cost-conscious householders were aware that dark papers had the advantage of not showing the dirt created by airborne industrial pollution. New methods of production and the repeal of duty in 1845 likewise made mirrors less expensive, and buttoning, which emphasized the depth of upholstery, was introduced from the 1850s.

It was not only furniture and textiles which were affected. Prints and etchings became cheaper and adorned many walls, while the demand for paintings grew.

Sometimes this was in response to a genuine appreciation of art, with the number of serious middle-class art collectors increasing sharply in the Victorian years.[236] But often it arose from a desire to add colour and distinction to a room rather than from any more aesthetic motive. Small 'cabinet' paintings might be sold by jobbing artists for as little as £3 or £4 apiece, so that when householders tired of them they could be discarded without too much expense. Alternatively, cheap second-hand paintings or prints could be acquired. When Alfred Tennyson and his wife moved into their new home in 1856 they found their existing pictures did not cover all the stains on the wallpaper. Rather than undertake repapering Mrs Tennyson appealed to a friend to look out at 'pawnbrokers' for paintings of 'red and flesh colour and bright frames'. She preferred 'oldest copies of oldest pictures to be sold for one farthing each barring the discount on ready money'.[76]

A further alternative was suggested by an advertisement in the *Western Mail* in February 1872, when 'John Frost's Gallery of Fine Arts' in Bristol offered to sell oleographs 'produced by an entirely original process', which had 'already attracted much attention for their extreme cheapness and truthfulness as copies'. They had 'in all respects the appearance of original oil paintings, and can be confidently recommended not only as cheap and excellent art for wall adornment, but as admirable studies for young artists'.

In addition to embellishing the walls of socially aspiring householders, the collecting of prints might play another role. Preserved in portfolios on the drawing-room table they could be 'leafed through on rainy days for the entertainment of guests (including daughters' suitors, who found the examination of prints side by side on a sofa the closest one could get to one's beloved)'. In this way they offered a pleasant and relatively inexpensive diversion.[77]

Over the years, however, there were fashion changes in what was considered desirable in furniture, wallpaper and textiles. This was particularly true from the 1860s under the influence of reformers such as William Morris and the Arts and Crafts movement. Although traditional styles remained more prevalent than the progressive schemes of the innovators, their desire to restore craftsmanship, natural designs and medieval artistic values to industrial society proved influential with many.

Morris was much affected by the views of John Ruskin and by the latter's belief that goods produced by mass-manufacturing methods were degrading symbols of a 'slave' social system. Initially, Morris's interest in the decorative arts had been inspired by dislike of what he saw as the degenerate and shoddy goods of commercial producers. In 1861 he and some friends established the firm of Morris, Marshall, Faulkner & Co. (later Morris & Co.) to make available 'Fine Art . . . in Painting, Carving, Furniture and the Metals'.[338] Their aim was to revive craft skills and to introduce simple, naturalistic patterns for textiles, wallpapers, furniture and stained glass, the latter being produced in large quantities not merely for churches but for domestic interiors as well. To many middle-class householders anxious to protect the privacy of their domestic lives, stained glass had the advantage of letting in the light and providing colour while excluding the prying eyes of outsiders. By the end of the nineteenth century it was claimed that examples of 'stained or transfer-painted glass' could be found in almost every

Two ladies reading quietly in the sitting room at The Elms, Hartley Wintney, Hampshire, in the late nineteenth century. The photograph shows a cluttered interior, so beloved by well-to-do Victorians. (Sulham Collection, Rural History Centre, University of Reading, and Mrs Iris E. Moon)

English 'artistic interior worthy of the name'.[90] In bringing that about Morris & Co. had played a significant role.

Morris's own approach to home furnishing was simple, as in his oft-quoted advice to have 'nothing in your house that you do not know to be useful or believe to be beautiful'. He disliked the clutter of the average well-to-do Victorian residence, declaring in 1882 that he had 'never been in a rich man's home which would not have looked better for having a bonfire made outside of nine-tenths of all it held'.[90] Contents should be kept to an essential minimum, which he defined as 'a cupboard for books, a table sturdy enough to work at, a few comfortable chairs, a couch to lie on, and a fireplace to keep warm'.[90] In practice, his own London drawing room scarcely met these austere standards, and that was still less the case with most of his clients. But his influence was important in emphasizing the value of naturalistic design and painted decorations, often with a medieval or allegorical motif applied to major items of furniture. In artistic circles, in particular, the firm's simple, black rush-bottomed country chairs drove out the heavily upholstered French-polished articles produced by more conventional manufacturers. However, it was with wallpapers and textiles that the company achieved its greatest success. The firm began to sell wallpaper from 1864, while chintzes and the first carpet designs appeared in 1875. Many had patterns of flowers or leaves, with the highly popular rose trellis design for wallpaper inspired by the trellis in Morris's own garden.

Following on from these ideas there developed in the 1870s the 'aesthetic' movement which emphasized the importance of art and beauty within the home. It found expression in the use of subtle colours and angular shapes in decoration, and in the purchase of foreign accessories and ornaments, particularly from the Near East and from China and Japan, or derived from Japanese designs. In promoting these ideas the firm of Liberty played a major part from its establishment in 1875. Initially it concentrated on selling oriental silks and embroideries, which were imported in large quantities, and by the end of the 1870s the shop had become a haunt of poets, painters and others with artistic pretensions. By the 1880s carpets, furnishings, fabrics, jade, china, pottery, tapestries, wrought ironwork and furniture were all on offer. In 1883 Furnishing and Decorating Studios were opened to advise potential clients, and within a few years the growth of orders for decorating meant that paper-hanging was also added.[115] By the 1890s, as an historian of the firm has argued, Liberty's unique contribution lay in having 'created an entirely new taste in fabrics, dress and interior decoration', which drew inspiration from all over the world and differed greatly from the solid furniture and heavy fabrics of mainstream Victorian fashion. At the turn of the century it offered a complete interior decorating service, including the labour to carry out its schemes. It appealed primarily to the wealthy, the aesthetic and the avant-garde rather than to mass consumers. One appreciative client was the Crown Princess of Greece. In a letter to her mother written in July 1896 she described with excitement a visit to the shop to buy furniture for an English cottage she was building near Athens: 'We spent I don't know how many hours at Maple [another furniture store] and Liberty! I *screamed* at the things . . . but they were too lovely: *No*, these shops I go mad in them! I would be ruined if I lived here longer!'[71]

Although the aesthetic movement was taken up most vigorously by the affluent, those of modest means but artistic inclinations could have some share of it. When Linley Sambourne and his new wife moved into their Kensington home in the mid-1870s not only did they purchase wallpaper from Morris & Co., but their most expensive single item of furniture was a sideboard with inset panels of mirror, tiles, carvings and paintings of fruit, in the dining room. The olive-green paint they chose for this room and the division of the walls into three bands of colour, with William Morris wallpaper on the central section, were typical of 'aesthetic' ideas.[257]

For the nouveaux riches who wished to learn how to furnish their home in the best style in order to impress their friends and provide comfort for themselves, a wealth of advice books appeared. These included Charles Locke Eastlake's *Hints on Household Taste* (1868) and the popular *Art at Home* series, published by Macmillan in 1876. That described in detail the function and contents of each of the major apartments in a house.[90] Even late Victorian advertisements for such consumer goods as chocolate biscuits and alcoholic drinks could offer incidental hints on how a well-furnished interior should look. Similar guidance was provided by fashionable shops like Liberty's or Maple, and by the new department stores. These were particularly useful in providing help for the lower middle classes. Potential purchasers could walk around inspecting the displays of furniture and fabrics, discovering what was fashionable and with prices clearly marked. At the same time they might see other items, such as ornaments, pictures and mirrors, which suggested purchases they had not previously thought of and they would be thus educated in the diversity of semi-luxuries available 'in the pleasantest manner imaginable'.[149] One of the earliest of these stores was established by William Whiteley in Bayswater during the 1860s. By 1875 he had started to sell and repair furniture, carpets, china and glass and in the following year began to undertake building and house decoration. In a district filled with large stucco-fronted houses requiring cleaning and repairing at regular intervals, this latter initiative proved particularly lucrative.[226]

Even the less affluent expected improvements in their living standards. At the end of the century the status symbols aspired to were a separate parlour with a piano, an overmantel covered with ornaments, and an upholstered suite. Many were unable to attain their goals but a 'velvet plush cover with tasselled ends might conceal a cheap, deal table-top', and a pair of American rocking-chairs served as substitutes for the upholstered suite.[198] In the bow window might be displayed a potted palm, while a table in the middle of the room, covered with a bright cloth, would be laden with books, prizes and 'souvenirs of sundry trips to the seaside'.[106]

Another aspect of the domestic pleasures and pastimes of these years was the increasing attention paid to the entertaining of friends. That was true not merely of the upper classes, who had always had the will and the means to do this, but of those lower down the scale. It was especially true of the middle classes who were increasingly able to afford to employ servants to carry out the laborious tasks of preparing and serving meals. Books of advice on household management and etiquette proliferated to guide hostesses about menus, table arrangements and similar matters. Many, including Marion Sambourne, found difficulty in organizing dinner parties in their early married life and they resorted to books such as Mrs Isabella Beeton's *Book of Household Management*, published in 1861, and *Family Fare, or the Young Housewife's Daily Assistant*, which first appeared in 1864 and was Mrs Sambourne's favourite.

The extravagance of the meals offered was an indication of the rising expectations of a class once noted for its thrift and frugality. This applied not merely to the food itself but to the table linen, crockery, cutlery, crystal and table decorations. In her diary, Marion Sambourne commented on the menus at the dinner parties she attended, as well as those she gave herself. In January 1878, for example, she noted a 'charming dinner' at Mrs Marcus Stone's, at which were served: 'Spring soup. Filleted soles, brown gravy. Filet de boeuf, thimble potatoes. Goose pieces in tomato sauce, garlic & parsley. Saddle of mutton, artichokes. Rice meringue, mince pies.'[257]

The Sambournes themselves favoured fairly small dinner parties of eight to twelve people, as in June 1880 when the menu included kippered cod's roe, capers, bread and butter as well as 'Julienne soup. Cold trout, sauce piquante. Pigeons with asparagus. Forequarters of lamb, mint sauce, tomato salad, potatoes. Beans aux francais. Ducklings, green peas. Coffee savoy, plum tart, cream.

Anchovies, parmesan cheese, etc.'[257] Such over-indulgence may seem deserving of censure to modern critics, but to aspiring Victorian hostesses, keeping a good table, and being seen to do so, was a sign of success.

Floral decorations for the dinner table also needed consideration. The anonymous author of *Party-Giving on Every Scale* (1882) advised that flowers like hyacinths, syringa and jasmine, which had a powerful perfume, should be avoided and preference given to those with a refreshing scent. In a small dining room guests could easily feel overpowered 'and the relish for the good dinner is destroyed'. He suggested, too, that firm limits be placed on the time spent upon the meal: 'the best of dinners should not be prolonged beyond an hour and a quarter'.[271]

In the late Victorian years large retailers like Harrods offered hostesses additional services, such as entertainers or the hire of marquees to serve as temporary ballrooms. Banjo quartets and musical jugglers were among the performers available for hire at private parties by the more frivolous. Edison's Phonograph, which 'Reproduces the newest Songs, Bands, Speeches, Recitations, Dialogues, &c.' could be secured at £2 2s for up to two hours.[73]

During the century the fashionable dinner hour crept forwards from 4 or 5 p.m., with a light supper served at 10 p.m., to around 7.30 or 8 p.m. by the 1850s. 'Formal dining', concludes Leonore Davidoff, 'became the centre of social life, possibly once a week for the aristocracy, once a month for those further down the scale. Elaborate dinner arrangements, the mixture of guests and correct organisation of precedence in the procession from drawing room to dining hall, were part of the upper-class hostess's preoccupations.'[145] Certainly Consuelo, Duchess of Marlborough, remembered the intricate arrangements made for the twenty-five to thirty guests who assembled for weekend parties at Blenheim Palace during the 1890s. Not only had menus to be approved, but hours were spent considering how best to place the guests for the 'three ceremonial meals they would partake with us, for the rules of precedence were then strictly adhered to, and not only in seating arrangements but also for the procession in to dinner'.[89]

'At homes' were another domestic social ritual involving the upper and middle classes. 'Calling' was an important activity for most better-off Victorian ladies, and although calls could be made on any day, many women fixed a time each week when they held open house for friends who cared to visit for conversation and perhaps light refreshment. Marion Sambourne made a list of such days at the front of her diary, indicating the range of her social circle. Her own 'at home' was on a Tuesday, and she normally received about four or five visitors. They were offered tea and cakes and a pleasant chat, although they were not expected to stay long. 'Sometimes gentlemen called too, and then the conversation took a more lofty tone. Occasionally the visitors were very boring, "Mr. Emery & sister called, both densely slow".'[257]

Mrs Beeton stressed the importance of making the right contacts on these occasions:

A gossiping acquaintance, who indulges in the scandal and ridicule of her neighbours, should be avoided as a pestilence . . . Friendships should not be hastily formed, nor the heart given, at once, to every new-comer . . . It is not advisable, at any time, to take favourite dogs into another lady's drawing-room,

A comfortable working-class home in London, with pictures on the wall, ornaments, an ornate clock and a sewing machine, c. 1900. (The author)

for many persons have an absolute dislike to such animals; and besides this, there is always a chance of a breakage of some article occurring, through their leaping and bounding here and there.[52]

This advice was particularly necessary in the later Victorian years when lap dogs had become a fashion item for some women, with animals imported from China and Japan 'to satisfy a demand for novelty which could quickly be transformed into a social imperative'.[362] Less exotic dogs were kept by many families at a time when pet ownership (including the keeping of caged songbirds) was seen as adding to the pleasures of domestic life.

Lower down the scale formal entertaining was important, too, with the parlour being carefully set aside in the late Victorian years as a place to be used on Sundays when family and friends came to tea. In Walter Southgate's home it was always known as 'Mother's parlour', and in the window fronting the street there stood a table with a pot holding the aspidistra, together with a Bible and a brassbound album of family portraits.

> Only on Sundays did we have a fire in the parlour grate. 'Just to air the place' was the reason but we could never escape the odour of camphor, camphor balls hung above each picture frame as an antidote against mildew and bad smells. The purpose of 'the airing' enabled the family to have a Sunday dinner together.[319]

Among women, pastimes and pleasures were often centred upon the home, with needlework, sketching, music and similar 'accomplishments' the norm for the better-off, together with letter writing and perhaps the keeping of a diary. Ann Staight, the daughter of a Gloucestershire blacksmith, regarded her diary as one of her principal recreations. She was friendly with an Enfield publican's daughter and one way in which they kept in touch during the early 1880s was by writing long entries in their respective diaries and then exchanging these regularly.[260] In August 1860 Sarah Thomas, daughter of a Baptist minister in the quiet Gloucestershire market town of Fairford, made wax flowers, sang and played the piano when a friend came to stay with her for several weeks.[230]

A Miss Child, who lived in Salisbury during the early Victorian years and wrote a book of verse entitled *The Spinster at Home in the Close of Salisbury*, conveyed the simple, mundane pleasures enjoyed by many of these women:

> I have friends . . . who frequently ask me to dine,
> When I taste of choice viands and sip the best wine;
> But full oft I decline these kind invitations,
> Of my home being fond and my own meditations.
> On my sofa I lounge with illustrious dead,
> And rejoice there are so many books to be read.
> I've sharp-pointed needles, a well-polished thimble
> To enweave slender threads with fingers right nimble:
> I've long letters to read, and still longer to write . . .

Mrs Beeton made clear that the mistress of a household should devote time to the 'pleasures of literature', 'the innocent delights of the garden, and to the improvement of any special abilities for music, painting, and other elegant arts, which she may . . . possess'. When receiving calls, occupations like drawing, music and reading should be set aside. 'If a lady, however, be engaged with light needlework, and none other is appropriate in the drawing-room, it may not be, under some circumstances, inconsistent with good breeding to quietly continue it during conversation, particularly if the visit be protracted, or the visitors be gentlemen.' Light or fancy needlework frequently formed part of the evening's recreation for female members of the household, too, perhaps diverted 'by an occasional game at chess and backgammon'.[52]

Even working women were influenced by this cult of domesticity. In 1849 Angus Bethune Reach described his meetings with Manchester factory girls who not only made their own clothes but were 'very fond of sampler work. I have seen a great many of these samplers. In nine cases out of ten they commemorate the death of a relation. . . . They exhibit a tombstone and a weeping willow, with a verse of poetry or a sentence from the Bible beneath.'[83]

Reading, including reading aloud by one member of the family to the rest, was a common diversion, while card and board games were played, including at the end of the century ludo, draughts, dominoes, and snakes and ladders. In 1851 the *Halifax Guardian* published an advertisement for a book entitled *Family Pastimes or Homes Made Happy* which included anagrams, enigmas, charades, conundrums, fireside games and various puzzles. Impromptu plays were staged, especially by young people, perhaps with the aid of a toy theatre, while even poor children played with cheap rag or wooden dolls, and with a little imagination a piece of cord fastened to the back of a chair might become a pony and trap. During the Boer War, at the end of the century, it was possible to buy for a penny a variation on the hand-held 'get the ball into the socket' game in which the player knocked out the teeth of one of the Boer leaders depicted, with a flick of the wrist. Twopence secured a jigsaw map of Africa with Boer defeats clearly, if sometimes inaccurately, marked.[214]

In better-off households, with sufficient space, 'games of action' like Blind Man's Buff or Hunt the Slipper were popular among the young and frivolous. In the early 1860s when William and Jane Morris moved into their new home in Kent shortly after their marriage, they entertained their friends by taking them out for drives over the surrounding countryside during the daytime and at night playing practical jokes or indulging in boisterous games of hide-and-seek. Visitors were expected to help decorate the half-furnished rooms and one of them recalled the sounds of merriment as they

> painted the walls with scenes from the Round Table histories; laughter sounded from the fragrant garden as the host, victim of some ingenious practical joke, fulfilled the pleased expectation of his guests by conduct at once vigorous and picturesque under the torment; laughter over the apple-gathering; laughter over every new experiment, every fantastic failure of the young housekeepers.

For the more serious minded, there were hobbies such as the collection of ferns and the pressing of flowers, which could be kept in elaborate albums. Botanizing became a favourite recreation, even among working people.[3] In 1849 the science of plants was described as 'a passion with the Manchester weaver. It is as common here as pigeon-fancying in Spitalfields. Every holiday sees hundreds of peaceful wanderers in the fields and woods around, busily engaged in culling specimens of grasses and flowers'.[281]

Stella Spencer, who lived at Higher Crumpsall near Manchester, one of the ten surviving children of a commercial traveller of uncertain income, remembered that for youngsters such as she there were not many toys and those they had were often improvized. Older siblings made dolls out of skittles for small sisters or dolls' beds out of cardboard boxes, while sets of tiny furniture could be constructed from horse-chestnuts, with stout pins forming the legs of the chairs and tables.[147] To amuse themselves and the rest of the family, the older children assembled a magic lantern from the spare parts of some broken ones they had bought second hand for a few pence, and they took it in turns to read aloud from books like *Swiss Family Robinson* and *Robinson Crusoe*.[147]

But perhaps the most important accomplishment for all young females was the ability to play a musical instrument, especially the piano although the banjo and mandolin were less expensive alternatives. One writer has described the 'piano mania' which existed during these years and has claimed that by the early twentieth century there were between two and four million pianos in Britain.[156] In 1899 even the *British Medical Journal* expressed concern: 'All – except perhaps teachers of music – will agree that at the present day the piano is too much with us.' The 'ineffective strumming of the amateur, and the damnable iterations of the learner' had 'sundered ancient friendships' and 'driven studious men from their books to the bottle'.[156] When William Morris's two young daughters began to play the piano their practising drove their father 'nearly frantic' and soon it was agreed they would play only when he was out of the house.

But these critics apart, most well-brought up girls were expected to entertain company by their musical talents. Inevitably there was a massive demand for sheet music, too, with sentimental ballads such as the *Lost Chord* enjoying sales of half a million copies between 1877 and 1902, while *The Holy City* was selling fifty thousand copies a year in the 1890s. Even simple instrumental pieces could have major success, like the undemanding *Myosotis* ('Forget-me-not') waltz which sold more than a quarter of a million copies.[156]

Such sales, when combined with the proliferation of cheap lessons and inexpensive instruction manuals, were evidence that piano purchases were moving down the social scale. To the Victorians, as Cyril Ehrlich notes, a piano 'symbolized respectability, achievement and status'. Hence a South Yorkshire miners' leader, giving evidence to the Select Committee on Coal in 1873, summarized the signs of material progress in his district as the existence of 'more pianos and perambulators', with the piano ranked 'a cut above the perambulator'.[156]

In contributing to this situation the so-called 'three-year' system played a part. Under it a piano could be hired for three years, after which it became the hirer's property. In the *Bethnal Green Times* of 5 January 1867 a firm that claimed to have pioneered this system was offering 'pianettes' for hire at 2½ guineas per quarter, piccolos at 3 guineas, cottage pianos at £3 10s and a drawing-room model cottage at £3 18s. Such 'pretentious nomenclature' was intended to disguise the identity of variously sized cheap, upright pianos. Five years later Thompson and Shackell of Cardiff and Carmarthen were also offering pianofortes for sale and hire 'on easy terms', on the three-year plan. They had introduced the 'now celebrated . . . SYSTEM' to the principality and with their thorough knowledge of the business claimed to be able to exclude all instruments of inferior make from their stock.[47]

Music lessons were offered on a wide scale by teachers of variable quality. In 1863 the *Musical Standard* commented sourly on unqualified instructors like the 'Gilder and Pianoforte Tuner' who offered lessons in dancing, the violin and the piano at sixpence a time. Similarly in February 1872 the *Western Mail* included an advertisement from Charles Cooke, 'professor of the pianoforte and violin' and leader and conductor of the Swansea Instrumental Philharmonic Society. He gave lessons on the piano and violin either at his own home or those of his pupils but he also tuned

Playing the piano was an important female accomplishment. Punch *(1884) contrasts the way few guests were interested in 'good' music but preferred low-brow comic songs instead. In this case 'Am I The Cheese?' was to be performed.*

and repaired instruments and was prepared to offer musical accompaniment at balls and evening parties 'with Pianoforte or Band. All Orders promptly attended to.'

For many women and some men music was a pleasant and soothing pastime. One writer in 1871 claimed that it provided females with an important emotional outlet as well: 'A good play of the piano has not infrequently taken the place of a good cry upstairs; and this was important . . . when a woman's life was "often a life of feeling" rather than of action . . . and society, whilst it limits her sphere of action, frequently calls upon her to repress her feelings.' Even males were assured in 1895 that 'for an educated man to seat himself at the piano is no longer thought effeminate'.[111]

The biography and letters of the novelist George Eliot confirm her lifelong attachment to playing the piano, both for recreation and as a source of spiritual refreshment. When her work began to yield a comfortable income one of her first ambitions was to purchase a grand piano – partly for the status of owning such an impressive instrument but also because of her desire to practise her musical skills, even though some of her contemporaries were less than complimentary about these.[111]

Other instruments were popular, too. The immature Dora in Charles Dickens's novel *David Copperfield* was too inept to play the piano so she learnt the guitar instead, while Dickens himself opted for the accordion, a suitably cheerful instrument.[111] Violins, harps, banjos, concertinas and harmoniums also formed part of the Victorian domestic music scene. In 1851 a Manchester firm of musical instrument makers advertised a 'large assortment' of concertinas at prices ranging from £1 11s 6d for one with twenty-two keys, to £10 10s for the largest and most complex instruments.[32] Likewise Druce and Gerring, a Witney firm of musical suppliers, in July 1883 offered tuition in organs, harmoniums, violins, flutes, melodeons, concertinas and banjos, among other instruments.[48] Around a decade later Walter Southgate remembered that in his area families did not own pianos – doubtless because of their cost – but played accordions, concertinas and mouth organs. 'Both father and my brother William could play the English concertina; my grandfather too, who had his own music book', this latter being seen as confirmation of his musical commitment.[319]

GARDENS AND GARDENING

During the Victorian years private gardens became accepted as part of the general amenities of family life among the upper working classes and those in the middle ranks of society, much as they had long been for the aristocracy and gentry. As early as 1841 a gardening expert declared them to be 'an indispensable part of the domestic establishment of every person who can afford the expense'.[131] Symptomatic of these developments was the appearance in 1867 of a new magazine, *The Gardener*, whose avowed aim was to concentrate on

> that large and increasing class of the community who, previous to the development of our railway system, lived in cities, but who now live in the country, and who occupy their hours of relaxation from city business in managing, with or without the aid of a common labourer, their suburban garden.[131]

To the growing business and professional classes the possession of their own plot of land was confirmation of their success in escaping from the pressures and pollution of city life. That feeling was intensified when a greater use of plate glass made possible the installation of large windows and glass doors in houses. In that way the garden almost seemed an extension of the dwelling itself. Gardening enthusiasms were stimulated, too, by the introduction of large herbaceous borders and the construction of glasshouses, with pineapples enjoying central heating long before human beings did so. Even in humbler properties, shrubs around the area railings and ferns in a glass 'Ward case' on the parlour table could enliven urban terraced houses.[146] Accompanying this was a proliferation of gardening publications, ranging from practical manuals devoted to the craft of garden-making to more general texts like Samuel Beeton's *Dictionary of Every-day Gardening* and lesser known works such as *Villa and Cottage Gardening*, offered by a Swansea seedsman, along with collections of vegetable and flower seeds. Encouragement was given to this new interest by experts who stressed its therapeutic effect. 'The culture of flowers is one of the most delightful and healthful recreations to which man can devote the powers of his mind and body', declared an enthusiast in 1857.[131] Another spoke of gardening's 'health-giving properties, both to body and mind' and that was a view with which

Sarah Thomas would doubtless have agreed. When she was worried about her sister's ill health or anxious about events in her personal life she often went out to the garden, and was sufficiently skilled to win prizes at the local flower show.[230]

The distinguished historian Thomas Carlyle and his wife, Jane, were also keen gardeners. When they moved to their Chelsea home in the mid-1830s they determined to get the neglected plot into order. After writing all the morning, Thomas often dug until their 4 p.m. dinner hour. By the end of the first summer he and Jane could admire a garden in which marigolds bloomed, vines were in full leaf and once-sickly roses had been freed from weeds. Soon they began growing vegetables as well and it was in the garden that the normally prosaic Jane was able to express her nostalgia for her native Scotland. Blooms were planted that reminded her of family and friends, and despite repeated disappointments she never returned from a trip north of the border without bringing a bundle of plants. After her mother's death a friend sent slips and cuttings from some of the plants which Mrs Welsh had grown – polyanthus, jessamine and sweet brier. The latter refused to grow in London soil, despite Jane's repeated efforts, but for her the garden was a way of linking herself with the people and places she loved.[189]

The growing preoccupation with gardening led to a rapid increase in the number of nursery businesses and promoted a sophisticated advertising and sales system designed to create further demand for plants and seeds. The importation of new

Pride in the cultivation of a small back garden at a terraced house in Walworth, c. 1900. (The author)

specimens became an industry in itself, with expeditions going all over the world to search for 'green treasure'. The famous Veitch nursery, founded in Exeter in 1832, maintained collectors overseas continuously from 1840 to 1905, and in 1853 it took over the firm of Knight and Perry in Chelsea. The new business became the Royal Exotic Nursery and was visited regularly by members of fashionable society and their gardeners.[250] Among the trees and plants introduced during these years were conifers from the Pacific coast of America, dahlias and fuchsias from South America, orchids from central America, Africa, India and the Far East, forsythia and large flowering clematis from China and lilies and chrysanthemums from Japan. Many well-to-do families built spacious conservatories and glasshouses to contain exotics like orchids, camellias, Eastern azaleas and Brazilian fuchsias.[250] For some, including the leading Victorian political figure Joseph Chamberlain, the growing of orchids became an absorbing hobby.

Within the house, the importance of private entertaining led to a demand for elaborate floral arrangements. The wealthiest had orchids in the drawing room and on the dining table, and there were tea roses by the score for bouquets and buttonholes. Potted palms were displayed in the hall, and even humble homes had asparagus ferns and aspidistra, which were able to withstand the atmospheric pollution of town life. Plants and flowers were accepted not merely as luxuries for grand occasions but as year-round necessities for 'homes of refinement and taste'.[250]

The popularity of luncheon and dinner parties stimulated demand for vegetables, too, and increased attention was given to the kitchen garden. Peas were regarded as 'the prince' of the new season's vegetables and essential accompaniments for duckling and lamb. In 1884 at Longleat, home of the Marquess of Bath, peas were served from late April until October, while the chef expected French beans to be available every week. This meant that boxes of beans had to be grown under glass from November until the following May. Cucumbers and tomatoes were similarly grown all the year round. For those who could afford it, hothouses ensured a supply of dessert fruit, including pineapples, grapes and melons. Strawberries, too, were popular, and during 1866 the glasshouses at Sandringham kept the Prince of Wales supplied with the fruit from 18 February until the outdoor crop ripened in June. To do this five thousand pots of plants were forced.[250]

But the garden was an important source of pleasure beyond its floral and culinary aspects. Not only could children play games there but they sometimes cultivated small plots of their own. Affluent families also had facilities for playing croquet (particularly from the 1860s) and lawn tennis (from the 1870s), to say nothing of archery and bowls. In May 1870 the curate of Clyro in Radnor, Francis Kilvert, noted that after luncheon at Clyro Court 'we had croquet and archery and I played bowls with Baskerville, an old set that were rummaged out of an outhouse for the occasion'.[273] Garden parties were a pleasant, relatively informal way of offering hospitality to friends, and during the summer tea might be served on the lawn. In August 1870 the newly married Lady Knightley and her husband held their first big party for the neighbours in the garden of their home, Fawsley Park: 'we asked every lady we could think of for miles round to come to croquet from 4 to 7 – wh. they did to the extent of about 100', wrote Lady Knightley in her diary, adding, 'we had a band & gave them refreshments in the old Hall'.

By the end of the century, under the influence of the gardening expert Gertrude Jekyll and other pioneers, the old-style enthusiasm for regimented flower beds, where bright splashes of colour lasted for three or four months of the year only, was giving way to more naturalistic displays.[211]

Gardening was welcomed as possessing important moral advantages, too, by countering any tendency for leisure to be associated with the vice of idleness. This aspect was emphasized by the editor of *The Gardening World* in 1884, when he expressed the belief that 'gardening is as essential to the welfare, pleasure, and happiness of the poorest as of the richest'. For that reason encouragement was given to the lower orders to take it up as a leisure pursuit. Although the expansion of towns had reduced the amount of land available for use as garden and allotment ground by working-class families, stimulus was given by the formation of local horticultural societies which awarded prizes in a separate 'cottager' class. This applied at Ealing, where a society was formed in 1864. Specially low subscription rates of 5s a year were available to wage-earning members who cultivated their own plots in Ealing. The awards in 1901 ranged in value from £1 1s for a first prize for the best-kept flower garden in the cottager class, to 5s offered for the best dish of strawberries or gooseberries. At the summer show held in July of that year it was stated that the cottagers' vegetables had 'never been in better condition'.

In the later Victorian years legislation encouraged local authorities to provide allotments and in 1892 there were estimated to be 445,000 of these in England and Wales alone.[165] By that time, the encouragement of gardening had become an integral part of the wider housing reform movement. But few towns could match Nottingham, where in 1871 the *Gardener's Chronicle* estimated that ten thousand allotments were available, rented at between 10s and 30s a year.

Elsewhere a minority of industrial employers built model cottages with gardens attached for their workers or, as at Halifax, supplied allotment land and set up horticultural societies. By the end of the century these initiatives were gaining fresh converts. At Port Sunlight, begun in 1888, the soap manufacturer William Lever provided comfortable homes with sizeable gardens for employees, and the chocolate firm of Cadbury adopted a similar policy in 1893 on their new estate at Bournville near Birmingham.[131]

Where no such initiatives existed, societies were formed with the modest aim of encouraging window-box gardening. One such was the Society for Promoting Window Gardening Amongst the Working Classes of Westminster, which held flower shows in the 1860s and 1870s.[131] By the end of the century a commentator noted that back-street window gardeners were not content merely to display a plain box or a simple row of pots. Instead they rigged up an archway or miniature palisade and even a minute greenhouse. At the end of the summer bedding season it was common for the London parks to be cleared of their plants and these were often given away. This was 'the slum gardener's opportunity': with these acquisitions, supplemented perhaps by a few bulbs picked up at a stall near Smithfield Meat Market, and by some odd roots purchased from a costermonger's barrow in the spring, he could do wonders.[314]

In rural areas, gardening was both an economic activity and a recreation, with the fruit and vegetables grown forming an important part of the daily diet. The

The ingenuity of window-box gardeners is shown at this house in a London mews, c. 1900. Note also the caged birds on a ledge above the doorway. (The author)

struggle by farm workers in Tysoe, Warwickshire, to secure large allotments was indicative of the value attached to such plots by villagers. But there was pleasure to be gained as well. At Juniper Hill in Oxfordshire Flora Thompson remembered the men's pride in their produce, and the spirit of competition between them to see who could grow the earliest and the choicest items.

> On light evenings, after their tea-supper, the men worked for an hour or two . . . The energy they brought to their gardening after a hard day's work in the fields was marvellous. Often, on moonlight nights in spring, the solitary fork of some one who had not been able to tear himself away would be heard and the scent of his twitch fire smoke would float in at the windows . . . Very little money was spent on seed; . . . they depended mainly upon the seed saved from the previous year. Sometimes, to secure the advantage of fresh soil they would exchange a bag of seed potatoes with friends living at a distance, and sometimes a gardener at one of the big houses around would give one of them a few tubers of a new variety . . . Most of the men sang or whistled as they dug or hoed.[342]

Gardening in the countryside. (From P.H. Emerson, Pictures of East Anglian Life, *1888)*

Nor did they neglect the more frivolous pursuit of raising flowers. In the 1880s Flora Thompson's neighbours were growing wallflowers and tulips, lavender and sweet williams, and 'pinks and old-world roses with enchanting names'. Certainly Gertrude Jekyll was in no doubt that the double strip of flower border which led from the road to the cottage door, and which was common in many country gardens, was not only 'absolutely right' but served as a useful lesson 'to gardens of some pretension'.[211]

In the industrial villages of the Midlands, florist societies were formed in the early nineteenth century, with working men, mostly artisans, competing for prizes. In 1858 Samuel Broome, a writer on urban horticulture, claimed to belong to twelve different floral societies, with membership varying from fifty to one hundred in each. There was 'not one shabby man amongst them. Very rarely do you find a man who is fond of flowers taken up for a misdemeanour of any kind.'[165]

During the second half of the century these specialist bodies waned, perhaps because the prosperity of their members was undermined by industrial change. But flower and horticultural shows continued to be popular and exhibitions of every kind proliferated from the 1860s. In London the shows held by the Royal Botanic and Horticultural Society became important events in the social calendar.[250] But even at a humbler level flower shows had their appeal and could, on occasion, encourage female participation – as in the case of Sarah Thomas of Fairford.[230] At Northleach, in Gloucestershire, a flower show held in August 1872 included two prizes subscribed by local bachelors for the two best bouquets by ladies. The competition was open to unmarried women only, and according to *Jackson's Oxford Journal* there was keen competition for the prizes – a 'splendid gilt inkstand and a smelling bottle'. In the newspaper's view this showed that if organizers provided suitable and innovative attractions, there were 'many prepared to enter the lists who [had] hitherto kept aloof'.[35]

Additional Sources Used

Sheila Ayres, Richard Holder, Tamar Jeffers, *Linley Sambourne House* (London, 1992).
Richard W. Bailey, *Nineteenth-Century English* (Ann Arbor, 1996), for the Virginia Woolf quotation.
Ealing Horticultural Society, Annual Report for 1901 at London Metropolitan Archives and Library.
J.M. Golby (ed.), *Culture and Society in Britain 1850–1890* (Oxford, 1986).
Halifax Guardian, 1 February and 3 May 1851.
Jackson's Oxford Journal, 24 August 1872.
Lady Knightley's Diary for 1869–70, K.2893 at Northamptonshire Record Office.
Jan Marsh, *Jane and May Morris. A Biographical Story 1839–1938* (London, 1986).
Edith Olivier, *Four Victorian Ladies of Wiltshire* (London, 1946 edn).
Western Mail, 1 and 10 January and 10 and 14 February 1872.
Witney Gazette, 21 July 1883.
G.M. Young, *Victorian England. Portrait of an Age* (London, 1953 edn).

CHAPTER 3

Fashion and the Wider Social Scene

The empire of fashion widened year by year and it was no longer possible to draw distinctions between Mayfair and the suburbs, or even between the capital and the provinces . . . Shop-girls . . . in small country towns, were clothed in the prevailing mode . . . There was also a good deal of sham jewellery and imitation fur worn by the women of the working classes, and the aspect of a London crowd on a bank holiday was calculated to make the judicious grieve.

Cassell's History of England, Vol. VIII
(London, n.d. [*c.* 1898]), 304–5

FASHIONABLE DRESS AND SHOPPING

The Victorian years saw increasing importance attached to fashion by women of all classes. Even in Flora Thompson's remote Oxfordshire hamlet in the 1880s farm labourers' wives and daughters insisted that their Sunday best must be 'just so. "Better be out of the world than out of fashion" was one of their sayings' – although in their case the height of fashion was a year or two behind that of many other places.[342] And if a woman were accused of hoarding her best clothes, she would reply with a laugh: 'Ah! I be savin' they for high days an' holidays an' bonfire nights.'

This interest in dress could be attributed partly to growing prosperity, first among the middle classes and then among those lower down the scale. As a result, more people were able to afford stylish goods, and fashions themselves altered with greater rapidity thanks to better communications and other factors. This trend was further encouraged by the falling price of some mass-produced articles, especially underwear and men's clothing. But by the late 1860s firms like Sélincourt and Colman in London were supplying ready-made ladies' mantles, waterproofs, costumes, shawls and children's clothes to a number of major retailers. In 1866 John Harvey & Son of Ludgate Hill, also in London, advertised 'Coloured serge costumes' from 25*s* 6*d* to 50*s* each and Redmayne & Son of New Bond Street and Conduit Street offered 'Made-up skirts for walking'.[72] The introduction of sewing machines in the mid-1850s not only made possible this large-scale manufacture of garments but allowed home dressmakers who owned a machine to copy the latest fashions, with the aid of up-to-date paper patterns. The latter, too, came to the fore

A French fashion plate of the early 1850s, giving details of the suppliers of the articles shown, for the benefit of possible purchasers. Mlles Romain provided the bonnets, Mlle Elise Chevalier the dresses, the corsetry was provided by Mme Dumoulin, and the gloves were from Faguer and Laboulée. (The author)

from the middle of the century, along with inexpensive fashion magazines. Among these was *The World of Fashion*, which in 1850 began including full-size patterns for bodices, mantles and underwear in its monthly issues.[114] Another pioneer was the *Englishwoman's Domestic Magazine*, first published in 1852 by Samuel Beeton and distributed monthly at twopence. Samuel's wife, Isabella, not only contributed notes on the latest models but visited Paris to cover the spring and autumn collections. She also arranged for attractively tinted French fashion plates to be used as illustrations in the magazine and offered a postal paper pattern service, which was an immediate success.[320] Others followed, such as *Weldon's Ladies' Journal* and *Myra's Journal of Dress and Fashion*, which appeared in the mid-1870s with fashion plates and paper dressmaking patterns.[380] Even those women's magazines and general newspapers which did not supply patterns gave details of the latest fashions and advice on dress.

Clothes served as indicators of social status, and their subtle nuances had to be weighed up carefully. Outfits considered suitable for one occasion could be seen as unacceptable for another:

The bonnet sufficiently gay for the Park would be flippant in church. Certain materials might be worn up to Easter, but not after; . . . And always there was the haunting fear lest [a woman] should be slightly behind the fashion (and therefore dowdy) or in front of it (and therefore fast).[141]

To the socially ambitious, the provenance of clothing was important and a visit to a prestigious 'court dressmaker' was a noteworthy event. Marion Sambourne, whose husband's income as a *Punch* cartoonist was limited, nonetheless made every effort to patronize the exclusive Madame Bocquet for evening dresses, despite the high prices. 'Went to Madame B's, paid her £38 for making me blue evening dress', Marion noted in her diary on one occasion. This meant that her quarterly allowance of £25 was quickly spent, but when she ordered garments from a less expensive source she was rarely satisfied. Sometimes a seamstress was employed to come to the house for a few days: 'Napper here, don't think dress will be a success, shall never fancy myself in any but Madame's dresses', she commented discontentedly.[257] Favourite clothes, like a red velvet evening gown, were repeatedly remodelled, and this practice of restyling outmoded but expensive dresses and millinery was a device commonly adopted by ladies of restricted means.

The many opportunities for leisure and pleasure which existed gave added impetus to the preoccupation with fashion, since the garments worn were often part of the enjoyment of an event, as well as a source of discreet competition between those present to see who was the most stylish. That applied not merely to special events like weddings, christenings and the ever-popular fancy dress balls, but to smaller diversions like garden parties and evening entertainments. Even Jane Carlyle, who was not particularly fashion conscious (she refused to tight-lace, for example, or to wear a crinolene), nonetheless in 1862 recorded with satisfaction the favourable impression she had made at a dinner party at Lord and Lady Ashburton's. 'Elise got me up in a rose coloured petticoat, with black tunic (good god!) which made me the envy of surrounding women.'[189]

Each engagement required an appropriate outfit and in the mid-1890s ladies were advised to ensure that their style of dress was suitable for the time of day. Small wonder that leading socialites such as the Countess of Warwick went away for country house visits accompanied by mountains of trunks. 'We changed our clothes four times a day at least. This kept our maids and ourselves extra-ordinarily busy.'[372] Similarly during Ascot week the Duchess of Marlborough recalled the fortunes spent each year on dresses chosen on a graduated scale of elegance, so as to reach a climax on the Thursday: 'fashion decreed that one should reserve one's most sumptuous *toilette* for Gold Cup day . . . We spent our mornings donning various dresses in accordance with the vagaries of the weather, and by noon we were apt to be not only cross and tired but probably attired in the wrong dress.'[89]

It was not only the ladies who needed to take care. Mrs Humphry in *Manners for Men* (1898) warned that those who did not dress well would never be a social success. The man who committed 'flagrant errors in costume . . . will not be invited out very much . . . If he goes to a garden party in a frock-coat and straw hat, he is condemned more universally than if he had committed some crime.' Two years later another writer on male etiquette advised readers to avoid wearing tan boots or shoes with a black coat of any kind, while 'no gentleman ever wears a made-up tie'.[271] In 1878 *The Tailor and Cutter* observed severely, 'it is the correct thing to vote a showily dressed man a snob'.[142]

Associated with these strictures was a widespread belief in the importance of class distinctions in clothing, and only in the final years of the century did that begin to disappear.[227] The term 'finery', for example, was often used pejoratively to describe attire that was perhaps elegant and striking in itself but was worn by a woman seeking to ape her social superiors. 'The same dress', writes Mariana Valverde, 'could be considered elegant and proper on a lady, but showy and dishonest on her maid.'[354] This applied even though many mistresses gave cast-offs to their servants, either for personal use or for transmission to friends and relatives. Middle-class moralists feared that girls preoccupied with fashion might slip into prostitution in order to obtain the cash needed to appear stylish. William Acton, in discussing the causes of prostitution in the late 1850s, maintained that 'vanity, vanity and then vanity' was the prime factor. According to him, love of dress and a craving for admiration were major causes of 'tens of thousands of the uneducated' going astray.[354]

Yet if a love of fashion gave rise to exaggerated moral concerns, especially as regards the lower orders, there was anxiety, too, about its physical implications. The wearing of heavy skirts, confining corsets, vast crinolines, bustles, and hampering tied-back skirts, which in successive decades characterized female attire, not only underlined women's subordinate social role but led to inactivity and idleness.[167] In the middle of the century females seemed almost imprisoned by their clothes, as well as isolated from their fellows by the large dimensions of their skirts. Although on grounds of practicality the working dress of lower-class women escaped the worst excesses of such fashions, in leisure hours they, too, followed the trend. Only towards the end of the Victorian era did these restrictive aspects of dress start to diminish as females began to exercise a degree of independence and to wear more 'masculine' garb, such as tailored skirts and jackets, shirts with collars and ties, and straw boaters.[114]

The poor, meanwhile, were heavily dependent on the second-hand market for many of their clothes, at any rate before mass production cut the price of new garments and placed them within the reach of most people. In Flora Thompson's Oxfordshire hamlet even in the late 1880s the older women relied on other people's cast-offs. Often these were sent by daughters or other relatives in service and when a parcel arrived there was much excitement. Fashion in the hamlet not only lagged behind that in the outside world but was very limited in scope. Hence garments given by a daughter's mistress were often less welcome than the girl's own discards because they were too far in advance of the 'hamlet vogue':

Then they had colour prejudices . . . Only a fast hussy would wear red. Or green – sure to bring any wearer bad luck! . . . nobody would wear it until it had been home-dyed navy or brown. Yellow ranked with red as immodest . . . To the mothers the cut was even more important than the colour. If sleeves were worn wide they liked them to be very wide; if narrow, skin tight . . . *The* Sunday garment at the beginning of the decade was the tippet, a little shoulder cape of black silk or satin with a long dangling fringe. All the women and some

ADVANTAGES OF MARSUPIALISM.

"I'M SO TIRED, MUMMY. I WISH YOU WERE A KANGAROO!"
"WHY, DARLING?"
"TO CARRY ME HOME IN YOUR POCKET!"

*Mother and son on an outing to the zoo. The mother is able to benefit from the less restrictive styles of the late Victorian era and is wearing a plain skirt and jacket with a simple blouse. (*Punch, *1892)*

of the girls had these, and they were worn proudly to church or Sunday school with a posy of roses or geraniums pinned in front.

Hats were of the chimney-pot variety, a tall cylinder of straw, with a very narrow brim and a spray of artificial flowers trained up the front. Later in the decade, the shape changed to wide brims and squashed crowns. The chimney-pot had had its day, and the women declared they would not be seen going to the privy in one.[342] Sometimes, as with the Gloucestershire blacksmith's daughter Ann Staight, judicious home dressmaking could be combined with loans from family members to give a stylish appearance. In August 1882 when Ann was preparing to go to Pershore Show, her sister lent a black flower taken from her own velvet hat to put on Ann's white one 'and I wore it and merino dress . . . had Mother's cloak to ride in. Sis lent me her old blue silk umbrella.'[260] In villages people often formed their ideas of the latest fashions by observing the clothes worn by members of the squire's or clergyman's family for Sunday service at church.

Early in Victoria's reign, bell-shaped skirts were all the rage. The desired outline was achieved by wearing multiple petticoats, including those lined with stiff horsehair, which came into use from the late 1830s. The ideal woman was seen as modest, gentle and demure, 'absorbed in acquiring the art of expressing emotions by graceful attitudes rather than by movement', since the weight of her clothing made activity difficult.[141] As late as 1855 it was not uncommon for fourteen cumbersome layers of petticoat to be worn under a ball gown, and ladies determined to be in the height of fashion were obliged to stand in their carriages en route to their destination, as well as between dances on their arrival, because of the physical impossibility of sitting down.[382]

Around the mid-1850s the situation changed with the introduction of the artificial crinoline. Initially it was made from a cotton or linen petticoat reinforced by hoops of cane or whalebone. But with the production of cheap steel from 1856 sprung steel hoops were used instead. The petticoat foundation was no longer needed and the metal hoops, increasing in diameter towards the bottom of the skirt, were linked by vertical bands of wide webbing. An opening was left at the front so that the frame could be put on and tied round the waist with tapes.[114] This met the current vogue for wide skirts without impeding the legs and reduced the necessity for tight lacing, since the wide skirt tended to make all waists appear slender.

The crinoline quickly became popular, reaching its largest dimensions around 1860, by which time it was said that 'with three or four of these giantesses in a room a diminished man could not creep in beyond the door, powerless under the domination of this new Colossus'.[142] But the women had a different perspective. 'Oh it was delightful . . . I've never been so comfortable . . . It kept your petticoats away from your legs and made walking so light and easy', declared one enthusiast. But the benefits were counterbalanced by several disadvantages. Not only did the crinoline take up a great deal of space, so that an unwary movement might upset an occasional table, but in windy weather there was a danger of being blown off one's feet. Most serious of all was the risk from fire, especially when flimsy frocks were worn near candles or an open grate. Once alight it was impossible to extinguish the flames by compression. Crinolines were difficult to manage, too, when travelling on trains or other public vehicles, and much fun was poked at them in *Punch* and elsewhere.[40] At Chester, for example, it was reported in July 1858 that fashionably dressed ladies were unable to get through the public entrance to the local cattle show, and had to be admitted by the gate usually reserved for the exhibits.[382] Nevertheless, at the height of its popularity the crinoline was adopted by all classes and was worn on almost all occasions except for riding. Those like Queen Victoria and Jane Carlyle who rejected it were very much in the minority.[114]

It was around this time that the first of the chemical dyes appeared, to supplement those made from vegetable sources. During the 1860s the new purple, mauve and purplish-pink or fuchsia shades were widely adopted, as was a vivid emerald green, itself produced from chemicals. When worn in combination these colours created a bold, garish effect displeasing to some observers. In the 1860s the French writer Hippolyte Taine commented on the 'want of taste' in British women's attire: 'Their dress, loud and overcharged with ornament, is that of a woman of easy virtue or a *parvenue* . . . The colours are outrageously crude, and lines ungraceful.'[167]

Others, such as Mrs Lynn Linton, condemned the growing use of artificial aids to beauty, especially by older women. She particularly criticized the application of powder, rouge, and bistre for the eyelids.

A REAL DIFFICULTY.

"WELL, DEAR, IF THIS IS THE USUAL STYLE OF THING IN DERBYSHIRE, THE FARMERS HAD BETTER
WRITE UP 'NO THOROUGHFARE' AT ONCE; THEN PEOPLE WOULD KNOW WHAT TO DO."

Punch *(1864) mocking the problems associated with wearing large crinolines.*

Dressed in the extreme of youthful fashion, her thinning hair dyed and crimped and fired till it is more red-brown tow than hair, her flaccid cheeks ruddled, her throat whitened, her . . . lustreless eyes blackened round the lids, to give the semblance of limpidity to the tarnished whites . . . there she stands, the wretched creature who will not consent to grow old.[183]

Over the years this intolerance towards cosmetics weakened, even though before the turn of the century it never entirely disappeared. But it is interesting to note Lady Lytton's approving comment in October 1896 at Balmoral that 'the Princess of Wales looked lovely at dinner . . . and she is so wise to put even a little help [*sic*] to give her a good colour'.[114] Interestingly in the 1890s companies like the soap manufacturer Pears were using famous faces, such as that of the actress Lillie Langtry, to advertise their wares.

WONDERS OF FASHION.

"WEAR MY HAT ON MY HEAD! IMPOSSIBLE, GRAND'PA DEAR! HAVEN'T DONE SUCH A
THING FOR AGES! IT'S PINNED ON WITH MY HAIR!"

*The use of artificial hair became common in the early 1870s as a way of balancing the large backward protuberance of the bustle. (*Punch, *1871)*

By 1868 the crinoline age was at an end, at least among the fashionable, as the vast skirts of the early 1860s were transformed into overskirts, looped up at the sides to cover decorative petticoats and bunched out behind to signal the arrival of the bustle in the early 1870s. As if to balance the bulk of the skirt, the hair was arranged in a large chignon at the nape of the neck, with false hair added to give it the necessary bulk. 'The new line of women's dress with its bustle projection at the back called for a characteristic posture which was popularly known as the Grecian bend,' notes Penelope Byrde. 'This served to accentuate the rear fullness by throwing the head and bust forward and the hips backwards.' The stance was encouraged by the shape of the longer, tighter corset now worn and by the high heels which had become fashionable.[114]

In the mid-1870s the bustle was itself discarded, and the ideal dress now fitted the body tightly from shoulders to hips in the so-called Princess line. Tapes were sewn inside skirts so that they could be pulled back behind the body, to keep the front of the dress close to the figure, while the remaining drapery and trimmings cascaded into a train. The narrow skirts made walking difficult and such dresses were primarily designed for women who had maids to do the work, thereby acting as a status symbol. Those who led an active life were expected to wear dresses that were narrow but without a train. However, many women outside the affluent 'carriage class' followed the mode and allowed their trains to trail in the street. This caused John Ruskin to comment sourly in 1876 that he had lost faith in the commonsense and personal delicacy of Englishwomen, 'by seeing how they will allow their dresses to sweep the streets'.[167] Nor was that the only disadvantage of the tied-back skirt. 'No-one but a woman knows how her dress twists around her knees, doubles her fatigue, and arrests her locomotive powers,' complained the novelist and historical writer Margaret Oliphant in 1878. There were also many accessories to take into account, including fans, bags and parasols, the latter designed to protect ladies' faces from the sun and to stop them getting freckles or, worse still, an unfashionable tan.

Around this time tailor-made suits began to make an appearance. The fashion started with blue serge yachting costumes, but was soon adopted for other purposes, including walking in the country and joining the guns at shooting parties. They proved practical for women who were beginning to travel around on horse omnibuses and horsedrawn trams, or were taking up committee work and similar duties. As such, they signalled the emergence of fashionable females from the confines of the boudoir and the drawing room into the wider world. Another indication of this was the use of rainproof clothing, including waterproof Ulsters, costumes and cloaks.[167]

Redfern's in London was the most prestigious tailoring house for the female élite, specializing in costumes for fishing, hunting, shooting and driving, but also running a creative dressmaking section. But the fashion soon reached the provinces, with the exclusive drapers Browns of Chester advertising tailormade costumes in 1879.[168]

During these years a number of intellectual women became determined to reject contemporary fads, especially the discomforts of the narrow Princess line. Their ideal was the simple attire of medieval times or the classical draperies of Ancient Greece and Rome. The waist was to be in a natural position and tight lacing eschewed, while skirts were to be loose enough to allow the wearer to walk or sit in comfort. In 1878 Mary Eliza Haweis, an advocate of this 'aesthetic' style argued in *The Queen* magazine that the prime purpose of a beautiful dress should be 'not [to] contradict the natural form of the human figure'.[388] Also condemned by aesthetes were the bright aniline dyes popular in conventional circles. Instead they favoured soft greens, blues, browns and pale golden yellows, made from vegetable dyes. Liberty's became their favourite shop and in 1884 one enthusiast claimed it was 'inappropriate to regard Liberty's merely as a place of business. . . . Liberty & Co. is as much a feature of the metropolis as the National Gallery or the Grosvenor Gallery.'[71] Its silks, embroideries and cashmere shawls were especially coveted.

Outside artistic circles, however, these clothes won few friends and the colours chosen were mocked by, among others, W.S. Gilbert in *Patience* (1881) as 'greenery-yallery, Grosvenor Gallery' colours. Some girls, like Jeannette Marshall, daughter of a leading London medical man, took up aspects of aesthetic attire, such as the characteristic amber necklace and the sage or olive-green dresses, partly because they were attracted to a 'tamed' version of aestheticism and partly because it was a way of dressing modishly for those unable to afford conventional high fashion. Accessories such as Liberty silk handkerchiefs and peacock feathers could be purchased out of a limited budget, and embroidery, a prime feature of aesthetic decoration, was Miss Marshall's favourite craft.[311] But in her diary she mocked the more extreme proponents of the new movement.

For those unwilling to accept the eccentricities and the ridicule associated with aesthetic garb, relief from the tight lacing fashionable in the 1870s and 1880s was found by the adoption of loose tea-gowns. In these, married women (although not girls) could relax for the new custom of five o'clock tea. Lady Warwick remembered the decorative tea-gowns of the late nineteenth-century as 'more beautiful than the evening gowns worn for dinner', and they were certainly a good deal more comfortable.

The health hazards associated with women's dress came under increasingly critical scrutiny at this time. They arose both from tight lacing and from the weight of the clothing itself, particularly in the winter when sealskin coats and jackets were worn by those who could afford them. In January 1888 the *Isle of Wight Times* drew attention to a report in the medical journal *The Lancet* which condemned female attire for being too heavy, especially when cloaks and mantles of sealskin and plush, with quilted linings, were put on during cold weather.[34] It called on doctors to remonstrate with their female patients over this, and to remember that many who complained of fatigue in walking were not suffering from physical weakness but merely the 'natural exhaustion from carrying a burden few strong men would care to bear'. In addition, metal-boned corsetry ensured that the waist was encircled with a load 'heavier than a felon's chain . . . and the shoulders and chest are compressed. Breathing is laboriously performed . . . We have reason to think that not a few of the maladies from which women suffer acutely, and the general weakness and depression of the muscular and nervous system of which they very commonly complain, will be placed in an entirely new light when the facts . . . are fully known.'[34]

It was in these circumstances that in 1881 Viscountess Harberton initiated the Rational Dress Society to promote 'a style of dress based upon considerations of health, comfort, and beauty'. It campaigned against tight lacing, hampering skirts, and high-heeled or narrow-toed shoes and boots, but one of its main aims was to reduce the weight of underclothing to a maximum of 7 lb.[44] It encouraged the wearing of divided skirts, too, along lines advocated unsuccessfully about thirty years earlier by the American Mrs Bloomer and her supporters.

Despite holding a successful international exhibition in 1883, its campaign was widely condemned as unfeminine. Mrs G. Armytage in the *Fortnightly Review* described the divided skirt as 'so utterly opposed to all the true spring of feminine action as regards apparel that it is morally impossible that it can ever be made popular. The principles which underlie the Rational Dress Association are false to nature.'[31] One of the benefits claimed by advocates of the new fashion was that it would ease female participation in sport. Hence, although the organization faded away in the late 1880s it was revived a few years later as a result of the

Rational dress (including the wearing of trousers) was recommended for riding a bicycle in the Catalogue of the International Exhibition of Rational Dress, *held in 1883. (The author)*

unprecedented popularity of cycling among women, especially from the mid-1890s. 'Rational dress', including the wearing of knickerbocker suits, quickly became popular among female cyclists in the USA, Germany and France, although it had less success in Britain. Undeterred, Lady Harberton helped to form a new Rational Dress League in 1898, together with an associated magazine. The league encouraged dress reform for both men and women, and especially the wearing of 'some forms of bifurcated garment' by women for cycling, tennis, golf, walking tours and other athletic pursuits.[300] Trousers had been an 'invisible' part of female riding dress since the early nineteenth century and continued to be worn beneath riding habits until the 1890s, when they were replaced by breeches. Similarly, long tweed trousers were worn under matching skirts when following a shoot or walking on the moors.[114] But it was the proposal to adopt them as outer garments that roused hostility and ridicule in society at large. One reformer claimed in August 1897 that a female cyclist needed 'nerves of iron' to ride through a London suburb in rational dress. 'The shouts & yells of the children deafen one, the women shriek with laughter or groan & hiss & all sorts of remarks are shouted . . . some not fit for publication.'[300] Few women adopted the new costume but the widespread use of bicycles did lead to the wearing of less cumbersome skirts. In fact it was claimed that almost every tailor had invented a 'bicycle skirt' of some kind.

Early in the 1880s the bustle had been reintroduced but by the end of the decade it was finally abandoned. During the last years of the century daytime skirts were plain and fitted at the waist, while the main emphasis was on the bodice or blouse. Sleeves became wider, with the so-called leg of mutton fashion popular in the mid-1890s. Tailor-mades, in the form of coat and skirt worn with a blouse, were widely adopted. The New Woman was more independent than previous generations and she wanted practical clothes, suitable for walking and travelling, or even mountain climbing. Nevertheless, emancipation had its limits. Women entered the twentieth century still wearing a full-length skirt, tightly laced corset and boned bodice, with a highly decorated hat and hair 'long and elaborately dressed'.[114] Even for new sports like tennis, serge or flannel skirts were normally worn, with a blouse or shirt, a stiff belt and a hat.

Among men, meanwhile, 'understatement and sobriety' became linked to a generally utilitarian approach to clothes during the Victorian years.[114] If women's garments, especially early in the queen's reign, had emphasized their 'dependent' social role, those of men responded to the need to work in urban offices and factories. There was widespread adoption of a more uniform, 'democratic' appearance. In 1874 the *Tailor and Cutter* pointed out that a quarter of a century earlier the different classes of society had been more clearly defined than was currently the case:

> on the street, the promenade or other place of resort, a man's position in society could more easily be traced from his dress and appearance than now. In these days, the clerk with a very moderate salary can appear on the promenade with all the airs and appearance of those very much his superiors.[114]

Characteristic regional outfits and even the wearing of smocks by agricultural workers became rarer. Already in the late 1860s it was claimed that a 'smockfrock is not to be seen in all Cumberland; every man on Sundays and holidays wears broad cloth'.[1] By the 1880s two main styles of coat for formal day wear had emerged – the frock coat, which was worn with a high silk hat, and the morning coat with the less formal hard felt bowler. But the frock coat even at that date was coming to be regarded as old fashioned for all except the most formal occasions, with a morning coat the popular garment for day and business wear. Hence the embarrassment of Lupin Pooter in *The Diary of a Nobody*, when his father insisted on wearing a frock coat with a straw hat while on holiday at Broadstairs.[400] There were other sartorial conventions to observe as well: 'to expose an inch too much shirt-front (by day) was a social stigma indicating that the wearer was "not quite."'[142]

Lounge suits, consisting of jacket, trousers and waistcoat, and made from tweed, serge, or flannel material, became increasingly popular. From around the middle of the century they were worn by the better-off for leisure pursuits, while they were rapidly adopted by lower middle-class men and artisans as best wear. In addition, variations of the short, double-breasted 'reefer' jacket were widely worn around this time by labourers and the like.

Another version of the lounge coat emerged in the early 1860s with the advent of the Norfolk jacket, cut with box pleats on either side of the centre front and at the centre back, and with a belt at the waist.[114] Unlike an ordinary lounge suit, the Norfolk jacket, frequently worn with knickerbockers, was confined to country pastimes. It became extremely popular for shooting and later on for golf, cycling and climbing. In the late 1850s knickerbockers were also worn by little boys, although by the end of the century they were replaced in popularity by sailor suits for girls and boys alike.

Spotless white linen was still the hallmark of a gentleman, and late in the century an increased use of starch added to its crisp appearance, giving an air of stiff respectability. Those unable to afford substantial laundry bills sought to create the same effect by using artificial shirt fronts, which were easier to clean and cheaper to discard.

The setting up of large department stores in the second half of the period increased the availability of fashionable clothes for men and women alike. At William Whiteley's store in Bayswater, the self-styled 'Universal Provider' claimed to be able to supply anything from 'a pin to an elephant'. It was said to be possible to enter Whiteley's gentlemen's outfitting department wearing 'one attire and come out in another, instantly equipped for wedding, garden-party, racecourse, funeral, or evening party'.[226]

Books of etiquette for men warned of the importance of 'correct' dress. In 1900 one such pointed out that although lounge suits were no longer restricted to sports and country wear, they were still inappropriate for an afternoon in London. 'When you are in town,' it advised, 'you mustn't appear in a lounge suit and a bowler after lunch, and of course if you have any business appointment in the morning, you would wear a frock or morning coat with a silk hat.' Other lapses to be avoided included wearing a silk tie with tennis and boating flannels, or a silk hat with a navy blue jacket.[271]

One further sartorial development was the blazer, which in the late nineteenth century was usually a brightly coloured or striped flannel jacket. It was widely worn at the seaside by the mid-1880s and for summer sports such as tennis, cricket and rowing.

Men's clothes, therefore, and to a lesser extent those of women, were modified by changing life styles and by the growing informality in social relations. The increased opportunities for leisure and pleasure, including seaside holidays and sports, influenced fashions and called for a wider variety of outfits. Clothing remained an indicator of status and class, with the wearing of hats or bonnets and gloves essential symbols of respectability for all Victorians. Among the working classes the ownership of special Sunday clothes remained important, and every effort was made to obtain these by all except the very poorest. The use of stiff best clothes for children could also be seen as an indicator of firm discipline. That applied even in well-to-do families. Sarah Sedgwick, who worked as a nursemaid in a large household near Doncaster at the end of the Victorian era, remembered the large quantity of clothes the children had to wear and the frequent changes that took place.

> Little girls at that time wore in winter a vest, a woollen binder, drawers, a bodice, a flannel petticoat, and a cotton petticoat; and on top flannel dresses. In summer the flannel petticoat was exchanged for one of lighter weight, the binder was cotton instead of wool, and the frocks cotton, linen or muslin. But whatever the season they never wore the same clothes in the morning as they wore in the

afternoon, and of course there was a complete change from top to bottom when the dressing-up to go downstairs [to see their parents] took place . . . At that time no little girl went outside the house without gloves of wool or cashmere . . . The little boys . . . used to look a picture in velvet knickers, and silk or crêpe-de-chine shirts with frills down the front and long sleeves . . . All the children, if they were dressed up for a party, quite understood being tied on to their chairs, or when older sitting perfectly still, so that nothing would get creased.

Associated with the growing attention paid to fashion was that given to shopping, which became accepted as an important leisure pursuit by all classes, particularly among women. As a result of transport improvements, distinct areas developed in towns and cities which catered for a particular class of clientele. That applied as much to the industrial Midlands and the north as to centres like Bath, Cheltenham and Brighton, which were the resort of well-to-do residents and holidaymakers, and, of course, to London itself. In the West End élite shopping during the Season took place between 2 p.m. and 4 p.m. In the late 1850s Augustus Sala described the 'innately fashionable' shops in Regent Street, which he labelled the 'great trunk-road in Vanity Fair': 'Fancy watchmakers, haberdashers, and photographers; fancy stationers, fancy hosiers, and fancy staymakers; music shops, shawl shops, jewellers, French glove shops, perfumery, and point lace shops, confectioners and milliners . . . these are the merchants whose wares are exhibited.'[72]

As the stylish world flocked to see the goods on offer, in carriages and on foot, people stopped to talk with acquaintances and to flirt with friends of the opposite sex, 'regardless of other carriages trying to proceed'. But respectable ladies had to be careful to avoid locations where they might be mistaken for prostitutes. Hence Jeannette Marshall, duly chaperoned, had to confine shopping trips to the 'heavenly' Burlington Arcade to the mornings, as from lunchtime it became a well-known haunt of street walkers.

According to Lady Jeune, each shop in these fashionable areas had its speciality, and the more expensive the merchandise the more conservative its business methods:

Jones sold the best silks, Smith the best gloves, Brown the best bonnets, Madame X was far and away the only good milliner and dressmaker . . . We bought our goods at these various shops, and dutifully followed in the steps of our forefathers, paying for the things we had at the end of the year, for no well-thought-of firm ever demanded or expected more than a yearly payment of their debts. If residence in the country made a visit to London to choose what was wanted an impossibility, Jones, Brown, or Smith knew the need of their particular customer, and the orders sent were executed and despatched with unfailing accuracy.[61]

However, the ritual of shopping in such establishments was both solemn and lengthy and those who entered were expected to make a purchase rather than merely look around.

There were also some large retail stores run along the lines of a market or bazaar. They consisted of a big central hall with galleries or upper floors in which were found additional stalls and counters. The Soho Bazaar was one such. It occupied several houses in a corner of Soho and brought together vendors of millinery, lace, gloves, jewellery and other articles. Nor was the Bazaar designed merely for those of limited means. At the height of the Season the long rows of carriages strung out before its doors confirmed its popularity with the affluent. A similar enterprise was the Pantheon Bazaar in Oxford Street, which sold accessories, cutlery, jewellery, toys, children's books and clothes, ornaments and artificial flowers. On one side of the toy bazaar was an aviary selling caged birds.[72] The stalls were rented by individual traders but together they provided the potential purchaser with a large range of competing merchandise from which to make a selection.

It was from these businesses that the department store developed, supplying a large number of speciality lines under its own roof. The Paris store Bon Marché, which opened in 1852, is often credited with inaugurating the new era. But in practice, many of the principles it applied had already been adopted in English provincial shops. These included Kendal Milne & Faulkner in Manchester, which began offering drapery, millinery, upholstery, carpets and mourning outfits from the late 1830s. Similarly Bainbridge's of Newcastle upon Tyne by 1845 contained departments for dress and furnishing fabrics, fashion accessories, furs and family mourning, as well as 'sewed muslin dresses', an early form of ready-to-wear clothing. All the merchandise was displayed at fixed prices, thereby eliminating the older system of bargaining, and customers were encouraged to walk around without any obligation to buy.[72]

It was in the 1860s and early 1870s that department stores grew to major importance in Britain.[263] Drapers like Whiteley's in Bayswater, Marshall and Snelgrove in Oxford Street, and Barker's in Kensington expanded into large businesses, together with Broadbent's in Southport[276] and Harrod's in London, which started as grocery shops, and Lewis's of Liverpool, which began as a boys' and youths' outfitter.[149] The ability of the stores to buy in bulk and their high rate of turnover allowed them to undercut more traditional competitors. They also carried varied merchandise and their encouragement to customers to 'shop around' gave a chance to stroll from department to department within a single store, or to visit the corresponding department in competing stores in order to compare quality, price, styles and value. By 1877 Barker's of Kensington were publishing in their Christmas calendar the welcome recommendation of *The Queen* magazine that, 'For good Drapery at a moderate price there is no better establishment in London than Barker's.'[266]

As a result of the wider transport network women could travel from the suburbs or even further afield to spend a day shopping. In the 1870s Lady Jebb came up to London for this purpose from Cambridge, and her niece, Maud Darwin, did the same a decade later.[72] Some firms, like Whiteley's, began to provide a restaurant where customers could enjoy a rest and refreshments, as well as a ladies' cloakroom. The latter facility was particularly appreciated, since although the Ladies Lavatory Company opened its first premises at Oxford Circus in 1884, there were few others available and most well-to-do women were unwilling to be seen entering them. By 1872, the year Whiteley's opened its restaurant, the firm was serving around four thousand customers daily, of whom perhaps five hundred to a thousand came from outside the capital.[226] From 1880 the opening of the ABC tea shops also enabled ladies to eat in town by themselves with perfect propriety and to meet their friends. The first Lyons' tea shop, offering a similar service, opened in Piccadilly in 1894. In the department-store restaurants, dainty teas and luncheons were served, 'perhaps with music by a pianist or even a ladies' string quartette' to put customers into a spending mood.[72]

Certainly Lady Jeune, an enthusiast for the attractions of department stores, described shopping in the 1890s as an 'unsuccessful struggle against overwhelming temptations':

We look for a ribbon, a flower, a chiffon of some sort or other, and find ourselves in a Paradise of ribbons, flowers, and chiffons, without which our life becomes impossible, and our gown unwearable . . . There are many shops in London into which one cannot safely trust oneself. There are the drawbacks of noise, heat, and

Eager bargain hunters at the sales at Peter Robinson's Department Store in London, c. 1900.
(The author)

overcrowding, but they are more than counterbalanced by the brightness of the electric light and the brilliancy of colour, and the endless variety on every side. There are two very important changes which have contributed to the temptation of spending money nowadays. One is gathering together under one roof all kinds of goods – clothing, millinery, groceries, furniture, in fact all the necessaries of life . . . And the other is the employment of women as shop assistants in the place of men . . . What an amount of trouble and expense is avoided where one can order one's New Zealand mutton downstairs, buy one's carpet on the ground-floor, and deck oneself out in all the glory of Worth or La Ferrier, on the top floor, to all of which one is borne on the wings of a lift, swift and silent.[61]

Even those like Marion Sambourne, who preferred to order special outfits from an exclusive dressmaker or tailor, patronized the department stores for smaller and less important purchases. Household shopping took up a good deal of Mrs Sambourne's time, and entries in her diary often began, 'To stores morning.' That usually meant a visit to John Barker's or one of the other shops along the newly rebuilt Kensington High Street. Everyday food for the kitchen was ordered by the cook on account, with Marion merely paying the bills from time to time, but she liked to select luxury items for dinner parties. 'Went to stores, bought crayfish, chicken, cherries, ordered ice' reads one entry.[257] She inspected ready made clothes in the department stores, since these could be altered to fit by dressmakers on the premises, or she might take advantage of specialist tailoring and dressmaking departments where outfits were made up to meet the customer's requirements. To do this she was prepared to travel considerable distances, going by the Metropolitan Railway to visit Whiteley's in Westbourne Grove, and Maple's and Shoolbred's in Tottenham Court Road. Marshall and Snelgrove was an omnibus journey away in Oxford Street, and Barker's was within walking distance. She was a finicky shopper, returning 'grey dress to Snelgrove, promised to send credit' on one occasion. 'Changed jersey at Marshalls, fits so badly' was another diary entry. Shopping could be tiring so breaks for refreshment were part of the routine. 'To Bond Street, had cup of chocolate at Charbonnels', and 'To Gunters for ices' were two typical comments.[257]

Many department stores were anxious to maintain the standards of individual service associated with smaller specialist retailers.[256] In September 1880 John Barker informed one customer, Mrs Edward Chesterton, that they would 'wait upon' her at her home 'for the purpose of offering for your selection a Bonnet of the latest Parisian taste, of which we have a large assortment ready for your choice; or can, if preferred, make you one to order.' The assistant would call on Mrs Chesterton at any time she desired, 'unless you would prefer to pay a visit to our Millinery Department yourself'.[266]

Debenham and Freebody, who in 1870 owned Cavendish House in Cheltenham, offered five different services for ladies' garments. The first was made-to-measure in their high-class dressmaking salon; then there were part-made clothes, which could be completed by the purchaser herself or by her dressmaker; thirdly there were complete ready-to-wear items; fourthly there was a dressmaking service, which supplied fabric and paper patterns; and finally there was a mail order facility for all of these. Catalogues were sent to potential

Ladies lunching at the Empress Club, the most luxurious female club in London, c. 1900. Members could read newspapers and magazines in the comfortable sitting rooms, meet their friends, or rest for a while during a shopping expedition. They could even stay overnight. (The author)

purchasers by this and other firms, and they not only stimulated the mail order business but gave recipients ideas of current fashion.

For all drapery shops with pretensions to fashion leadership it was important to emphasize connections with Paris, since the French capital held 'the sceptre where feminine dress' was concerned.[314] The large department stores could afford to buy imported silks and millinery, as well as model dresses from fashion designers such as Worth and Doucet, and these were then copied to meet the requirements of English customers. Even provincial drapers sought to establish their French credentials, as with Mrs J.L. Tucker & Sons of Exeter. In April 1880 the proprietors announced 'their return from PARIS with a Beautiful Assortment of the Choicest Productions for the Season. Their suites of showrooms are now re-opened. And the favour of a visit is respectfully solicited.'[30] Similarly Green & Son, court dressmakers of Exeter, reported that they had 'imported from the First Houses in Paris, Models of the Newest Styles in Dresses, from which Ladies can select in accordance with individual taste'.[30]

As early as the 1840s Browns of Chester, which catered for county society in Cheshire, claimed their outfits were 'personally selected' in Paris by the proprietors. Many of their customers came to Chester for a week's shopping, staying at one of the best hotels and buying enough dresses to last for the next three months. According to a former employee, who worked in the fur department, orders worth several hundred pounds would be placed. 'They used to come in: "Now the very best. I leave it in your hands." And Mr. Holmes would select a skin and I would make up a model in calico . . . The customers would come in as many as three times for one coat.'[382]

So great was the fascination with French fashion that some proprietors such as Margaret Cameron of Edinburgh, added a French-sounding (and entirely bogus) name to their business in order to attract prestigious customers. In Miss Cameron's case the firm of milliners, dressmakers, stay and corset makers was known as Cameron and Violard and she herself visited London and Paris regularly to purchase goods and learn of the latest fashions.[256] Similarly Helen Bagrie, an Aberdeen costumière, made it her business to visit London and Paris before returning with model dresses and bales of material in preparation for the coming season. At her establishment, as at most others, the selection of new clothes was regarded as a pleasant entertainment, and the initial fitting for a made-to-measure garment could take half a day.

Only the wealthiest had dresses personally made for them by the French fashion leaders. Lady Warwick remembered that Worth of Paris was the idol of the socially ambitious.

Taking tea at Slater's Restaurant in Piccadilly, London, c. 1900. Note the elaborate decor. (The author)

Twice I consulted Jean Worth regarding a costume for a fancy-dress ball . . .
A Worth frock was, of course, very costly. I never had one for which the bill
was less than a hundred guineas, and often his gowns were half as much again.
But against this, I always set two facts, that they were the creations of a man
of genius, and that the materials would never wear out.[371]

For day gowns and lingerie she patronized Doucet. 'I had my special . . . *vendeuse*, at
Doucet's, and she knew almost as surely as I did myself just what would please me.'

For the male élite, Savile Row was the major destination, with firms like Henry
Poole clothing 'two-thirds of the *beau monde*' in the mid-nineteenth century.
Poole's combined the skills of a high-class tailor with some of the benefits of a
club. Henry Poole himself returned to Savile Row at about 3.30 in the afternoon
and remained until 5 p.m. playing the genial host to 'sundry sporting nobility in a
candelabra-lit parlour behind the showroom'. Here cigars, hock and claret were
liberally dispensed. By the 1860s the firm enjoyed the patronage of the Prince of
Wales as well as members of a number of other European royal families.[361]

Davies & Son of Hanover Street was another exclusive tailoring establishment. It
counted prime ministers among its clients and was also a popular rendezvous for
the social élite. By 1850 it had begun to offer guest bedrooms for customers on the
top floor and there were those who maintained that this was merely a cover for
prostitution, with 'a discreet eye turned to the ladies who accompanied' the
guests.[361] Others have claimed that one reason why gentlemen arranged so many
fittings with their tailor was because 'in the back, or round the corner, would be
something else – in lots of cases that's where all these dozens of fittings came from'.
The fitting was merely an excuse for activities of a 'more personal nature'.[361]

For working-class purchasers such conspicuous consumption was impossible.
Few could even afford to patronize the new department stores, which were aimed
primarily at a middle-class clientele. Nevertheless, in the humbler ranks of
society, too, shopping could be a pleasure as well as a necessity.[70] It could also be a
way of expressing status, as Geoffrey Crossick has pointed out for artisan families
in Kentish London. There the wife of a lighterman on the London riverside felt
she was with her equals when she went shopping with the wife of a stevedore or of
a shipwright, 'but never with the wife of a docker or an unskilled labourer'.[134]

The Victorian years were the heyday of the little corner shop and the wives and
daughters of local families would run in and out of the shop nearest to them to
make small purchases of tea or jam or treacle, or merely for a gossip. The fact that
few groceries were ready packaged meant a long wait while each item was
weighed out. Customers took their time, too, ordering the next thing on their list
only when its predecessor had been bagged up. In the interim they would talk to
one another and make jokes which 'might spark along the line of assistants and
backfire through the customers'.[340] In Bolton the young Alice Foley remembered
one neighbour who would go into a nearby shop and, seating herself on an
upturned box by the counter, would call out, 'It's nobbut me, Mrs Walker;
I dur'nt want owt, I've only cum' eaut o't road o' yon lot.' Once she had escaped
from her domestic burdens she would spend a good half-hour chatting to the
customers, and then she would depart, 'nourished and refreshed for further bouts

"wi' yon lot"'. Mrs Walker, the shopkeeper, for her part claimed that she 'wouldn't leave this place even if I were losing money; it's worth it for't entertainment'.[161] In such neighbourhoods the shop acted as a community centre for wives who had few other opportunities for a break in the drudging daily routine, or the chance to discuss their problems.

There were door-to-door vendors, too, and women were believed to be particularly susceptible to the blandishments of the tallyman. Charles Booth claimed it was the salesman's 'power of talk' which persuaded wives in 'better' working-class neighbourhoods to buy. They were left at home all day, and along would come a tallyman 'with an oily tongue; they like a gossip, and don't have a chance of seeing many men, so they talk, and then buy.' Subtle flattery and sexual innuendo were part of the successful tradesman's routine.[340]

A different kind of entertainment was provided by cheapjack salesmen like 'Pot Bailey', who auctioned crockery at night on a piece of spare ground near Alice Foley's home. Each item was attractively displayed on a bed of straw, illuminated by flickering paraffin flares. Pot Bailey himself was a bluff, good-humoured man, who promoted his wares with infectious gusto and displayed the china with fascinating skill. 'This performance, accompanied by rich banter always swayed the crowd, and money and crockery readily changed hands.'[161] But for Alice herself, the shopping trip she enjoyed best was to be taken into the centre of Bolton on a Saturday evening, when life was

> at its gayest and rowdiest; the open shop fronts lit by paraffin flares, competing traders bawling their wares, and narrow streets crowded with buyers or gaping sight-seers . . . The covered market was a mecca for the townsfolk . . . Wonderful penny stalls attracted old and young as did the adjoining open food stores where elders sat on upturned mineral boxes devouring ham sandwiches or black-puddings daubed with mustard whilst their off-spring licked ice-cream out of tall glasses. Up in the gallery crowds milled round the cages of live-stock, of puppies, pigeons, rabbits, doves and chickens . . . all contributing to the pervading warmth, smells, noise and gaiety of life caught in a moment of time.[161]

PUBLIC HOUSES, BEER SHOPS AND DANCES

During the nineteenth century public houses and beer shops were major providers of refreshment and recreation for working-class people, particularly the menfolk. Following the passage of the Beer Act in 1830 numerous beerhouses were set up in the poorer areas of town. They were cheap to open, and although forbidden to sell spirits they were at first relatively free from magisterial control. Publicans reacted to the competition in the larger towns by opening gin palaces, with plate-glass windows, ornate frontages, gilded lettering and brilliant illumination. Their splendour was in marked contrast to the often squalid and dingy buildings around them, and there were complaints that they offered temptations injurious 'not only to the grown-up people, but to the children. The lower class of children are tempted into them.'[17] Indeed, not until 1872 was legislation passed forbidding sellers of alcohol from allowing children under sixteen to consume spirits on the premises; fourteen years later the prohibition was extended to beer – but only for youngsters under thirteen.[179] In many cases the restrictions were flouted.

In the early Victorian period consumption per capita of beer and spirits continued to rise, officially peaking in 1874 and 1875 respectively. Spirits consumption in the latter year averaged 1½ gallons per annum for every man, woman and child in the country. It was an indication of the large quantities purchased by some adult males.[234] Such trends caused drinking houses to be condemned by many as centres of debauchery and brawling, and helped to promote the temperance movement. The fact that they were primarily used by labouring people gave rise to fears that the lower orders were losing the benefit of 'contact with persons of superior stations', that they were, in some senses, inhabiting a secret world which their social superiors did not share.[333] In response to the criticisms some publicans began to sell non-alcoholic drinks, including ginger-beer, lemonade and soda water. Already in the early 1860s one temperance reformer noted that a teetotaller asking a publican for a non-intoxicating drink was now treated with courtesy, whereas twenty years before he would have been insulted.[179] At the end of the century Charles Booth observed that ginger-beer was available at many London public houses, although in a number of cases customers wanted it mixed with spirits!

However, public houses and beershops did more than sell drink. To the poor and unlettered, declared the psychologist William James, they stood 'in the place of symphony concerts and of literature' as providers of entertainment.[179] In them were found companionship, comfort (with regular clients often having their special seats), and a wide range of activities such as the organizing of excursions, the setting up of savings clubs – usually for a particular purpose, like the 'goose clubs' formed around Christmas or for outings – and the holding of flower shows, sporting competitions and musical events. At a time when few public rooms were available for hire the club room at a pub was an attractive venue for the meetings of friendly societies, debating groups and even musicians. The Halifax Philharmonic Society, for example, rehearsed at the King's Head, Cow Green, and the Accrington Choral Society met in the assembly room of the Black Bull or the Red Lion Inn. In 1844 the Red Lion was used for theatrical productions, too, including classical drama. Similarly, at this time the principal theatre in Burnley was attached to the Hall Inn.[406] In Nottingham it was even reported in 1851 that several 'working men's libraries' were held in public houses. At two of these, 'political discussions [were] also held under judicious regulations'. Reports in Bolton newspapers similarly reveal the various organizations centred on the public house or its gardens. Among them were bowling, quoits and glee clubs, as well as 'free and easies', the forerunners of music halls. There were plays, fruit and vegetable shows, sweepstake clubs, and opportunities to play cards and dominoes.[85] In 1855 when the Star Inn in the town was rebuilt after a fire its evening entertainment included a string and brass band, madrigal singers, comedians, a black melodist and 'histrionic sketches', as well as food and drink.[406]

In Flora Thompson's Oxfordshire hamlet the single public house attracted almost all the adult male population. They gathered each evening to sip half-pints, 'drop by drop, to make them last', and discuss local events or politics or the latest farming methods. They would also sing a few songs 'to oblige'. Those who did not take part were known either to 'have religion', and therefore to disapprove of public houses on moral grounds, or were suspected of being 'close wi' their ha'pence'. The rest went as a matter of course, each appropriating his particular seat on the settle or bench and enjoying the roaring fire, red window curtains and well-scoured pewter, which were a welcome contrast to their own poverty-stricken cottages.[342]

In the larger towns the entertainment was far more varied and included the holding of tavern concerts, where amateur and professional musicians, impersonators, ventriloquists, tap dancers and 'Ethiopian' minstrels provided amusement as well as stimulating drink sales.[151] By the 1840s London had a substantial body of semi-professionals working in the singing saloons. Among them was Charles Rice, who combined this with employment as an attendant at the British Museum. His diaries reveal the large number of public houses in which he worked, sometimes with several engagements carried out on a single evening. A typical entry relates to 5 March 1840:

Child performer in a Liverpool public house, 1895. (Liverpool Libraries and Information Service)

. . . worked all day at Museum . . . Went in evening to Horse & Dolphin: —
Singers Engaged: Mrs. Cluett, Jackson, & me. — The Room was very fairly filled,
and the singing went off with great success . . . In the course of the Evening, I
went to Tom Martin's Benefit at Furzman's Catherine Wheel, Windmill St
Haymarket. The Room was not full; — met Charley Sloman, Coulson, & Mrs.
Chell. — I sang 'St. Anthony,' encore 'Billy Taylor;' — and by desire of a party of
gents in the room, I sang 'The Wolf,' which went off immensely, and I sang 'Tom
Noddy.' . . . Horse & Dolphin closed at ½ past Eleven, got home about ¼ past 12.
  Called in at The Grapes Compton St. and settled with Sigrist, to go there every
Monday, with Ryan, Mrs. Ryan, & Myers. To Commence next Monday Evening.[309]

In Brighton wives accompanied their husbands to the pubs on Saturday
evenings, and on other nights when there were 'free and easies', involving musical
entertainment, the whole family would join in. A few women also visited at other
times, perhaps drinking with female friends at midday on Mondays, when there
was still some housekeeping money left.[234]

But many of the public houses and beershops had their darker side, with
clandestine gambling, prostitution and brutal sports part of the regular
programmes. The RSPCA frequently found army officers involved in cruel sports
in drinking places, especially in the earlier Victorian years,[179] while at Preston in the
1850s cockfighting was said to linger on in the beerhouses, despite its illegality.
According to the chaplain of the Preston House of Correction there were several
men imprisoned for cockfighting: 'the beerhouse-keepers supply the cocks . . . It is
one of the inducements, out of many, that the beerhouse-keepers resort to, to attract
custom; cock-fighting, dog-fighting, and badger-baiting.'[17] Ratting was another
dubious diversion, with the vermin released into a pit where a trained terrier was
waiting to pounce. The sport consisted of competitions between the dogs as to the
number of rats killed within a fixed time. One champion terrier, about which Henry
Mayhew heard in the 1850s, could kill two hundred barn rats in a session. He was
such a favourite with his owner that he wore a lady's bracelet as a collar.[63]

Prostitution, too, was an important service provided by the shadier publicans
and beerhouse-keepers. In 1862, at a time when there were 101 beerhouses and 80
public houses in Halifax, a local police superintendent claimed that nineteen of the
former and four of the latter were the 'known resorts of thieves and prostitutes and
I am sorry to report that many of the beer houses are little if anything better than
common brothels'.[375] The situation was worse in garrison towns like Aldershot,
Devonport and Portsmouth, where publicans were heavily involved in meeting the
servicemen's sexual needs. At the Battle of Inkerman pub in Portsmouth the
landlord specialized in providing young girls, thus leading to the house being
known as the 'Infant School'. Young girls also predominated at the Good Intent in
the town, while at the Fortune of War four adjacent tenements were all used as
brothels. Significantly Mr Russell, owner of the Fortune, professed complete
ignorance of any such activities.[287] According to government statistics, in 1865
23 public houses and 61 beershops in Portsmouth were operating as brothels or
offered accommodation for 'immoral purposes'. By 1876 the enforcement of new
licensing laws had led them to abandon the practice, although many doubtless

RATTING—"THE GRAHAM ARMS," GRAHAM STREET.

A ratting match in a London public house in the 1840s. Note the mixed class of spectator. Ratting remained a popular sport to the end of the century, with large wagers changing hands. The supply of rats usually came from the sewers. (From Henry Mayhew, London Labour and the London Poor, *1861 edn)*

encouraged 'pot house' girls to frequent their premises, in order to attract male customers. Certainly the number of street walkers remained at a high level, with 913 at work in the town in 1875 and 942 in 1881. At the latter date Devonport, another major centre, had 655 prostitutes officially recorded and Aldershot 292.

Even before the passage of the Contagious Diseases Acts of 1862, 1868 and 1869 required the medical inspection of prostitutes in garrison towns and ports (until their repeal in 1886), Aldershot publicans employed surgeons to ensure that women on their premises were clean. 'Better-class prostitutes', notes Brian Harrison, 'usually rented adjacent or nearby cottages from publicans on the understanding that they would pick up custom only in his taproom; lower-grade prostitutes merely rented a room.'[179] In 1868 a witness to a parliamentary inquiry described a visit to one 'notorious house' in Aldershot. He and his companions entered a long room in which about two hundred soldiers and around thirty-five to forty women were gathered. The room was fitted out with chairs, forms and narrow tables, and at one end a fiddler was playing a lively tune to which a few couples 'were dancing a merry accompaniment. Three or four persons, acting as waiters, were briskly engaged in seeking and attending to orders, bringing in beer, &c., which was shared by the soldiers with their female companions, who either sat by their sides, or, as was more frequently the case on their knees. But, amidst all the loud talking, drinking, and singing, I heard no quarrelsome language used . . . and everyone appeared in good humour.'[179]

In the early 1880s, as pressure grew for the repeal of the Contagious Diseases Acts, there was increased activity among the 'social purity' movements in garrison and seaport towns. In 1888 the National Vigilance Association achieved the closure of twenty-two Aldershot brothels. According to the association's newspaper, after the closure ninety women paraded the town's streets in protest at losing their livelihood and claiming that they would have to swell the ranks of the unemployed as a result of this exercise of middle-class morality.

In London, too, public houses offered music and dancing, as well as the services of prostitutes. Though, as Donald Thomas points out, the 'panorama of sexual opportunities' available in the capital in the 1860s was a great deal wider than that. At a time when the number of prostitutes in London was computed variously as between 8,500 and 80,000 they plied their trade in cafés, cigar divans, dancing academies and pleasure gardens in the West End and Chelsea, as well as in the seedier surroundings of opium houses in Stepney, the tavern rooms 'of the White Swan in Shadwell and the dance halls of the Ratcliffe Highway'.

Happily, in many cases a public house's connections with dancing had no unsavoury associations. In Cumbria, where the services of itinerant dancing masters were an integral part of traditional social life, the club room of a public house was a common venue for dances. One of the migrant teachers who travelled around during the summer months was Oliver Cowper. He charged 6*d* per lesson for children and 1*s* for adults and insisted that pupils at his town classes wear white gloves, although in the villages they were excused. At the end of each course a 'finishing ball' was held so that parents could see how well their children had learnt. Like the other instructors he seems to have taught country dances as well as waltzes and quadrilles. Music was supplied mainly by local performers on an ad hoc basis, although there were a few quadrille bands based in towns such as Kendal, Maryport and Carlisle, and these were joined in the last years of the century by a small number of string bands.[253] The maids on Cumbrian farms spent a large part of their wages on clothes for the balls. In the late 1860s it was claimed that a girl 'whose ordinary costume' comprised a coarse petticoat, 'pinned close round her body, and wooden clogs', would appear at a dance in a white muslin dress, white kid boots and gloves, and with 'a wreath of artificial flowers on her head'.[1]

Other districts may have lacked the Lakeland's enthusiasm for dancing, but especially in the early Victorian years the larger inns and hotels served as centres for balls and dinners even for the well-to-do. In Banbury, Oxfordshire, for example, the social season revolved around balls held at the major public houses during January and February. Some were sponsored by organizations like the Oddfellows Friendly Society or the Yeomanry Cavalry, but there were two annual public balls. One, for the aristocracy and gentry, was held at the Red Lion and was attended by over a hundred people, with feasting and festivities lasting late into the night. The other was for tradesmen and those of lower social standing. It was held at the Flying Horse, where 'the absence of *bon ton*' among the assembled company was more than compensated for 'by a profusion of beauty and bonhomie'.[178]

But with the growth of the temperance movement and of middle-class concerns about the respectability of public houses, it came to be seen as undesirable for females to enter even the best inns for purposes of entertainment. New venues were sought and in the case of Banbury, as in many other towns, this meant a resort to the town hall and corn exchange.[178] In some places assembly rooms served a similar purpose and in villages the schoolroom or a large barn might be used. Likewise parties could be held in private houses, as in Thomas Hardy's novel *Under the Greenwood Tree*. There, the living room of the tranter (or carrier), Reuben Dewy, was cleared for a Christmas celebration and men and women jigged madly round to the squeak of the fiddles, as dance followed dance in an endless sequence.[196]

To some Victorians, dancing was frivolous and immoral, even when it took place in private homes. This view was held particularly by Nonconformists and supporters of the temperance cause. Nonetheless it was a pastime enjoyed by large numbers of young people and it was accepted as an essential part of the London Season of the social élite. *Harpers* magazine in 1886 noted that some of the smaller dances held in private residences at that time could be dismal, with mothers and daughters ranged two or three deep round the walls, many of them standing, and the middle of the room, intended for dancing, reduced to only about ten feet by six. Here 'struggling couples beat one against another . . . The floor oscillates; wax candles sprinkle their substance liberally about; hot young men open windows, and chilly dowagers shut them.'[158] This was in sharp contrast to balls in large houses, where impressive rooms, hung with historic pictures, would open out from one another to give long vistas. Two or three of these would be cleared for dancing, while the rest were left 'in their everyday state of comfort, where non-dancers can stroll or sit as luxuriously as if no ball was going on. There is probably a terrace, balcony or garden, lit with Chinese lamps, where those who are hot can breathe a cooler air', and where discreet flirtations could be conducted.[158]

In the country, when friends met together to enjoy themselves, such gatherings could be pleasantly informal. In January 1873 Francis Kilvert went with his two sisters to a 'jolly party at Sir John Awdry's', near his Langley Burrell home.

> Almost everybody in the neighbourhood was there . . . [and] when we drove up the harp and the fiddles were going. 'Bang went the drum, the ball opened immediately, and I knew not which dancer most to admire,' . . . The dining room was turned into the ball room, beautifully lighted overhead, and the smooth polished oaken floor went magnificently, just like glass, but not a bit too slippery, though Eliza Stiles came down with a crash full on her back in Sir Roger de Coverley, and there was a roar of laughter which, combined with Eliza's fall, shook the room . . . Madder and madder screamed the flying fiddle bows. Sir Roger became a wild romp till the fiddles suddenly stopped dead and there was a scream of laughter. Oh, it was such fun and Francie Rooke was brilliant. When shall I have another such partner as Francie Rooke?
>
> An excellent supper and we got home about one o'clock, on a fine moonlit night . . . 150 or more altogether, and they fell to playing the game of catch-as-catch-can.[273]

By the end of the century the dances in vogue were the quadrille, lancers, waltz, schottische, Highland reel, polka, which had largely replaced the formerly

Children's fancy-dress ball at the
Mansion House, London, 1901.
(The author)

popular gallop, and the cotillon, with which a ball closed. Certain of the wealthier
hostesses during the London Season gave expensive presents to guests in the
course of this dance. Girls attended the balls carefully chaperoned and it was
thought improper for any of them to dance more than three times with the same
partner. The chaperons, meanwhile, acted as 'gatekeepers', vetting who was or
was not acceptable as a partner and perhaps a future husband.

For the socially ambitious, fancy-dress balls were regarded as the most desirable
means of celebrating special events and of making a mark. Large fancy-dress balls
were widely reported in the press, and Debenham and Freebody even published an
advice manual on what to wear on such occasions. By 1900 it had gone into several
editions. Part of the attraction of fancy dress was that it gave its wearer the chance to
assume a totally new personality and behave in a different way. This was especially the
case when masks were worn. Nor was it only the rich and famous who joined in. In
one issue of *The Queen* on 14 January 1893 there were accounts of a fancy dress ball
for children at the Assembly Rooms, Southsea, in aid of a local hospital and a similar
ball for adults at the Drill Hall, Merthyr Tydfil, in support of the town's General
Hospital, to say nothing of several private dances. Even socialist organizations joined
in. *The Clarion* newspaper of 23 November 1895, included an invitation for cyclists
belonging to its associated cycling club in the Manchester area to attend a fancy-dress
ball organized by the Pendlebury and Swinton branch, in order to clear a debt on the

Labour Hall. Tickets were 1s each and those attending were advised that the pierrot costumes they wore in their cycle parades would be quite suitable.

However, the most famous fancy-dress ball of the century was probably that held at Devonshire House in London in 1897 to celebrate Queen Victoria's Diamond Jubilee. Lady Randolph Churchill considered it 'more than a ball, it was a spectacle. Everyone of note was there, representing the intellect, beauty and fashion of the day.' The several hundred guests, who included the Prince and Princess of Wales and other royalty, were asked to come dressed as famous historical personages. Lady Randolph herself appeared in a large Byzantine head-dress, with a golden orb in one hand and a huge lily in the other, as Empress Theodora. These accessories successfully prevented her from taking any part in the actual dancing. There were eight duchesses present, the richest of them choosing to come arrayed in a simple costume as Charlotte Corday, in a mobcap. The Duke and Duchess of Devonshire themselves were attired as the Emperor Charles V and Queen Zenobia of Palmyra, as they greeted their guests at the top of the marble staircase.[229]

The young Duchess of Marlborough also attended, despite being in an advanced state of pregnancy. She regarded it 'a fitting climax to a brilliant season'. The ball lasted into the early hours of the morning and the sun was rising as she walked through Green Park to Spencer House, where the Marlboroughs were then living. But a jarring note was struck when on her way she passed the shabby forms of men sleeping rough, 'too dispirited or sunk to find work or favour, they sprawled in sodden stupor . . . In my billowing period dress, I must have seemed to them a vision of wealth and youth, and I thought soberly that they must hate me. But they only looked, and some even had a compliment to enliven my progress.'[89] Yet she recognized sadly that they were 'pitiful representatives of the submerged tenth' of the population who had no share in the pastimes and pleasures available in increasing abundance to their more fortunate fellow citizens.

Additional Sources Used

Mrs G. Armytage, 'Modern Dress' in the *Fortnightly Review*, September 1883.
Devon Weekly Times, 30 April and 7 May 1880.
Isle of Wight Times, 12 January 1888.
Anthea Jarvis, ' "There was a Young Man of Bengal . . ." The Vogue for Fancy Dress, 1830–1950' in *Costume*, No. 16 (1982).
Pittville Pump Room Museum of Fashion, Cheltenham, displays, etc.
Rational Dress Society's Gazette, October 1888, in the Bodleian Library, Oxford, Per.1676.d.8.
Report on the Operation of the Contagious Diseases Acts, for 1881, Parliamentary Papers, 1882, Vol. LIII.
Return of Public Houses and Beerhouses used as Brothels or Houses of Accommodation for Immoral Purposes within the Districts subjected to the Contagious Diseases Acts during 1865 to 1881, Parliamentary Papers, 1882, Vol. LIII.
Sarah Sedgwick, 'Other People's Children' in Noel Streatfeild (ed.), *The Day Before Yesterday* (London, 1956).
The Clarion, 23 November 1895.
Donald Thomas, *The Victorian Underworld* (London, 1998).
Myna Trustram, *Women of the regiment. Marriage and the Victorian army* (Cambridge, 1984).
Judith R. Walkowitz, *City of Dreadful Delight. Narratives of Sexual Danger in Late-Victorian London* (London, 1994 edn).
Judith R. Walkowitz, *Prostitution and Victorian Society. Women, Class, and the State* (Cambridge, 1980).
Ann Whyte, 'Helen Bagrie, Costumière, 343 Union Street, Aberdeen: Reminiscences of a dressmaker's workroom' in *Costume*, No. 16 (1982).

CHAPTER 4

Traditional Recreations

Traditional recreation was rooted in a social system which was predominantly agrarian, strongly parochial in its orientations, marked by a deep sense of corporate identity; it could not be comfortably absorbed into a society which was urban-centred, governed by contractual relations, biased towards individualism, increasingly moulding its culture in a manner appropriate to the requirements of industrial production. In the new world . . . recreational life had to be reconstructed . . . and the reconstruction was only gradually accomplished over a period of several generations.

Robert W. Malcolmson, *Popular Recreations in English Society 1700–1850*
(Cambridge, 1973), 170–1

COMMUNAL CELEBRATIONS

Many traditional festivities were rooted in the day-to-day round of the countryside. They arose out of the needs of agriculture, the passage of the seasons and the broader rhythms of rural life. They were often a means of cementing local ties and acknowledging mutual responsibilities, as well as a way of bringing together people who lived in isolated communities and who otherwise had few opportunities to socialize. Sometimes they were wholly informal, such as the summer evening gatherings of boys and girls outside the smithy at Westrigg on the Scottish borders. There they staged impromptu dances on the road, or the boys would engage in trials of strength in order to impress their female companions. They also devised practical jokes to play on unpopular older people, like tarring a cow or pig and then turning it loose, so that the owner became covered with tar when recapturing it.[231] In the Highlands these communal links were further reinforced by a vigorous culture of oral Gaelic story telling which survived into the Victorian years, and by the reciting of traditional ballads.[154]

Such activities found a pale reflection in the singing and dancing games played, especially by girls, in some towns even in the 1890s. Alice Foley remembered the quaint rhymes sung to familiar tunes which she and her friends chanted on the streets of Bolton. In spring May Queen processions were organized and in the evenings, when it grew too dark for further play but was still too early to go indoors, they would huddle together in the entrance of an empty shop or house. 'I then became the story-teller and for forty darkling minutes we lived in a fantasy world where knights battled with ogres, where beauty and goodness prevailed, and life was forever fair.'[161]

But in country areas not only were these communal entertainments preserved more tenaciously but they were often associated with particular seasons, such as Christmas, New Year, Easter and Whitsun, or with special agrarian tasks, such as sheep shearing, when there would be food as well as music and dancing for the shearing gang. At Westrigg all the shepherds in the parish and most of the farmers took part, moving from flock to flock and following a well-established ritual in the way they went about their labour. Thus it was usual to arrive for work in clean clothes rather than in dirty ones, as might have been expected. And at the end of their daily stint the men ate together before joining in an informal round of singing and dancing to the music of a fiddle. The last day's clipping was marked by a special party.[231]

Similar arrangements were common in mid-Wales, with the best china and cutlery brought out for the celebratory evening meal and the women spending long hours preparing the food while their menfolk worked outside. One former maid, employed on a large moorland farm, recalled the drudgery that was involved in catering for a hundred people over two days while seven thousand sheep were being sheared. Preparations began a week beforehand and included the baking of special cakes and pies. Much the same was true of the corn-threshing gangs in lowland areas, while at haymaking and harvest not only was food taken to the fields when work was in progress but the intervals for refreshment were seized by harvesters to engage in jokes, horseplay and mild flirtations with female helpers. These included games at haymaking time when the men chased the girls 'around the hay cocks, and young men [vied] with each other in feats of strength'.[344] Despite the heavy labour carried out and the long, exhausting working day, there were always opportunities for fun. Often the men and their families would have an evening meal in the farmhouse and afterwards there would be dancing and games. Anything miserly was frowned upon and most hosts made great efforts to extend generous hospitality.

In south-west Wales such get-togethers were also organized to raise cash for needy families, through the holding of a *cwrw bach* (literally 'small beer'). If someone suffered a sudden financial crisis friends would arrange for the brewing of a supply of beer and then neighbours would attend the party without formal invitations being issued. They would partake of the beer and refreshments in return for a small charge. On occasion tea would be served instead of beer, but in all cases the cash obtained was passed on to the beneficiary to help him or her over a difficult period. However, despite this ostensibly charitable purpose there were claims that the festivities led to immorality, through the drinking and flirtations they encouraged. There is some evidence that this could be the case, as in 1859 when a paternity suit involving a Carmarthenshire butcher revealed that he and a male friend had called at a house to look for girls to take to a *cwrw bach* held somewhere else. It was to aid a young woman, the putative father of whose illegitimate child had disappeared. The four young people stayed at the party, drinking and enjoying themselves, from nine in the evening until three the next morning, before they returned to the girls' home. It was then that they had the sexual intercourse which was the cause of the subsequent paternity suit.[261]

Similar procedures were followed to celebrate a wedding, with guests invited to attend by a 'bidder', who was usually a well-known local character. Here, too, the selling of food and drink formed part of the proceedings. The sums of money given by each guest were duly recorded and the couple whose wedding it was would be invited, in their turn, to feasts at which they would be expected to repay the 'debt' due to the respective families.[344] If no cash were paid, gifts in kind might be offered. At one Carmarthenshire 'bidding' it was suggested guests might send:

> a waggon full of potatoes, a cartload of turnips, a hundred or two of cheeses, a cask of butter, a sack of flour, a winchester of barley, or what you please, for anything will be acceptable; jugs, basins, saucepans, pots and pans, . . . gridirons, frying pans, tea-kettles, plates and dishes . . . or even a penny whistle or a child's cradle.[261]

In this way business and pleasure were mixed, as guests celebrated while, at the same time, helping young neighbours to set up home.

In areas of Britain where commercial agriculture was more highly developed these informal means of giving aid did not apply, but communal junketings were still common. In the Huntingdonshire fens in the 1880s Kate Edwards remembered the Molly Dancers who came round at Christmas clad in outlandish costumes. 'One would have a fiddle, and another a dulcimer, or perhaps a

A midday meal in a harvest cornfield in Wales, c. *1900. (Museum of Welsh Life, St Fagans, Cardiff)*

concertina and play while the rest danced.' They went from pub to pub and 'when they'd finished there, they'd go to any houses or cottages where they stood a chance o' getting anything. If we ha'n't got any money to give 'em, at least they never went away without getting a hot drink . . . Sometimes the Molly Dancers got home-made elderberry wine, well sugared and made scalding hot and spiced with cloves . . . a good tumbler full of that, all sweet and hot and spicy, were worth dancing for, and kept the cold out till they got to the next cottage.'[241]

However, agriculture began to decline in national importance as a result of industrialization and urban expansion. New attitudes developed and a new morality took hold. The old-style celebrations were increasingly shunned as uncivilized and irrelevant. Some were able to evolve into more acceptable forms, as was the case with sports like football and prize fighting. But to most middle-class urban dwellers traditional amusements, especially those involving trials of strength and wagers, were crude and pointless. 'In an age of progress,' writes Peter Bailey, '. . . it was frankly incomprehensible that people should amuse themselves by eating scalding porridge with their fingers or stripping the wicks from a pound of candles with their teeth, all for the sake of a wager and the applause of an audience of like-minded boobies.'[85] Such contests were held regularly at the annual Halshaw wakes near Bolton. Also to be condemned, in the eyes of many, were feats of strength like that undertaken at Goole, Yorkshire, in June 1851, when a young local man backed himself 'in £25 against £50 to wheel a wheelbarrow . . . to London in six days'. He was accompanied by a 'minder' to ensure that he did not cheat, and duly completed the task in five days twelve hours. According to the *Halifax Guardian* on his return from London by train he was greeted at Goole railway station by a large crowd of wellwishers. The fact that such events were usually accompanied by heavy drinking, as well as gambling, reinforced 'respectable' people's disapproval of them.

Old-style festivals like Plough Monday, held on the first Monday after Twelfth Night and originally marked by farm lads going round the parish in fancy dress with a plough to beg for money, food and drink, were similarly condemned as 'rude diversions' and 'vulgar games' which had little place in urban society. In January 1847 the *Stamford Mercury* commented acidly that 'the silly pagan custom, happily sinking into desuetude, of men's [sic] parading the streets dressed in colored [sic] rags and white external petticoats, was practised at Louth by half a dozen money-hunters on Monday last (Plough Monday)'.[240]

To town residents these practices seemed mere excuses for rowdiness and intimidation. This was true in 1868 in Bradford, where at the New Year large numbers of men and boys dressed as mummers, with blackened faces and bizarre clothes, roamed middle-class neighbourhoods and even, in a few cases, entered homes uninvited. When demands for gifts were rejected some of them resorted to harsh words and violence, as happened when a couple were assaulted on their own doorstep by a young man angered by their refusal.[330] Whereas mumming had once been accepted as a way of reaffirming communal solidarity around Christmas time, in towns like Bradford such folk rituals had long since ceased to be genuine expressions of neighbourliness. The protection of property and the control of public spaces became basic law and order issues for Victorian local authorities and it was precisely these which were challenged by such festive demonstrations.[331]

'Christmas Boys' at Netley Abbey, Hampshire, 1891. The play they performed was of the 'hero-combat' type. As part of the disguise their hats were covered with flowers, and paper scales or strips were attached to jacket and trousers. They also wore long white sashes, crossed at front and back, and each carried a sword. The 'hero', St George, is wearing a taller hat than the rest and it is adorned with streamers (Rural History Centre, University of Reading)

The resultant sense of alienation was partly an outcome of population growth and the consequent social and spatial divisions which appeared in urban communities. This led to alarm about the potentially destructive powers of an anonymous 'mob'. Partly it arose from the new morality associated with the rise of evangelical religion, and from a dislike of the disruption of business which accompanied these events. This was made clear at Derby in 1845 when a number of the clergy, tradesmen, manufacturers and members of the respectable working class complained to the mayor about the annual Shrovetide football match, with its mass involvement of men and boys over several miles of streets. It led, they declared

> to the assembling of a lawless rabble, suspending business to the loss of the industrious, creating terror and alarm to the timid and peaceable, committing violence on the persons and damage to the properties of the defenceless and poor, and producing in those who play moral degradation.[137]

A year earlier another critic had claimed that the match was a 'relic of barbarism . . . wholly inconsistent with the intelligence and the spirit of improvement' which currently characterized the people of Derby.[240] In 1846 the celebration was banned, and despite initial opposition that decision was accepted. The fact that alternative amusement was provided, first in the form of athletics and then, more successfully, horse racing, aided the reconciliation process.

There were complaints, too, of immorality and illegitimacy being encouraged among young people who lost all restraint when they joined in such feasts and celebrations. In the Lathe of Scray in Kent during the 1860s, Whitsun entertainments, parish festivities, friendly society club days and hopping festivals were all blamed for the downfall of women who were engaged subsequently in paternity suits. One nineteen-year-old girl was said to have been with a local blacksmith, the alleged father of her child, at Boughton Feast and had also been seen with him at Whitsun in a Hernhill public house. In another case the girl concerned referred to a tea party at a local inn where she had 'danced with a young Gentleman who did not act in a gentlemanly manner. He offered me money to go for a walk with him. I refused.'[283]

These links, real or imagined, between festivities and immorality were pinpointed by the clergy and by other disapproving Victorians. As late as 1890 Accrington's August Fair was condemned as a 'carnival of vice' and a 'horrid nuisance' by Nonconformist opponents, while many evangelicals denounced fairs as 'popish festivals' and promoters of 'violent vulgar sports'.[179] In the late 1860s the rector of Kirkby Stephen in Westmorland advised the setting up of flower, poultry and dog shows in order to wean young people from less desirable diversions such as racing, wrestling, dancing and similar amusements, 'all innocent enough in themselves, but fruitful of evil owing to the conditions under which they are available'.[1] He had established one such event in his own parish, where there was a 'band of music and the people dance on the green sward, but no drunkenness nor incivility in word or act would be tolerated'. The most successful aspect of it was a dog show, at which local shepherds displayed the skills of their animals in rounding up sheep and other tasks. Prizes were awarded for the best-looking and most accomplished dogs and in this way the shepherding expertise of both man and animal was recognized.[1]

But it was not just on grounds of vulgarity and sexual impropriety that criticisms were levelled at traditional festivals. They were also felt to promote drunkenness and fighting. At Stalybridge wakes in the middle of the century, 'Lord' George Sanger, a well-known showman and circus proprietor, remembered witnessing terrible violence when men and women were 'literally kicked to fragments by the formidable iron-tipped clogs which formed the general footwear. Lancashire men in those days gave very little attention to the use of their fists. The clog was their weapon, and they considered there was nothing unmanly in kicking and biting to death . . . any person who had the misfortune to incur their anger.'[306] In Sanger's view, there was 'a callous brutality about a Lancashire mob in those days that . . . strikes one as simply appalling'.

This brutality found expression, too, in the pursuit of blood sports such as cockfighting, bull-baiting, badger-baiting and dogfighting, despite the fact that they had been outlawed in 1835, with a further measure passed in 1849 against cockfighting. James Macaulay, in an *Essay on Cruelty to Animals* (1839), argued that much of the misery and crime of the English countryside was attributable to the influence of cockfighting, 'which has trained many a victim for the gallows, and reduced many a family to want and begging'.[240] But the sport was certainly not confined to villages and although prosecutions were instituted, often at the instigation of the Royal Society for the Prevention of Cruelty to Animals (itself founded in 1824) and by other animal protection societies, covert contests continued.[180] In April 1875 the *Annual Register* reported a police raid at Aintree racecourse near Liverpool where about a hundred 'gentlemen' had assembled to witness a cockfight. On the arrival of the police the assembly tried to disperse and several of those present sustained serious injuries when they leapt through the windows.

> The names of many persons present were obtained, and proceedings were instituted against them; seven of the party were eventually fined £5 each. It is believed that the fight had been going on for some hours, as several dead cocks were found, together with about thirty live ones, which were trimmed in the usual fashion ready for fighting. The stakes are said to have reached £3,000, and the persons present, many . . . occupying high positions, are reported to have come from various parts of the kingdom and also from the continent.[25]

Although the patronage of the well-to-do, once prominent in cockfighting circles, was now on the wane, vestiges remained.[180] In his reminiscences Sir John Dugdale Astley described attending a contest involving birds belonging to his brother. After a circuitous journey he arrived at a country house where the floor of a shed had been covered with green turf. The gamecocks were produced and a number of battles were fought. Then suddenly 'the birds were thrust into bags, and these were gently pushed into a large hole in the wall, and some straw piled over it; the turfs were carried away'. This was completed so quickly that there was no evidence left when the police, 'of whose coming the cockers had received warning from watching scouts, arrived on the scene'.

In Cumbria cockfighting continued to the end of the century, with contests held on isolated farms. Sometimes the matches involved individual birds, as one breeder challenged another. On other occasions, as at Eskdale and Kirkby in 1880, they were between competing communities, with heavy gambling on the birds. As late as 1890 there was a South Cumberland and Furness Cockfighting Club run on lines similar to a football league and with matches arranged between member villages.[253] The excitement of the competition, the heavy wagers, and the sport's illegality all seem to have added to the enjoyment, as did the satisfaction of outwitting the police. Cockfighters often used county boundaries, particularly that between Lancashire and Cumberland, as a way of defeating the authorities, so that if they were disturbed at one location they would hastily move to another in a different county, thereby evading capture.[253]

Dogfighting presented similar problems. In the mid-1850s a Liverpool commentator noted that although the police had tried to put an end to it, the sport had simply been driven underground: 'Not a week elapses . . . in which several dogfights do not take place, some more or less openly, many, particularly those involving large sums of money, strictly private.'[332] According to him, before the match the participants talked 'in the coolest manner' about fighting their dogs, but they would never name publicly 'the trysting place'. Nor did they mention the hour at which the fight was to take place. 'The time chosen is generally early in the morning, when the police are going off duty, and we were told that Sunday was a very good time.'

The establishment of the new police forces around the middle of the century brought an end to these sports in a number of places. This was so in the West Riding of Yorkshire in 1857, where the county police were accused of making themselves 'obnoxious' by tackling cockfighting at Wibsey near Bradford, among other places. Again, in 1843 Manchester Council formally prohibited dogfighting, cockfighting and bull- and badger-baiting.

Sometimes, as with the famous bull-running at Stamford, suppression only occurred after pressure was exerted for several years. In this case the event was ended in 1840 as a result of intervention by the military, the magistrates and 'respectable' members of society, aided by the RSPCA, and with substantial financial penalties imposed on the local community for policing costs.[137]

Yet it was not just external influences and the law which caused the decline of these brutal sports. The teachings of evangelical religion and new approaches to discipline promoted by industrial capitalism caused many people to turn against such activities, while the effects of land enclosure restricted the amount of space available for them. This was true of Deritend Wake near Birmingham, which became a victim of urban growth. Its most prestigious event was the holding of steeplechases and when that was no longer possible, the wake itself faded away.[285] By 1861 the area it had formerly occupied was covered by housing development and metalworks, and within a few years the whole festival was described as 'not noticeable outside two or three of the lowest public houses'.

More significant than repression in driving out traditional celebrations was, therefore, the attitude of the local populace. There gradually emerged an artisan sub-culture which rejected such rowdy amusements and preferred to patronize the new commercial recreations on offer, such as railway excursions and the music hall. The larger, more orderly fairs did survive, with new-style amusements to give pleasure to the increasingly sophisticated tastes of the later Victorians. But even in the early 1840s men in Birmingham were said to prefer saving up their spare cash to spend on outings rather than, as they had once done, on bull-baiting and cockfighting at the wakes.[285]

Some old-style sports were able to adjust to the new situation. This was true of horse racing, which overcame its decadent image partly because it enjoyed

Advertisement for a fête, gala and horticultural show at Llanidloes, 1885, as new-style amusements ousted some of the traditional entertainments. (Museum of Welsh Life, St Fagans, Cardiff)

support from the aristocracy and gentry. Still greater changes occurred in football, where a new, rule-governed game emerged as the traditional mass participation sport went into decline, surviving only in residual fashion in a few smaller market towns such as Ashbourne in Derbyshire.

The world of prize-fighting, too, was transformed as the excesses of the old regime were driven underground and eventually disappeared. One of the most notorious and disreputable of the later contests took place near Farnborough in 1860 between the massive American fighter J.C. Heenan and the small native champion, Tom Sayers. It was a vicious contest that ended only with the arrival of the police, by which time both men had been badly injured.[125] The long-established aristocratic link with gambling on prize-fighting was broken, and racing became the preferred sport of late Victorian gentlemen, while a series of legal judgements from 1825 to 1882 outlawed the prize-ring. Hence two fighters were arrested at Aintree in 1875, while the customary contests held at the Derby were stamped out by the police and the Jockey Club. But clandestine contests continued, as in the spring of 1888 when Alec Roberts succeeded in defeating Jem Hayes 'for £100 a side' at a venue near Bainham in Kent. According to a hostile account in the *Isle of Wight Times* the two men fought for an hour and forty-seven minutes, neither being prepared to give in despite being severely injured. 'Hayes hurt his hand against the stakes, and it was not until he was in an almost unconscious state that his seconds threw up the sponge.' The newspaper called the proceedings 'revolting in the extreme' and expressed surprise that they should have been allowed to continue for so long without the police interfering or making any arrests.[34] By the 1890s, however, the barbarity of bare-knuckle contests had largely been replaced by boxing matches, with the first gloved heavyweight championship taking place between Sullivan and Corbett in the USA in 1892. This was conducted in accordance with rules drafted in 1867 under the name of the Marquess of Queensberry. Professional boxing contests were staged in England under the aegis of the National Sporting Club, itself formed in 1891.[191]

Some traditional events undoubtedly declined as a result of police action, and at first their role was viewed with suspicion by all social classes. A number of critics argued that the campaign against blood sports was class biased, since the field sports of the aristocracy were allowed to continue unchecked. As a correspondent to *The Animal World* (the journal of the RSPCA) declared in 1870:

> We denounce the barbarities of ignorant, or half-ignorant cattle-dealers, butchers, &c., and other plebeian cruelties, but so long as the more aristocratic pastimes . . . continue, may not the lower-classes retort against us who by birth and education are presumably imbued with some sentiment of humanity . . .?

Equally, even towards the end of the Victorian era there were those who blamed oppressive action by the police for the decline of harmless old-style amusements. In 1882 a commentator from Batley, Yorkshire, regretted the time when

> the first policeman came into our midst, to plant the thin edge of the wedge, which was . . . to revolutionise our manners and customs. Since he came . . . we have lost all trace of mumming: all trace of Lee Fair, . . . most of our mischief night; . . . If mummers were to be seen upon the street now, the police would interfere . . . I put a deal of this severance from ourselves of old custom down to the advent of the policeman in uniform.[332]

Walter Rose of Haddenham, Buckinghamshire, similarly attributed the demise of the village's traditional mumming performances to the 'zeal for conventions'. 'The police made it their duty to hover on the heels of the players, keeping a watch on their conduct; so that they became fearful of making unannounced entry to a private house. Thus it was, that, in the last years of the Mummers, the public-house became almost the only place where the play could be rendered correctly.'[295]

But while some lamented these trends, for most people the establishment of a law-abiding society was the prime goal. Already in the 1840s letters to the Bolton press show that ratepayers were anxious for the police to stop young men playing pitch and toss (a gambling game) on the main streets and to clear away the crowds of youths who gathered to cheer on pedestrian or foot races, thereby obstructing rights of way.[85] There was impatience, too, at the survival of the ancient Lancashire custom of begging for eggs, or 'pace-egging', at Easter since this became an excuse for gangs of lads to dress in 'outlandish garb and march in procession from pub to pub, blowing trumpets and banging on the tables till free drink was brought'. Respectable passers-by would be pestered until they contributed drink money.

In certain places the social divisions which led to these festivities being stigmatized as menaces were mitigated by a taming of the celebrations themselves. This happened in the southern counties with some Guy Fawkes events, at which for years unpopular local individuals had been burnt in effigy, property had been damaged and mass demonstrations had taken place, accompanied by demands for money. For example, at Chelmsford in 1888 a middle-class initiative led to the holding of a monster bonfire and town carnival on 9 November instead. A procession was organized in which the mayor and corporation took part and provision was made for female members of the audience to be seated in a ladies' enclosure. So popular did this event become that by the early 1890s the rowdy celebration of the 5th had dwindled away and the transfer of activities to the 9th had been accomplished. A similar approach was adopted at Reigate in 1890, with the Watch Committee offering a 'tolerated and expensive demonstration in return for good order'. At Dorking, Nutley and Walton, too, celebrations were successfully reorganized. By such means a carefully regulated opportunity was given for people to indulge in their fondness for fancy dress and bonfires, while the celebrations were channelled along lines designed to reunite class with class.[331]

FAIRS, MARKETS AND STREET ENTERTAINERS

As transport and marketing facilities improved during the Victorian years, many wakes (linked to the commemoration of the patron saint of the local church) and fairs lost their former economic roles as occasions for the sale of livestock and as rudimentary labour exchanges. Some did continue these roles, particularly in the north where hiring fairs fulfilled a labour exchange function for the hiring of farm servants. At a customary meeting place those seeking work would gather, each wearing a distinctive symbol to indicate his or her particular skill. A waggoner would have a bit of twisted cord on his hat, horsemen attached a scrap of horse-hair to their coat collar, and shepherds wore a piece of wool. As they waited to be hired the men would exchange information about past employers and occasionally, as in Scotland, mean or unjust masters would be derided publicly by the singing of specially composed mocking rhymes.[121] Fred Kitchen, who attended Doncaster Fair in the early twentieth century, recalled it as crowded with men from south Yorkshire, north Nottinghamshire, north Lincolnshire and parts of Derbyshire. It 'represented the biggest babel of dialects since the time of Noah'. But the fairs had their 'merry bucolic side', with the young, newly hired workers spending their 'fastening penny', received from their future employer, at boxing booths, coconut shies and roundabouts, or in flirtations with the servant girls. 'Many a match was made at the Hiring Fair' was a familiar claim.[197] Music and singing rang out from every pub, and Fred Kitchen remembered hearing familiar tunes like *Farmer's Boy*, *Sweet Marie* and *Annie Laurie* 'sung by voices over-fresh with too many "liveners"' and played on concertina, melodeon, mouth-piece and tin whistle.[225]

Elsewhere some fairs, such as at Atherton or Adwalton in West Yorkshire, continued their old function as events for the sale of farm produce and livestock. Farm horses and dray horses would show their paces as they were led up and down the main street, and every entrance and open space would be filled with stalls selling brandysnaps, sweets and nuts. Local families and friends would take the opportunity to have a reunion, with hospitality offered usually in the form of cold beef and pickles. At Haworth Tide Fair the roads would be filled with sheep pens, some with animals on their way to winter in Derbyshire, and there would be gipsies trotting their horses and geese and poultry noisily awaiting new owners.

Alongside these, manufactured goods of variable quality would be offered. At Portsmouth Free Mart Fair in the 1840s one man recalled cheap jacks cajoling the unwary into buying 'tin saws that would not cut, . . . everlastingly pointed pencils that failed to draw a line, . . . [and] razors that were a torture to the user'. St Giles's Fair in Oxford had a better reputation, with clothing and material of reasonable quality always to be found, together with stalls selling baskets, glass and china ornaments, cheap tools, cakes, sweets and gingerbreads. There would also be barrows offering fruit and nuts, as well as canaries and other caged birds. In 1892 there was even a display of the well-known Singer sewing machines.[74]

But it was the entertainment the fairs provided which attracted most visitors, with roundabouts, menageries, dancing booths, displays of curiosities, circuses, theatres

Crowds enjoying the fun at St Giles's Fair, Oxford, c. 1900. (The author)

and many other specialities. At Portsmouth Free Mart one youth remembered the large number of freaks on display, and these seem to have been a mainstay of all early Victorian shows. At Portsmouth albinos 'blinked their pink Eyes at the gaping crowd; . . . the dwarf . . . thrust into the doll house box hardly bigger than a footstool, . . . rang his tiny bell out of the bedroom window.' Then there were 'bleared old women who fried their bread bloated sausages on the little charcoal fires . . . [and] the broken-down race-course gamblers, who haunted this fair with their antiquated roulette tables, or their clumsy, spurious thimble rigging'. There were dancing booths, too, known as 'Vauxhalls', where couples jigged on 'rickety boards to the gloomy strains of a harp, a fiddle and a trombone; . . . decorous tradesmen, and people of respectability who came out to "enjoy the fair" danced quadrilles and country dances cheek by jowl with very questionable partners, with the gravity of judges.'

In the London area these migrant performers spent the winter on the fringes of the capital and then occupied their spring and summer by following a circuit of the various metropolitan and provincial fairs. 'Lord' George Sanger remembered the difficulties of the winter months when he and his family had to live on the little they could scrape together as savings until they could take to the road again.[306]

For the people of London, meanwhile, the fairs offered a welcome break from their accustomed routine. In 1836 Charles Dickens described the road to Greenwich for the Easter fair as a scene of noise and bustle, with cabs, hackney-coaches, carts, wagons, omnibuses and a multiplicity of other vehicles all hastening in the same direction, crammed with passengers. He compared it to a three-day fever which cooled the blood for six months afterwards and allowed the capital's inhabitants to settle once more into their normal 'habits of plodding industry'. Amid the general excitement there was a loud cacophony as women screamed, boys shouted, gongs clanged, pistols fired, bells rang and speaking trumpets bellowed. Then there were the deafening rhythms of the bands, 'all playing different tunes from the wildbeast shows', while in the centre of the fair was a large booth, with a stage in front, offering a melodrama '(with three murders and a ghost), a pantomime, a comic song, an overture, and some incidental music, all done in five-and-twenty minutes'.[398] It was the rowdiness of Greenwich Fair that led critics to condemn it as a centre of 'London iniquity', and a 'barbarous relic of a bygone age'. In 1857 they succeeded in having it banned.[139]

In other cases restrictions were placed on the running of the fairs. This happened with St Bartholomew's in London, where as early as 1819 swings and roundabouts were abolished. The doubling of stall rents in 1840 by the City of London's Markets Committee had the effect of banishing the larger shows and exhibitions, so that only pedlars and minor performers remained. The fair ceased to be a popular festival and it was finally ended by the Corporation of London in 1854.[220]

There were allegations, too, that the authorities allowed excesses to run on unchecked so that they would have an excuse to close down a fair. In some instances the closures which had taken place within London itself, coupled with general transport improvements, meant that by the 1850s many people were travelling a considerable distance in search of entertainment. For example, in the late 1870s thousands of visitors came from the East End to Harlow Bush Fair. Those favouring abolition of the fair argued that problems had arisen since 'the

London roughs' had 'taken possession of it'. Interestingly, however, when the matter was referred to the police, a superintendent who had worked in the area for eleven years gave it a favourable report. He claimed to be unaware of any 'Disorderly conduct or Immorality' and considered this unusual with 'so large an assemblage of persons principally from the East-end'. According to him, the pleasure seekers, numbering around fifteen to twenty thousand, prepared for their day's outing by subscribing to a penny a week fund organized by bus and van proprietors, with each van accompanied by one or more musicians. They arrived at the fair at noon and began their homeward journey around 4 p.m., so that by 7 p.m. only about fifty or a hundred people remained, mainly from the local community. He considered abolition would seriously interfere with the enjoyment of all these people.[139] But neither his superiors nor the chairmen of local Quarter Sessions accepted his arguments and in 1879 the fair was suppressed by order of the Home Secretary.

It was symptomatic of the hostility and prudishness of many of the better-off towards these entertainments that in 1871 an Act was passed to facilitate the closure of fairs. Its preamble declared:

Whereas certain of the fairs held in England and Wales are unnecessary, are the cause of grievous immorality, and are very injurious to the inhabitants of the towns in which such fairs are held, . . . it is therefore expedient to make provision to facilitate the abolition of such fairs.

As a result of this measure almost three hundred closures took place between 1871 and 1898.[366]

But if these negative reactions led to the demise of a number of fairs during the second half of the nineteenth century, more positive influences were at work, too. Many fairs enjoyed a new lease of life as railway excursions were run to them and as technical advances widened the attractions they had to offer. The first railway excursion to St Giles's Fair, for example, was organized by the Great Western Railway Company in 1850. It ran between Banbury and Oxford, picking up passengers at the intermediate stations as well. In its first year it brought about nine hundred visitors, but once the precedent had been established the catchment area for cheap day ticket holders widened rapidly. Soon it reached as far as Cardiff, London, Birmingham, Gloucester and other large towns.[74]

A similar transformation took place in the amusements which the fairs had to offer. People were no longer satisfied with playing skittles, gawping at freaks and riding a donkey, as they had been in the early years of Queen Victoria's reign. They wanted something more exhilarating, and during the 1870s the first steam-powered roundabouts began to appear. A decade later the switchback was introduced, built initially using boats or gondola cars. Kate Edwards, who visited Ramsey Fair in the 1890s with her mother, remembered the atmosphere of excitement, with dancing booths, conjurors, and much else besides: 'there were a boxing-booth, and a waxwork show, where . . . I see the sad sight o' Queen Victoria and all her children round Prince Albert's death bed. One thing I shall never forget, because it seemed so very wonderful, were paying 6d. to go into a booth to hear the first phonograph

A marksman trying his skill at a sideshow, c. 1900. (The author)

as ever come our way. Other music come from the hurdy-gurdy with its little monkey to collect the pennies . . . Mother 'ould go with us for a ride on the "Sea-on-Land", as were nothing really but a boarded floor made to rock from end to end and from side to side. But we went in the "swing boats" by ourselves.' The flying-horses were another attraction, though, as Kate drily commented, they 'di'n't exactly fly, because they were only cranked round by a man by hand'.[241]

Alongside these were the scientific and mechanical innovations like the riband-making process shown at St Giles's Fair in 1856, with the machinery operated by a miniature steam engine. There were also clockwork hummingbirds on display. Two years later the exhibits included Clapton's Exhibition of Scenic and Mechanical Art and Norton's Patent Incubator, or Egg-hatching Machine. The Clapton display included views of Florence and Verona, as well as a representation of a ship on fire at sea and other events. A local newspaper described it as 'one of the most pleasing and intellectual exhibitions that has attended this or any other fair'.[74] Such exhibits widened visitors' general knowledge and informed them of the world outside. In 1855 engravings of the recent storming of Sebastopol during the Crimean War were sold at two a penny at the Michaelmas Fair in Banbury, and the following year peep shows offered 'all the Russian battles'. In 1861 'every important engagement in the present American war was truthfully represented', and by 1868 stereoramas depicted such varying events as the death of Abel and the Abergele railway disaster.[350]

Most exciting of all to many fairgoers was the appearance of 'living pictures' during the 1890s. At St Giles's Fair in 1898 a visitor reported entering a tent to see a bioscope show of Mr Gladstone's funeral procession. Outside, dancers, acrobats and other performers drew the attention of the potential audience to the picture being shown inside. 'From the 1890s until the First World War,' writes Sally Alexander, 'the joy-ride and living picture shows vied with each other for supremacy and popularity.'[74]

A similar educational role was performed by the menageries which toured the country. At a time when zoological gardens were still rare (that at Regent's Park only opening in 1828), they showed a wide range of exotic animals to the inhabitants of even small communities. Wombwell's, the best known, called themselves 'the wandering teachers of Natural History'. In 1880 in Devon they went still further with a claim that the gorilla, 'or hairy wild man', they had just acquired was 'Dr. Darwin's MISSING LINK!! The nearest approach to Man of all animals. The only one in Europe.'[30] Six hundred other beasts, birds and reptiles were also on display, together with the daring deeds of 'Cardono, The American Lion-tamer', who worked with lions, tigers, leopards, bears, wolves and hyenas. 'The transatlantic reputation of this great *artiste*' was said to be 'a sufficient guarantee of his excellence in this peculiar art'.[30]

Even the Clyro curate, Francis Kilvert, was attracted by the Wombwell menagerie. In May 1871 he noted that he had gone to see an elephant ride upon a bicycle, as promised in an advertisement. 'This elephant is said to have killed a boy at the Potteries, but whether he did it by driving the bicycle over him or not did not appear.' Kilvert and a companion went along the road to meet the procession of caravans, but he was disappointed to discover that the elephant was 'a very small one and three camels or dromedaries came shuffling and splashing along the muddy road in the heavy rain looking cold and miserable'. The menagerie arrived at 4 p.m. and the show began two hours later, but failed to live up to Kilvert's expectations:

> There was a fair lion and a decent wolf, which looked as if it had been just freshly caught, his coat was so thick and good and he was so strong and restless. A laughing hyena set us all off laughing in chorus . . . A dwarf three feet nothing pointed out to us 'groups of wolves', stirred the beasts up with a long pole and made them roar. There was no bicycle forthcoming . . . I soon went away.[273]

In the final decade of the century a more tolerant attitude was displayed towards fairs and showmen and their exhibits, as fears of civil disorder faded and policing became more effective. In 1885 the Home Secretary, Sir William Harcourt, ordered the Metropolitan Police 'not to interfere with steam roundabouts, "these innocent amusements of the poorer classes . . . even if such amusements are presumed to constitute unlawful fairs within the Police Acts"'.[139] Nine years later it was the police who helped to ensure the survival of Pinner Fair, despite the wish of local magistrates, the vicar and other leading residents for its abolition. According to the police, over the previous twelve years there had been 'no summons or charge in connection with the fair, no case of felony reported to the police, and no disorder or case of immorality'. Furthermore, it was eagerly awaited by 'several hundreds of the poorer classes living at and around Pinner, as their only holiday in the year'. Abolition would 'interfere with the enjoyment of the poorer classes of the community'. And when opponents argued that the Metropolitan railway extension through Pinner had brought in 'the rough element and disorderly and disreputable men and women' to the fair, the police responded that those who came from a distance were mainly 'the respectable though poorer classes' who had come for a day's pleasure. The Home Office examined the evidence and allowed the fair to continue.[139] This decision accorded with the view of Sir William Harcourt that a fair should not be discontinued merely because it was no longer needed on commercial grounds or because it gave trouble to the police, provided that once or twice a year it offered 'popular amusement for poor people'. There was a balance to be struck between public order and personal freedom, and increasingly by the end

Children riding an elephant in Regent's Park Zoo, c. 1900. The Zoological Gardens had opened in 1828 and taken over the animals from the royal collection at the Tower, which had attracted Londoners since the Middle Ages. (The author)

of the century this was being determined in a way that favoured the continuance of
fairs and wakes for which there was substantial demand.[139]

In the meantime new fairgrounds began appearing at the seaside, to meet the
requirements of growing numbers of day trippers. In Norfolk T.H.S. Escott
described the rapid transformation of one holiday beach when an excursion train
was expected:

> You look round and find that upwards of a hundred men have suddenly invaded
> the place, are setting up booths, furnishing them with eatables and drinkables,
> are establishing Aunt Sallies . . . In less than fifteen minutes . . . what was
> absolute solitude now presents the appearance of a fair . . . Puff-puff is the
> warning sound of the steam-engine in the distance, and the wreaths of smoke . . .
> are significant of the cloud of humanity that in a few seconds will settle down
> upon the shore. Out they troop from the carriages which have just drawn up at
> the platform – men, women, boys, and children, a good thousand strong . . . It
> is by no means an uncommon thing to see the shore . . . covered by three
> thousand human beings, restlessly moving to and fro . . . Fun and frolic reigns
> all day until the moment for departure on the return journey arrives . . . The
> last notes of the excursionists' songs die away on the wind; . . . and the
> hucksters who have waited on the great army of pleasure-seekers pack up their
> belongings . . . [and] steal away as silently and swiftly as they alighted.[57]

Developments at popular resorts such as Blackpool were still more extensive
and a good deal more permanent. In the late 1870s stallholders on the foreshore at
Blackpool's South Beach increased rapidly, to cater for trippers from the West
Riding of Yorkshire and East Lancashire. They provided everything from
shooting galleries and fortune-tellers to cheapjacks and vendors of Bibles and
herbal remedies. Despite efforts by the authorities to restrict their activities they
continued to flourish. Even when in 1897 the corporation managed to clear the
beach of its most disreputable quacks and showmen, they merely set themselves
up in front gardens let out to them by South Beach residents. By 1899 freak
shows were moving in, and fairgrounds were appearing elsewhere in the town.
From the late nineteenth century 'the fairground amusements of the Lancashire
Wakes migrated to the coast with their patrons, and found a congenial home at
Blackpool'.[363]

Associated with fairs, but also operating on their own account, were circuses,
many of them moving laboriously from site to site. The arrival of a circus was a
memorable event in the life of any community, both because of residents' excited
anticipation of the performances they would witness and because of the sheer size
of the processions as they travelled around the country. In July 1842 when the
American lion tamer Isaac Van Amburgh arrived in Redruth, Cornwall, he was at
the head of a procession of forty horses and carriages and drove eight horses in
hand himself. His arrival attracted a crowd of more than seven thousand. A year
later in Hartlepool a public holiday was declared so that people could watch his
arrival.[137] He was reputed to have been the first performer to put his head into the
mouth of a lion, and a contemporary rhyme celebrated the feat:

He sticks his head in the lion's mouth
And holds it there a while;
And when he takes it out again,
He greets you with a smile.

In 1848 a playbill for the Theatre Royal, Edinburgh, featuring Van Amburgh and his animals noted that these included a 'rare black tiger' and a performance of the 'Grand Final Triumph of the Arab. Going to the Derby.'

However, the heyday of the travelling circus was between 1850 and 1900, when performances were staged at Windsor, Balmoral and Sandringham for the royal family by leading proprietors. At the end of the century it took at least one hundred and fifty draught horses to move 'Lord' George Sanger's circus around the country, and the cavalcade stretched for miles, completely blocking narrow roads. Sanger specialized in military displays, and when in the 1880s his show required 'some new element' he produced the 'Relief of Khartoum' and the death of General Gordon. For this spectacle he used field artillery, ambulance wagons and rifles, while members of his company appeared as doctors, Red Cross nurses and other characters.

One young circus enthusiast during the 1890s was particularly impressed by the bands in their smart uniforms. 'I never knew any band that could equal a circus one for noise.' As they headed the procession into a town, behind them would follow members of the company riding on coloured horses and dressed as jockeys, cavaliers and their ladies, clowns, cowboys and any other characters for whom costumes could be found. They would be followed by five or six large processional or tableau cars.

Initially circuses had concentrated on equestrian displays and that remained an important part of their programme. However, by the mid-1870s growing concern was expressed about the welfare of the child acrobats who were performing in them, and particularly about the early age at which their training began and the harsh treatment they received. In 1879 after several attempts Lord Shaftesbury succeeded in getting a Children's Dangerous Performances Act passed which made it illegal to employ a child under fourteen in any 'public exhibition or performance' which could endanger its life and limb. Unfortunately the Act had serious weaknesses. It was left to magistrates to decide what constituted a potential danger and it related only to *performances*, not the training which preceded them. The plight of child acrobats continued to cause anxiety, with allegations that youngsters were being sold by parents to trainers. The charges were vigorously denied by circus proprietors. 'Lord' George Sanger, for example, declared that not only did he never have more than half a dozen young people under training at any one time, but claims that they had been purchased were absurd. On the contrary, he had been offered premiums as high as £100 by parents anxious for their children to be trained. Furthermore, almost all the children who were taken on belonged to artistes and assistants in the circus or in similar places of entertainment:

it often happens that one of the parents is present on the premises when the training is in progress . . . When the training of a child commences, it is first, for a month or two, left to play in the ring, while the other children are being taught horse-riding, so that it may get accustomed to the surroundings and acquire confidence. Then it is taught riding . . . A child is not asked to stand upon the horse's back until it has had some weeks' practice . . . and in most instances the pupil has often besought the riding-master's permission to stand up before it is allowed to do so. The training of a child in dancing and other feats on horseback usually lasts from six to nine months . . . When a child fails to show any capacity for horsemanship – and the experience of a day or two is sufficient to furnish the proof – it is put upon the tight rope; and should it prove unfitted for that sphere, it is put to trial at walking upon the hands and in tumbling, when it is tended with great care, the trainer, for instance, holding up the legs in the case of walking on the hands.[38]

According to Sanger, harsh treatment was contrary to the trainer's interests, since for successful performances, courage and confidence were needed. Cruelty not only unnerved a child but the fear engendered would materially diminish the strength it was so important for the child to possess. Despite these reassuring comments, and those by other leading proprietors, accusations of the mistreatment of some child performers continued. In 1890, for example, Stephen Etheridge of the Ethardos acrobatic troupe was prosecuted for ill-treating a ten-year-old member of his three-girl group. She had a heart condition but was required to balance on her sister's head, turn somersaults and do the splits. Her father, a plumber by occupation, claimed in court that Etheridge had agreed to teach the girls dancing, music and calisthenics, not contortions. In the end a fine of 20s was imposed, with £5 5s costs.[27]

These were issues with which the newly formed National Society for the Prevention of Cruelty to Children became involved in the 1890s. In 1894, under NSPCC pressure, the law was strengthened by a new Prevention of Cruelty to Children Act. It forbade the training of children under sixteen as acrobats, contortionists and circus performers, although exemptions could be granted, subject to a magistrate's licence, provided they were over seven. Unfortunately licences were not required for children employed by their own parents, as often applied in circus families. However, in 1897 a further step was taken when dangerous performances were prohibited for boys under sixteen and girls under seventeen.[294] In this way hesitant progress was made in eliminating some of the darker aspects of circus life, at least as far as child performers were concerned; the animals were less fortunate.

Meanwhile, the moral concerns which had affected public attitudes towards fairs in the earlier Victorian years were extended to the London pleasure gardens, of which there were at least sixty-five during the first half of the century.[136] Some were very small and were attached to public houses. Others, according to their resources and the season, offered music, fireworks, balloon ascents, zoos and shady paths along which visitors could stroll. The best-known of them were Vauxhall Gardens and Cremorne Gardens, which both earned a growing reputation as places of ill-repute. At the beginning of the century Vauxhall was still a centre of fashion but in 1836 Charles Dickens, who paid it a daytime visit, was disillusioned by its tawdriness:

We paid our shilling at the gate, and then we saw . . . that the entrance, if there had been any magic about it at all, was now decidedly disenchanted, being, in fact, nothing more nor less than a combination of very roughly-painted boards and sawdust . . . We walked about, and met with a disappointment at every turn; our favourite views were mere patches of paint; the fountain that had sparkled so showily by the lamp-light, presented very much the appearance of a water-pipe that had burst; all the ornaments were dingy, and all the walks gloomy. There was a spectral attempt at rope-dancing in the little open theatre; the sun shone upon the spangled dresses of the performers, and their evolutions were about as inspiring and appropriate as a country-dance in a family vault.[398]

In 1841 the first auction of Vauxhall property was conducted, but between 1842 and 1859 galas and masquerades continued to be held. A grand Venetian Carnival, illuminated by sixty thousand lamps was arranged in 1849, but four years later Vauxhall was being frequented by disreputable visitors and disturbed the peace of local inhabitants. By 1859 the gardens had been closed and the entertainments dismantled.[151]

Vauxhall's rival, Cremorne, had in the interim risen in popularity. It was opened in 1831 as a stadium to teach 'the manly sports', as well as to provide entertainments. Within eight years, however, the amusement gardens had taken over. There was a Chinese orchestra, a circus, a crystal grotto, a maze, a theatre and a tent for a gipsy fortune-teller. There were also 'naughty little arbours' for sexual dalliance and refreshment bars scattered through the grounds. Soon balloon ascents added to the entertainment as well as 'Dancing on the Parisian Platform', archery, rifle shooting, concerts, ballet and a 'Mythological Spectacle with Pyrotechnic and Hydraulic Adjuncts'.[307] Tight-rope walking and an appearance by 'Kaffir Chiefs from their Native Wilds' were other entertainments on offer, and in the mid-1850s Cremorne still attracted large numbers of fashionable visitors.[151] But within two decades its reputation as a haunt of prostitutes and a 'nursery of vice' had grown. There was rowdiness and vandalism, with critics claiming sourly that it offered three attractions only – drink, dancing and devilry. In 1877 it was closed and the *Standard* newspaper, for one, welcomed its passing. While admitting that 'the sort of man who used to frequent Cremorne will be always with us' and that the loss of the gardens also meant the loss of its trees, the latter 'were not the kind of beauties which caused Cremorne to be visited'. An attempt had been made to carry on the entertainment without dancing, but the musical and theatrical attractions had not been sufficient to tempt the public. 'It had to exist in its accepted form or not at all; and of the two alternatives the latter was undeniably the best.'[307]

Finally, for many poorer Victorians, denied the pleasures of feasts, fairs and festivals by lack of funds, there remained the amusements provided by street performers.[94] Charles Booth in the 1890s claimed that the itinerant vendor played a part in the life of London which was unparalleled in any other city that he knew.[101] But all towns and many villages were visited by travelling showmen – Punch and Judy men, buskers, ballad hawkers, patent medicine salesmen, magicians, jugglers and many more besides. Their performances were a welcome diversion for people unable to afford even cheap theatres, and they provided a livelihood for the showmen themselves in the form of a kind of disguised begging.

Around the middle of the century a London performer told Henry Mayhew that he estimated there were about a thousand musicians working on the streets of the capital. This represented nearly 250 street bands, to say nothing of hurdy-gurdy men, barrel-organists, and non-musical entertainers.[63] The performers included young Italian musicians brought to England by their masters or *padroni*. They played on barrel-organs, harps, fiddles and accordions, and often displayed white mice or other small animals as well. Some residents welcomed the music they provided, but others, especially in middle-class neighbourhoods, would have agreed with the German writer Theodor Fontane when he described such 'street virtuosos' as a real horror of London life. In the early 1860s one aggrieved lady wrote to Michael Bass MP to back his campaign to end the nuisance:

> I live in a house from which, in *three different directions*, the disturbance which goes by the name of 'street music,' can be distinctly heard. It begins at nine in the morning, and continues till late at night, without intermission. I have frequently heard, *at one and the same time*, WITH EQUAL LOUDNESS, the several well-known airs of 'Annie Laurie,' 'The Last Rose of Summer,' and the prison song from the *Trovatore*.

"PREVENTION'S BETTER THAN CURE."

Jeames (excitedly). "HERE—HERE—HERE'S THE SHILLIN'! QUICK—QUICK—OFF WITH YOU!"
German Impostor (affecting concern). "DERE IS SOME VUN ILL?"
Jeames. "WELL, NOT JUST YET! BUT THERE PRECIOUS SOON WILL BE, IF YOU DON'T KNOCK OFF!"

Punch *(1869) drawing attention to the general unpopularity of street musicians, especially in affluent neighbourhoods.*

The hour of family prayer has been changed four times, in the vain attempt to get a quarter of an hour *un*interrupted by noise; and is . . . daily broken in upon by this wretched nuisance.

There is evidence, indeed, that street musicians were sometimes used by the malevolent to pursue personal quarrels. Charles Babbage, the mathematician and inventor, claimed that noisy street organists were paid to play in front of his house or next door by his neighbour in order to annoy him. In other cases servants secretly encouraged the organ-grinders to continue with performances which drove their employers to despair.[396]

Yet, despite sporadic attempts to reduce the nuisance (including the passage of an Act in 1864 requiring a street musician in London to move away from a house when asked to do so by the occupier, his servant, or a policeman), the number of performers continued to rise. During the final decade of the century the number of Italian street musicians alone rose from 1,441 in 1891 to 2,237 according to the probably conservative figures collected for the population censuses.[322]

Much the same was true of other street entertainers. At the end of the Victorian era one commentator claimed that in London performers could be found both in the heart of the city and in its most distant suburbs. A trio sometimes enlivened 'such a centre of bustle as the neighbourhood of the Stock Exchange', playing a dulcimer, harp and violin. But in his experience no street performers, however hackneyed, failed to draw an audience.

The 'street Irishman' belongs to the most primitive order of low comedians. Nevertheless, the Londoner is too desirous of being amused to leave him quite unnoticed. He sings and dances, and while recovering his breath fires off a volley of well-worn jokes . . . Sometimes one sees . . . crude attempts to emulate the 'tableaux vivants' of the theatre. The street boxers, for instance, attitudinise to the strains of a piano-organ. They attire themselves in fanciful costume and assume poses indicative of the most striking incidents in a prize-ring encounter . . . The fire-eater manages to command an audience even in sceptical London. Like the . . . juggler, and the thought-reader, he enjoys the prestige which belongs to the man who not only amuses but bewilders . . . Men who eat pebbles, nails, broken glass, and similar delicacies are so numerous . . . as to suggest the reflection that their diet is quite nourishing![314]

Outside the capital reactions to street entertainers varied. Jane Carlyle, staying at Ramsgate in 1861, was exasperated not only by the cries of vendors of 'prawns, shrimps, lollipops – things one never wanted, and will never want', but by the large number of itinerant musicians:

a brass band plays all through our breakfast, and repeats the performance often during the day, and the brass band is succeeded by a band of Ethiopians, and that again by a band of female fiddlers! and interspersed with these are individual barrel-organs, individual Scotch bagpipes, individual French horns![59]

Some of the more genteel seaside resorts, such as Bournemouth, were particularly hostile to the street performers and took action to discourage them. Nevertheless in 1884 the *Bournemouth Guardian* gave a grudging welcome to a troupe of Ethiopian minstrels, 'somewhat above the average merit' who had been amusing visitors to the town. 'A novel departure from the usual run of such performances is their "drill," which they go through with remarkable precision, to the great amusement of the on-lookers.'[26]

Cagliardo Coraggioso, who came to England as a child in the late 1890s together with his father and some other Italians, remembered the unfriendly reception he received in certain districts. 'Almost every day, wherever I went, the boys and girls followed me in large numbers, laughing at me, throwing stones, shouting and making a fool of me.' Coraggioso played the accordion and felt he was being treated so badly because he was a foreigner. However, one day he caught sight of himself in a shop window and realized that his bizarre appearance was partly to blame for the mockery with which he was greeted. At the age of about ten and a half years he was wearing a man's hat, about three sizes too big and nearly covering his ears. His hair was long and his suit was designed to fit a large man, with the jacket sleeves and trouser legs cut down:

> My boots had been picked out of a bucket. They were large navvy's boots, full of huge nails . . . A big greasy muffler was wound round my neck, tied in a knot, and, to complete the disaster, I wore in my ears a pair of ear-rings with three tiny balls hanging to each . . . not even a scarecrow would have frightened birds as I could.[132]

Later he and other members of the troupe toured the North Wales coast, where they received a warmer welcome. At Colwyn Bay the town was crowded with visitors and Coraggioso 'started to play, sing, and dance on the promenade. Pennies and threepenny bits were coming from all directions.'

But in many places reservations were expressed about these young musicians. In August 1877 a resident from Seacombe in Cheshire wrote to the Home Secretary to complain of the number of '*beautiful* [Italian] children of from 14 to 15 years of age going about this neighbour-hood dressed in showey [*sic*] attire and jewellery, "as their national costume", *professing* to be musicians, they are sent over daily to our watering place, New Brighton, . . . and I believe these poor girls are sent to earn money as best they can, and by illicit purposes, or any way, so that they bring home to the Padrone their daily gains'. His complaint was referred to the Cheshire Constabulary by the Home Office, but after investigation the police concluded there was no evidence of the 'slightest impropriety' in the girls' conduct; 'if accosted by men [they] invariably turn away and repulse any attempt at familiarity'. It was conceded that they earned a good deal of money by performing on the streets and on the sands, but they were not, as the complainant had maintained, beautiful, nor were they all girls: 'great numbers of both boys and girls, both Italians and Savoyards frequent Eastham, New Ferry and New Brighton during the summer'.

There the matter was allowed to rest, although from time to time, particularly in London, both performers and *padroni* were arrested for begging, with the latter imprisoned and the children returned to Italy. Between July and December 1877 alone, thirty-three *padroni* and eighty-three children were dealt with in this way, according to the *Annual Report* of the Charity Organization Society which had taken an interest in the matter.

So attitudes towards street entertainers varied. Some people welcomed the skills and the gaiety they offered, while others condemned them as noisy idlers and exploiters of vulnerable children.[49] But particularly among the young there must have been many who shared the enjoyment of Margaret Fletcher, daughter of an Oxford don, as she watched from her nursery window the comings and goings of itinerant entertainers in the crescent where she lived. They included dancing bears with their keepers, performing dogs, Punch and Judy, acrobats, 'gaudily-dressed children dancing on stilts and endless Italian organ-grinders, each with their attendant monkeys cap in paw held out for pennies'.[198]

Additional Sources Used

An Act to further amend the Law relating to Fairs in England and Wales, 34 Vict. 1877.
Annual Register for 1875 (London, 1876).
Michael T. Bass (ed.), *Street Music in the Metropolis* (London, 1864).
Bournemouth Guardian, 14 June 1884.
Charity Organization Society, *Annual Report for 1877* at the London Metropolitan Archives, A/FWA/c/B2/7.
Child's Guardian, May 1890.
Correspondence between Cheshire Constabulary and the Home Office on Italian Street Musicians in 1877 at the Public Record Office, H.O.45/9366/36003.
Devon Weekly Times, 16 and 23 April 1880.
T.J. Edelstein, *Vauxhall Gardens* (New Haven, Connecticut, 1983).
Theodor Fontane, *Ein Sommer in London* (Frankfurt am Main and Leipzig, 1995).
Halifax Guardian, 21 June 1851.
Marie Hartley and Joan Ingilby, *Life and Tradition in West Yorkshire* (London, 1976).
Isle of Wight Times, 24 May 1888.
Pall Mall Gazette, 8, 13 and 28 April 1885.
William H. Saunders, *Things I have seen: men I have known. A Portsmouth Retrospect*, manuscript at Portsmouth City Record Office, A/22/3.
George Ryley Scott, *The History of Cockfighting* (Liss, 1975).
Ian Starsmore, *English Fairs* (London, 1975).
The Animal World, 1 February 1870.
Theatre Museum, London: collection of circus posters.
Sir Garrard Tyrwhitt-Drake, *The English Circus and Fair Ground* (London, 1946).

CHAPTER 5

Country Pursuits

[My grandfather's] preoccupations were fox-hunting, shooting and coaching, and the catching of pike, perch and eels in the lake at Compton on off days. He had no taste for . . . any other business except the business of being a country gentleman . . . Although not quite at the top of the class as a horseman, he was a Master of Foxhounds whose woodcraft could not be denied in the field, while in the kennel he bred up a fine pack of foxhounds during the seventeen seasons for which he hunted the Warwickshire country. As a game shot he was second to few, if to any of his contemporaries; . . . He was among the three or four most accomplished whips of his day, having learnt to drive on the road coaches from such renowned coachmen as Harry and Charles Ward.

> Richard Greville Verney, Lord Willoughby de Broke, *The Passing Years*
> (London, 1924), describing the 17th Baron Willoughby de Broke
> (1809–62), 9–10

COUNTRY SPORTS

Much of the leisure of the Victorian landed classes was devoted to sporting activities and it was these which often formed the basis of country-house parties. Fox-hunting, shooting (including deerstalking in Scotland) and game fishing were followed with enthusiasm, and the horseman who displayed skill and daring across country or who was an expert marksman at a shoot enjoyed high prestige among his peers. In October 1878 a contributor to *The Field* extolled the virtues of wild fowling:

> the self-reliance which the wild-fowl shooter must place upon his individual resources, and his perpetual struggle against all the elements combined – everything tends to make of the pursuit one which I have no hesitation in calling the most manly and the most fascinating of all the pursuits which the sportsman may addict himself to.

A few months earlier the magazine had comforted itself that a recent spate of hunting accidents was unlikely to discourage 'high-spirited youth or enthusiastic middle-age from following a sport that is the best possible training for a . . . career which may demand resolution, pluck, and readiness of resources, and the best means of preserving in their freshness qualities that add a robust charm to mature manhood'.[43]

In the final quarter of the century hunting was even advocated as a means of achieving imperial success, to the benefit of the nation at large. In 1899 the historian of the Belvoir Hunt argued that by sharing the sport of his social superiors, a young middle-class Englishman would acquire 'the virtues and good qualities of a governing race'. By combining sturdy common sense with 'aristocratic boldness' such men would be equipped to rule 'an immense dependency of mixed races'. In this way fox-hunting nurtured the strength of the English character and the power to command.[18]

For some of the nouveaux riches the acquisition of a sporting estate became an essential status symbol and a means of entry into the higher levels of society. As Raymond Carr explains, 'ancient parks and baronial halls' were used to sanction 'the social position of "cotton spinners, cotton brokers, brewers, ironmasters and engineers overflowing with ready cash"'.[119] In 1894 Sir Edward Guinness celebrated his elevation to the peerage by purchasing the Elveden estate in Suffolk. This was famous for its prolific game, and under the new Lord Iveagh's regime staff in the game department rose to seventy. Among them were twenty-four gamekeepers who patrolled nineteen 'beats'. At the close of the first season the head keeper was able to report that his employer and guests had shot 15,100 pheasants, 1,978 partridges, 679 hares, 6,778 rabbits, 74 woodcock, 19 snipe, 13 ducks and 80 'various' – a formidable total even at a time when the annual game bags of estates ran into thousands rather than hundreds.[193]

It was indicative of the growing interest in shooting that the game room became a characteristic feature of country mansions, with its walls adorned by cases of stuffed game and fish and its racks stocked with firearms. Game books were meticulously kept and the number of birds and animals killed was regarded as a measure of the enjoyment of a shoot. Those who failed to make a satisfactory contribution to the total would be conscious of a sense of inadequacy. Thus at Eaton Hall every guest at a shooting party would find a printed game card before him at the dinner table in the evening. This bore the Grosvenor crest and inside would be details of the day's bag, and the share attributable to each member of the party: 'whereas a persistently poor score might bring social diminution, consistently long lines of furry and feathered corpses aligned upon the grass conferred a social cachet which made endurable the splitting headaches suffered from the recoil of "hot guns"'.[193]

Equally, hosts who were unable to provide the expected tally of fish or game felt the omission keenly. In September 1889 Sir Edward Hamilton expressed sympathy for his host, Arthur Sassoon, whose grouse drives had been 'very bad' and 'the river though in beautiful order produces no fish'. As a consequence they had been 'flogging the river, though without success, & playing Lawn Tennis'. But in compensation, his fellow guests were congenial and 'there could not be a better host & hostess'.

Once grouse shooting began on the 'glorious Twelfth' of August, details of bags would be published in the sporting press. A contributor to *Country Life Illustrated* in August 1897 described how after the first morning's sport he and his fellow guns went off happily to lunch. When they arrived all the dead birds were laid out in long lines for inspection, 'and we find that sixty-five brace and a hare is the sum total'. After consuming a sumptuous repast, they lounged lazily in the bright

Pheasant shooting at Studley Royal, Yorkshire, 1901. (Rural History Centre, University of Reading)

sunshine, 'half buried in blossoming heather, chatting and smoking until warned by the keeper that it is time to get to our places', and to resume the slaughter.

In the final quarter of the nineteenth century, when agricultural depression caused a drop in farm incomes, the earnings secured from the rental or sale of estates for sporting purposes gave a welcome cash boost to landlords, especially in the arable Eastern Counties and in Scotland. In Norfolk one estate took £500 a year from its farm rents and £2,000 from shooting leases, while in Scotland it was common for a landed proprietor to derive a quarter or more of his rent roll from letting shooting rights to outside tenants. Among the latter was Walter Shoolbred, of the London furniture-making firm, who rented Carriehall Forest. He built a large lodge there, and included two game larders, for grouse and deer respectively. He even brought a steam launch to the loch, to take him to suitable positions from which to shoot.[193]

In these circumstances the number of gamekeepers in Britain rose sharply, as sporting landlords strove to protect their investment in birds and coverts from the attacks of poachers and animal predators. In England and Wales alone the total of gamekeepers reported in the population censuses rose from 7,542 in 1851[12] to

16,677 in 1901,[15] a rise of 121 per cent over fifty years; for Scotland the figures were 1,944 in 1851[12] and 5,367 in 1901,[16] making an increase of 176 per cent over the half century. In both cases there was a particularly sharp rise in the 1850s and 1860s. On the Harpur Crewe estate in Staffordshire, for example, where the number of gamekeepers employed rose from four in 1838 to ten in the 1870s, a summary of the 'vermin' killed for threatening the partridges and pheasants over the period 1860–80 included 5,701 cats, 2,256 stoats, 2,073 weasels, 1,784 magpies, 23 foxes and 9 polecats, to say nothing of many hundreds of crows and hawks.[130] Often gamekeepers constructed a so-called 'graveyard', a pole fixed between two trees, on which some of the corpses were hung to act as a deterrent and to demonstrate the keeper's diligence.

The frequently cruel means adopted in capturing these predators led the Royal Society for the Prevention of Cruelty to Animals to offer prizes for improved traps to avoid unnecessary suffering. The competition was unsuccessful, however, and for the rest, the RSPCA refused to condemn game preservation, doubtless in deference to the views of most of its landed supporters.[180] In 1884 the society president, Lord Aberdare, told its annual general meeting that there was 'something to be said' in favour of both hunting and shooting: 'Hunting often involves great personal courage and danger. Shooting generally requires the expenditure of considerable energy resulting in fatigue. It takes men out in the open field, and, at least, is a healthful pastime.' But individual members were less sympathetic. In 1890 one contributor to the society's journal, *The Animal World*, commented sourly on the common phrase 'which describes one Englishman as saying to another, "It's a fine day; let us go and kill something!"'

> I am not altogether alone in thinking that when killing and wounding have ceased to be enjoyed for their own sake – when, to find pleasure or acquire skill in hitting a mark, it is no longer necessary that the mark should be a living creature, English sport will have lost nothing of the undenied healthiness of its influence.[42]

Despite such arguments, the RSPCA maintained an equivocal stance towards field sports until the end of the century.

The link between these sporting activities and the renting of landed estates by wealthy incomers was underlined by advertisements in the property pages of *Country Life Illustrated* and similar publications. Thus on 19 June 1897 a Suffolk estate of 2,800 acres 'shooting' was offered, 'with or without a Furnished MANSION, one and a half miles from town and first-class station; 1,400 to 1,500 pheasants, 700 partridges, 150–200 hares; boating and fishing in river.' A few weeks later 'grouse and low ground shooting and salmon fishing' were offered at Kirkby Lonsdale, Westmorland. The property included '250 brace grouse moor, 500 acres rabbit warren, and 500 acres of most conveniently arranged covert. Also some six miles of good salmon and trout fishing in the most picturesque portion of the Lune.' It could be hired with or without a 'capital lodge of three sitting rooms and seven bedrooms'.[29] Countless similar offers appeared during the late Victorian period and those estates with easy rail access to London were specially sought after. According to one commentator, although Norfolk and Suffolk were the prime shooting counties Sussex at the end of the century could command higher rents, partly because of improvements made in the preservation of game but also because of its proximity to the capital. 'It is quite an easy matter for a dweller in the metropolis to breakfast in London at eight o'clock, look through his letters, and begin shooting on his Sussex ground at 10.30.'[124]

For ambitious politicians there were wider social implications. Benjamin Disraeli drily pointed out in *Coningsby* that the higher a man rose in the political world the more important well-stocked game preserves became, since they offered a means of cementing new alliances and ending old rivalries within the hospitable framework of a shooting party. As Lady Aberdeen delicately phrased it in her *Memories of a Scottish Grannie*, 'An informal and pleasant mode of intercourse sprang up which . . . had important results to the country, for when politicians of different parties were fellow guests under the same roof for a week, differences were apt to be smoothed over, and compromises effected.'[301]

Unlike hunting, shooting made few demands on a man's courage or stamina, and even those like the future prime minister Arthur Balfour, who had little love for the sport, felt it necessary to attend the more important parties. When the newly married Duke and Duchess of Marlborough held their first shoot at Blenheim in 1896 the Prince of Wales and other members of the Royal family were among the guests, and so was Balfour. In a letter to a close friend he described the journey from London by special train with others in the party, and their reception with 'illuminations, guards of honour, cheering and other follies . . . Today the men shot and the women dawdled. As I detest both occupations equally I stayed in my room till one o'clock and then went exploring on my bike, joining everybody at luncheon. Then, after the inevitable photograph, I again betook myself to my faithful machine . . . So far you perceive the duties of society are weighing lightly upon me.'[89]

In this way pleasure and politics could be neatly combined. Yet they were not a low-cost option, especially when royalty was involved. According to the Countess of Warwick, who was intimately associated with the Prince of Wales in the early 1890s, some men and women economized for a year or even fell into debt so that they might entertain members of the royal family for a weekend. Not only was there the cost of entertainment, but cohorts of servants had to be accommodated:

> In certain houses of unlimited wealth, it had become customary to have a Royal suite specially refurnished on the occasion of each visit, in order that the note of novelty might be maintained. The chef who served for ordinary occasions would be replaced by a specialist, whose skill was equalled only by his wastefulness.[371]

Lady Warwick's own hospitality was lavish. Guests' bedrooms were fitted with beautiful furniture and hangings, large comfortable armchairs and sofas, as well as the finest linen, and shaded lamps to make reading 'as you rested a joy'. The house was comfortably warm, unlike many others where ladies in low-cut evening dresses were chilled in draughty passages even when the rooms were adequately heated. There were also plenty of opportunities for discreet flirtations. According to Elinor Glyn, who visited Lady Warwick's Essex home, Easton Lodge, in the 1890s, by the end 'of the first evening you usually knew which member of the

A SHOOTING LUNCHEON AT EASTON, OCTOBER, 1895

H.R.H. the Prince of Wales; Mrs. Ralph Sneyd; Lord De Lisle and Dudley; Blanche, Countess of Rosslyn; Mr. and Mrs. Menzies; Col. Mark Lockwood, M.P., and Mrs. Lockwood; Lady Lilian Wemyss; Lord Rosslyn; Lady Angela Forbes; Col. Sir Arthur Paget; Lord Herbert Vane Tempest; Miss Muriel Wilson; Mr. and Mrs. R. Woodhouse; Sir Walter Gilbey; Sir George Holford; Myself and my husband

The Countess of Warwick entertaining at her luxurious home, Easton Lodge in Essex, in 1895. Standing in the middle of the guests is the Prince of Wales, with whom she enjoyed a close relationship at this time. (From Frances, Countess of Warwick, Life's Ebb and Flow, *1929)*

party intended to make it his business to amuse you . . . during the rest of the visit, in the hope of who knows what reward? . . . The beaux of the 'nineties were experts at arranging pleasant things and were full of self-confidence.'

During the autumn and winter, the country sports pursued usually involved killing something; in the summer they were associated with ball games and, in some parts of the country, with race meetings. In south-west Wales H.M. Vaughan remembered that the lawn-tennis club at Newcastle Emlyn was a convenient meeting place for the younger members of gentry families during the summer months. On the shady lawns beside the River Teify they assembled each Tuesday to play tennis and croquet, 'to gossip, to drink tea, to flirt, to quarrel and generally to disport themselves'. But the club was anxious to maintain its social exclusiveness and carefully guarded against any but the gentry and their visiting friends.[148]

In other cases, as for the young George Cornwallis-West, it was attendance at house parties in the late summer on estates with a private cricket ground in the park which gave special pleasure. These parties lasted for a week and involved not only long hours of gentle exercise and much talk and laughter, but in the evening an opportunity for the enthusiastic trout fishermen in the party to rush to the river to take advantage of the evening rise. Dinner followed and then dancing, music, games and practical jokes. Another cricketing enthusiast, H.D.G. Leveson-Gower, considered that ideally the game should be sufficiently competitive to interest the participants but not so absorbing that it became 'a nuisance to the fair sex'. He was not in favour of the lavish cricket lunches, including champagne, which were becoming common. 'Men do not play good cricket on Perrier Jouet, followed by Crème de Menthe, with two big cigars topping a rich and succulent menu. No, give us some big pies, cold chicken, a fine sirloin of English beef, and a round of brawn, washed down by good ale and luscious shandygaff. That is all cricketers want, and kings only fare worse.'[337]

Cornwallis-West's wife, the former Lady Randolph Churchill, was less enthusiastic about these summer gatherings, dismissing them as marriage marts rather than real sporting occasions:

Innumerable are the country house parties with golf, lawn-tennis and the river to amuse and keep one out of doors. Mothers with broods of marriageable daughters find this kind of entertainment a better market to take them to than the heated atmosphere of the ballroom, which the desirable *partis* shun for the greater attraction of air and exercise.[280]

A quiet afternoon on the River Cherwell, Oxford, c. 1900. (The author)

Most of the élite country sports relied on a select social network, with invitations issued to a limited group of people who moved from one house to another. Only in the case of hunting was this not so true, since theoretically all those equipped to ride to hounds were able to do so. In practice, many would-be participants were excluded on grounds of cost – or at best were reduced to following the hunt on foot (as was the case with humble stockingers in Leicestershire, where whole villages emptied to follow the hounds).[119] Nevertheless in the early and mid-Victorian years farmers, in particular, were likely to join in. It was said that no man could be a successful master of hounds without the backing of the farmers, since it was over their land that the hunt galloped and it was they who had to preserve the foxes, despite the threat posed to their hen-roosts. Some were as keen as the sixty or seventy farmers, all in red coats, who rode regularly with Lord Yarborough's Brocklesby Hunt. There were also less prestigious packs which were owned by farmers, such as the Essex Invincibles and Hempstead Hounds.[103]

In Cumbria there were two quite distinct types of hunt. On the one hand the members of the Cumberland Foxhounds and their like hunted on horseback and adopted the conventions of the prestigious Shire counties. On the other the fell packs would be followed on foot, on account of the difficult terrain. Although the huntsman of the latter wore a red coat and velvet riding cap, doubtless for reasons of prestige, most of the field would be clad in weatherproof clothing and stout boots. Comparatively little expense was involved, since the hounds were 'trencher fed', that is they were kept on separate farms in ones and twos and were only brought together for a meet. In this way small farmers, shepherds and country tradesmen could afford to take part alongside members of the local gentry. Among the humblest of the packs was the Eskdale, founded in 1857 by Tommy Dobson, a bobbin turner. He combined the roles of master and huntsman for over fifty years.

Many of the humbler hunts met not at crossroads or market places nor on the lawn of a manor house, as was usual with the prestigious packs, but at a public house. This was the base to which they also returned at the end of the day for refreshments. The occasion would finish with a good deal of music and general jollification; indeed, hunting songs were regarded as folk-songs in Cumbria. In these, hunt followers were mentioned by name and their exploits related with admiration or humour.[253] John Peel, who died in 1854 and whose skills were celebrated in a popular song, was one of the most famous. Like many other fell-pack men, he chased hares and mart (i.e. polecats and pinemarten) as well as foxes. By the end of the century, however, these joint hunts had waned, as increasingly hares were pursued with beagles.[387]

Even in Cumbria many of the masters of fell packs were local gentry, and that was certainly true of the more prestigious mounted hunts. They relied on the patronage of important landed families or upon those, like the well-to-do Mr Puffington in R.S. Surtees's *Mr. Sponge's Sporting Tour*, who could contribute much-needed cash. Puffington was the son of a 'great starchmaker of Stepney' and felt that mastership of the Hanby hounds would give him 'consequence'. He had no natural inclination for hunting but when he saw friends without any taste for the turf becoming stewards 'he saw no reason why he should not make a similar sacrifice at the shrine of Diana'.[402] It was probably with such men in mind that *Country Life Illustrated* in 1897 commented sourly on those who hunted in a 'cramped country', which had no difficult fences. They took up the sport simply

> because the riding does their livers good, because it is pleasant to say in society that they 'hunt,' because they wish to make an impression amongst their neighbours. The last thing they want is a good run across country, since they are probably unable to jump a fence of any sort and are afraid to take the slightest risk.

For an expert horseman such an approach would be disastrous. The timorous example of his companions would undermine his own nerve. He would 'lose his dash . . . He may even take to golf'.

Hunting brought excitement and a sense of purpose to the daily lives of many landed families during the winter months. Already by the 1830s the country had been divided out among the regular packs, with territories clearly defined and it was considered highly improper for any master to enter a neighbouring territory. One who attempted to do so in 1844 was firmly rebuffed by the landowner to whom he had appealed:

> You would . . . make me consent to the greatest mischief that could be aimed at foxhunting . . . , by subscribing to the doctrine that owners or occupiers of coverts could take those coverts from one hunt and add them to another at their own will . . . ; so that no master would know from one season's end to another what did, or what did not belong to his country.[103]

Over the years, as hunts became more numerous, territories were sub-divided by agreement, while the total of hunt followers rose sharply. In 1866 there were 125 packs of hounds in Britain, of which about a dozen were in Scotland.[341] By the end of the century there were 161 packs of foxhounds in England and Wales plus 11 in Scotland. In addition there were 19 packs of staghounds, 125 of harriers in England and Wales and 3 in Scotland, 49 packs of beagles, 18 of otter hounds, and 2 of basset hounds, as well as 7 packs of draghounds – all of the latter being in England and Wales. As the figures show, foxes were the main quarry, but stags, hares and otters were pursued in certain districts. In south-west Wales a number of larger estates had their own otter hounds to safeguard the fishing.[148] In the south of England, too, otters were hunted to protect trout streams. According to Richard Jefferies, by the early 1880s they had been 'almost beaten off the Thames itself'.

At the beginning of the Victorian period it was feared that railway building would disrupt hunting territories and would lead to a decline in the sport, even within its heartland in the Shire counties of middle England. In practice, the reverse proved to be the case. Not only did railways increase the size of hunting fields but it became possible to travel to distant meets in special compartments, with six to twelve men provided with their own saloon carriage, including a dressing room and cooking facilities.[232] One enthusiast, William Chafy, noted in his journal the distances he had travelled by rail and horse to attend meets on 2,822 hunting days. He sometimes covered 100 miles but usually returned home

*Lord Tredegar, Master of the
Tredegar Hunt, 1884.
(Museum of Welsh Life,
St Fagans, Cardiff)*

for tea. According to Raymond Carr, railways 'saved hacking heroic distances at dawn and dusk and enlarged the choice of meets'.[119]

It became possible to hunt with ease from London and in 1894 the Duke of Beaufort pointed out that this could be accomplished either by keeping horses in town and taking them down by train on hunting mornings or by stabling them at some hunting centre and meeting them there or at the covert side.[51] Of the two possibilities the first was more convenient for the rider but the second was better for the horse. The duke himself was one of a dynasty of huntsmen and his country seat, Badminton, was considered the 'great metropolis' for horse and hound.[117] Under his mastership the Beaufort Hunt went out on six days a week until the 1880s, when economic pressures forced a temporary reduction to four days a week and led to part of the hunt's territory being lent to Captain John Spicer and the new Avon Vale Hunt.[264] At the end of the century, under the mastership of his son, that arrangement was ended and hunting was resumed on six days a week. A young relative claimed that at this period 'the main thing' at Badminton was following the hounds. Sport commenced in the middle of August with cubbing and continued through to May. 'We would get off very early in the morning – breakfast at six o'clock, because one was out on a horse at half-past six.'[373] When the railway from Paddington to Bath opened in 1841 the Beaufort became accessible from London and sport had to be provided for ever-growing fields. Badminton lawn meetings could attract as many as five thousand spectators, with the 8th Duke entertaining a thousand at breakfast. His successor at the turn of the century spent lavishly, too, keeping twenty 'magnificent hunters' for his own use.[119]

For participants there was not only the excitement of the chase but a sense of achievement when it was brought to a successful conclusion by the death of the fox. The 19th Lord Willoughby de Broke, himself an enthusiastic master of hounds, compared the hunting instinct with that which drove a literary collector to search for first editions. The bringing of the quarry 'to hand at the end of an arduous chase' was the consummation most hunt followers desired, although he denied there was any 'lust of blood'.[358] Despite criticisms from opponents such as Dean Inge, who condemned field sports as 'barbarous and immoral', the pleasure derived by most of those taking part was undeniable. This is confirmed in the diary entries of Dearman Birchall, a Leeds merchant who in 1869 purchased a small estate, Bowden Hall, in Gloucestershire. Soon after taking up residence he went out with the Berkeley. One typical comment relates to 20 December 1870, when the hunt met at Fretherne Court: 'Found in covert behind the House. Soon lost; but picked up another at Withy Bed, Frampton. Ran him with great speed to within 2 miles of Sharpness Point, a fine sight on the sands. A most enjoyable day, 9 hours in the saddle, about 40 miles.'[357]

The diary nonetheless indicates the dangers for inexpert or unfortunate riders. On 25 January 1870, when the Berkeley hunted from Norton, one man's horse fell and kicked him on the head and four other animals were killed or died. Again, on 8 February, despite a 'capital lunch' at Stonehouse Court and a sharp run to Whitminster, they ended up 'without killing our fox. Many casualties and very hard riding.'[357]

So great was the enthusiasm of the 18th Baron Willoughby de Broke for the sport that when he married in October 1867 he and his bride dispensed with a honeymoon so that they could return to their estate at Compton Verney and ride with the Warwickshire Hounds. According to their son, the new Lady Willoughby de Broke was 'rightly bred to marry into a fox-hunting family', being the daughter of a former Master of the Cheshire Foxhounds and coming from 'good fox-hunting stock'. After the marriage she was 'well mounted on horses who were fit to carry a lady; and in her husband she had the very best pilot in England. So these two rode at the head of the hunt for some seasons.' As for Lord Willoughby de Broke himself, his life was spent 'within ear-shot of the singing of the hounds', and hunting four times a week for seven months of the year left him scant time for other interests. Although an expert shot, his love of the chase meant that he had little opportunity to join country house parties and he 'gradually dropped out of the shooting world'.[358]

Not until the later 1850s did women begin to hunt regularly. This was partly because at a time when the speed of hounds was increasing and the new fashion of galloping at fences was being adopted it was considered too dangerous for them, especially as they rode sidesaddle in cumbersome riding habits. But in the second half of the century attitudes began to change. Among the new generation of enthusiasts was Lady Brooke, later the Countess of Warwick. When she and her husband stayed at Warwick Castle she ignored her father-in-law's disapproval of women who hunted. Immediately after breakfast with the family she would rush off to change into appropriate garb and slip out by a side door to the stable. At various times she followed four of the most fashionable hunts in the famous county of Leicestershire and visited Ireland from time to time so as to be able to hunt with the Ward and Meath packs.[98] She also went out with the Essex Hounds when she was living at her own seat, Easton Lodge, and her 'social *cachet* lent a reflected glow to the country gentry who made up the bulk of its members'. When hunting was over for the season Lady Brooke took up another sport, driving a four-in-hand. This was a light, high carriage drawn by four spirited horses and required great skill to control. According to her biographer, she adopted this recreation, then very unusual for a woman, in order to show her independence rather than from any particular love of it. Before she married, her step-father had refused her the smart pony cart she had set her heart on, arguing that no lady could be seen in any vehicle but a sober four-wheeled carriage and pair. But soon after her marriage she began driving guests around her estate on the high box of the four-in-hand, with two coachmen in attendance at the back.[98]

Lady Randolph Churchill was another keen horsewoman. When her husband quarrelled with the Prince of Wales she spent part of the six years of their social exile hunting in Ireland. It became something of a passion for both her and her husband:

> Whenever I could 'beg, borrow or steal' a horse I did so. We had a few hunters of our own which we rode indiscriminately, being both of us lightweights. Some of my best days with the Meath and Kildare Hounds I owed to a little brown mare I bought from Simmons at Oxford, who negotiated the 'trappy' fences of the Kildare country, and the banks and narrow doubles of Meath . . . Many were the 'tosses' I 'took', . . . but it was glorious sport, and, to my mind, even hunting in Leicestershire later on could not compare with it. With the exception of the Ward Union Staghounds and the Galway Blazers, I think we hunted with nearly every pack of hounds in Ireland.[92]

The Earl of Warwick was not alone, however, in having reservations about women who hunted. R.S. Surtees, for one, admitted that while females had better hands than men in controlling a horse, he disliked having them in the field. 'A man does not like riding before them, or leaving them in the lurch; and even if they do "go along", the whole field is kept in alarm lest an accident happen.'[103] He enjoyed having them at the meet, to which many drove in their carriages, but maintained they were 'as much in their place' there as 'they are out of it tearing across country'.

To achieve success hunts had to have the co-operation of farmers, not only because of the damage which riders and foxes could do to holdings but to deter tenants from using wire as a cheap form of fencing. The latter was anathema to the hunting fraternity, even before barbed wire began to appear in the 1880s. By a judicious mixture of flattery, patronage and cash payments, successful masters were able to avoid these problems. Hence the normally unsociable Lord Scamperdale, Master of the Flat Hat Hunt in *Mr. Sponge's Sporting Tour*, took care to make 'things pleasant' by taking breakfast with farmer Springwheat and his wife when the hunt met on the Springwheat property. Without such attention, comments Surtees, 'Springwheat would have trapped every fox on his farm, and the blooming

Mrs. Springwheat would have had an interminable poultry-bill against the hunt; whereas . . . Springwheat saw his corn trampled on, nay, led the way over it himself, and Mrs. Springwheat saw her Dorkings disappear without a murmur.'[402]

Outside the pages of fiction, the landed classes were remarkably successful in persuading country people of the evils of vulpicide. Many of the great hunting landlords included a clause in their leases forbidding the destruction of foxes, but in most cases tenants willingly accepted the need for preservation. Indeed, it was claimed that farmers of Mr Farquharson's hunt in early Victorian Dorset refused to sit at the same table in the Dorchester ordinary as a man suspected of destroying foxes. And at the end of the century an Essex tenant instilled into his children the maxim that it was better to kill a man than a fox.[119]

Initially most packs were privately owned but by the 1860s, with the rise in hunting costs and an increase in the size of fields as a result of railway construction, subscription hunts became the norm. According to Anthony Trollope, himself an enthusiastic rider to hounds, most independent fox hunters preferred a subscription pack, since in this way they could 'pay their own proportion of the expenditure, and feel that they [followed] their amusement without any other debt to the Master . . . than that which is always due to zeal and success in high position'.[119]

In the early days of subscription hunting, the compensation paid to farmers for fox damage was often inadequate. But it was realized that serious difficulties would arise if proper provision were not made, and by the final quarter of the century satisfactory payments were normal practice. Another problem, however, was the growing popularity of game preservation, particularly of pheasants. While few preservers closed their coverts to hounds or had foxes trapped, since this was generally condemned, they did turn a blind eye to their keepers' vulpicide.[232] When shooting rights were let to absentees, tensions could become particularly acute, since shooting rents and keepers' tips often depended on eliminating foxes. Hence the fury of the Duke of Cleveland's agent when he discovered that an absentee was allowing 'foul play with foxes'. This was 'an unlooked for and shameful outrage that has taken place in a foxhunting country . . . a tenant of yours has made it his business to destroy foxes on Anniscliffe Moore.'[341] Yet despite the agent's protests and those of others who shared his feelings, friction between shooters and hunt members continued in a number of districts to the end of Queen Victoria's reign and beyond.

Agricultural depression added to the difficulties of the hunting fraternity in the final quarter of the nineteenth century. As we have seen, the number of hunts in private hands was diminishing. Even the Duke of Beaufort was obliged to ask for subscriptions in 1888, while the Duke of Rutland reduced his hunting from five days a week to four in 1891 on cost grounds. When he retired from the mastership of the Belvoir in 1896 the sporting press described it as a 'national calamity'. Others shared such financial dilemmas:

Lord Spencer had to borrow £15,000 to cover his excess hunting expenses in 1879, and refused to contemplate a fourth term as Master of the Pytchley in 1900 on account of the cost . . . Lord Lonsdale was obliged to resign as Master of the Quorn in 1898 because his trustees effectively ordered him to do so . . .

George Luttrell was a West Country gentleman, who had hunted in Somerset at his own expense: but in 1881, he simply gave up. Three years later, Lord Haldon took over the South Devon and promised to provide all the necessary funding. But in 1886, he was compelled to sell the hounds.[117]

It was against this background that new men from commerce and industry became involved, as they sought to establish their credentials as country gentlemen. As early as 1870 the fashionable Quorn hunt had a Liverpool shipbroker as master. He had hunted with hounds in India and under his leadership the Quorn flourished. At the same time many businessmen and manufacturers from Leicester could be found in the field. Two decades later a Midlands journalist claimed that whereas in the 1860s the Warwickshire, Staffordshire and Worcestershire hunts had enjoyed little support from city men, in the 1890s hundreds of Birmingham magnates and businessmen were devoting much of their leisure to 'the prince of sports'. Similarly, Albert Brassey, son of the major railway contractor, ran the Heythrop as master on a lavish scale in the late Victorian and Edwardian years. When out hunting Mr Brassey wore a very long red coat and a buttonhole of white violets. He hunted four days a week with his own hounds, and those who rode with the Heythrop did so by invitation.[119]

To instruct the new men in the etiquette of the sport various guides and manuals were published. Among them was *Thomas' Hunting Diary for 1899–1900*, edited by the Earl of Rosslyn. This stressed the importance of proper dress. 'Going out hunting in mufti is on the same lines as going out to dinner in a suit of dittoes.' If a man were visiting a distant pack he should always take care to avoid any carelessness in his apparel. 'If he is visiting the most out-of-the-way pack in the world he should dress as if he were hunting at home . . . Nothing is in such bad taste as the "anything will do for these fellows" sort of air which some men give themselves when hunting with what they are pleased to call a provincial pack.'

Equal care must be taken when out in the field:

If there is a rush or a crush through a gate, you must abide by your position and show no undue eagerness to get before others . . . When you open a gate you must not allow it to close in the face of the next comer, and you should stop to catch a man's horse when he falls. It is rudeness to rush by a man at a fence, or through dirty ground, though you may chance to have a faster mount . . . There is nothing more unbecoming to a sportsman than . . . to rush for the brush, which is vulgar.

Friendships struck up on the hunting field could lead to the establishment of networks of congenial parties and other events. Hunt balls, for example, were major features in the local social calendar and were a means of promoting good relations as well as raising funds for the hunt itself. Women who took little part on the hunting field might be tempted to try to stop their menfolk, particularly their husband, joining in. But attendance at a hunt ball could change their minds. Similarly keen game preservers were regarded as unreliable protectors of foxes, but if their daughters wanted to go to the ball, that encouraged a conciliatory spirit. The railway also helped to make hunt balls a success by bringing down from London first-class orchestras and additional luxuries such as Mr Gunter's cakes, purchased from that famous metropolitan confectioner.[119]

Steeplechasing, too, grew up in part as a way for hunts to woo farmers and their families by offering them an entertaining day out. But it soon became a means for young men to find greater excitement than was provided by hunting alone. Steeplechases began as races between 'friends and rivals across country between two points'. At first it was rough riding and there were no rules, but gradually this changed. In 1836 a Grand Liverpool steeplechase was held at Aintree and eleven years later it was renamed the Grand National. It became a national institution and from 1867 a Steeplechase Calendar was published by the National Hunt Committee, giving details of such events. But many members of the hunting fraternity disliked the new sport. 'Nimrod', a famous contemporary writer on the subject, described it in the *Sporting Magazine* in April 1840 as the 'most cruel, the most *cocktail* pursuit ever entered into by English gentlemen'.[119] Even more than the toll taken of the horses by dangerous fences in the Grand National and other races, the widespread gambling encouraged was strongly condemned. This applied

Croquet at Hurlingham, c. 1900. This was a sport that was enjoyed by many country house ladies. (The author)

especially when local publicans were involved in the staging of races. *Bell's Life* called these 'instruments of fraud and barefaced swindling'. In the 1870s the National Hunt Committee finally established rules for steeplechases and then sought to eliminate dishonest racecourse managements and stewards. In the 1880s individual hunts also ran point-to-point races under the aegis of the National Hunt Committee and by 1900 about fifty of these were being held.[191]

Despite its problems, then, hunting did much to maintain the solidarity of the rural élite during the nineteenth century. But by the final quarter of that century increasing numbers of the rich, led by the Prince of Wales, came to prefer shooting to the hazards and discomforts of the hunting field. Shooting has been described as 'the sport of the plutocracy *par excellence*'.[191] Participation was by private invitation and the sport proved divisive not only through the barriers it created between rich and poor, or between preserving landlords and their tenant farmers, but within the sporting community itself, between hunters and shooters. After 1831, when restrictions on shooting rights were eased and it was possible for anyone to purchase a game licence, tenants were rarely allowed by their landlords to shoot even ground game. Hares and rabbits, the latter kept in enormous numbers in warrens on some estates, did much damage to crops yet it was not until the 1881 Ground Game Act that farmers were entitled to shoot these without seeking their landlord's permission. Even then there is evidence, for example from Scotland in the 1880s, that farmers who took advantage of their new rights were given short shrift by owners or their agents.[5]

The Prince of Wales was an early enthusiast for the sport and after buying Sandringham in 1863 he turned it into one of the most prolific game estates in Europe, while driving some of his tenant farmers to despair in the process. Queen Victoria disliked such excesses and appealed in vain to the prince 'to do a little away with the *exclusive* character of shooting . . . With hunting (much as I dislike it on account of the danger) this is the case, and that is what makes it so popular.'[126] Despite the payment of compensation to tenants for damage done by game and the custom of giving presents of pheasants, partridges and hares to local people, it was rare to find ordinary countrymen who sympathized with game preservation.[341]

Traditionalists deplored the development of *battue* shooting, whereby pheasants and partridges were driven in vast numbers over the guns. In 1868 one critic compared the almost tame pheasants raised by hand on many estates to 'Shanghai roosters . . . in the neighbouring farmyard'.[41] He believed (wrongly) that 'the taste for wild and adventurous shooting' was so deep seated that it would require 'a long course of luxury, and of battue-shooting, and of hot luncheons among the brown fern' to eradicate it. He was equally hostile to the practice of driving partridges and grouse so that they could be shot from behind a hedge or peat-stack, as they flew overhead:

> It is notorious that there are many estates in England, especially in the moorland districts of Derbyshire, Yorkshire, Lancashire, Cumberland, and Westmoreland [*sic*], where, in former times, a moor, beaten in the ordinary way, yielded at most twelve or fifteen brace of grouse in a day, picked up by the laborious exertions of two or three good shots . . . But the same moor, if driven

according to the modern fashion, will now yield without difficulty, to the same number of guns, 130 or 150 brace in a day.[41]

The adoption of the breech-loader gun to replace the old muzzle-loader was similarly condemned on account of its superior killing power. One commentator argued that to destroy game as a pastime, without reference to the value of the birds or animals killed as articles of food, 'must be pronounced by a severe moralist . . . in the highest degree reprehensible'.[67] But such criticisms were brushed aside and by the later years of the century the slaughter of a thousand birds a day was considered normal for a good shoot. Lord Walsingham quoted the game book of a Norfolk estate which had registered 39 pheasants killed in 1821 and 5,069 in 1875.[118] At Audley End Park, too, a dramatic change occurred, with the annual total of game killed rising from 2,872 in 1820 to 12,908 in 1884–5.[213]

Good shots were welcome members of house parties and those who were particularly expert, such as Lord de Grey or Lord Walsingham, practised incessantly. At one gathering a fellow guest had occasion to go down to the library late at night to get a book. She was surprised to find de Grey there, too, practising changing guns with his two loaders. He was, she noted drily, 'not too pleased at being discovered'.[92]

But while the menfolk enjoyed the competition and camaraderie of shoots, as well as the sense of achievement when they were successful, for females they had less appeal. Few women shot, since this was considered inappropriate and unfeminine. In 1882 Queen Victoria commented disapprovingly to her daughter, Princess Victoria, that while it was acceptable for a lady to be a spectator on such occasions, 'only fast women shot'.[301] Even Lady Randolph Churchill, who saw no harm in females shooting game, nonetheless could not 'admire it as an accomplishment'.[133] Some did ignore the disapproval. In the late 1880s and early 1890s Princess Radziwill shot regularly with Sir Frederick Milbank at Barningham, although with little success.[301] Far more consternation was caused when Lord and Lady Ribblesdale visited the Duke of Westminster's estate in Sutherland. This probably possessed the finest deerstalking and salmon and sea-trout fishing in the world, and great was the surprise when Lady Ribblesdale announced that she was to accompany her husband on a stalking expedition. She wore no hat and her buttoned boots and long skirts seemed ill suited for such a venture. Certainly some of the duke's sons gloomily predicted that such an apparition would so alarm the deer that it would ruin the stalking for years to come. 'Contrary . . . to all expectation, the Ribblesdales returned with a fine stag, extolling the glorious day they had enjoyed, though Lady Ribblesdale's hair was wringing wet, all the buttons were off her boots, and the lace in her petticoat hung in shreds.'[205]

Far more common, however, was Lady Warwick's unenthusiastic reaction to shooting parties. Her husband was a crack shot and so they were asked to all the important houses.

The average party might number sixteen, as too many guns spoil the shoot. We began the day by breakfasting at ten o'clock . . . There was enough food to last a group of well-regulated digestions for the whole day. The men went out shooting after breakfast and then came the emptiness of the long morning . . . I can remember the groups of women sitting discussing their neighbours or writing letters at impossible little ornamental tables . . . We were not all women. There were a few unsporting men asked – 'darlings'. These men of witty and amusing conversation were always asked as extras . . . to help to entertain the women; otherwise we should have been left high and dry. The 'ladies' . . . rarely took part in the shoot, not even going out to join the shooters until luncheon time. Then, dressed in tweeds . . . we went out together to some rendezvous of the shooters. A woman who was very bloodthirsty and sporting might go and cower behind some man and watch his prowess among the pheasants. But there were very few even of those brave ones. After a large luncheon, finishing up with coffee and liqueurs, the women preferred to wend their way back to the house. They would spend the intervening time until the men returned for tea once more, changing their clothes . . .[372]

At tea, conversation was 'slumberous', with the men discussing their successes and the women expressing dutiful admiration. Only with the introduction of bridge in later years were the hours between tea and dinner rendered less tedious. Otherwise it was sheer boredom for most of the women until the time came to dress for dinner. Eventually Lady Warwick avoided attending many of these parties, letting her husband go alone. 'I knew that this was no hardship, as a few odd men always help to make a party merrier. I preferred to remain among my own pursuits at Easton.'[372]

Certainly a visit to Lowther, seat of Lord Lonsdale, can have appealed to few females. Not only was the dinner menu unexciting but when the time came for the ladies to retire from the dining room they had to accompany Lady Lonsdale to the drawing room for an hour of stilted conversation, while the port decanter circulated among their menfolk in the dining room. Once the men rejoined the ladies it was the signal for Lady Lonsdale to lead the way to bed, while the men repaired to the billiard room for games and brandy. 'The most ladies would be offered after dinner might be a glass of lemon barley water.' To add to their discomfort, there were vast unheated corridors to traverse before they reached their rooms and the only lighting was a candle for each of them, plus a box of matches. As draughts whistled along the corridors it was difficult to keep the candles burning.[336]

It was the Prince of Wales's interest in shooting which helped to popularize it, and it was through royal example that deerstalking became a highly prized pastime for the rich. When Queen Victoria and Prince Albert settled at Balmoral on Deeside in 1848 the male members of the royal party devoted much of their time to this hitherto little-known sport. Even at the end of her life Queen Victoria took an interest in the shooting although she was no longer able to go out with the guns herself. Each evening the head stalker came to tell her exactly how every member of the party had performed and any bad marksmen were unwise to try to make excuses to her. The fact that plentiful supplies of whisky were available to both servants and guests at Balmoral may have contributed to the poor accuracy of some of the shooters.[92]

Red deer were too prolific for the scanty Highland vegetation to sustain and yearly culls were needed to control their numbers. Yet they were too wild and wary to be approached easily and it was the skill needed to surprise them on the rough terrain that gave the sport its special fascination. With the fall in wool prices during the 1870s the letting of Highland shoots became an important source of income for landowners. Holdings previously devoted to sheep were converted into deer forests and by 1892 the deer forest area in Scotland exceeded 2.47 million acres, compared to about 1.97 million acres nine years earlier.[7] Crofters and their sympathizers argued that the forests not only deprived them of cultivatable land but made it difficult for adjoining properties to be farmed, since the sheep sometimes wandered into the forests and were lost, while livestock was attacked by foxes which found a refuge there. During an outbreak of crofter unrest in the mid-1880s, over the growing use of the Highlands as a recreational resource, one protest, basing its message on Oliver Goldsmith's *Deserted Village*, summed up the attitude of many:

> Ill fares the land, to passing ills a prey, when deer
> Accumulate and men decay.[154]

But the protests had little effect at a time when sporting tenants offered rents far higher than any farmer could pay. Sometimes, too, wealthy landowners purchased land with the express aim of converting it into deer forest.[7]

As the railways penetrated further into the Highlands and the attractions of deerstalking and grouse shooting became better known, growing numbers of wealthy English sportsmen travelled north. As the *New Book of Sports* put it in 1885: 'On one day you may be lounging along the hot pavements of Pall Mall . . . the very next afternoon you may be in the heart of the Highlands.'[118] Many of the more permanent migrants, such as the Duke of Westminster, carried out extensive building works to make shooting lodges comfortable for the weeks in August and September that they spent in Scotland. By the 1880s the duke's Sutherland estate had four roomy lodges, and the long hours spent fishing and deerstalking were interspersed with picnics and trips on the duke's steam launch.[205]

To go stalking was physically demanding, since anyone engaged in it had to be fit even to climb to within sight of a stag. And that was only the beginning of the enterprise. The real business commenced when, under the guidance of a local expert an approach route to the animal was worked out. Lady Randolph Churchill, with the aid of powerful field-glasses, witnessed the efforts of one female hunter. First she 'crawled on all-fours up a long burn; emerging hot and panting, not to say wet and dirty, she then continued her scramble up a steep hill, taking advantage of any cover afforded by the ground, or remained in a petrified attitude if by chance a hind happened to look up.' Finally she fired her rifle, but failed to shoot the stag cleanly, thereby condemning him to a painful death, as the dogs were set on him.[133]

To an enthusiast like Lord Willoughby de Broke there was 'nothing very much better' than a deerstalking expedition on a fine day. And while there was a deep sense of humiliation when the rifle missed and the deer galloped away, 'if you have killed a good beast, everything is all right. The whole establishment, from the head forester down . . . is delighted.'[358] Particularly valued were beasts with 'grand branching antlers', since these were well suited to hanging on the wall as trophies of a successful expedition.

Scotland also appealed to fly fishermen. The catching of salmon and trout became a fine art in the late nineteenth century and both the cost of tackle and the rental of good stretches of river rose sharply. In the 1890s a season's rent for salmon fishing could be as high as £1,500, although those with more modest incomes might prefer to get their sport at hotels for £1 a day all found.[118] By the turn of the century many of the 56,000 registered trout anglers in Britain were joining together in syndicates to secure the best fishing rights, and it was in this context that Scottish and Welsh rivers became attractive.[191]

One West Highland property which fell into English hands was the Achranich estate at Morvern, which was purchased in 1845 by Octavius Smith, a London distiller. When the estate's fishing books began in 1853, the catches were mostly of trout, but soon the tally of salmon began to increase, with thirty fish killed in 1863 and fifty-two in 1864. Among the guests invited to share the sport was the philosopher Herbert Spencer, who was a friend of Smith. He visited for the first time in 1856 and in a letter home on 16 August, about a fortnight after his arrival, he expressed pleasure at the informality of the daily round. 'Fishing, and rambling, and boating, and bathing, form the staple occupations; varied, occasionally, with making artificial flies and mending fishing rods.'[164] So successful was the visit that Spencer was asked to extend it to six weeks. During that period there were more picnics and boating excursions, as well as a sketching trip to Killoonden Castle, and many days spent on the banks of the River Aline and on Loch Arienas, where he caught large numbers of sea trout.

By the end of the century the growing cost of game fishing in Scotland led some enthusiastic anglers to travel to Norway, where there were plentiful opportunities to pursue the sport. They included the 18th Lord Willoughby de Broke, who for many years rented a salmon river in that country. According to his son, he rated the successful playing of a salmon and the winning of a steeplechase second only to a good run with the foxhounds, and regarded a battle with a salmon 'full of fight' as having a 'high place in the list of the things that are thrilling'.[358]

Fishing was more popular as a sport than either hunting or shooting and its appeal spread beyond those living in the countryside. Professionals and businessmen of a reflective turn of mind often took it up. In the late 1860s Anthony Trollope noted that 'many an enthusiastic fisher' had to be content with 'an hour or two's permissive sport on the ornamental water of the London parks'.[67] Some of the better-off hired the services of a professional fisherman and his punt and were guided to a likely spot where they could remain peacefully in the middle channels of a river, only moving aside when steam launches and other craft appeared. This became increasingly common on major rivers at the end of the century, with the keen Thames fisherman James Englefield complaining of the disturbance caused by the 'wash and hurry and turmoil' of 'the endless procession of every description of floating craft'.[100]

Also increasing were the numbers of proletarian anglers, concerned with coarse fishing from the bank and coming mainly from manual- and white-collar groups, with a fringe of tradesmen. A majority of these were concerned with competitive 'match' fishing and that was often linked to gambling. In Sheffield, for example, the total number of registered fishermen rose from about 7,000 in the 1860s to over 20,000 in the early 1900s. They were not seeking a quiet, solitary day by the river, as an overstretched businessman or lawyer might do. Instead they joined clubs, mostly based upon public houses, and arranged matches which were used to bond membership as well as promote the sport. Sometimes special excursion trains were hired, with Sheffielders frequently fishing up to 90 miles away in Lincolnshire, where lengthy stretches of river were 'pegged down'. Prizes were awarded and there was a vast network of bankside and domestic betting, both on and between competitors.

Yet this sport, too, had its contemplative side, as men sat for hours by canal or river waiting for a bite, perhaps in the company of a son or friend. Just before the First World War there were estimated to be between 150,000 and 200,000 working-class anglers in the country.[191] That ignored the countless children who took part, armed with a homemade rod, and perhaps interspersing the activity with forays in search of wild strawberries, mushrooms, blackberries, and nuts to supplement the family diet. As a Norfolk girl remembered of her childhood in the early twentieth century, 'We knew where all the best chestnut and walnut trees were and rubbed our fingers nearly raw to remove the tell-tale stain before going to school.'

The enthusiasm of the British landed classes for field sports led them to visit other parts of the world in order to add to their trophies. In 1898–9 the future 19th Baron Willoughby de Broke spent the winter in India and Ceylon with his wife and a friend. During these months they shot 'Nilghiri ibex and, I regret to say, an elephant in Cochin; snipe and ducks in the Deccan, partridges and black buck at Umballah, and hunted and killed deer with a pack of English hounds and a Cingalese huntsman on the Horton plains in Ceylon.'[358] Later he stalked chamois in Styria, in the wildest part of the Austrian Alps.

For some sportsmen this 'ritualised slaughter' became even more ambitious. From the 1870s British gentlemen travelled to the western parts of North America on shooting expeditions. They included Hugh Lowther, the future Lord Lonsdale, and a friend who in 1879 returned to England loaded with trophies of buffalo, bison and bear. Between 1869 and 1896 Lord Dunraven regularly visited North America to shoot moose, caribou, elk and buffalo in Montana, Wyoming, Nova Scotia and Newfoundland. But the Indian sub-continent was perennially popular, with its abundance of sport ranging from pig-sticking to tiger shooting. In December 1882 the Duke of Portland, accompanied by Lord de Grey (son of the viceroy, Lord Ripon) and two other friends went on a major shoot in Nepal. They had with them seven hundred elephants and in six weeks killed fourteen tigers and eight rhinos, as well as a crocodile. This was considered 'good fun'. They then joined another shooting party and killed a further 3 tigers, 28 buffalo and 273 pigs.[117]

Kashmir in 1900 was dubbed the 'sportsman's paradise' by *Country Life Illustrated* because of its wide opportunities for shooting, although visitors were advised to plan in advance what they intended to hunt. 'If markhor, ibex, and red bear are your game, go to Baltistan in the spring. If ovia ammon are the object, take Ladak in the spring, for the finest rams move elsewhere before autumn. Bear will be found in the forest belt pretty well everywhere. But the vertical range of these hills is so immense, that it is no use settling down for a "general" shoot on them.'[29] At the end of the century Kenya and Uganda, too, proved attractive destinations for big-game hunters, with elephants, lions and giraffe among the selected prey.

Somewhat bizarrely, a few of these expert shots combined an interest in hunting with a love of natural history. Lord Walsingham, probably the second-best sporting marksman in the country in the late nineteenth century, was a keen ornithologist. Even here his gun proved useful. All the hummingbirds in the Natural History Museum were shot by him, using powder shot so as to prevent too much damage. He was awarded several academic distinctions and in 1879 was elected to the Literary Society. He also became a director of the British Museum and a founder member of the Castle Museum at Norwich.[301]

Sir Vauncey Harpur Crewe of Calke Abbey in Derbyshire was another specialist in ornithology. In his youth he went on a bird-watching expedition to Egypt but his vast collection of stuffed birds was almost entirely composed of British specimens or of rare migrants which had strayed into the British Isles. Some he shot himself and had preserved, but many were purchased from dealers and correspondents all over the country. He was an avid egg collector, too, and in 1894 paid 300 guineas at auction for the Great Auk's egg which was the pride of his collection. Although he became a member of the British Ornithologists' Union, his approach was scarcely scientific. For him, bird-watching, shooting and collecting were complementary activities.[130]

Sir John Harpur Crewe, Sir Vauncey's father, preferred more bucolic pastimes. His great interest was the breeding of longhorn cattle and Portland sheep, and the prizes won at agricultural shows were the only recognition he valued.[130] Other country gentlemen shared his concern for improved animal breeding and to that end supported the growing numbers of agricultural societies and shows, as well as taking an interest in the activities of their farmer tenants. According to Kenneth Hudson, the leading agricultural societies were primarily clubs for major landowners, with peers taking a prominent part in most of them. An examination of the members and officers of the Bath and West Society for 1852 shows that the patron was the Marquis of Lansdowne and eight vice-patrons were all members of the peerage. They included the Dukes of Wellington, Somerset and Bedford and the Earls of Mount Edgecumbe, Fortescue, Digby and Fitzhardinge. It was their role to add lustre to the society and to attend occasional meetings, dinners and the annual show.[203] It formed part of the social network which played such an important part in the pastimes and pleasures of the landed élite.

POACHING

The lower orders participated in field sports as beaters at shoots and sometimes as foot followers at a hunt. The latter were particularly numerous in Yorkshire and the north of England. Thus in the industrialized Badsworth territory in the mid-1860s there were colliers who ran for miles and were able to keep very close to the hounds. 'Their principal sin was to holloa too much, getting hounds' heads up or on to the line of fresh foxes, hares, curdogs, cats or other game.'[232] A few of these humbler enthusiasts even had their own packs of hounds, as in the Cumbrian fells or, around the middle of the century, in the Saddleworth area of Yorkshire. There, many of the country weavers kept beagles, for which local gentlemen, who subscribed to the hunt, paid the relevant tax. There were no foxes, but hares abounded and occasionally there would be a 'trail' or drag hunt, with the quarry taking the form of a herring or a bit of rag dipped in some strong-smelling oil and pulled across the ground by an energetic runner.[83] The weavers followed on foot, trusting to their sound lungs to enable them to keep within sight of the hounds.

Shooting party at Whomerly Wood, Stevenage, Hertfordshire, showing the tally of game killed, as well as the beaters (some of them very young) and the sportsmen themselves, 1894. (Rural History Centre, University of Reading)

But with the coming of the factory system the freedom to join in these frivolous pursuits was steadily eroded.

Some working people, however, experienced the excitement of the chase in another, less legitimate fashion, through poaching. Although legislation in 1831 had reduced the penalties for the daytime pursuit of game, those found to be so engaged at night were still severely punished. Under the 1844 Night Poaching Act they could face imprisonment or transportation, at least up to the 1850s when transportation was phased out. Even in the later nineteenth century punishments were harsh, with those found guilty of the offence facing three months' imprisonment with hard labour, and at the expiration of that time they had to find two sureties in £5 with themselves 'each in £10 that they will not so offend again for a year'. In default of meeting this requirement they could be further imprisoned for six months.[197] Many, unable or unwilling to find the extra sum, opted for an additional prison term. Yet, despite this, in the 1890s around 5 per cent of all game offences fell into the night poaching category. In addition, the

1862 Poaching Prevention Act authorized the police to search any person on the road or in a public place whom they suspected of poaching or of having in their possession a gun, nets, or snares for the purpose of killing or taking game. If discovered, they faced prosecution and the confiscation of their gear.[197]

Nonetheless men were prepared to take the risk and continued poaching, with an annual average of 7,838 game law convictions recorded over the period 1895–9 (6,348 of them involving the daytime pursuit of game). But that was a considerable reduction on the annual average of 11,144 recorded between 1878 and 1882 (of which 9,458 had been daytime offences).[197] Some poachers were driven by hunger and poverty to engage in their illicit activities. Others were concerned to profit by selling ill-gotten gains to hawkers or nearby town traders, and others again acted on the principle that the wildlife of the countryside, particularly hares and rabbits, was part of Nature's largesse in which all should share, rather than being the property of an individual landowner. In 1891 James Watson, in his book *Poachers and Poaching*, described villages where almost everybody from cottage wives to postmen, blacksmiths and parish clerks was involved, spending winter evenings mending nets, making wires and breaking in the lurcher dogs which were an integral part of their activities.[216] However, for a minority of poachers the chief attractions were the thrill of the chase and a desire to humiliate those in authority. This was true of salmon poachers on the River Wye who in January 1880 fixed a stale salmon to the Market Hall in Rhayader with a mocking note attached, asking:

> Where were the river watchers when I was killed?
> Where were the police when I was hung here?[215]

A few days later other salmon were nailed to the Market Hall, one with a five-pronged spear used for catching fish and a second with the inscription, 'To Supt. Arthur Williams, with . . . compliments.' Williams was the head of the local police.

Many of the perpetrators refused to accept that poaching was theft. As Griffith Evan Jones, a Welsh salmon poacher, declared in 1877, 'I never stole anything in my life.' Yet this did not prevent him from regaling at length his adventures as a poacher. According to him, community sympathy for the activity was so widespread that two members of his own gang were magistrates. His philosophy was: 'Laws grind the poor, yet Welshmen rule the Law.'[148]

Some, like James Hawker from Daventry, Northamptonshire, first took up poaching because of poverty but then became addicted to it. Hawker began in 1850, aged fourteen, by catching pike with a ball of string, hooks and a bait, but he soon turned to catching partridges, hares and rabbits. According to his biographer, he continued with this all his life because it 'thrilled his whole being':

> Once a man has grown adept at using a gun and a gate-net in the not so silent hours of the night, it becomes hard for him to lie in bed when the wind is just strong enough to make the Scots pines sound like the sea . . . Hawker might stay indoors in a hard frost when a poacher's footsteps could sound through the silent air to the ears of rabbits and hares hundreds of yards away; but he was often out with the

long net as the skies darkened and the wind stirred without beating down the leaves and twigs from the trees. On moonlight nights he learned to walk the woods and copses, never treading far from cover and always keeping within the shadows . . . Again and again he wrote: 'If I am able, I will poach till I die.' And he did.[128]

Freddie Rolf, the self-styled 'King of the Norfolk Poachers', was another enthusiast. Like Hawker, he began by seeking food for the pot but then succumbed to the thrill of the chase. In his autobiography he claimed that poaching was 'something like drug taking – once begun no goen back, it get hold of you'. He maintained he would rather have 'a night out with either gun or dog, than go to the best Diner (*sic*) Party ever Provided'. He particularly enjoyed outwitting gamekeepers and the police:

> that went a long way towards recompence for the danger and risk run. Of corse wen I got had, I took it as part of the Bargin, but that did not happen verry often . . . Some times the Maderstrates rubbed it in pretty hot for me, and I got a pretty good name, but I gloried in that.[174]

Rolf was proud of the woodcraft skills he had acquired – the ability to understand the vagaries of the weather and the call of the birds. Any poacher entering a wood must have the wind in his face, for the wind and the stars were his guide: 'I could run like a hare once I had got a start . . . and him who cant run cant poach.'[174]

'Blacky' Tapper, who worked on the Berkshire Downs among other places was another poacher who prided himself on his abilities. He was able to walk across a field setting a dozen hare snares without any spectator being able to detect the operation. Blacky was short and bent with very long arms, and as he walked he would drop the snare, complete with 'tealer' or 'pricker' in a run. Then with an almost imperceptible stoop he would place the peg and tread it as he continued on his way.[196]

By the end of the nineteenth century poaching was far less violent than it had been at the beginning of Queen Victoria's reign, when hunger had been the major motivation for many offenders. Nonetheless battles between gamekeepers and poachers still took place, with men on both sides killed or injured. Between November 1880 and July 1896 there were at least thirty serious affrays involving poachers and keepers in different parts of the country. In seventeen of them either poachers or keepers were killed.[196]

Again, on the River Wye between 1875 and 1881 skirmishes involving salmon poachers became so serious that in 1881 the Inspectors of Fisheries investigated the situation. The gangs, numbering as many as a hundred people, would go out with blackened faces, handkerchiefs or bonnets on their heads and white undergarments or nightshirts over their everyday clothes.[215] They would be armed with bludgeons and guns and called themselves followers of 'Rebecca', the legendary focus of unrest in the principality during the 1840s against the high tolls charged on turnpike roads. In the 1870s and 1880s the grievances were different, but some of the methods adopted were the same. A particularly unpleasant incident took place on 6 December 1880 at Llanbadarnfynydd, when about a hundred armed men gathered together. In the subsequent struggle a constable's arm was broken and shots were fired at the local police station. The cause of the unrest was local resentment at the introduction of new restrictions on fishing by the Board of Conservators of the Wye, supported by a group of 'better class . . . people in Radnorshire and Breconshire who . . . conceive that they have been unjustly deprived by the inclosure of commons of ancient rights of fishing which they had previously enjoyed'. Eventually the conservators were persuaded to modify their restrictive policies and the disturbances subsided.[197]

Overall, however, poaching remained a cause of tension in the countryside to the end of the nineteenth century. It was partly a bitter reaction to the restrictions which arose from landed society's preoccupation with game preservation and partly a working-class recreation with its own economic and social imperatives, including the thrill of the chase.

Additional Sources Used

Country Life Illustrated, 14 and 21 August, 4 September 1897, and 24 March 1900.
Daily Telegraph, 7 November 1980.
East Kent Federation of Women's Institutes, *East Kent Within Living Memory* (Newbury and Canterbury, 1994 edn).
Eleanor Glyn, *Romantic Adventure* (London, 1936).
Diary of Sir Edward Hamilton for 1889, entries for 2 and 5 September, at the British Library, Add. MSS. 48,651.
Richard Jefferies, *The Life of the Fields* (1884; this edn, Oxford, 1983).
John Lowerson, 'Brothers of the Angle: Match Fishing, 1850–1914' in *Bulletin of the Society for the Study of Labour History*, No. 50 (spring 1985).
Gordon Mingay (ed.), *The Victorian Countryside* (2 vols) (London, 1981).
Norfolk Federation of Women's Institutes, *Within Living Memory. A Collection of Norfolk Reminiscences* (King's Lynn, 1972).
Rosslyn, Earl of, *Thomas' Hunting Diary 1899–1900* (London, n.d. [1899]).
Royal Society for the Prevention of Cruelty to Animals, Annual Reports for 1884 and 1885.
The Animal World, June 1890.
The Field, 19 January and 12 October 1878.

CHAPTER 6

Excursions, Holidays and Foreign Travel

The development of travel and recreation for other than the wealthy classes, for whom Paris and the Italian tour had long been a social and cultural necessity, was a conspicuous feature of Victorian life. The engineers . . . with their roads, bridges and railways, laid the foundation for the almost ritualistic addiction of the English to the annual holiday. For the rising artisan class this was symbolised by the steam-boats that took them to Southend, Margate and Ramsgate. The comfortable self-conscious lower middle classes found solace at Folkestone, Brighton and Bognor . . . It was the age of the bandstand, the bathing-machine, the pier, and the guide-book all evocatively depicted in the literature and art of the period . . . Europe represented the zenith of the holiday adventure and was characterised by complicated arrangements, exhausting local tours and a spirit of romance and sentimentality.

Kenneth Neale (ed.), *Victorian Horsham. The Diary of Henry Michell 1809–1874* (Chichester, 1975), 17–18

EXCURSIONS AND HOLIDAYS IN BRITAIN

It was in the Victorian era that day excursions and annual holidays became facts of life for countless Britons. In 1869 the *Standard* newspaper claimed that large numbers of people 'from the heir to the throne to the humblest greengrocer' were adopting the 'good wholesome practice' of taking a summer vacation.[107] A quarter of a century later another writer maintained that with the 'high pressure of . . . keenly competitive modern life' an annual break was 'not a luxury of the wealthy, but a necessity of the workers as much to be reckoned with as the universal need of food and clothing'.[68] For many it was questions of prestige and pleasure rather than health which were the guiding factors in the choice of holiday venues, since personal standing with friends and acquaintances was influenced by the kind of resort patronized. In 1895 there were claims that middle-class visitors heading for Margate, which was associated with rowdy day trippers, hid their luggage labels and prevaricated about their destination when going off on holiday.[365]

In the latter part of the century seaside resorts were among the fastest-growing towns, at a time when rising living standards, cheaper transport and the establishment of regular holidays (including the creation of the new August Bank Holiday in 1871) were combining with a mass press to broaden horizons and thereby stimulate the flood of visitors. By the 1870s virtually all the nation's major resorts had been created and the 1871 Census of Population drew attention to their individual characteristics:

> London throws its weight into Margate, Ramsgate, Hastings, Brighton, and other towns on the south coast which has the attractions of the sea in all its varieties of mood; further west is Torquay and Torbay with the charms of an Italian lake; to the west lie Ilfracombe and the Welsh towns by the sea and mountains; to the north-east Scarborough, the fair mistress of that coast.[13]

Surprisingly the list omitted the rapidly expanding resorts in the north-west, such as Blackpool, Morecambe and Southport, which were closely linked to the textile towns of industrial Lancashire and Yorkshire. Already in the early 1850s Blackpool, with fewer than three thousand inhabitants, was playing host to around twelve thousand visitors during an August weekend.[367] Thirty years later, when the population had risen to about thirteen thousand, its railway stations were receiving 1.3 million visitors a year.[367]

Even before the railway age this recreational revolution had been initiated by the steamboats which plied along the estuaries and navigable rivers. In the 1840s the Firth of Forth, the Firth of Clyde, the mouth of the Mersey and, in particular, the Thames from Chelsea and Greenwich to Gravesend, Margate and Ramsgate were traversed by steamboats busily carrying passengers from one side to the other, or taking holidaymakers to the seaside and short-term pleasure seekers to places of local interest.[95] In the early 1850s Theodor Fontane whiled away what he called the 'great tyranny' of an English Sunday by going on steamer trips to Kew, Richmond and Hampton Court.

Initially it was professional families, tradesmen and white-collar workers who predominated among the holidaymakers. At the seaside they bathed, walked, rode, gathered botanical specimens, collected shells and visited ancient monuments, or they simply spent their time idling on the sands, as Charles Dickens noted at Ramsgate:

> ladies . . . employed in needlework, or watch-guard making, or knitting, or reading novels; the gentlemen . . . reading newspapers and magazines; the children . . . digging holes in the sands with wooden spades, and collecting water therein; the nursemaids, with their youngest charges in their arms, were running in after the waves, and then running back with the waves after them; and, now and then, a little sailing boat either departed with a gay and talkative cargo of passengers, or returned with a very silent and particularly uncomfortable-looking one.[398]

A little later another visitor to the resort commented on the vast number of itinerant salesmen offering their wares to the visitors. These ranged from books, coloured seaweeds, and seashells, to toys and spades for the children and sand-

A middle-class family enjoying their seaside holiday at Ramsgate, c. 1850. (Kent County Council Arts and Libraries Department: Ramsgate Library)

shoes for the ladies. 'Every chair that can be hired, and every lump of chalk or jutting stone that can be used for a seat, is filled by an occupant. Every bathing-machine has a tenant; and all jammed in solid phalanx . . . they are immersed up to their axles in the water', he wrote in *The Leisure Hour* in 1852.

However, if the first stimulus to resort growth came from the visits of middle-class families for two or three weeks in high summer, they were soon joined by skilled manual workers and their relatives. In addition, the growing availability of inexpensive rail and steamboat excursions enabled the less affluent to go for day trips if they could afford nothing better. In the 1890s Alice Foley's family were able to manage only a day's outing during Bolton's August holiday season. New Brighton was the chosen destination because it provided the most attractions for their money.

Having risen at a very early hour on the great day mother was to be found busily cutting piles of sandwiches and currant cake; father bustled about doing nothing in particular . . . Finally, like a flock of excited birds, we set off for the station. Excursion rates were extremely modest . . . 2/9d. for adults, half-price for children, and free for infants. Before I grew too tall for evasion it was customary to wedge my small person between father and mother whilst the rest of the family shoved us quickly through the barriers. Once safely in the compartment I had to be prepared for a sudden duck under the seat should a ticket inspector appear but, apart from this small indignity, it was usually a day of complete happiness.

We had the adventure of the great docks [at Liverpool], the boat and river crossing and the eager landing at New Brighton, to be followed by long hours paddling, gathering sea-shells, making sand-pies, eating shrimps and sandwiches washed down by sweet tea. Such was our brief summer holiday.[161]

Similarly in York at around the turn of the century Seebohm Rowntree discovered that even among the poor many took the opportunity to crowd into Scarborough on day and half-day excursions run by the North-Eastern Railway Company for August Bank Holiday.[297]

The vogue for holidaymaking by the sea started during the craze for medicinal sea-bathing around the middle of the eighteenth century, and like the earlier – and overlapping – fashion for visiting spas, it spread from the aristocracy and gentry to the prospering industrial middle ranks of society.[367] Fashionable resorts like Brighton or Scarborough and inland spas like Bath, Buxton and Harrogate enjoyed the patronage of the well-to-do who sought to improve their health by taking the waters while engaging in an active social life. Dr Granville, writing on *The Spas of England* in 1841, claimed there was 'a fragrance of aristocracy in the very air' of Buxton, while Scarborough, which combined the attributes of a seaside resort with those of a spa, provided wider 'intellectual amusement' for visitors than its competitors. This included libraries, a large shell collection and a museum.[60] The sands were 'incomparable' and the use of bathing machines in the open sea was particularly advantageous for the ladies. Boats could be hired for the moderate charge of a shilling an hour to take parties on sea trips, and horses, donkey carts and other carriages offered opportunities for drives and excursions into the surrounding country.

In the early years of the century many aristocrats still went on lengthy tours of Europe, concentrating especially on the cultural and social pleasures of France and Italy, or they moved around in this country, visiting friends and relatives on their landed estates and migrating to London to join in the pleasures of the Season during the late spring and early summer.

For those lower down the scale, visits to relatives or short excursions to a nearby town provided a break in the daily routine although, as we have seen, the middle-class demand for seaside holidays was also growing sharply. London had a good steamboat connection with Gravesend (described in 1825 'as the goal of every young Cockney's Sunday excursion'), and with the Kentish resorts of Margate and Ramsgate. In the mid-1830s around 100,000 passengers a year came by boat to Margate, while in 1852 the journal *The Leisure Hour* dubbed Ramsgate 'one of the lungs of London and something more – its favourite bathing machine'. Charles Dickens, a frequent visitor to that town, described the excitement in the resort when the London steampacket arrived at the pier:

crowds of people promenaded to and fro; young ladies tittered; old ladies talked; nursemaids displayed their charms to the greatest possible advantage; and their little charges ran up and down . . . There were old gentlemen, trying to make out objects through long telescopes; and young ones, making objects of themselves in open shirt-collars; ladies, carrying about portable chairs, and portable chairs carrying about invalids; . . . and nothing was to be heard but talking, laughing, welcoming, and merriment.[398]

Even at the end of the century, when good rail links had been long established, around a quarter of a million passengers were still landed each year by steamboat on Margate jetty. This was nearly half the resort's annual visitors and as a local newspaper pointed out, the efficient transport links enabled scores of people to come to the town daily, thereby boosting trade: 'consequently one meets brighter faces, lighter hearts and heavier pockets on all sides'.[36] Even more ambitious excursions were also offered, such as cross-Channel days trips to Boulogne, available twice weekly in the early 1880s.

On a local basis, clubs and societies continued to organize day trips by wagon or boat, so that parties from London's East End travelled by van to Hampton Court, attracted by its free admission and its picnic facilities. Often they took a

The crowded beach at Ramsgate in the 1890s, with sideshows and hawkers of various kinds on hand to serve the holidaymakers. (Kent County Council Arts and Libraries Department: Ramsgate Library)

fiddler or trumpeter along to play an accompaniment to their songs as they travelled the two or three-hour journey.[281] Similarly youngsters from Manchester were taken by canal boat on Whitsun outings.[228]

But the widening of the railway network enabled more elaborate journeys to be made, and special excursions were offered by the rail companies themselves or by agents such as Thomas Cook. Cook began his commercial career by organizing a trip for Leicester temperance supporters to a convention at Loughborough early in July 1841. He believed this would not only gain publicity for the cause but would serve to encourage more attractive and wholesome forms of recreation than the alehouse. He later suggested that the arrival of a railway 'in an ignorant and barbarous district' was 'an omen of moral renovation and intellectual exaltation. The prejudices which ignorance has engendered are broken by the roar of a train of carriages, and the whistle of the engine awakens thousands from the slumber of ages.'[107] Over five hundred excursionists assembled at Leicester station for the first trip. There they were greeted by a uniformed brass band and a crowd of two or three thousand onlookers, before they climbed aboard the train. Once it was on its way every bridge along the route was thronged with spectators and when they arrived at Loughborough they were met by a crush of fellow temperance advocates. They went in procession for a bread and ham lunch before setting off for further parades, speeches and jollifications in a local park.[107]

Cook did not initiate railway excursions, however. As early as 1831 the Liverpool and Manchester Railway ran a Sunday school trip and the Preston and Wyre Railway offered cheap fares during August from its first season in 1840.[367] Crowds of spectators were taken to sporting events, the opening of parks and public buildings and even to public executions, while many early trips were organized by Sunday schools or local philanthropists anxious to promote 'rational' recreations among the lower orders. Sunday schools, in particular, sought to remove young people from the temptations of the fairground and when fairs were set up in the popular seaside resorts they went elsewhere. At Blackburn, for example, most of the Sunday schools preferred long-distance trips to small, scenic resorts and historic towns to the 'fleshpots of Blackpool'.[365] Many of these outings were arranged at Easter, Whitsun or, later in the century, on the August Bank Holiday.

However, if Thomas Cook did not pioneer day trips by rail, the publicity that his efforts generated undoubtedly gave a boost to the whole movement, and for several summers he busied himself organizing temperance society trips and Sunday school outings throughout the region served by the Midland Counties Railway.[389] But it was the Great Exhibition of 1851 which gave a major stimulus to rail travel. For the first time people became aware of the true potentialities of the new means of transport and its ability to transform leisure. It accustomed people to going long distances for pleasure and particularly to visiting London. Overall, more than six million tickets were sold to entrants at the Crystal Palace and, allowing for foreign and double visits, this probably meant that around a sixth of the British population made the trip.[252] Savings clubs were set up for the purpose, often based at the workplace or at a public house; sometimes, as at Beverley in Yorkshire, they were formed with the direct encouragement of the local authority.[150] In Leeds a special sub-committee was established to encourage working men to see the exhibition, and

Thomas Cook and his son themselves toured the Midlands creating Exhibition Clubs among working men. The availability of special, cheap rail fares and shilling entrance days helped the promotional cause, as did the provision of cut-price accommodation in London and the advertising skills of agents such as Cook or Grant & Co. of Manchester.[389] Cook even organized accommodation for visitors, ranging from a Mechanics Home in the Pimlico area, which accommodated a thousand people in dormitory style for 2s a night with breakfast included, to rooms in private houses.[389] He also launched a penny journal called *Cook's Exhibition Herald and Excursion Advertiser*, which soon became known as *Cook's Excursionist*, to give details of travel arrangements. This paper was destined to be a major source of information for tourists for decades to come.[107]

Many commentators, such as a reporter with the *Leeds Times*, emphasized the great educational value of the exhibition to all classes, though there was anxiety that the lower orders should not waste their visit to the capital in frivolities like 'panoramas, shows and paltry theatres'. Instead they should concentrate on the British Museum, St Paul's, Westminster Abbey, Green Park and similarly worthwhile venues.[252]

Some employers followed the example of the Horsham brewer Henry Michell and arranged for their workers to go to the Crystal Palace, as well as encouraging local children to attend and making many forays themselves. The aristocratic landowner Lord Willoughby d'Eresby was even reported to have rented a house in London to accommodate his tenants.[150] Henry Michell's enthusiasm is evident in his 1851 diary:

> We did not go any tour this year but made a point of devoting all the time and money we could spare in visiting the crystal palace and studying its contents with our children and all our servants and dependants at the Brewery, Farm and Brickyards, and on the 24th of September we went with all the school children in the parish to the number of 380.[254]

A special train was chartered to take the party to London Bridge and from there they travelled by steamboat to Westminster Bridge, 'whence we marched in procession to a large tree just outside the palace and every child was instructed to come again to the same tree by 4 o'clock p.m.'. When they returned at that time each was given a penny bun before the homeward trip began, after what had been 'a day of great pleasure to every one concerned'.

Occasionally whole villages became virtually deserted as the inhabitants clubbed together to visit the exhibition and to marvel at the wonders of British industrial achievement, as well as the benefits of modern travel. At Topsham in Devon many of the 'respectable shopkeepers' went off in this fashion, informing customers of their intention by posting a notice on their door: 'Gone to the Royal Exhibition, to be reopened when we come back.'[32]

Already in the 1840s seaside resorts like Brighton, Margate and Ramsgate had begun to benefit from the new mode of travel, as had Blackpool with its numerous visitors from industrial Lancashire. Over the years other towns, too, formed industrial linkages, so that Morecambe attracted visitors from the West Riding of Yorkshire and

Bridlington and Cleethorpes were favoured by Sheffield steelworkers and cutlers. Indeed Bridlington became known as 'Sheffield-by-the-sea'.[364] Inland destinations benefited, too, as with the 'gipsy parties' organized by firms in Birmingham which began in the railway era. Favourite destinations for these were Kenilworth, with its castle ruins, and the Clent Hills. According to a correspondent with the *Morning Chronicle*, one mid-century outing organized by the firm of Hinckes and Wells was financed by the females each paying a penny a week for a year towards the cost, while the men paid twopence and the employers contributed a 'handsome sum'.

> The party mustered no less than 350 people. About 130 stayed away, some because they could not afford the money, and others because they stated that they had no clothes to go in. The party started from Birmingham at seven o'clock on a fine summer morning to Hagley and the Clent Hills to pass the day. They filled forty-five cars, which were gaily ornamented with banners and devices, and they were accompanied by a band of music. The whole of the party breakfasted in the open air, in tents, at the Hagley Arms. They walked in procession up to the Clent Hills and enjoyed the beautiful view into Wales. Quadrilles and country dances were got up and these and other amusements continued until dinner time. The whole party dined under tents in the open air, the band of music played all the time.[281]

A careful moral note was also struck when it was pointed out that although it was not 'a tee-total festival, . . . the party were very temperate'.

The vogue for 'literary tourism' played a part, too, with Charles Mackay's *The Scenery and Poetry of the English Lakes* (1846) among the first of many books to use literature as a guide for directing visitors where to go and what to admire. In this context Wordsworth's writings acted as a major attraction for the Lake District, as did the poet himself while he was alive. According to Harriet Martineau, he was receiving about five hundred people a year in the 1840s. Stratford-upon-Avon, too, reached new heights of popularity as a result of its carefully nurtured links with William Shakespeare. In the second half of the century there was a sharp increase in the number of visitors to the birthplace itself. In 1891 its custodian resigned his post, disillusioned at being expected to 'act the part of a common showman'. To add to his problems, he quickly discovered that 'not a single one of the many so-called relics on exhibition could be proved to be Shakespeare's – nay, that the Birthplace itself is a matter of grave doubt'. But his reservations had no effect in stemming the flood of visitors to it and to the other Shakespeare attractions that Stratford-upon-Avon had to offer. As Ian Ousby points out, such 'lionisation' fitted well with the Victorian cult of hero-worship.

However, those anxious to escape the 'tripper' element were encouraged by the widening railway network to visit more remote destinations on the coast of west Wales or in the west of England and East Anglia. Lyme Regis was a resort 'eagerly sought after by quiet families who prefer the beauties of nature to noisy amusements and dress parades'.[365] It afforded scope for visitors interested in geology and fossils and, according to one satisfied commentator in 1882, it was 'far enough from a railway station to be out of reach of cheap trips which render life unbearable in larger and more accessible places.'[405]

Visitors enjoying the quiet dignity of the promenade at Bexhill-on-Sea, c. 1900. (The author)

Other, bigger resorts, like Bournemouth, Ilfracombe, Eastbourne, Torquay and Paignton, sought to discourage boisterous excursionists by clamping down on the entertainments likely to appeal to them. In 1885 the *Paignton Observer* loftily noted: 'Here you will find no rollicking horseplay or boisterous fun such as you may have been accustomed to on Ramsgate Pier or Margate Sands . . . Paignton prefers to be dignified and discreet.'[347] Eastbourne even in the early twentieth century was determined to maintain its exclusive image, as a tongue-in-cheek account made clear:

> This is the most miserable place on the south coast for the half-day tripper . . . no whelk stalls in the street, no sixpenny dinners or ham and beef teas, no crowds of yelling bathers, no ventriloquists, phrenologists, cheap-jacks, fortune-tellers . . . anywhere in sight . . . Its policy is to preserve itself from the jolly greeting of cloth-capped thousands – and until now it has succeeded very well.[116]

By the end of the century some concessions had been made and amusements offered which were likely to attract excursionists. But in the town generally, accommodation was reserved for the middle-class families such resorts were anxious to retain. Sometimes, as with the growth of Hove alongside Brighton, or Cliftonville and Westgate alongside Margate, élitism might take the form of developing new 'marine suburbs'. Cliftonville firmly disassociated itself from its vulgar neighbour, and fashionable lady visitors were advised 'to pack at least 40 dresses for a holiday here'. Westgate was even stricter, adopting a firm code of behaviour and dress for its visitors. Minstrels, hawkers and other distractions were not permitted by the parochial committee, which even had to approve the repertoire of music played by the ladies' orchestra. There were bye-laws restricting donkey rides to children under the age of fourteen and excursion trains were not allowed to stop at the station. 'We do not want to be as noisy as Margate' was the general attitude.

Other places adopted different solutions. At Great Yarmouth, while the masses congregated in the town centre, those seeking quieter amusements went to either end of the seafront. Great Yarmouth segregated its visitors by season, too. In 1895 it was described as 'a great place for trippers . . . during August, but a large number of the better class of visitors may be found during the other summer months'.[365] Brighton had similar arrangements, with excursionists coming in July and August, family holidaymakers in the spring and late summer and the 'fashionable' season for the well-to-do occurring in the autumn. However, as the resort's reputation declined in the final years of the century, this more aristocratic trade was lost to rivals as far apart as Biarritz and Bognor.[234]

Bournemouth and Torquay relied on the demands of a winter season to fuel their expansion, with both resorts popular among wealthy invalids suffering from a weak chest. In the case of Bournemouth, anxiety to provide suitable entertainment led to the establishment of an attractive Winter Garden and a municipal orchestra in the 1890s.[289] However, by the end of the century a summer season of 'inferior standing' was emerging as well, with excursionists coming from as far away as the Midlands. On 5 July 1884 the *Bournemouth Guardian* noted that four hundred 'members and friends of the Bible class connected with Christchurch, Sparkbrook, Birmingham, . . . arrived at the West Station at an early hour. Dinner and tea were provided at the Town Hall.' In the same week more than a thousand employees and their relatives from Fry's huge cocoa works at Bristol 'inundated' the town, many of them going for a short cruise to Swanage and Totland Bay on local steamers and others going out in rowing boats or bathing in the sea.[26]

Weston-super-Mare experienced influxes of rail trippers, particularly from Bristol, as early as the 1850s. It attempted to separate the excursionists from its middle-class clientele by providing a separate platform at the railway station for the former and opening a special hall where tea could be bought at $1\frac{1}{2}d$ a cup or else made with ingredients brought from home. In April 1853 the local newspaper commented on trains that were bringing in one or two thousand passengers apiece.[405] With the opening of a pier in 1867 the excursionist trade was further boosted by the expansion of steamer traffic from south Wales. As in other towns anxious to maintain both an élite and a mass clientele, an element of social zoning was applied. In 1894 a guide to Weston boasted that while the Birnbeck Pier, with its swings, gymnastics and other entertainments, was 'a place of popular resort for what are known as the "day trippers"' the convenience and peace 'of the invalid and more sedate visitor – whose favourite haunts are elsewhere' were little disrupted by the presence of excursionists who sometimes numbered twenty thousand a day.[405]

One way of controlling potentially rowdy elements was to restrict activities on the foreshore, thereby eliminating the undesirable fairground atmosphere created by a multiplicity of hawkers, musicians, Punch and Judy showmen and the like. At the same time, esplanades and seafront gardens were provided for the more genteel. At Weston-super-Mare in the 1880s such initiatives gave rise to opposition from the tradespeople who had formerly sold goods and services on the sands. One 'poor widow' even wrote to the Board of Trade in July 1886 to complain that for years she had earned a living hiring out donkeys on the foreshore but recently the town commissioners had required her and the other donkey keepers to take out a licence. A special place has been allocated for them to ply their trade 'and if wee [sic] move a way they have got 3 men a watching and they summon us and fine us'. The town authorities, for their part, explained that action was needed to protect their recent investment in a seafront promenade:

> the noise and annoyances on the foreshore had become intolerable thro' the Rabble that frequented there with Swing Boats, Shooting Stands and Galleries, Games of 'Aunt Sally', Throwing sticks three a penny for Cocoanuts, Costermongers, Likeness takers, Shows of every description . . . which had become injurious to the welfare of the Town.

After consideration the Board of Trade refused to intervene and the new restrictions remained.

Prior to the 1870s few working-class families had been able to take more than a day or two's break at any one time, although among white-collar workers a week or a fortnight's holiday at the seaside during the summer was increasingly the norm. For most this meant staying in an apartment, where they supplied the food and the landlady and her servants cooked and served it. In other cases, as with the *Punch* artist Linley Sambourne and his wife Marion, a mother and her children might spend several weeks away, perhaps staying in a house rented for the purpose, while the husband came to visit them at the weekend. Mrs Sambourne also had wealthy relatives who invited her and the children to stay with them and she much enjoyed the unaccustomed luxury. 'Heavenly day, sat on sands while all the little ones paddled', is one typical diary entry. As the children grew up there were more energetic pursuits, as when her husband and son played tennis together or her brother-in-law went off to Cowes for the regatta.[257]

There was a slow growth of large hotels at seaside resorts to cater for affluent visitors. These purpose-built properties represented a change from the old-style apartments (where private suites of serviced rooms were the norm), to a wide-ranging provision of services and facilities, including public restaurants and smoking rooms. The 119 hotels and boarding-houses listed in a Bournemouth directory in 1891 included the Bourne Hall, with 125 bedrooms plus a library, ballroom, theatre, billiard room and ten bathrooms; the Mont Dore with medical baths, ballroom, winter garden and covered tennis courts; and the Grand Fir Family Hotel, which boasted furnishings by Messrs Shoolbred of London.[365] Then there was the luxurious Ilfracombe Hotel, which opened at the Devon resort in May 1867 with over two hundred rooms, including a smoking room, a library and reading room and specially segregated ladies' coffee room, dining room and drawing room. A number of bedrooms were set aside for visitors' servants, and each morning, except on Sundays, a special four-horse omnibus would leave the hotel at 9 a.m. to take guests to Barnstaple railway station. It would return at 5.30 p.m. after the arrival of the London express. Advertisements boasted of the 5 acre ornamental grounds and the terrace which afforded 'the finest marine promenade attached to any hotel in the United Kingdom'. The Ilfracombe Hotel proved so successful that within a few years an additional wing was built. Later visitors included members of the German royal family and American plutocrats like the Vanderbilts.[243]

But while these large hotels stressed the presence of nobility, gentry and, on occasions, royalty among their guests, most visitors were far less exalted. As H.G. Wells slily noted, some middle-class couples stayed at hotels purely to practise their social skills.[85] Many more doubtless wished to avoid the trouble of catering for themselves in rented apartments or lodgings and turned instead to hotels and boarding-houses, especially in the latter part of the century.

At the bottom end of the market, overcrowded lodging-houses in resorts like Blackpool and Morecambe accommodated many visitors from the textile districts of Lancashire and the West Riding of Yorkshire, while London families concentrated on the arc of seaside resorts along the Kent and Sussex coast or spread out into resorts like Southend and Clacton in Essex. At Ramsgate in 1861 a commentator pointed out that while there were high-class lodging-houses on the cliffs, accommodation in the lower town near the harbour catered for 'a vast number of other people, a class of an inferior kind'.[364]

Blackpool was the first resort to appeal specially to the working classes. Its expansion was helped by the employment structure in the textile industry, whereby the widespread labour of women and children created a joint family income able to support a holiday. One boy who began work as a weaver when he was thirteen, in 1894, remembered that when trade was good he and his family saved enough to take a modest break at Blackpool or Morecambe:

> You did not board, but took your food with you. It meant a busy week beforehand for Mother, baking all the bread and fancy cakes needed for seven people for a week. You could get good beds for half-a-crown a night! We had a much battered oblong tin box in which we packed all the provisions, and any surplus baggage was shared by the family.[198]

Holidays in the cotton towns began to lengthen from the 1840s. Already in the middle of the century, Burnley textile workers had two free days beyond the July weekend fair and in 1899 the fair holiday was extended to a week for these workers, to say nothing of an extra long weekend in September, secured in 1890. Oldham and Darwen obtained a full week's summer break in 1899, while Chorley and Nelson, too, benefited from the trend.

This holiday pattern affected the resorts patronized by the workers, such as Rhyl in north Wales, Douglas on the Isle of Man and, above all, Blackpool. The making of seaside visits would be spread over several weeks of summer, corresponding to the different wakes weeks. Excluding Whitsun, itself a popular

The pleasures of paddling in the sea, c. 1900. (Kent County Council Arts and Libraries Department: Ramsgate Library)

time for excursions, the working-class holiday season in industrial Lancashire lasted from Burnley Fair in early July to Oldham Wakes in early September.[364] This made it worthwhile for resorts to supply entertainments for the visitors, and these included selling local newspapers from the holidaymakers' own towns. Going to the seaside became a norm in the close-knit cotton communities, and the modest architecture of Blackpool helped to make the visitors feel at home.

To finance their stay, most of the cotton workers relied on savings schemes, which had themselves developed from earlier thrift funds. During the 1880s 'going-off clubs' proliferated in the textile towns, with Oldham among the pioneers. There, by 1882 savings of £23,000 were being paid out for the wakes, and in 1889, when (unpaid) holidays in the town were officially extended to a week, £40,000 was distributed. In 1892 that had risen to around £80,000. In other cotton communities finances followed a similar pattern.[364]

The practice of going away for several days had no parallel, at least on this scale, among other industrial workers in Victorian Britain. However, holidays away from home were taken by some of the better paid in the woollen industry and among certain craftsmen in the Sheffield and Birmingham metal trades. Rail employees, who were given special travel concessions, also participated. In Swindon Alfred Williams remembered that men in the Great Western railway workshop began planning their July trip as soon as they returned from the annual Whitsun outing.

On the plates of the forges and walls, and even outside in the town, the words 'Roll on, Trip,' or 'Five weeks to Trip,' may be seen scrawled in big letters . . . Whichever way one turns he [*sic*] is greeted with the question – often asked in a jocular sense – 'Wher' gwain Trip?' the reply to which usually is – 'Same old place,' or 'Up in the smowk;' i.e. to London, or 'Swindon by the Sea.' By the last-named place Weymouth is intended . . . 'Trip Day' is the most important day in the calendar at the railway town. For several months preceding it, fathers and mothers of families, young unmarried men, and juveniles have been saving up for the outing. Whatever new clothes are bought for the summer are usually worn for the first time at 'Trip' . . . and the children come . . . equipped with spade and bucket and bags full of thin paper, cut the size of pennies, to throw out of the carriage windows as the train flies along. A general exodus from the town takes place that day and quite twenty-five thousand people will have been hurried off to all parts of the kingdom in the early hours of the morning, before the ordinary traffic begins to get thick on the line. About half the total number return the same night; the others stop away till the expiration of the holiday, which is of eight days' duration.[383]

Guide books proliferated to meet the demands of the new mass tourism, advising on famous beauty spots and how they could be reached. Information was given, too, on the sights to be seen in the towns through which the trains passed.[113] Many resorts began to draw attention to places of interest in their vicinity, so that a guide of Ramsgate, published in 1897, mentioned the 'capital service of brakes' which would take visitors 'to all parts of Thanet, and even as far as Sandwich, Canterbury, and Dover'. Closer at hand was Pegwell Bay, where at the Belle Vue Hotel they could sit in the marine gardens to watch shrimps being netted and then enjoy a plate of them for tea. Minehead in Somerset referred not only to the stag-hunting available in the area but to the proximity of Exmoor. The publication of R.D. Blackmore's novel *Lorna Doone* in 1869 brought great publicity to the district and an article in the *Sheffield Weekly Telegraph* even referred to Minehead as being 'in the land of Lorna Doone'.[405]

This approach was further stimulated when Thomas Cook began conducting tours to Scotland, the west of England and other destinations. The Scottish trips appealed particularly to admirers of the novels of Sir Walter Scott and to those influenced by the royal family's devotion to Balmoral. Cook's Scottish trips began in 1846 and fourteen years later his organization had conveyed around fifty thousand tourists north of the border. One satisfied Cambridge client wrote to his local paper to describe the 'three weeks of thorough enjoyment' he had experienced in Scotland, and concluded: 'Hurrah for the Excursion Trains, say I! – They are a fine invention for men like myself of small means and not much leisure.'[107] Thomas Cook himself insisted that 'unprotected females' need have no fears about going on his tours, and in this way he not only helped widen the leisure opportunities of single women but promoted the broader cause of female emancipation. He referred to himself as a 'travelling chaperon' and mentioned that his wife often accompanied him on tours to Scotland.[107] Later, similar arrangements were to be applied when he began conducting tours overseas during the 1850s. One young woman, making her first trip to Scotland in 1855, referred to the 'pleasant and home-like' atmosphere of the excursion, and by the mid-1860s women were in the majority on most of Cook's tours.[389]

But as yet the majority of holidaymakers chose to stay at a seaside resort and enjoy the pleasures associated with this. For the greater part of the period sea bathing was carefully segregated by gender, with the bathing machines used by men and women placed some distance apart. Initially the menfolk bathed naked, while the women's bathing dress consisted of a long, loose, sacklike garment. In 1856 the *Observer* commented critically on the improprieties to which this had led at Ramsgate when the sea was rough and females lay on their backs in shallow water instead of venturing further in. As the waves came in they not only covered the bathers but carried their dresses up to their neck, so that 'as far as decency is concerned, they might as well be without any dresses at all . . . and all this takes place in the presence of thousands of spectators'. Furthermore, not only did 'the gentlemen come to look at the ladies bathing' but 'the ladies pay as much attention to the performances of the gentlemen. The portion of the beach allotted to the men is crowded with well dressed females . . . who calmly look on without a blush or a giggle.'[143] The newspaper called on the authorities 'to compel gentlemen to wear, as in France, caleçons', while the ladies' dresses should be so made that there could be no 'wholesale exposure of their natural perfections or imperfections, as now momentarily takes place'.

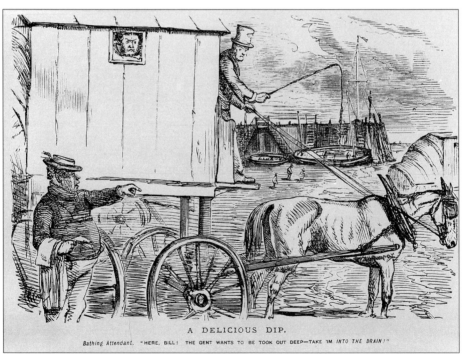

A DELICIOUS DIP.

Bathing Attendant. "HERE, BILL! THE GENT WANTS TO BE TOOK OUT DEEP—TAKE 'IM *INTO THE DRAIN!*"

*A bather being driven into the sea in a bathing machine. Apart from the jolting ride, users of bathing machines remembered their characteristic smell of damp clothing, seaweed and horses. (*Punch, *1857)*

As these criticisms intensified, women's bathing dress from the 1860s increasingly comprised long trousers covered by a blouse or tunic, and with serge the recommended material. By the 1890s bathing caps were coming in and it was around this time that mixed bathing began to be accepted in some resorts.

Meanwhile, pressure was exerted on the menfolk to wear bathing drawers. In 1860 the novelist R.S. Surtees commented on the 'great naked men' who proceeded 'from Underdown Cliff to the sea' in order to exhibit themselves in a way that 'in a secluded wood in the country' would have caused an uproar. 'But because they come down upon the open coast with a grand sea before them people think nothing of it.'[143] But change was under way. In 1867 the authorities in Scarborough decided to make the wearing of drawers obligatory for men and brushed aside the objections of the bathing-machine proprietors that 'first-class visitors' would refuse to wear such garments. They pointed out that similar regulations operated at other watering places, as well as on the Continent, and they had been

> credibly informed that at Brighton the regulation has been enforced with the most successful results, and that, although it is not unusual there to see 1,000 persons bathing in the morning before 8 o'clock, but one conviction only for violation of this regulation has occurred during the past year.

Among those objecting to the new trend was the Anglican curate Francis Kilvert. In June 1874 when staying at Shanklin he was annoyed to discover that male bathers had to adopt the 'detestable custom of bathing in drawers. If ladies don't like to see men naked why don't they keep away from the sight? To-day I had a pair of drawers given me which I could not keep on. The rough waves stripped them off and tore them down round my ancles [sic]. While thus fettered I was seized and flung down by a heavy sea which retreating suddenly left me lying naked on the sharp shingle from which I rose streaming with blood. After this I took the wretched and dangerous rag off and of course there were some ladies looking on as I came up out of the water.'[273]

But by then the practice was generally accepted and when mixed bathing was adopted in some resorts during the 1890s there were prudes who argued that even the 'loin cloth' worn by many men was too disgusting a costume in which to meet and bathe with ladies. At Paignton, where mixed bathing was introduced in 1897, it was declared that any dress 'which did not completely cover the body from the neck to the knees' would be judged indecent and therefore banned. Hence the all-concealing costumes worn at Continental resorts became a required form of dress for male bathers at Paignton and at other English resorts which adopted the new practice of mixed bathing.[347]

If going into the sea was one pleasure enjoyed by Victorian holidaymakers, especially the younger ones, walking over it was another. Initially piers were constructed as landing stages for boats and as promenades where visitors could enjoy the sea air without the danger of getting wet. But as they proliferated in the 1860s many became centres of amusement in their own right. In 1863 Blackpool's first pier, the North Pier, was opened amid great celebrations and proved an immediate success as visitors paraded up and down, showing off their best clothes. By 1875 it was registering almost half a million admissions a year. This led to the building of a second pier, which was opened in 1868. At first the new South Jetty, or Central Pier as it later became, did little business but in 1870 a new manager took over. He organized cheap steamer trips and arranged for dancing to take place on the pier deck. That set the pattern for future development, with sideshows provided as well. Polkas, quadrilles, barn dances and the Lancers were all played by bands on the Central Pier for three sessions daily, sometimes starting as early as 5.30 a.m. to cater for day trippers. According to a contemporary, the dancers took themselves seriously. 'Wearing thick boots their tread is something short of a pile-driver and the stoutest-hearted flooring quakes and trembles beneath the percussion.' Complaints were made that dancing lowered the tone of the area, but the 'people's pier', as supporters dubbed it, maintained the popularity of its open-air entertainment to the end of the century and beyond.[219] The North Pier, meanwhile, concentrated on more genteel pursuits, with refreshment rooms and concerts.

Other mass entertainments available in Blackpool included the Raikes Hall pleasure gardens, which from the 1870s offered trippers 'dancing, fireworks, acrobats and alcohol, with an unofficial admixture of prostitution'. Later the resort's Winter Gardens, initially opened in 1875 to cater for a better-class clientele by supplying an 'all-weather promenade and up-market concerts', provided similar entertainments to Raikes Hall. By the 1880s it featured music-hall and spectacular acts, such as a 'female human cannonball'.[367]

Most resorts had band concerts and performances by itinerant musicians on the sands, including the Christy minstrels with their faces blackened by burnt cork and playing cornets, concertinas and banjos, as they sang comic songs and told jokes. Their simple entertainment was designed to appeal particularly to children. Alfred Bourne, who as 'Uncle Bones' led a troupe of minstrels at Margate for over thirty years, claimed never to have uttered a word unfit for youngsters to hear, 'for it is out of the children's pennies and halfpennies that I have bought my little house'. He added to his income by selling copies of the songs he wrote or purchased from their composers, and claimed that his troupe seldom took less than £50 a week during the season. This was divided into eleven shares, one each for the ten performers and the remaining share set aside in a reserve fund to provide against sickness 'or other disaster'. But some of the more genteel resorts frowned upon the minstrels. At Westward Ho! in Devon it was boasted in 1872 that visitors were never 'annoyed by the vulgar discordant songs of Ethiopian serenaders'. During the 1890s the minstrels faced a challenge from pierrots, introduced from France in 1891. More refined and carefully dressed than their minstrel counterparts, with faces whitened by oxide of zinc, they were immediately successful.[347]

Musical entertainment at the resorts was provided by German bands, military bands, light orchestras and individual performers. But, as in inland towns, their competing sounds were not always welcome. In 1847 Charles Dickens, then staying in Broadstairs, confessed that he would have to leave unless it poured with rain as he could not write for half-an-hour 'without the most excruciating organs, fiddles, bells or gleesingers. There is a violin of the most torturing kind under the window now (time ten in the morning) and an Italian box of music on the steps – both in full blast.'[93] At Llandudno in 1863 three rival bands played in the resort, each providing different sorts of music and sometimes within hearing distance of

Alfred Bourne – 'Uncle Bones' –
performed on Margate sands as leader of a
minstrel troupe from 1865 until the early
twentieth century. (Kent County Council
Arts and Libraries Department: Margate
Library)

one another.[365] But the financial rewards gained at even small resorts were sufficiently attractive to fuel this musical competition.

By the end of the century seaside entertainments in the larger towns had expanded beyond these simple diversions to include more sophisticated fare. At Blackpool, alongside the multiplicity of theatres, music halls, waxworks, fairground amusements and public houses, there appeared the Tower in 1894 and the Gigantic Wheel two years later. The Tower, which was lit by electricity, included a circus, an aquarium, a menagerie and refreshment rooms, as well as space for dancing, promenading and exhibitions.[365] Another all-embracing entertainment centre was opened at Margate in the 1870s by the circus proprietor 'Lord' George Sanger. In 1883 it, too, was lit by electricity, and advertisements boasted that for a sixpence entrance fee visitors could wander through the Italian and zoological gardens, inspect the 'choice collection of statuary', and enjoy all the fun of the fair with swings, shooting galleries, waxworks and the like. 'Every comfort and convenience, and free from all chance of danger' was the boast, to say nothing of its role as 'quite a CHILDREN'S PALACE OF RECREATION'. Dancing was held weekly on Thursday evenings, for which an entrance charge of 1s was made.[36]

Some resorts even began to advertise moving pictures. Films were shown at the Pier Pavilion in Ramsgate in August 1896, as the *Thanet Advertiser* reported:

The latest attraction at the Pier is the cinimatographe [*sic*], a wonderful instrument which gives living pictures of the Prince of Wales' horse winning the '96 Derby, the bustle and traffic of London's streets, recreation on Hampstead Heath, a French railway scene etc. This nineteenth century marvel should be seen by all.

A year later Rhyl, too, was announcing its first 'living picture' show, with many of the early films coming across the Atlantic from the USA.[368]

Holidaymakers seeking quieter destinations, perhaps to pursue self-improving hobbies such as fossil gathering and butterfly collecting, were also catered for. Ilfracombe, for example, stressed the availability of rock pools for the collecting of shells, while a guide to resorts in 1876 recommended Weymouth, Freshwater, Southwold and Sheerness for geology, 'Falmouth for shells and seaweed, and West Lulworth for lepidoptera'. The fashion for marine biology was stimulated by Philip Gosse's *A Naturalist's Rambles on the Devon Coast*, published in 1853, and by similar volumes. But Gosse's son later described his father's 'chagrin' at the pillaging of the pools which had followed, thereby destroying many of their beauties.[365]

For others seeking peace and tranquillity there were the inland spas, which continued to provide hydropathic treatment in comfortable surroundings until the end of the century. A brochure for the Rockside Hydro in Matlock,

Excursionists on the pier at Ilfracombe, making their way to the steamboat, c. 1890. (The author)

Derbyshire, around 1900 stressed that it was located in a district 'justly called the "Switzerland of England"'. As well as offering various baths and treatments administered by qualified medical attendants, its indoor amusements included concerts, 'dramatic recitals, theatricals, tableaux, dancing, bridge, whist, chess, badminton, [and] billiards'. There were also tennis courts, croquet lawns and bowling and putting greens for the more energetic, while Matlock golf club was only a short walk away. One satisfied client from the nearby Smedley's Hydro claimed that he had arrived in Matlock 'a wreck' after a too active social life in London, but had been restored to health within two weeks:

> the atmosphere and tradition of Smedley's is gaiety – pure, quiet, serene, but unclouded, amiable and persistent. It is understood that quiet enjoyment is part of the cure, and everybody is also tacitly requested to add his or her share to the common stock . . . Those who desire rush, or tumultuous pleasure, or smart society had better keep away from Smedley's, but to all who crave for quiet, natural, healthy, serene life, it is the best place I have yet seen.

For energetic holidaymakers, hiking, climbing and a new interest in nature conservation began to emerge, epitomized by the founding of the National Trust in the mid-1890s. Some families, like Beatrix Potter's parents, chose the Lake District or Scotland, where they could enjoy field sports or ramble over the countryside. For a number of years during the 1880s Mr Potter took a house on the wooded shore of Derwentwater near Keswick, where the lake provided a perfect setting for fishing and boating, the woods were alive with red squirrels, and to the north the rugged, heather-clad slopes of Skiddaw dominated the landscape. There were many opportunities for long walks, and it proved a stimulating environment for the young Beatrix to develop her interest in wildlife and the countryside.[339]

By this time the Lake District had become a centre for well-to-do residents and there was an element of 'social zoning' in that although there were rail excursionists, few of them had sufficient time to wander far from the station. Those who came to stay in the area for a week or so tended to concentrate on the main beauty spots and to travel along clearly defined paths. This meant that more permanent residents could keep to themselves the district's wider aesthetic attractions. A desire to cater for the élite is indicated by the fact that when licensing hours at Windermere were extended for the season in 1873 it was emphasized that this was to benefit visitors wishing to meet their friends in 'well-conducted hotels' and did not apply to the 'low beerhouses'.[378] Nevertheless, the railway brought growing numbers of visitors to the Lakes, with half a million people riding in trains to the area each year at the beginning of the twentieth century. Nine-tenths of them travelled on third-class tickets, and three decades after the Kendal–Windermere Railway was completed John Ruskin, a lover of the rugged scenery, complained of the 'stupid herds of modern tourists . . . emptied, like coals from a sack, at Windermere and Keswick'. He argued that further expansion of the railways would make the region 'a steam merry-go-round', with 'taverns and skittle grounds round Grasmere'.[389] But many found such attitudes unacceptably élitist, seeking as they did to restrict a beautiful region to a select few.

Deep emotional commitment to the scenic values of the Lake District was expressed in the writings of William Wordsworth, John Ruskin and others, as well as in the work of the Lake District Defence Society. In a letter to the local press one correspondent described Windermere in florid terms as 'a great temple of nature adorned by all the wealth of mountain, crag, sylvan shores and limpid streams' which had been given by 'an over arching providence . . . to lift up the hearts and minds of people from Nature to Nature's God'.[378]

This belief in the moral benefits to be derived from the countryside was echoed by the social reformer Helen Dendy. To her, a major drawback of urban life was its remoteness from the country. So one of the main aims of the education of town children should be 'to get them back to a proper reverence for Nature'.[198] To that end she strongly supported the Children's Country Holiday Fund, which sent deprived youngsters from city slums to enjoy fresh air in a rural environment. The fund was set up in 1884 under the auspices of the Charity Organisation Society and by 1889 was sending around twenty thousand youngsters to the country each year. Among later beneficiaries were Walter Southgate of Bethnal Green and his sister, who went to Stock in Essex for a fortnight. Walter was nine and this was his first sight of fields of grass and wild flowers and of sheep and cows grazing.

> Another boy and I were taken to a cottage where the lady made us welcome immediately by putting before us hot dumplings soaked in beef fat. Her first injunctions . . . were that we must *not* climb the fruit trees in her garden. It was about the first thing we did as soon as her back was turned and had the intense pleasure of seeing real red apples growing on trees. They were not ripe; we got a tummy ache and were sent to bed early for disobedience.[319]

But that did not mar the little boy's pleasure at his introduction to country life: 'It was all very strange and exciting to a child from another world.'

Even among middle-class families there were those like the Gaskells who took their children away not merely for health and enjoyment but to give them an insight into country life. As Mrs Gaskell wrote to a friend from the farmhouse where they were lodging, it was important that the children 'learn country . . . ways of living and thinking', since these were very different from Manchester where much of their time was spent.[198]

Holidays, therefore, varied widely according to the social class and the interests of those taking them. For some, enjoyment lay in quiet rural scenes in the Lake District or other beauty spots away from the main tourist routes. For others, there was greater appeal in the constant round of excitement in resorts like Blackpool and Margate, which catered particularly for working-class tastes. And for many middle-class families it was the genteel atmosphere of one of the élite resorts like Bournemouth, Torquay and Eastbourne that appealed. For the latter this was epitomized by the church parade which took place on the Sabbath.[116] Most holiday centres had a wide range of churches and chapels to cater for the different tastes of visitors and it was noted that at Bournemouth members of the evangelical wing of the Church of England were discouraged from coming prior to 1867 because of the High Church monopoly in the town.[365] But from a social standpoint it could be more important to *appear* to attend church than actually to do so. At Eastbourne, one man remembered that

> it was the done thing from twelve to one o'clock to parade in front of the Grand Hotel with a prayer book under the arm. This showed that you were the kind of person who went to church (whether you had been there or not) and, equally important, that you were the kind of person who did not need to cook his own dinner.[116]

FOREIGN TRAVEL

By the Victorian years the old-style aristocratic Grand Tour, with its emphasis on the culture of the Ancient World, was no longer in vogue. In part this reflected a change in approach from the leisurely pattern of eighteenth-century life for the well-to-do, and in part it was the result of improvements in transport, notably the building of the railways on an increasing scale in Continental Europe from the 1840s. As Christopher Hibbert points out, in the 1860s Rome could be reached from London within sixty hours and 'a man could go all the way round the world in a shorter time than it had taken him to get to Naples and back in 1750'.[184]

Many landed families continued to visit the Continent on lengthy tours for pleasure or health reasons, even if the regulation pattern of earlier decades no longer applied. Some, influenced by the writings of Byron and Wordsworth, came to appreciate the beauties of the natural landscape. The Alps began to be admired rather than dreaded and Switzerland became a tourist venue in its own right, as did the Rhineland region of Germany for similar aesthetic reasons. A number of British travellers chose a journey on a Rhine steamship as part of their route home from Italy and Switzerland.[389]

The Lucys of Charlecote Park, Warwickshire, set out on one of these new-style Grand Tours when they travelled through Europe between October 1840 and March 1842, accompanied by servants and much luggage. Their belongings included two beds for the children and two baths, as well as a vast array of bed linen, towels, books, tea, arrowroot and 'everything we fancy we could want'. Italy was the principal destination, as it was for most grand tourists at this period, and they spent time in Naples, Florence, Milan, Verona, Perugia and Venice. 'I have walked round galleries till my legs ached intolerably and I was ready to *scream* with fatigue', complained Mrs Lucy, noting that her husband was 'perfectly happy with his sketch book, making drawings of the pavements of varied marble in which his soul delights'. They spent the winter of 1841 in Rome, where Mrs Lucy had distinct reservations about some of the exhibits in the galleries they visited: 'I confess that more often than not I had to hurry the girls past statues of naked gods that their native innocence might not be impaired; and as for myself, the blushes rose to my cheek when looking on Canova's recumbent marble figure of Pauline Borghese.'[159] They became acquainted 'with all the best families in Rome, from whom we receive endless invitations . . . We have an Italian coachman too and a Roman open carriage, and make excursions most days.'

Florence also became a favoured destination for the British during the 1840s, with many spending the winter there. So great did the invasion become that the city supported an English church, a newspaper and a reading room stocked with newspapers from London. The migrants recreated their own kind of social life, too, including morning calls at each other's rented flats and horse racing.[389]

Later in the century there were far more ambitious itineraries. Dearman and Emily Birchall, for example, visited Russia in 1883, staying with a friend of Mrs Birchall's in Moscow and making a leisurely tour of Holland, Denmark and Germany on the way. When they arrived in Moscow on 24 May they were struck by the strangeness of the city:

> We walk about . . . staring and gaping . . . It is so entirely different from all other cities, so unique . . . It is the liveliest place we have ever seen rather like Naples in this respect, crowds of people, droschkys [*sic*] darting about . . . and the coachmen shouting wildly as they gallop along . . . The Russian common people all dress in very bright colours . . . These bright colours give a very gay appearance to the streets. Moscow is . . . a curious mixture of gorgeous splendour and semi-barbarism. You see the wildest looking people about, and in many of the best streets the palaces of princes are next door to the shabbiest of little hovels.[357]

From there they went on to elegant St Petersburg, which seemed tame by comparison, before returning to England in June.

Travel opportunities, however, were also widening for the less affluent, with visits to France and Switzerland becoming popular among the middle classes in the 1850s and 1860s. 'The quietest sort of people are uncomfortable unless they, at least once a year, tie themselves together in batches and go prowling over the tops of unexplored Alps,' commented the *Saturday Review* acidly in April 1860.[85] The appeal of Switzerland was intensified in the early 1850s by lectures given at the Egyptian Hall, Piccadilly, by a middle-aged journalist, Albert Smith, following his own ascent of Mont Blanc in August 1851. His presentations combined instruction with entertainment, and the stage was festooned with 'chamois skins, Indian corn, Alpenstocks, vintage baskets, knapsacks, and other appropriate matters'. During the interval St Bernard dogs patrolled the room carrying chocolates in barrels under their necks. In his first two seasons Smith lectured to almost 200,000 people, including Queen Victoria, and by 1856 *The Times* was concluding a 'perfect Mont Blanc mania' had gripped 'the minds of our countrymen'.[177] After more than two thousand performances spread over five seasons, Smith's show closed, not because of declining popularity but because he was bored with it. 'For diversion he went on a trip to China.'[389]

For the energetic, mountain climbing became associated with the new middle-class status symbols of sport and summer holidays. The formation of the Alpine Club in 1857 to promote links between those who had similar tastes was a further boost. Of its almost three hundred charter members, most were Oxford- or Cambridge-educated professional men, over a third being lawyers or clergymen.[389] To some enthusiasts, such as the barrister and social reformer Frederic Harrison, the Alps engendered a sense of almost mystical exaltation. 'I was carried out of all good sense and self-control by the fascination of this new transcendent world,' Harrison wrote on one occasion. 'I raced about the crags and

The hazards of travel abroad in the early Victorian years: two parties of tourists try to pass one another on a narrow mountain ledge. (From Richard Doyle, The Foreign Tour of Brown, Jones and Robinson, *1854)*

rattled down the snow glissades, tramped through the night, rose to see the dawn in midsummer, and behaved like a youth in a state of delirium. . . . To know, to feel, to understand the Alps is to know, to feel, to understand Humanity.'[272] New resorts were established, like Zermatt whose growth was stimulated by the desire of mountaineers to climb the nearby Matterhorn.[389]

Soon the construction of mountain railways made the High Alps accessible to the less adventurous, and more exclusive resorts like St Moritz were established, offering luxury accommodation, climbing clubs and a mountain guides' association. St Moritz hoteliers catered for wealthy visitors who were anxious to remain apart from the main tourist trade, and they arrived for the season with their families, servants and a great deal of luggage. Initially the resort, like others in Switzerland, concentrated on the summer months, but from the mid-1860s a winter season began to be established. It grew steadily in popularity and spread to other places as well. Davos, which was particularly patronized by those suffering from tuberculosis, was able to extend its season when it became clear that the sunny and relatively mild winters were just as beneficial as the summers.[389] New specialist sanatoria were opened for the invalids, and in order to occupy themselves some of the more energetic took up skating and tobogganing. These diversions were later adopted by the young and fit, as at St Moritz, although it was skiing, a pastime imported from Norway and popularized by a small group of English enthusiasts, which most advanced winter sports during the 1890s.[272]

For those with a delicate constitution, winters in the south of France became increasingly attractive and at the end of the century there were complaints in Torquay that changing fashions had caused some of the wealthiest winter invalids to transfer their allegiance to more exotic locations, like Switzerland, Egypt, the Canaries and the Riviera. The demands of the winter visitors inevitably influenced the character of these resorts. Thus in the early Victorian years English visitors to Nice had occupied their own villas and spent their days out of doors, on foot, on horseback, or driving in carriages. In the evenings they had met together to discuss politics, drink tea and socialize. Prior to the 1870s there was almost no public entertainment in the town other than a sedate opera.[181] But in the final quarter of the century that changed. In 1876 the famous 'Battle of the Flowers' was created, consisting of a parade of carriages elaborately decorated with flowers. The carriages drove up and down the Promenade des Anglais, giving their occupants a chance to throw bouquets and flowers at one another. The carnival rapidly became the high point of the winter season and its emphasis on elegance, luxury and celebration attracted sophisticated visitors. The building of luxury hotels and gambling casinos was another sign of the changing times, as was the appearance of prostitution in the town, itself an indication of the altered nature of winter society. By the end of the century Nice provided opportunities for the new, cosmopolitan visitors to spend money and enjoy the pleasures and pastimes on offer.

> For the men, the days were filled by trips to clubs, casinos, cafés and restaurants. The women engaged in endless rounds of formal visits or, in turn, received visitors 'at home'. They spent an enormous amount of time selecting, purchasing, arranging, and changing their clothes and jewelry [sic]; preparing for balls and parties; and planning for the festivities that surrounded the carnival.[181]

Most of the other Riviera resorts followed a similar pattern, although Menton remained a relatively quiet refuge for invalids. For those interested in gambling, Monte Carlo was the focus of attention, although by the more respectable members of society its preoccupations were severely condemned.[351] The Revd Sabine Baring-Gould, for example, described Monaco as 'the moral cesspool of Europe'. As a result of the principality's flourishing casino, it was given over 'to harlots and thieves, . . . to rogues and fools of every description'.[200]

There were also the pleasures of Paris to enjoy at all times of the year. The Prince of Wales liked to break his journeys either to or from the Riviera by spending a few days in the French capital. There he became such a familiar figure 'in certain quarters that on entering a music-hall he was liable to be greeted with the cry of "'Ullo Wales"'.[200] On the Riviera he took part in regattas in his yacht or made excursions to Villefranche, Monaco and Menton. He also played golf, but aside from these intermittent sporting activities his enjoyment was found in 'gambling, tobacco, food and sex', as one writer has caustically expressed it.[200] Many of his wealthy fellow countrymen shared those interests.

During the summer months some of the most affluent visitors to the Continent went on cruises in private yachts. Others followed the example of the Prince of

Wales and took 'cures' in various spa towns in Europe. As the Countess of Warwick pointed out:

> Nerves, indigestion, sometimes plain obesity, due to too many meals and too little exercise, generally ended the season. Then the cure at a foreign spa became a necessity, and London society was compelled to visit such places as Homburg, Marienbad, or Wiesbaden.
>
> In the years when King Edward, as Prince of Wales, used to go to Homburg, he was followed by society. He had his own table at Ritters Park Hotel . . . Wonderful balls were given at Homburg for the Prince, some by the Duke of Cambridge, who shared his liking for the town.[371]

The taking of baths, the drinking of large quantities of spa water, a restricted diet, and plenty of walks in the surrounding countryside were part of the routine. In the view of a German commentator, 'Idleness without boredom' was an essential ingredient of a successful cure.[376]

There was, of course, more to taking a cure than a rigid regime of dieting, bathing and taking the water. Wealthy socialites were able to meet and exchange news and gossip, as well as display their smartest clothes, attend concerts and make excursions

Visitors taking the cure at Wiesbaden, c. *1860. (The author)*

into the countryside. The Countess of Fingall, who visited Bad Schwalbach in 1897 with a friend, remembered meals eaten out of doors among the flowers, and although they were supposed to be 'doing the cure' the food was delicious:

> When anybody wanted to pay you a compliment, as a gallant friend of mine did, they offered you a rose bath. For this, the petals would have been picked from hundreds of roses and strewn on top of the glutinous water. You lay in your bath with roses up to your chin and presently a tray was laid across the bath on which was placed a cup of delicious chocolate and *brioches* for your enjoyment.[160]

Later she moved to Wiesbaden, where she had treatment for her eyes.

Among middle-class families visits abroad could allow a greater degree of informality than was possible in Britain and, in the case of the womenfolk, a measure of emancipation. Jeannette Marshall, the daughter of an eminent London doctor, seized the opportunity of Continental visits with her family to engage in flirtations with men to whom she had not been formally introduced, in a way that would have been impossible at home. For example, in 1887, when the Marshalls were staying at St Luc in Switzerland, she complained in her diary about the uninteresting company: 'I am on friendly terms with 3 parsons!' she noted on the third day, adding ruefully, 'Very dreadful, but the best there is.' Only when they moved to the Riffel-Alp, above Zermatt, did prospects improve, as she became friendly with a middle-aged barrister, Arthur Stone, whom she had met on an earlier holiday. But her efforts, both in Switzerland and later in London, to turn this into a permanent relationship proved as unsuccessful as her previous holiday flirtations had been.[311]

Margaret Fountaine, the daughter of a Norfolk clergyman, travelled extensively when she came into a modest fortune in her late twenties, and she had even more complicated relationships.[120] Sometimes she travelled with members of the family but mostly she toured alone, striking up close friendships with several men whom she met along the way, including an Italian doctor and, at the end of the century, a Syrian dragoman, with whom she travelled the world for almost thirty years. Margaret used her interest in butterfly collecting as an excuse to escape from the conventions of English provincial life. Even when she spent time in Menton with one of her sisters, who was suffering from tuberculosis, she preferred this to England, rejoicing 'exceedingly that the dead days in Bath', where she had been living with her mother, 'had come to an end once more'.[120]

For those lower down the economic scale, less extravagant tours were available. For example, Henry Gaze organized a cheap tour to Paris in 1844 and in the late 1850s he launched excursions to Switzerland. He accompanied this with a guidebook entitled *Switzerland and How to See It for Ten Guineas*.[389] But it was the intervention of Thomas Cook on the European scene that made the major impact. Cook began taking tourists to France from the mid-1850s and also became associated with tours to various international exhibitions.[65] These included the 1867 Paris Exhibition, when he accommodated in specially provided lodgings about half the twenty thousand people who went to the French capital under the firm's auspices. Still more impressive was his effort in 1878, when 75,000 passengers were taken to Paris by Cook & Son and more than 400,000 tickets were issued through their various offices. This represented about a thirtieth of all the admission tickets sold at that particular exhibition. Special trains and steamers were chartered to carry the passengers and, as before, boarding and hotel accommodation was supplied by the firm to some of the visitors. About twenty thousand of the tourists also went on carriage excursions arranged by Cook in and around Paris.[11]

In 1855 the firm began escorting longer Continental tours, the first, led by Thomas himself, involving a trip to France, Belgium and Germany. The party of about forty people included the four Lincolne sisters from Norwich, who ran a boarding school for young ladies.[318] Later Matilda Lincolne sent an account of the trip to *Cook's Excursionist*. In it she admitted that many friends had thought they were 'too independent and adventurous' in going away in this fashion without a 'protecting relative'. But such fears were unjustified:

> Often when we should have felt alarmed or nervous if alone, we only found a cause for merriment among so many. Did we come to a halting place and find no coaches, we each took up our carpet bags and marched off in a troop, laughing at our novel appearance . . . It was pleasant to meet at the long breakfast table and relate where we had been and what we had seen, and arrange plans for the day.[28]

She was particularly grateful to Thomas Cook and her fellow travellers for their help and was anxious to encourage other unattached females to follow their example. Over the years many thousands did so, and the speed with which the tours proliferated in the 1860s led the *Morning Star* newspaper to claim at the end of the decade that Cook's tourists were 'pervading the whole globe'.[107]

Not all welcomed these developments. Some snobbish English people whom the tour groups encountered abroad referred to them as 'Cook's Circus' or 'Cook's Hordes'. Those who began visiting Switzerland in the 1860s were condemned as a 'low vulgar' mob even though, in practice, most of them came from respectable business or professional backgrounds. To the *Pall Mall Gazette* these increasing numbers of tourists travelling under Cook's guidance were only concerned 'to "do" certain sights and scenes' so that they could talk 'glibly about places and things', familiarity with which they imagined would confer 'some kind of distinction'.[109] In the newspaper's view, the firm was encouraging people 'to travel above their station, to climb socially by climbing the Alps, to "go abroad on the principle on which a kitchen-maid distends her Sunday petticoat with a barrel-hoop because her mistress wears a crinoline"'.

In reality, although there were rumbustious elements on some of the tours most participants were serious middle-class people concerned with self-improvement, who consulted their Baedekers or Murray's *Handbooks* on the sights to be seen and behaved with perfect decorum. For women, in particular, the tours enabled them to visit places which it would have been impossible for them to have seen on their own either on grounds of cost or of social convention. Advice was also given on etiquette and on the possible pitfalls of particular journeys. Thus on the Easter 1868 tour of Italy participants were warned they would be unable to gain admission to the Sistine Chapel or to an audience with the Pope unless they wore 'black evening

Thomas Cook transformed the mass foreign-travel market. Here one of Cook's parties is returning from Karnak on an Egyptian tour, c. 1900. (Thomas Cook Group Ltd. Company Archives)

dress – ladies in black veils or scarves and gentlemen in black trousers and dress coats'.[28] Cook himself welcomed the new mobility, regarding it as an essential feature of democracy and freedom, and was proud of his part in promoting it. Although he appreciated the value of having smart clients this was not his prime objective. In 1873 he frankly admitted, 'We have gone in for numbers.'

However, Thomas's son, John Mason Cook, had a less populist approach and in the final quarter of the century the firm, while continuing to cash in on the cheap excursion business both at home and overseas, nonetheless promoted an increasingly élitist image. Advertisements began to refer to 'select first-class' parties of 'limited numbers', as did the mention in brochures that tours would be 'select and private'. Under the firm's auspices Egypt became a popular winter destination for the well-to-do, while from the late 1860s Cook offered package tours of Palestine and Syria for those anxious to visit biblical sites. No longer was Egypt merely the destination of those interested in the country's exotic past or of sportsmen anxious to shoot game along the banks of the Nile.[351] Now it also attracted those wishing to spend the winter in a warm, dry climate. Luxury hotels were constructed and in 1898 one of Cook's promotional brochures glibly described Cairo as 'no more than a winter suburb of London'.[389]

The widening travel opportunities led to a proliferation of guidebooks and publicity campaigns, as well as the appearance of rival operators such as the

Regent Street Polytechnic, which from 1886 began taking parties of students to Switzerland, France and Belgium at cheap rates and for educational purposes.[188] Many of these rivals were prompted by high-minded motives similar to those which had originally inspired Thomas Cook. The Arlington Travel Club and the Toynbee Travellers' Club were both connected with educational institutions and laid particular stress on the cultural aspects of travel. Intensive study courses preceded the foreign trips from Toynbee Hall. In the winter of 1887 club members prepared themselves for a visit to Italy by listening to lectures, examining photographs and reading books on Italian history and Florentine and Milanese art. 'Neither,' recorded a participant proudly, 'were the conditions of the countries passed *en route* neglected, and we were further instructed on Switzerland's government and Belgium's trade.'

Among the other agents who established themselves in the final years of the century were Dean & Dawson from 1871, John Frame from 1881 and Sir Henry Lunn from 1893.[389] (Frame was such a fanatical teetotaller that he asked his customers to sign the pledge.)[107] Even sea cruises became less expensive, with the Regent Street Polytechnic in the 1890s offering cruises to Norway at £8 8s and to Madeira at £12, while a number of steamship companies were entering the market, too.

The brochures issued by the various firms detailed the delights of travel and, less prominently, the problems which might be encountered. Cook's *Handbook to the Health Resorts of the South of France and Riviera* (1893) mentioned points to bear in mind when renting apartments and information on the charges to be expected. But it described in graphic terms the benefits to any traveller who, like one satisfied visitor to Cannes, was ready to abandon a dreary London winter for the sunshine of the Riviera. There breakfast could be eaten in the hotel garden 'under the shade of some orange trees, whose fruit, hanging in hundreds overhead, formed a picturesque contrast to the scarlet arbutus berries close by', and where the pungent perfume of geraniums and heliotrope hung in the air.[54]

For a number of people there was much personal satisfaction to be derived from the new opportunities to travel, and this extended far beyond the mere pleasure of holidaymaking, as the diary of the Horsham brewer Henry Michell, makes clear. After a second visit to Switzerland in 1865 he wrote nostalgically of a stay that had provided some of the highlights of his life:

> . . . it was altogether a source of heartfelt and unbounded satisfaction. If I look back to the days of my boyhood, early manhood, or even middle age, I always consider[ed] the advantages of travelling in foreign countries as blessings reserved for something like a different order of beings to ourselves, but prosperity at home, and facility of travelling by rail and steamboat abroad, opened my eyes to the fact that even we might partake of them; most thankful am I that we were permitted to do so, as the language, manners and customs of the people, the views, lakes and mountain scenery, of a continental country as compared with our Island home creates in one's mind a class of ideas, and affords a never-ending source for contemplation.[254]

Additional Sources Used

Cook's Excursionist, 6 August 1855 and 2 March 1868.

Theodor Fontane, *Ein Sommer in London* (Frankfurt am Main and Leipzig, 1995).

Halifax Guardian, 24 May, 31 May and 12 July 1851 for special excursions.

Alan Kay, *North Thanet Coast* (Bath, 1994).

Keble's Margate and Ramsgate Gazette, 5, 19 and 26 May and 25 August 1883.

'A Day or Two at Ramsgate' in *The Leisure Hour* (1852) in the Victorian Ramsgate Project File at Ramsgate Local History Library.

Lois Lamplugh, *A History of Ilfracombe* (Chichester, 1984).

Matlock, Bath: brochure for Rockside Hydro, D.1645 Z/B1; and letter from M.A.P., 23 June 1900 concerning Smedley's Hydro, 1397B/B.253. Both at Derbyshire Record Office.

Ian Ousby, *The Englishman's England. Taste, Travel and the Rise of Tourism* (Cambridge, 1990).

John Pemble, *The Mediterranean Passion. Victorians and Edwardians in the South* (Oxford, 1988).

Royal Ramsgate (Ramsgate, 1897). This guide is in the Victorian Ramsgate Project Collection at Ramsgate Local History Library.

Scarborough Local Board of Health to the Home Office: correspondence in 1867 at the Public Record Office, MH.13/162.

Edmund Swinglehurst, *The Romantic Journey. The Story of Thomas Cook and Victorian Travel* (London, 1974).

Thanet Advertiser, 15 August 1896.

'Uncle Bones', 'In the Days of my Youth', article from *M.A.P.* at Margate Public Library local history collection.

Penny Ward (ed.), *Margate 1736–1986. A Resort History* (Margate, n.d. [c. 1986]).

Weston-super-Mare: correspondence with the Local Government Board and the Board of Trade in 1886 at the Public Record Office, MT.10/443/H.627.

CHAPTER 7

The Sporting World

Lawn-tennis is the amusement of the hour; croquet and rinking have had
their day . . . Archery was a few years ago the favourite sport of society at
Cheltenham; but we move quickly nowadays, and archery was soon voted
slow. Later there have been contests from time to time for championships
and grand prizes at lawn-tennis, just as a few years before the game was
croquet at every place at which pleasure-seekers congregate . . . Within the
last five-and-twenty years cricket clubs and football clubs have been formed
in all the towns and most of the villages in England . . . In some counties . . .
wherever there is a fair expanse of level and unoccupied grassland, the
wickets are sure to be pitched, and the boys and men practise with bat and
ball.

T.H.S. Escott, *England: Its People, Polity, and Pursuits*
(London, 1885 edn), 98, 536–40

THE GROWTH OF MASS SPORTS

By the late nineteenth century Britain had become a nation of town dwellers and
for many, especially among the menfolk, it was sport which created and sustained
a new popular culture and a new kind of urban identity.[191] It also provided much
pleasure, and John MacFarlane, founder and patron of the first Stirling Boat
Club, was not alone in considering it was sufficient if the sole benefit of boat
racing for spectators was 'the excitement and enjoyment' it gave. Similarly the
aim of the working men who formed the crew of the Scottish Central Rowing
Club in the 1850s was to secure 'amusement after working hours'.[346]

On a wider basis the success of a local football team could engender pride in the
whole community, even if the players themselves had not been born there. When
Tottenham Hotspur won the Football Association Cup in 1901, three decades
after the competition was inaugurated and after years of dominance by northern
clubs, the huge crowd which gathered to welcome the team on its return was
unconcerned by the fact that it comprised five Scots, two Welshmen, an Irishman
and three northerners. The players' birthplace was 'of little significance to the
crowds that blew horns, threw confetti, and chanted snatches of popular songs
changing the words to celebrate the team', comments Richard Holt.[191] Many even
went the next evening to the club's White Hart Lane ground to watch an
animated picture show marking the victory.

The doings of a local club could also form the subject of heated arguments when men met at work or in the public house, and at major matches the noisy behaviour of the crowd shocked some observers. Football in the north, declared *Tinsley's Magazine* in the late 1880s, 'is more than a game. It excites more emotion than art, politics and the drama, and it awakes local patriotism to the highest pitch.'[242]

Yet if football was the most popular of all sports at the end of the nineteenth century, it was not the only one to enjoy strong support. Cricket, boxing, horse racing and many others were followed enthusiastically, while new sports such as badminton, cycling, field hockey, lawn tennis, table tennis and yachting were quickly taken up.[346] In 1899 a German visitor claimed that in England, 'All is sport . . . It is sucked in with the mother's milk.'[169]

Often the kind of activity pursued and the people engaged in it were indicators of social class. Sports involving the use of relatively expensive equipment, such as croquet, lawn tennis and golf, were largely the preserve of the upper and middle classes, while soccer, which required little more than a ball and a piece of open ground or even a street as a playing area, was increasingly the choice of the working classes. At the turn of the century Geoffrey Brady, whose father owned a Stockport cotton mill, remembered that although his parents were friendly with local shopkeepers they did not ask them 'to come and play whist or tennis'. His own home had a croquet lawn where friends were invited to play, but when the family wanted a game of tennis they went to the court at his grandparents' large residence.[343] In other cases the wealthy joined select clubs, like that in Hove where the Wick Lawn Tennis Club, formed in 1881, had eight courts, discreetly sheltered by trees from the intrusive gaze of passers-by. To ensure that the club's select nature was preserved members were chosen by ballot.[234]

Some organizations signalled their élite status by adopting the word 'amateur' in their title, as the Derby Amateur Bicycle Club did on its formation in 1878. The minutes note that a group of 'gentlemen' attended the inaugural meeting, and it was decided that the club uniform of chocolate serge jacket and breeches should be made by a London tailor.

The setting up of such bodies not only fostered congenial social contacts but enabled the sports to be followed more economically, through the use of shared facilities, than was possible on an individual basis. Interest arose at a time when many middle-class men were entering sedentary urban occupations and wanted to enjoy the fresh air by playing sports in their spare time. Membership could also confirm or consolidate social status. This aspect was exemplified by a correspondent to a Bolton newspaper in 1865 when he argued that there was a great need for a club for 'gentlemen' in the town. This demand was speedily met by the formation of a succession of associations:

> a rowing club was in existence in 1865, the year of the foundation of Bolton's cricket club (whose membership grew from 30 to 220 in six years); an amateur athletic club formed in 1870, followed by an amateur swimming club in 1871 . . . Subscriptions were beyond the range of any but a middle-class pocket, and there were several complaints about the exclusivity of the clubs.[85]

Lawn tennis at Onslow Gardens, London, c. 1900. Note the cumbersome clothing and elaborate headgear of the female players. (The author)

On another level, sport could influence society's self-perception. One archetypal (if fanciful) image of rural England was of a cricket match played on the village green, with squire, farmer and labourer all participating in a spirit of friendly rivalry.[201] Or, as a sports magazine of 1864 put it, 'Prince, peer, parson, peeler [policeman] and peasant all participate in the game.'[153] The reality might be very different, with clear distinctions drawn between 'gentlemen' and lower-class 'players', but the values of social harmony and good sportsmanship were the themes which promoters of this vision of the countryside wished to convey.

The factors which encouraged the growth of the mass holiday and excursion market in the Victorian years gave a similar impetus to the expansion of sporting activities. These included the greater spending power of many working people, especially towards the end of the century, extra leisure time, including the Saturday half-holiday and bank holidays, and better transport, with railway 'specials' running to major football fixtures and trams offering cheap and convenient services within cities.[88] Significant, too, were changes in the population's occupational structure, including the rise in middle-class employment which offered income levels and work patterns conducive to leisure pursuits. If sports were to prosper there had to be spare cash available to purchase the equipment needed and to pay the entrance charges to grounds which were increasingly imposed. Specialist firms emerged to produce balls, shin guards and playing boots. In 1851 Lillywhite & Sons were advertising 'newly invented leg guards' stuffed with horsehair for cricketers. The early pads were tied on with tapes or strings but in 1862 buckles and straps were advised.[143] In Glasgow the number of football outfitters rose from eight in 1885 to twenty in 1900 and increasingly departmental stores offered a whole range of football goods. Likewise cycle manufacturers sponsored meetings and riders in order to promote their products.[346] Even makers of herbal and patent medicines became involved, turning their attention to the thousands of players whose knocks and strains needed simple treatment. Elliman's Embrocation became the 'lubricant of football success. Tonics found in the footballing fraternity a new and greedy market.'[370] Instruction manuals on sports also proliferated, with around 260 books on golf alone published between 1870 and 1914.[346]

The increasing space devoted to sport in the press, and the appearance of specialist newspapers and magazines concerned with the various games, were

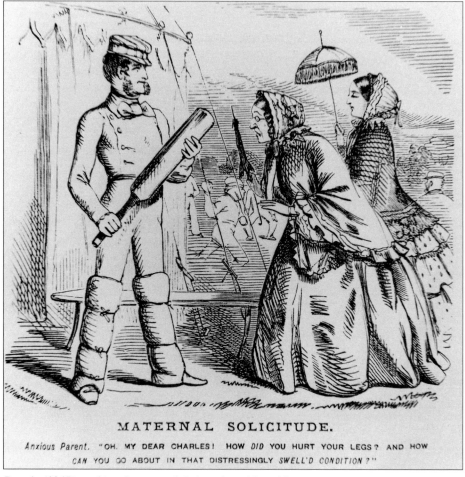

MATERNAL SOLICITUDE.

Anxious Parent. "OH. MY DEAR CHARLES! HOW *DID* YOU HURT YOUR LEGS? AND HOW CAN YOU GO ABOUT IN THAT DISTRESSINGLY *SWELL'D CONDITION?"*

Punch *(1845) mocking the new pads being adopted by cricketers.*

further signs of their importance and, at the same time, they reinforced the general enthusiasm. The same was true of the portraits of sporting heroes which were printed on cigarette cards and postcards at the end of the period.

In south Wales, where rugby became immensely popular from the 1880s, the *South Wales Daily News* described it as 'the one great pastime of the people'. Detailed accounts of leading players were published and methods adopted to stimulate public interest, including an appeal to readers to submit lists of their selections for the best Welsh representative team. When this was printed in January 1889, over 2,100 entries were received. The speed with which match results could be transmitted by telegraph helped to give sporting editions a special importance, while club rivalries were intensified, perhaps by local newspapers framing the report of a defeat in a derby match with black edging, like an obituary announcement.[317] It has been claimed that in the principality, rugby union played a significant part in shaping Welsh national identity and self-confidence, thereby helping to promote social cohesion. This was particularly important at the turn of the century when the south Wales coalfield was expanding rapidly and large numbers of workers were being sucked in from England and other parts of Wales.[384]

In Scotland it was soccer that induced a similar spirit of nationalism, with the first formal 'international' taking place in Glasgow between England and Scotland in 1872, before a crowd of four thousand. By the 1890s, when the international match between the two teams had become a biennial fixture, large numbers of Scots travelled south to support their side, with five thousand reported to be coming from Glasgow and Edinburgh alone in 1891. On this occasion the match was played in Blackburn and soon after their arrival in the early hours of the morning the Scottish fans caused alarm among townspeople 'by shrieking war whoops and riotous singing accompanied in several places with the crash of glass and smash of door panels'.[249] As one writer has put it, reports of Scottish football which concentrate on 'lurid accounts' of the rivalry between Rangers and Celtic, the two leading Glasgow clubs, need qualification since 'they do not allow for what binds Scots together – a dislike of the "English" which has historical, material and cultural roots'.[249]

Similarly, the revival of Highland Games events in Victorian Scotland has been attributed at least in part to a desire to stimulate a sense of national consciousness. 'Unless something is done to revive the popular spirit of the Highlands, its games and exercises, the sound of Gaelic language and the pibroch will soon disappear from the northern glens,' warned the *Stirling Observer* when announcing the date of the Stirling Highland Games assembly in 1855. In the same year the *Alloa Advertiser* complained that if Alva and Tillicoultry could have a Highland Games contest then Alloa should be able to do the same. Indications of the popularity of the new venture can be gauged by the fact that whereas there were just two Highland Games gatherings in Stirling and its immediate vicinity in the 1840s, the number had risen to thirty by the 1870s.[346]

Alongside these social and national influences, technological changes also contributed to the expansion in sport. Golf benefited from the replacement of feather-packed balls first by those using gutta-percha and later by machine-made, rubber-strip balls, while improvements in refining and working iron and steel produced iron-headed clubs. Lawnmowers and rollers helped to promote sports like bowls, cricket, golf and lawn tennis by producing the smooth playing surface needed, and vulcanized rubber was used to make tennis balls as well as the inner tubes for modern footballs.[346]

While these advances were under way, throughout Britain older, more brutal traditional sports like cockfighting and prize-fighting were in retreat, and there was an acceptance of the need for rules to be applied to the new or reformed sports which were growing up. This came at a time when the notion of regulation and accountability was being accepted in many areas of social and economic life, including elementary education and the professions. Its application was seen clearly in football, where by the 1850s the many different versions of the game played in local communities and at various public schools began to be divided into two distinct categories. These were the handling and tackling game, in which some kicking was allowed (this resembled the old-style 'folk' game that had fallen into disrepute), and the kicking and dribbling game, in which handling was frowned upon. The former version was played at newer public schools like Rugby and Marlborough and the latter at older foundations such as Eton, Shrewsbury, Westminster and Charterhouse. Efforts were made to produce a uniform code for the two types of game, but without success.[88] The division was recognized in 1863, with the formation of the Football Association to regulate soccer and the institution of the FA Cup eight years later. This not only boosted interest in the game but helped to promote uniformity, since all who participated had to observe the same national rules. When the first Cup Final was played in 1872 only fifteen clubs took part in the competition; by 1890 that had risen to 132, and there was a proliferation of local cup competitions throughout the country.[153]

During 1871 the Rugby Football Union was formed to assume a regulatory role for the handling game, and over the years ruling bodies were set up for croquet, lawn tennis, boxing and many other sports. In 1898 *Country Life Illustrated* even called for national regulation to be introduced for billiards, with 'a representative central authority of amateurs to control it, as cricket, golf, and polo are controlled by the Marylebone, St. Andrews, and Hurlingham Clubs respectively'. By 1890 fifteen sports had gained a large enough following to have their own national organization. Fifty years earlier only horse racing, golf, cricket and curling (with the formation of the Grand Caledonian Curling Club in 1838) had been subject to such arrangements.[169] In 1897 *Country Life Illustrated* called curling the 'national game' of Scotland 'as much as the thistle is the national emblem'. In the Stirling area alone the number of curling clubs rose from twenty-five in the 1830s to around one hundred, forty years later.[346]

In the past much of the credit for the upsurge in sport codification was given to the public schools and their former pupils, since it was they who manned most of the regulatory organizations. Behind their interest lay a belief in the values of 'muscular Christianity' and its associated moral virtues, both for school pupils and for adults. The Hampshire clergyman and author Charles Kingsley produced one of the classic arguments in favour of boys taking up games when he claimed that through sport they gained benefits which no books could give them:

> not merely daring and endurance, but, better still, temper, self-restraint, fairness, honour, unenvious approbation of another's success, and all that 'give

and take' of life which stand a man in good stead when he goes forth into the world, and without which . . . his success is always maimed and partial.[191]

Similarly the physician to Rugby School argued that games encouraged the young 'to excel in every phase of the battle of life'.[85] In this way courage, tenacity and team spirit would be promoted, and pupils would be equipped to withstand danger from all quarters, including insurgent tribesmen in the outer reaches of the Empire!

Some clergymen and philanthropists, enthusiastic about the sports they had played at school or university and anxious to promote the idealized moral attitudes associated with them, began to introduce team games to the working classes. A number of early football and cricket clubs grew up with church or Sunday school connections, and in the 1890s the social investigator Charles Booth commented drily that this could mean 'obligatory attendance at a Bible-class being administered medicinally with cricket and football to take the taste away'.[153] Hence in 1885 25 of the 112 football clubs in Liverpool had religious links, and a similar pattern emerged in other cities. In Birmingham 83 of the 344 clubs in existence in 1880 were connected with churches. For example, Aston Villa originated in 1874 from an initiative by members of the Villa Cross Wesleyan chapel who already played cricket in the summer and wanted a winter game as well.[370]

Recently, however, doubt has been cast on this simplistic view of the diffusion of sports from middle-class mentors to the lower orders.[169] Thus while some old-style games did decline, others, like cricket, quoits, professional rowing and pedestrian racing (professional athletics) continued to enjoy mass support over the years in many localities without external encouragement. Alan Metcalfe, in his research into the mining communities of south Northumberland, points to the 'pedestrian mania' of the early 1860s which was encouraged by the opening of commercial running grounds in Newcastle and Gateshead.[247] Crowds of up to ten thousand people would gather to watch and bet on the various events. Also important in the area was professional rowing, with highly paid oarsmen appearing on the River Tyne in the 1840s before 100,000 spectators. There was a further growth in popularity during the 1860s and the strong sense of community involvement engendered was expressed in the adulation given to sporting heroes. Thus when Harry Clasper died in July 1870 his funeral was held on a Sunday 'to meet the convenience of numerous bodies of working men' who wished to attend. Clasper, a former miner, became a champion professional rower and crowds estimated at between 100,000 and 130,000 lined the streets to witness the largest funeral held in Newcastle up to that date.[247] Rowing died out on the Tyne during the 1880s due to the disruption of courses by additional ship traffic, the growth of industry on the river and the appearance of other sports attractive to spectators – notably football.[247]

Ironically, when rowing became a major sport for 'gentlemen' from the mid-nineteenth century, competition from working-class oarsmen was firmly excluded. Amateurs from a public school or university background did not relish being beaten by social inferiors, nor were they prepared to mix with them socially. So when the Amateur Rowing Association (ARA) was formed in 1882, under the influence of the Henley stewards who had organized the exclusive Royal Regatta on the Thames from 1839, all manual workers were kept out. This applied not

Spectators watching a race at Henley Regatta in the 1890s. (The author)

merely to professionals of the Harry Clasper school but to working-class amateurs as well. Symptomatic of the general approach was the exclusion by the Henley Regatta stewards of the local town rowing club on the grounds that its members were not 'gentlemen amateurs', even though they had previously been accepted at other regattas.[175] In these circumstances it is perhaps not surprising that the American Richard Harding Davis could conclude that only 'a very small part of Henley' was actually concerned with racing:

> Henley is a great water picnic, not a sporting event; . . . the thousands of boats and thousands of people . . . , all on pleasure bent, and the green trees, and beautiful flowers of the house-boats, and the coloured lanterns at night and the fireworks, . . . make Henley an institution.[55]

A similar attitude of social discrimination was taken by the Amateur Athletics Club (AAC) when it was formed in 1866, to give 'all classes of Gentlemen Amateurs the means of practising and competing versus one another without being compelled to mix with professional runners'.[85] But the spread of athletics to new clubs in the north of England led to the dropping of the exclusion clause against working-class amateurs by the Amateur Athletic Association, formed in 1880 to replace the AAC. No such change occurred in rowing. In 1890 the National

Amateur Rowing Association was set up to represent manual workers who rowed for the pleasure of the sport rather than for cash, but despite pressure from the new body the ARA refused to change its rules. However, from the mid-1890s the two groups were at least allowed to row together for amusement or against each other in private contests, and at some provincial regattas less prestigious National Association members were able to compete against ARA oarsmen.[175]

Cricket was another old-style sport which survived into the new era. The crowd of twenty thousand, largely working men and their families, who watched Nottingham play Sussex at Nottingham in September 1835 were thoroughly familiar with the game, according to the writer William Howitt, who was present.[137] And in the 1840s William Clarke's All England XI of professional players toured the country with success. Cricket sent its first professional touring sides to North America in 1859, Australia in 1861 and South Africa in 1888. In 1878 the first fully representative team of Australians came to England and by the end of the century the biennial tours between the two countries to compete for Test Match glory were a major feature of English sporting life. 'Is it wrong to pray to beat the Australians?' one public schoolboy is supposed to have asked anxiously. 'My dear boy, anything which tends to increase the prestige of England is worth praying for', came the reply.[191]

Only in the 1860s, with changes in the rules to legalize over-arm bowling and with the emergence of the towering figure of W.G. Grace, did professionals cease to dominate cricket. Grace was able to outplay his professional opponents, and his stamina and enthusiasm were legendary. It is a tribute to his skills that of forty matches between the Gentlemen and the Players from 1865 to 1881, the Gentlemen won twenty-seven and lost only five. Prior to Grace's emergence the Gentlemen

An athletics competition in London between representatives of Oxford and Cambridge Universities, c. 1900. (The author)

had been beaten consistently. Through these successes the amateurs were able to reassert control over the game from their base at Lord's, home of the Marylebone Cricket Club, and could relegate the professionals to a subordinate position.

During the 1860s, too, the county game began to establish itself, again with amateurs at the helm, and this culminated in 1873 in the development of the county championship. The leisurely matches extending over several days made few concessions to working-class spectators whose free time was limited to Saturday afternoons and a few brief holidays. Indeed one of the attractions of cricket, in the eyes of *Country Life Illustrated*, was the opportunity it afforded the spectator to go away for a while and return to find 'the same cricketers in possession and the state of the game not materially altered. Even a player may enjoy a day's leisure in the midst of a match, and a fashionable crowd can picnic round for three days and yet witness no conclusion.'

But for those with a tighter schedule, new league and cup competitions were organized on a local basis. They ranged from the Heavy Woollen District Cup arranged at Batley, Yorkshire, in 1883 to the successful Lancashire League, inaugurated in 1890, and many others.[346] In the Lancashire League, whose fourteen clubs were concentrated within 20 miles of one another, a few matches each season around the turn of the century attracted more than five thousand spectators. As with the counties, clubs in the league allowed their members into matches free of charge.[386]

Nevertheless it was on the leisurely amateur game that the moral virtues of cricket were felt to rest. The Eton v. Harrow match at Lords formed part of the social round of the élite during the London Season, and it was 'gentlemanly' values that were considered beneficial to the wider community. In the 1880s Joseph Lawson wrote of the 'wonderful influence for the good' on the young men of Pudsey, Yorkshire, achieved by the game, whether they were players or spectators:

> By cricket, players are taught patience, endurance, precision and courage. They are taught self-respect and gentlemanly conduct in bowing to the decisions of the umpires, and derive physical benefit as well. The discipline taught by the game of cricket is great and invaluable . . .[137]

Other writers stressed the advantages that accrued where leadership was given to the 'players' by 'gentlemen'. According to *Bailey's Magazine of Sports and Pastimes* for 1861, cricket served a particularly laudable purpose from this point of view:

> The pent up citizen, the shopkeeper in a country town, the rustic or mechanic of the village, each and all feel a kindly influence spreading over them when (for instance in the company and under the immediate eye of the banker's son from the city, of the young squire and brothers from the hall or of the village rector's first born just fresh from college) they are enjoying a game full of healthy excitement and that in common with those from their wonted marks of respect, they consider it some privilege to be acquainted with, and whose presence we take it for granted would be sufficient guarantee against any bad conduct, swearing, drunkenness and such like malpractice.[406]

Dr W.G. Grace, the doyen of English cricket, c. 1900. Grace's enormous skill and enthusiasm transformed the game in the 1860s. (The author)

However, the reality was more complex. At local level many working men had long organized cricket matches on their own account. In Birmingham and Sheffield around the middle of the century some utilized 'St Monday' for the purpose. The workers at Messrs R. Timmins & Sons in the Birmingham steel implement trade took up cricket and archery in that way. They owned bats, wickets, balls, bows, arrows and targets in common, and in the summer turned out to play two or three times a week. At Sheffield, too, around the mid-century cricket, foot-racing, jumping and other sports were indulged in: 'on a Monday afternoon, when little or no work is done, the men of one establishment challenge those of another to a game of cricket, or something of the sort, and spend the evening pleasantly in this manner', commented one journalist.[281] Small wonder that Will Thorne considered one of the most remarkable features of Birmingham in the early 1870s the fact that 'no matter how hard men and boys worked, they were whenever possible always anxious to take part in sports'.[85]

Children, too, played games, even when they lacked proper equipment. Walter Southgate remembered that in his Bethnal Green home at the turn of the century no sports were allowed on Sundays, but during the rest of the week activities varied on a seasonal basis. 'We had no apparatus except what we improvised for ourselves – coats down in the road for goal posts; the lamp post for a cricket stump; a rough piece of wood shaped for a cricket bat; . . . balls of pressed paper and string.'[319] As they grew older he and some of the other lads organized their own football and sports club 'in an amateurish way to be sure but this directed and absorbed our interest'.

In other cases cricket teams were set up by football and rugby players in order to give themselves a summer game or, as in parts of south Wales, they grew up on a community basis. Cardiff, for example, had ninety-one sides formed between 1870 and 1885, and Swansea forty-three. Some took the name of the street on which they were centred, others were established in the expanding suburbs, and others again were organized by migrants to the area. For them a team gave a sense of identity and comradeship in an unfamiliar city. Hence in Cardiff a group of Yorkshiremen formed the White Rose Cricket Club, while some Scotsmen set up the Caledonian Cricket Club. In 1879 the South Wales Cricket Challenge Cup was inaugurated and although it raised interest in the game it also led to ill-tempered rivalry between some of the sides. Certain wealthier clubs, like that at Newport, which benefited from funds derived from a successful rugby team, began to employ professional cricketers, partly to train amateurs in the team but also to increase the chances of success in inter-club matches.[185] In 1886 the South Wales Challenge Cup competition came to an end amid acrimony, but professional cricketers continued to be employed by the more prosperous clubs to the end of the period. A similar policy of employing professional help was adopted by Lancashire League clubs and, of course, by county teams. Here they might spend a considerable amount of time bowling in the nets to give the gentlemen practice, and the numbers employed varied according to the attitude of the clubs. In the mid-1890s the Lancashire team included nine professionals and only two amateurs, while at Somerset the reverse applied, with nine amateurs and two professionals. From an early stage the latter club began courting Oxford and Cambridge blues to improve its playing strength, but it had difficulty in maintaining a settled team. Sometimes it was even a struggle to field a full eleven, and the county's treatment of its professionals remained paternalistic and even autocratic.

On occasion, as at Banbury, Oxfordshire, sports clubs were formed with the support of an employer. In this case the initiative came from the agricultural engineering firm of Bernhard Samuelson, with dinners, picnics and cricket matches arranged for foundry workers from the 1850s. In 1856 a Mutual Instruction and Recreation Society was formed and soon became a major provider of recreation in the town, with well over a hundred members. In April 1858 Samuelson rented part of the town's old racecourse for use as a sports ground and workers had half-holidays on Wednesdays and Saturdays during the summer, with matches played between different departments.[350]

Later in the century it was soccer that attracted most working men, although there were some areas, including parts of Lancashire, Yorkshire and south Wales, where rugby was the dominant sport. Significantly, even when they accepted assistance from other members of the community, including the churches, in setting up their clubs, once these were established many of the men went their own way. Thus although the original members of Aston Villa Football Club were connected with a Bible class at a Wesleyan chapel, they turned to a local butcher to obtain their playing field and a publican for their dressing room. Similarly, members of the Christ Church Football Club in Bolton abandoned their clergyman mentor four years after he had formed the club. They marched out of a meeting in the church schoolrooms, crossed the road to the Gladstone Hotel and 'reconstituted themselves as the Bolton Wanderers'.[85] Evidently would-be players saw these middle-class helpers as sponsors rather than as 'missionaries' whose message they must absorb.[169]

Once northern soccer clubs began to recruit working men to their teams financial problems arose. Before 1880 many of them were making compensatory payments to players for out-of-pocket expenses on match and training days, and to cover shortfalls in income where a player lost part of his week's wages in order to fulfil a club commitment. As attendances at matches grew and gate takings increased this seemed to many local people a fair arrangement. At the same time, their admiration for the close-passing team game developed by clubs north of the border led to a greater recruitment of Scotsmen to play in Lancashire sides. But to amateur administrators running the Football Association in London this was creeping professionalism. They reacted by forbidding any payments to players over and above *bona fide* expenses and loss of earnings. In 1884 aggrieved Lancashire clubs threatened to secede from the association if the ban were imposed. At a time when northern teams were dominating the game it was a threat to be taken seriously, and in 1885 the FA capitulated and agreed to accept professionalism.[88]

Three years later came the formation of the Football League, as a means of ensuring that top clubs had a regular supply of good quality opponents, and supporters were given predictable, high calibre entertainment. Attendances were boosted and whereas the average gate at a Football League match in 1888–9 was over 4,600 by 1899–1900 the average recorded at a First Division match in the league was 9,500.[386] However, the formation of the league was strongly criticized by supporters of the amateur game. Writing in the *Contemporary Review* in November 1898 Ernest Ensor referred to the professional footballer as 'an idler'. In his view, by caving in to financial pressure, the Football Association had

> touched pitch and been shockingly defiled . . . The effect of League matches and cup ties is thoroughly evil . . . The system is bad for the players, worse for the spectators. The former learn improvident habits, become vastly conceited, whilst failing to see that they are treated like chattels, and cannot help but be brutalised. The latter are injured physically and morally . . .[153]

Country Life Illustrated was equally scathing, condemning the failure of professional teams to demonstrate a true 'gentlemanly spirit'. In March 1900 it compared the cup ties of the late seventies and early eighties with the 'inexpressibly degrading . . . account' of the semi-final played at Crystal Palace before some forty thousand spectators in the recent past. This was 'a mere rough-and-tumble exhibition, in which the excitement of the players prevented them from doing justice either to the game or to themselves . . . It was not merely that they were rough . . . but they were also . . . tricky and mean in their roughness.' The fact that the two teams comprised players drawn from all over the kingdom it considered of scant importance: 'After all, it does not much matter where gladiators are bred.'

But the majority of the sporting public ignored these supposed moral dangers and turned up at cup and league matches, both in the major competitions and in local contests, in increasing numbers and with growing commitment.[246] For some this began at an early age when they went with fathers or older brothers to Saturday afternoon matches and it continued as they grew older, with football one of the principal topics of conversation for lads hanging about street corners. Impromptu games formed a large part of leisure time, as one youngster remembered: 'in those days, nearly every street that was any street at all had a football team', and rival gangs played one another.[127]

By the end of the century professional football had spread to the south of England, particularly London. According to a contemporary, when the season opened the capital's professional teams bounded away 'like hounds unleashed, and every camp is stirred with anxious thoughts'.[314]

The size of crowds for cup clashes grew dramatically. The first English Cup Final in 1872 had attracted 2,000 spectators; in 1888 the gates closed behind 17,000, and in 1895, when the Cup Final venue was established at the Crystal Palace, even larger numbers flocked there; a record 110,000 attended in 1901. By the turn of the century attendance at the top games of the 'new national sport was limited solely by the capacity of the stadiums and the interests of safety'.[370]

Increasingly, too, spectators refused to accept that the struggle should be confined to action on the pitch. In Scotland as early as 1876 a game between Queen's Park and Vale of Leven took place amid 'yelling, hooting and calling out to the players' as well as 'coarse and vulgar pleasantries'.[346] And at a purely local level, matches involving teams in the mining communities of east Northumberland during the 1890s could lead to violent confrontations between rival supporters. As the *Morpeth Herald* commented acidly in 1899:

> We are beginning to think . . . that football is exercising a great influence over the young people of our villages, and not a few who take up their newspapers read little or anything else. Take for instance matches that are played weekly between village clubs. Strong feelings are exhibited against each other, and it is no uncommon thing to see spectators in open conflict in support of their respective teams.

Meanwhile the administrators of Rugby Union were determined not to follow the path towards professionalism taken by their Football Association counterparts. Yet, as increasing numbers of working men took up the game in the north of England and south Wales, similar problems arose over the payment of expenses when players had to travel to games or when they lost part of their earnings in order to take part. The Rugby Football Union was not prepared to authorize so-called 'broken time' payments. As Arthur Budd, RFU President in 1888–9, put it, if a working man 'cannot afford the leisure to play the game he must do without it'.[384] Similar hostility was shown to proposals from Yorkshire and Lancashire for the formation of competitive leagues, since these were felt to be the thin end of a professional wedge. In 1895 the two counties responded by forming a Northern Union to regularize the payment of compensation for broken time and to develop their own version of the game. At this stage they wished to avoid full-scale professionalism. That only came in 1898, by which time the sport had increased in popularity among supporters in Lancashire and Yorkshire. But the split robbed the English national team of many gifted players, since they were firmly excluded from appearing with the strictly amateur, non-plebeian practitioners who dominated both the rugby establishment and the mainstream English and Scottish game.

Wales, too, remained loyal to amateurism, despite well-founded suspicions that financial inducements were being offered to some men to change clubs within the principality and that generous 'expenses' were being allowed to many players. A minority did defect to the professional game in the north of England, to the anger of Welsh fans. In 1899 when a scout from Wigan was detected approaching players from the Penarth club, local supporters dragged him from his cab, pulled him down the landing stage at the small seaside resort and threw him into the water.[384] So, as the historian of the Welsh game points out, despite 'the jibes of socially superior practitioners' from outside the principality, Rugby Union retained its hold and 'embedded itself . . . in popular culture and national consciousness'.[384]

The issue of professionalism, which proved so controversial in soccer and rugby, had little significance for élite individual sports like golf, croquet, badminton (developed from the old game of shuttlecock-and-battledore), and lawn tennis. Although professionals were engaged in golf and tennis, their function was primarily to coach amateur players and perhaps sell equipment or help look after the grounds. They played no part in the organization and administration of the games. Golf became increasingly popular in England from the mid-1860s, under the influence of Scottish exiles and particularly following the development of links at Westward Ho!, Devon, in 1864. Over the succeeding years many new clubs grew up, some making clear in their rules that 'the etiquette of golf as laid down by the Royal and Ancient Golf Club has been adopted as a bye-law'. This was to reassure potential members of their impeccable credentials. A few even specified suitable occupations for entrants, as with the Beccles Golf Club whose 1899 rulebook mentioned army and naval officers, clergymen and masters of endowed schools as being among the acceptable categories. In practice, such restrictions were hardly needed, since in England at least the high costs of club membership were normally sufficient to restrict entrance.[381] In Scotland some clubs were less élitist, although there, too, a number concentrated on recruiting professional people and leading businessmen.[171]

Although a ladies' section was formed at St Andrews in 1867, and at a number of other golf clubs over the next two or three decades, their position within the game remained inferior to that of the menfolk. Lawn tennis, by contrast, was freely taken up by both sexes, even though the cumbersome clothes worn by the women seriously hampered their mobility. In the 1880s it even became fashionable to wear an apron with pockets to hold the balls. Yet fear of being considered unladylike prevented most girls from adopting more appropriate outfits.

Tennis was patented in 1874 by Major Clopton Wingfield and proved an immediate success, especially in upper- and middle-class families whose gardens were large enough to accommodate its fairly modest requirements. The first code of rules was published in 1875 and two years later a tennis tournament was held at the All England Croquet Club at Wimbledon. Its popularity quickly relegated croquet to a minor role and by 1885 it was attracting over 3,500 spectators to the men's final.[191] The sport was also taken up at holiday resorts, with Exmouth staging a tournament in 1881, only four years after the first had been held at Wimbledon. The Exmouth competition, which was soon extended to a week, became an annual event and attracted players from all over the country.[347] Ladies had their own contest, and playing tennis quickly became an integral part of holidaymaking for visitors to most of the nation's seaside resorts. By 1900 about three hundred clubs were attached to the Lawn Tennis Association.

However, the importance of lawn tennis in the Victorian years was not its competitive aspect but the fact that in terms of gender it was the first truly national game.[191] Certainly *The Field* in 1885 was enthusiastic about the changes it had helped to promote: 'lawn tennis has taught women how much they are capable of doing and it is a sign of the times that various games and sports which would have been tabooed a few years ago as "unladylike" are actually encouraged at various girls' schools'.[143] These included vigorous sports like hockey, lacrosse and rounders as well as lawn tennis itself. But the game had a more intimate side, too. Social contacts between the sexes on the tennis court, or at the dances, picnics and concerts organized by clubs, could lead to marriage. 'Within the club there was room for . . . competitive play,' writes Richard Holt, 'especially for men at league and county level, but this rarely overshadowed the larger social purpose.'[191]

Bicycling and ice-skating (or rinking) also offered opportunities for girls to display their athleticism and their independence. In both, chaperons were rarely able to keep pace with their young charges and in the case of cycling, advertisers exploited the desire of young people to escape the confines of family life by emphasizing the opportunity it offered to explore an unspoiled rural world. 'There is a new dawn, a dawn of emancipation, and it is brought about by the cycle,' enthused Louise Jeye in the *Lady Cyclist*, August 1895:

> Free to wheel, free to spin out into the glorious country, . . . the young girl of to-day can feel the real independence of herself, and while she is building up her better constitution she is developing her better mind . . . How little and cramped seems the life before the cycle came into it![299]

Nevertheless, women cyclists experienced disapproval from older, more conventional individuals in the wealthier classes and unpleasantly strident hostility from certain members of the working classes. In crowded urban areas they would be greeted with jeers and derision and sometimes caps were thrown into their wheels in an effort to unbalance them. But these adversities did little to stop women from cycling once the sport took off in the mid-1890s. In the end public opinion was forced to accept this new expression of female emancipation.[299]

Among middle-class men cycling likewise offered an opportunity for independence at relatively modest cost, particularly after the development of the Rover safety bicycle in the mid-1880s, with its greater comfort and efficiency. In 1897 membership of the Cyclists' Touring Club alone reached 44,496 – an increase of almost 10,000 over the previous year.[29] However, it was at this point that a number of the social élite took up another craze – the motor car – and

This advertisement seeks to persuade potential purchasers of the pleasures and freedom of the open road offered by bicycling. (The author)

became 'ardent automobilists'. Significantly in 1897 the prestigious periodical *The Cycling World Illustrated* changed its name to *The Cycle and Motor World*.[267]

Even socialism spawned enthusiastic cyclists, the best known of them being associated with the *Clarion* newspaper. The first Clarion Cycling Club was set up in Birmingham in February 1894 and by April 1895, when the National Clarion Cycling Club was established, membership was rising rapidly, reaching seven hundred at the end of the year, divided among thirty-six local clubs. Two years later there were around two thousand members and the largest of the clubs in Manchester even published its own newspaper. 'Clarionettes' combined propaganda work for their political cause (distributing socialist literature and holding meetings with rural workers) with large meets and camps attended by several hundred cyclists. In August 1896 the Manchester club set up a camp near Knutsford with fourteen bell tents and two marquees. Members from as far afield as Birmingham, Bradford, Nottingham and London were among those seizing the opportunity to spend a weekend under canvas. Most Clarion club members were probably well-paid skilled manual workers or members of the lower middle class, together with a sprinkling of wealthier sympathizers, like the suffragettes Christabel and Sylvia Pankhurst.[299]

By the end of the Victorian era, therefore, not only had there been a great increase in the number of sports taken up but they were assuming a major role in the formation of social relationships in an increasingly urbanized world. Where problems were encountered in obtaining space to play games, the municipal authorities in many towns began to make provisions for them. Not only were swimming baths more common but there were ambitious schemes like the 90-acre Platt Fields park in Manchester, which contained 46 tennis courts, two bowling greens, nine cricket pitches, 13 football pitches, a boating lake and a paddling pool.[245] At the turn of the century the city's medical officer of health claimed that every field that could possibly be obtained had been 'snapped up all round . . . for football clubs and cricket or one game or another'. There was a 'great eagerness on the part of Manchester children to get spaces for games'. Swimming was particularly popular, with almost 340,000 visits to the baths being made by pupils from the city's schools during the year ending 7 November 1901. Over half the visits were made free of charge.[198]

Elsewhere educational institutions catering for adults became involved. In London the Regent Street Polytechnic had a wide range of facilities by the 1880s, including clubs for athletics, rowing, cycling, cricket, soccer, rugby, lawn tennis, gymnastics and lacrosse. Some sports even had separate organizations for teetotallers, and the college magazine included reports of students' achievements. In 1889 it was claimed that the Cycling Club was 'looked upon . . . as the leading path club in England, thanks to our brilliant string of racing men'.[39]

For women, meanwhile, sporting (and spectating) opportunities continued to remain relatively limited, despite the progress made. Nonetheless it was accepted that at least in middle-class circles female participation had helped along the cause of social emancipation. As Herbert Chipp, the first secretary of the Lawn Tennis Association, admitted with some reluctance, 'whether for better or worse, whether we disapprove with our grandmothers or approve with our daughters, times have changed, and we have to accept facts as we find them'.[191]

Above all, the rise of organized sport created a leisure 'revolution' in Britain. Not only did it provide pleasure and excitement for participants and spectators, but in the case of popular team games like soccer and rugby, success by a local side induced communal pride, while unsuccessful clubs saw their support drifting away.[386] In 1889 when Preston North End won the FA Cup a crowd of thirty thousand massed at the railway station for the team's return, while a band played 'See the Conquering Hero Comes':

'Around the team swarmed hundreds of fanatics, each of whom struggled to get a handshake with some member of the team.' When the trophy itself was revealed . . . 'the wildest enthusiasm prevailed. Hats were thrown up, handkerchiefs waved, and sticks flourished' and thus the huge and excited entourage made its way to the town hall where the team would be formally thanked for the distinction and celebrity they had brought the town.[191]

HORSE RACING AND BETTING

While most of the sports so far considered had their clearly defined bands of supporters, horse racing to some degree transcended class boundaries. Major races like the Epsom Derby were occasions for widespread celebration, while

Ascot and Goodwood were part of the social round of the élite during the London Season. When Richard Harding Davis visited Epsom in the early 1890s he was struck by the vastness of the crowd, with at least sixty thousand people present, and by the gaiety of the scene:

> There are dozens of . . . wagons and hundreds of bookmakers. Some in white flannel caps, clothes and shoes, others all in red silk with red silk opera hats and evening dress, others with broad sashes spangled with bright new shillings like shirts of chain armour, and others in velvet or Scotch plaids . . . They will take anything from a shilling to a five pound note, and they take a great many of both.
>
> But if you would get something for your money other than a ticket with 'Lucky Tom Tatters of London' printed upon it, you can throw wooden balls at cocoanuts in front of a screen, or at wooden heads, or at walking-sticks, and perhaps get one of the cocoanuts, or a very bad cigar. You can also . . . bet on which one of three cups the little round ball is under, or buy wooden doll babies with numerous joints to stick in your hatband, or coloured paper flowers and feathers to twine around it . . . There are also numerous vendors of tin tubes and dried peas, with which joyous winners on their way home pepper the legs of the helpless footmen on the back of the coach in front . . . or, if you are a sportsman, you can watch a prize-fight which is always just about to begin, or shoot at clay pipes with a rifle, or try your strength by pounding a peg into the ground.[55]

But if the Derby was a major festival for the London working classes, it also had a widespread appeal for the social élite. There were claims that half the male members of the peerage could be seen in the saddling enclosure on Derby Day and racehorse owners competed with one another for the prestige of breeding the winner of that race. Among them was the Prince of Wales, who acquired his own stable in 1886 although his enthusiasm for the sport long preceded this. Even in the 1860s Queen Victoria had repeatedly urged him to reduce the number of races he attended, though without avail. In 1896 the Prince's horse, Persimmon, won the much-coveted Derby; four years later another of his horses, Diamond Jubilee, did the same, as well as winning some of the other classics including the St Leger at Doncaster and the Two Thousand Guineas at Newmarket. After the latter victory the prince was said to be 'delirious with joy'.[237] As one of his biographers comments, he enjoyed both the excitement of the races and the 'raffish camaraderie of racing society'.[248] But it also proved a profitable enterprise. Between 1886, when he began racing, and 1910, when he died, his horses earned £415,840 in stud fees and stake money.[237] Punters who backed the prince's horses, or those of highly successful aristocratic owners like the Earl of Rosebery, the Duke of Westminster and the Duke of Portland, had logic as well as snobbery on their side. In 1889 alone the Duke of Portland won nearly £74,000 in stakes.

It has sometimes been argued by apologists for the turf that one of its merits was its promotion of social harmony because it appealed to rich and poor alike. But that claim is exaggerated. At most racecourses the upper ranks of society met their friends within the safe confines of the grandstand or their private carriages, where they were protected from contact with the lower orders. Their visibility helped to reinforce their superior social status but their inaccessibility served to protect their privacy.[204] This was very obvious at Goodwood Park, 'where the privileged enclosure round the grandstand excluded all that the most fastidious would desire to exclude' and racing could be enjoyed without 'its coarse and disgusting accessories, the degraded mob, the blasphemous, greedy, obscene Bohemianism that revels on Epsom Downs and ordinary racecourses'.[356] Likewise at Ascot, to gain entry to the royal enclosure was 'the true certificate of social standing'.[356]

Even at lesser events, like that at Stockton on Teesside where the summer meeting was regularly patronized by Lord Zetland, a special halt was constructed beside the course so that he and his party could descend from their personal train without encountering the 'roughs' at the main station. Frequently race meetings formed part of country house entertainment, and this applied to Redcar and Stockton, which were conveniently arranged on either side of the 'glorious twelfth' of August. Visits to the races could thus be interspersed with days out on the grouse moors, as was the custom with Lord and Lady Londonderry when they entertained at Wynyard Hall around the time of the Redcar and Stockton meetings.[204] Lord Zetland also had a house party to coincide with these races.

In the early Victorian period gate-money was not paid at races. Spectators could watch all the events free of charge and only had to pay if they entered the grandstand. Many smaller, less prestigious meetings were held to coincide with local holidays and workers were allowed time off to attend. In one part of Lancashire factory commissioners claimed in the 1840s that three or four days' holiday were normally allowed by employers to enable operatives to go to Ratcliffe Races.[85] At

Racing at Ascot in the early 1840s. (Illustrated London News, *1843*)

these meetings entertainment was provided by travelling shows, beer tents, boxing and wrestling matches, fortune tellers and acrobats, alongside the opportunities to place bets. Prostitution, too, was a common constituent of the racing scene, with the atmosphere of drink, gambling and holidaymaking producing a ready clientele. Some of the women travelled around the racing circuits. In Scotland there was a large influx of prostitutes from Glasgow and other major towns for the Musselburgh races while the Ayr meeting attracted those from Edinburgh.[356]

Alongside these established events there grew up a number of meetings in and around London organized by publicans and bookmakers for the purpose of encouraging crowds to come along in order to bet and to drink beer. Some of the worst elements in metropolitan society attended, and violence and hooliganism were commonplace. At Streatham, for example, a riotous mob tore up railings and flung them at a jockey whom they suspected of not trying, while at Bromley a pitched battle took place between punters and bookmakers when the latter tried to welsh on their debts.[356] Eventually this scandalous behaviour led to the intervention of parliament. Under legislation passed in 1879 all racecourses within 10 miles of Charing Cross had to be licensed by local magistrates. This meant that badly conducted meetings could be closed down.

However, it was the coming of the railways which most revolutionized racing, as it did so many other leisure pursuits. Not only could horses be taken by rail to more distant events, thereby widening competition, but spectators could travel long distances too. Soon special excursions were being run to 'any country places where races are held, and in every sporting paper at least half a column is dedicated to excursionists who want to go racewards'.[356] Those courses off the route of the railway or a long way from a station lost popularity, while others more conveniently placed or with a prestigious reputation, such as Epsom or Doncaster for the St Leger, gained in support. Over the period 1840–70 an average of six meetings a year vanished from the *Racing Calendar*, though others were substituted for them – some being purely speculative ventures which disappeared as rapidly as they had been set up.[356] There was a trend towards longer meetings on the surviving courses and to the holding of more than one meeting a year, so as to utilize facilities fully. In 1848 there were 61 one-day meetings and 56 longer ones in Britain; by 1870 the respective totals were 58 and 82. As a result of the changes more horses were being raced, with over double the number running in 1869 that there had been in 1837. The character of the races was also changed so as to appeal to working-class spectators, who wanted close and exciting finishes. This led to more racing by two-year-old horses and to a proliferation of sprints and handicaps.[356]

Up to this time despite the sport's popularity no real attempt had been made to collect course entrance fees from those attending. Sporadic efforts were made to charge gate-money at some of the rougher events but the normal practice was to impose a levy only for entry to the stands or for viewing the races from a private carriage. In 1875 that began to change, with the opening of Sandown Park as the first enclosed course to make a charge to all racegoers. Its success was immediate, with two meetings held in its first year. This rose to four by 1877 and five by 1880. Sandown's example was soon adopted elsewhere, with Kempton Park following suit in 1878.[356] By the end of the century racing was taking place at

Crowded platform at Waterloo station, London, with passengers preparing to travel to Ascot for the races, c. 1900. (The author)

enclosed courses all over Britain and attendances were rising, with crowds of ten to fifteen thousand not uncommon. Double that could be anticipated at major fixtures and as many as seventy to eighty thousand on bank holidays.

Enclosed courses appealed to two groups of racegoers – ladies (who had hitherto patronized few events beyond those, like Ascot and Goodwood, which were associated with the London Season) and working-class men. Sandown encouraged female attendance by setting up a club for carefully vetted male members who were allowed to bring lady companions. The other enclosed courses followed this example and at the end of the century several thousand females might be present at the most important meetings. The clubs offered racing, luncheon and a musical accompaniment, as well as the opportunity to stroll around the lawns and flower-beds in a pleasant atmosphere.[356]

Working men were attracted by the greater orderliness of the enclosed courses compared to some of their more raffish unenclosed competitors, and by the offering of Saturday afternoon racing. Sport was also of high quality, with good horses and jockeys taking part. With the revenue secured from entrance charges higher prize-money could be offered, and this attracted more, as well as better, horses.

Accompanying these developments the standing of the leading jockeys rose, especially of the most celebrated of them, Fred Archer. At his peak the champion jockey earned from £8,000 to £13,000 a year and during the final two decades of the century at least ten other jockeys could earn £5,000 a season – approaching one hundred times the income of an ordinary working man.[346] Even a young man could become a national hero by a sensational win, as was the case with Robinson in the 1887–8 St Leger. 'The commonest jockey-boy in this company of mannikins can usually earn more than the average scholar or professional man', wrote one contemporary disapprovingly in 1889, adding that they also received 'a good deal more of adulation than has been bestowed on any soldier, sailor, explorer, or scientific man of our generation'.[356]

It was Fred Archer's tragic suicide in November 1886 which showed most clearly the hero-worship his successes on the turf had engendered among some sections of Victorian society. According to *The Times*

> A great soldier, a great statesman, a great poet, even a Royal Prince, might die suddenly without giving so general a shock as has been given by the news of the . . . death of Fred Archer . . . Archer was known and admired by all that large proportion of the upper class that cares for racing; and to the populace his skill, his daring and his prodigious good fortune had endeared him . . . Consequently the news of his death has come with a sense of shock and almost personal loss literally to millions.[244]

Prior to his death Archer had mingled freely in high society and the reliance of owners upon his skills to win races meant, in the view of one critic, society 'went simply mad about him'.[244]

However, it was the close link between horse racing and gambling that led respectable Victorians to question the sport's morality.[58] Betting was not confined to the turf, since sports like athletics, rowing and even football had this darker side.[2] Miners, in particular, were said to be ready to back themselves 'against any other man in the world' in competitions and they rarely took part in sports just for the fun of it.[247] In soccer the alleged connection between some spectator misconduct and betting led the Football Association in 1892 to require clubs to take action to prevent spectator gambling. Five years later, after several court cases, bills were posted at all grounds warning of the illegality of betting on the terraces. Firmness on the part of clubs and the police led to a sharp decline in the practice, but it proved impossible to eliminate. At the same time competitions in which the results of football matches had to be predicted became a feature of the sporting press in the 1890s.[355]

But it was the link between betting and horse racing that was most pervasive. In 1892 L.H. Curzon, a noted writer on the turf, claimed acidly that so long as the 'sport of Kings' was 'surrounded by that army of gamblers, which now so fatly flourishes on all our racecourses, it will continue to be what it has long since become, a monstrous game of peculation'.[356] As early as 1851 £1,000,000 was estimated to have changed hands on the Chester Cup and heavy sums were pledged on such classics as the One Thousand Guineas, the Two Thousand Guineas, the Derby and the St Leger.[244]

It was the upsurge in working-class betting that caused most concern, and in the late 1840s the Attorney-General intervened to check the growing number of sweepstakes that were springing up. Although illegal under legislation prohibiting lotteries, they were often organized informally and many were advertised in the sporting press. On 3 September 1848 *Bell's Life* alone advertised forty-seven sweepstakes and it was around this time that the matter was raised in the House of Commons. The Attorney-General then announced he would prosecute any newspapers that printed sweepstake advertisements, and this led to a sharp decline in that particular form of gambling.[208] But soon a new breed of bookmakers came to the fore prepared to accept off-course bets in cash from all comers. Many posted lists of odds in public houses, billiard rooms and tobacconists' shops, and they were later published in the sporting press, too. Betting houses sprang up, especially in London where there were estimated to be between 100 and 150 of them around the middle of the century. The larger provincial towns also had their own establishments. Consequently in July 1853 the Attorney-General introduced a bill designed to outlaw all off-course betting for ready money. His reason for so doing was the temptation which the betting shops offered to servants, apprentices and workmen to wager their few shillings. If these individuals lost they often went on spending money, in the hope of recouping their losses,

> and for this purpose it not infrequently happened that they were driven into robbing their masters and employers. There was not a prison or a house of correction in London which did not every day furnish abundant and conclusive testimony of the vast number of youths who were led into crime by the temptation of these establishments.[270]

Whatever the intentions of the 1853 Act may have been, however, it did not eliminate off-course betting. Partly this was because where credit was involved rather than cash the practice was allowed to continue. It was a concession likely to benefit the well-to-do rather than ordinary gamblers. Partly there was a failure at first to apply the legislation to Scotland, so that some major commission agents simply moved their offices north of the border and conducted business by letter and telegraph with former clients in England. Circulars were also issued and advertised in the press. Thus the Cardiff-based *Western Mail* of 20 April 1872 included details of *The Premier Racing Circular*, produced in Edinburgh, and *The Private Turf Circular* of Glasgow, which both offered advice to potential punters. The former suggested beguilingly that 'Gentlemen wishing to win a few hundreds with a trifling outlay and a certainty of success, have only to send for this week's number, which contains some of the greatest "mounts" the world ever knew.' In 1874 this loophole was closed when the English law was altered so as to make illegal all public offers of advice concerning horse races or offers to take bets. In addition, the amended 1853 Act was applied to Scotland, too.[356] Some of the agents then moved to Boulogne and the Netherlands, where they continued in business as before. They also sent representatives to the major English race meetings so that they could take ready-money bets in the racecourse betting rings.[208]

But the services which these agents provided were beyond the means of most working men. For them the only recourse was the street bookmaker, along with the touts, scouts (employed to keep a look-out for the police) and runners (who carried betting slips from touts or other agents to the bookie) associated with him. 'For many,' comments Ross McKibbin, 'the first and sharpest memories of city streets' involved such 'hurried and agitated' transactions which made it seem as if betting had become 'the principal business of the country'.[244]

Many of those placing bets with street bookmakers never attended a race, but gained their information from the sporting press and the predictions of race tipsters who, for a fee, provided details not always published in the newspapers. The first of the new breed of racing papers was the *Sporting Life*, which began in 1859. It appeared twice weekly until 1881, four times a week from 1881 to 1883, and daily from then onwards.

Its rivals included the *Sportsman* and the *Sporting Times*, both introduced in 1865. Manchester had the *Sporting Chronicle*, established in 1871, and Birmingham had two sporting papers by 1880. During the late 1880s the *Sporting Life*, *Sportsman* and the *Sporting Chronicle* each had circulations in excess of 300,000 and their lesser-known competitors also sold in large numbers.[208] These newspapers gave information about the names and past performances of the horses entered in the various races and other details as well. Of prime importance in enabling them to give up-to-date guidance was the new electric telegraph. This not only allowed the press to publish racing results speedily but to give the starting-price odds, which were the basis of off-course betting. It was in these circumstances that in 1892 a London club steward told L.H. Curzon, 'Here everyone bets . . . everyone from the City to the West End; the cabman who brought you from the railway station, the porter who took your hat, the man who sold you that copy of the special *Standard* [that is, the racing edition], all bet.'[244]

Likewise the *Westminster Review* concluded in 1895 that the 'betting mania is all prevalent'. Individual bets might be as low as 2*d* or 6*d* on each horse and were rarely above 1*s* but it was the pervasiveness of the activity which aroused alarm. One writer in 1899 claimed that even children were able to 'lay their pennies and errand boys their sixpences'. For some punters the main motive was excitement; for others the knowledge that even if a successful gamble did not yield enough to pay off debts it might enable the winner to have a night out at the music hall or enjoy some similar pleasure. It was this aspect which was highlighted by George Moore in his novel *Esther Waters*, when he wrote of the people of Shoreham enjoying a 'happy, golden shower' following a racing success.

> In every corner and crevice of life the glitter appeared. That fine red dress on the builder's wife, and the feathers that the girls flaunt at their sweethearts, the loud trousers on the young man's legs, the cigar in his mouth – all is Goodwood gold. It glitters in that girl's ears and on this girl's finger.[401]

But for many it was not these motives which led them to speculate but rather a desire to exercise their personal judgement and intellect, as they studied form and decided on the probable outcome of a race. In Alice Foley's Bolton home a pink-backed copy of the *Racing Handicap* always hung above her father's armchair and he consulted it daily in his search for winners.[161] Likewise in Salford at the turn of the century Robert Robert's uncle spent most of his leisure 'sprawled on a sofa with the handicap book. An intelligent man, untaught in other ways of using his natural skill, he lived like countless others of the time for petty gambling.' According to Roberts, a number of men even made 'the breakthrough to literacy by studying the pages of the *One o'Clock*. Many a child, too, would spell out the list of "Today's Starters and Jockeys" for unlettered elders, making out their betting slips and so improve both in handwriting and in vocabulary.'[290]

Roberts also described the way the bookmakers went about their business in his district, as in most others,

> usually . . . standing on a chair behind a locked back-yard door. One handed up the betting slip while he, later in the day, handed down any winnings. At the catwalk end

his 'dogger-out' stood watch. This system facilitated the bookie's quick getaway in the event of a police raid. By gentleman's agreement the dogger-out allowed himself to be taken and fined at regular intervals. Old bookmakers, talking of the time, state categorically that they had to bribe the police frequently to stay in business at all.[290]

Sometimes touts stood outside factories when men left for their midday break, in order to collect their bets. In other cases apprentices were sent out to place bets when the men themselves could not manage this. Arthur Sherwell claimed that in the early 1890s touting was 'endemic in the craft trades of the West End' of London, and sporting papers were 'universal in tailor's workshops'.[217] In some places hairdressers, tobacconists and news vendors combined their legitimate business with illicit bookmaking, while elsewhere bookmakers went from door to door in working-class neighbourhoods when the menfolk were at work. They tried to persuade wives to place a bet and sometimes this did not end with the risking of spare cash: 'a woman very often takes the things of the house and pawns them to get the money to bet with'.[2] Yet, as Robert Roberts points out, despite condemnation by the respectable middle classes, betting on horses was virtually 'the only way, other than theft, that the worker knew of to get money without earning it'. Charles Booth, too, commented on the sudden excitement that manifested itself on the streets in London when a major race had been run and the latest edition of the newspaper was out:

> Boys on bicycles with reams of pink paper in a cloth bag on their back, scorching through the streets, tossing bundles to little boys waiting for them at street corners. Off rush the little boys shouting at the tops of their voices, doors and factory gates open, men and boys tumble out in their eagerness to read the latest 'speshul' and mark the winner.[101]

Yet if gambling on horses was the principal kind of speculation practised by the working-classes, it was not the only one. Charles Booth described gambling clubs which were raided by the police in London and perhaps closed down, only to be reopened shortly afterwards.[101] Elsewhere the street served as a forum for gambling, with 'pitch-and-toss' or halfpenny banker played on street corners. Alice Foley recalled older boys playing pitch-and-toss in the back streets of Bolton, with younger ones keeping watch, ready to give the alarm should a policeman approach. The youths would quickly scatter but periodically one would be caught and fined 5s by the magistrates. 'A street collection was usually organized and the fine paid in pennies and half-pennies.'[161] In some places pitch-and-toss 'schools' were run, often by local bookmakers. In Manchester C.E.B. Russell, who conducted a boys' club in the city, lamented that while the older lads played pitch-and-toss or bet with bookies, their younger counterparts, aged twelve to fifteen, played cards for cash, purchasing a cheap pack for a halfpenny and then wagering a few pence. It gave them 'a certain sort of excitement . . . in their lives'.[2]

Among the social élite there was also an upsurge in gambling at the end of the century, and the casino at Monte Carlo became particularly popular. Baccarat and roulette were much in favour, with the Prince of Wales an enthusiast for the former game. In May 1887 Sir Edward Hamilton noted that at the Duchess of Manchester's

'Derby' entertainment for the Princess of Wales and her daughters, one room was set aside for baccarat: 'gambling always delights H.R.H.'. The thrills of baccarat derived from the element of chance rather than from the exercise of skill, and as early as July 1889 the prince's love of the game brought him into conflict with the Duke of Richmond, with whom he was staying for Goodwood. Despite the duke's objection to its being played in his house the prince persisted and this led to a quarrel. Early in the following year Winifred Sturt, a daughter of Lord Alington, was disgusted to find baccarat being played at Sandringham into the early hours. 'I think it is a shocking affair,' she wrote, 'for the Royal Family to play an illegal game every night. They have a real table, and rakes, and everything like the rooms at Monte Carlo.'[194] In September 1890 this enthusiasm caused the Prince of Wales great embarrassment: a scandal arose over cheating by one of the participants in a game in which he was involved while staying in Yorkshire for the St Leger. In the subsequent publicity over the case the prince was heavily criticized, with *The Times* calling upon him henceforth to abandon all such undesirable pastimes. It seems that he did give up baccarat after this and turned instead to bridge. But he certainly continued to gamble. In the early 1900s George Cornwallis-West described a train journey he made with the former prince who was now King Edward VII. They played bridge to pass the time and when Cornwallis-West won, the king produced 'an enormous roll of notes from his pocket from which to pay me'.[194]

In the élite gentlemen's clubs of London wagers between the members were also relatively common. For example, the betting book at Brooks's Club includes an entry for 6 July 1896: 'Mr. Godfrey Benson bets Mr. Charles Trevelyan £5 that Home Rule will not be granted to Ireland within twenty years. Sir Edward Grey to be arbiter of what constitutes Home Rule.' At the St James's Club, opened in 1859 primarily for diplomats, there was a great deal of whist, piquet and éscarté played, with sums as large as £150 at stake. 'Sometimes there was trouble with members who did not pay their card debts. Other nuisances included sitting at card-tables till dawn.'[395] Sir Arthur Sullivan, composer of the Savoy Operas, was a member of the St James's and it seems that, as a keen gambler, he was attracted to the club by the high card stakes as well as by the congenial company and surroundings it offered.

Additional Sources Used

John Ashton, *The History of Gambling in England* (first publ. 1899; this edn, New York, 1968).
Country Life Illustrated, 6 February, 24 July and 4 December 1897 and 31 March 1900.
Derby Cycling Club Minutes for 1878–90 at Derbyshire Record Office, D.3987/1/1.
Christopher Dodd, *Henley Royal Regatta* (London, 1989 edn).
Peter Green, 'A Hundred Years of Tennis' in *Times Literary Supplement*, 1 July 1977.
Diary of Sir Edward Hamilton for 1887 at the British Library, Add.MSS.48,646.
Jennifer A. Hargreaves, ' "Playing like Gentlemen while Behaving like Ladies": Contradictory Features of
    the Formative Years of Women's Sport' in *British Journal of Sports History*, Vol. 2, No. 1 (May 1985).
Alan Metcalfe, 'Sport and community: a case study of the mining villages of East Northumberland,
    1800–1914' in Jeff Hill and Jack Williams (eds), *Sport and Identity in the North of England* (Keele, 1996).
Polytechnic Magazine, Vol. XII, 16 February 1888, and Vol. XV, 22 August 1889, in the archives of
    the University of Westminster, London.
The Clarion, 27 June and 22 August 1896.
John Twigg, review of David Foot, *Sunshine, Sixes and Cider. The History of Somerset Cricket* (1986)
    in the *International Journal of the History of Sport*, Vol. 4, No. 2 (September 1987).
John Woodcock, 'Amazing Grace, his fame still endures' in *The Times*, 18 July 1998.

CHAPTER 8

Music and the Theatre

The diffusion of a taste for music . . . may be regarded as a national blessing . . . In the densely populated manufacturing districts of Yorkshire, Lancashire, and Derbyshire, music is cultivated among the working classes to an extent unparalleled in any other part of the kingdom. Every town has its choral society, supported by the sacred works of Handel, and the more modern masters are performed with precision and effect, by a vocal and instrumental orchestra consisting of mechanics and work people: and every village church has its occasional holiday oratorio.

George Hogarth, *Musical History, Biography and Criticism*
(London, 1835), 430

. . . theatres are the exponents of what I may call cultured feeling and cultivated ideas. The attractions are the performance of a play; the attractions are not that you go there to smoke or to drink. When you take the music hall in its inception, it is simply a room attached to a public house; . . . it is a place to which you can go and have your glass, and have a song, and have a short dance, and a good many of the music halls have a sketch.

Evidence of William Fladgate to the *Select Committee on Theatres and Places of Entertainment*, Parliamentary Papers, 1892, Vol. XVIII, 56–7, Qu. 858

THE GROWTH OF MUSIC

In Victorian Britain music was an extremely popular leisure pursuit, ranging as it did from sing-songs around the piano at home or in public houses to grandiose performances in public parks, concert or opera houses, and music halls. Most major public events were marked by brass band or orchestral renditions and in the 1890s, at the peak of provincial musical life, there were perhaps 350–400 societies in existence in the Yorkshire textile districts alone devoted to brass bands, amateur orchestras, choral singing, concertina playing and even handbell ringing.[302] In 1897 an Italian government official on a visit to Britain claimed that there were 'few countries in the world where music is made the object of such enthusiastic worship'.[303] This was in marked contrast to the position half a century earlier when England was widely regarded on the Continent as devoid of musical sensibility. At that time the German visitor Theodor Fontane was certainly not alone when he called music England's 'Achilles's heel' and lamented the lack of appreciation of harmony.

The late Victorian commitment to the cause was confirmed not merely by the broad range of events staged but by the large number of instrument makers in business (particularly those manufacturing pianos) and the enormous sales of sheet music. Sir Arthur Sullivan's 'The Lost Chord' sold half a million copies between 1877 and 1902 and many popular 'hits' could expect to sell 200,000 copies. At the end of the century the onset of the Boer War boosted sales of 'Soldiers of the Queen' to 238,000.[155] Falling production costs helped the process along, and whereas a piano score of Handel's ever-popular *Messiah* had cost 21*s* in the 1830s fifty years later the price had fallen to 1*s*. With the growth of choral singing *Messiah* assumed almost cult proportions, and when in the summer of 1846 the music publisher Alfred Novello advertised 'the cheapest publication ever offered to the public' to be sold in twelve monthly parts, it was a serialized version of the *Messiah* which he selected.[369] Hymn books, too, sold massively during these years.[105]

Not only was music accepted as pleasurable in its own right but it came to be seen by middle-class reformers as having the added merit of moral and spiritual uplift as well as promoting general social cohesion. From the 1840s, declares Dave Russell, 'a scheme of rational recreation that did not include music, was no scheme at all'.[303] Through listening to 'good music' Christian values were promoted and temperance, patriotism and family ties encouraged. Or as John Hope Shaw, a Leeds solicitor, told an audience at a 'people's concert' in the town in 1857, it was 'impossible that all classes of society could mingle with each other week after week, as at these concerts, without feeling their mutual regard for each other strengthened and confirmed'.[303]

Similar sentiments were expressed at the end of the century, at a time when philanthropists were making major efforts to provide concerts in the poorer neighbourhoods of large cities. Among them was the London-based People's Entertainment Society, whose avowed aim was to offer 'high class amusement' in the hope of weaning working-class people from 'lower places of resort', as well as introducing 'an element of brightness into their lives, and to establish a better feeling between the different classes by bringing them into clear contact with each other'.[303] In Manchester this approach brought about the establishment of 'court and alley' concerts in the mid-1890s, and that initiative was taken up in other towns.

The music offered took various forms, from 'scarce-remembered folk songs, through to the . . . set-piece epics performed by . . . choral societies or orchestras', and there was also a widening in the overall scale of activity.[369] Whereas in 1856 there were only about half a dozen brass band contests in England, by 1896 there were over two hundred and forty. The growth and diversification which took place is exemplified by developments at Bradford. In 1840 the main interest was concentrated around a group of musicians who performed primarily sacred music. They 'sustained the local chapel choirs, a choral society and a number of "clubs"'. Concerts were staged periodically in the few available public halls and there were several singing-saloons within public houses in the centre of the town. By 1900 the climate had been transformed, so that the area within five miles of the town centre boasted almost thirty choral societies, some twenty brass bands, an amateur orchestra, six concertina bands, a team of handbell-ringers, two music-halls and a number of venues offering Saturday evening 'popular concerts'. The local theatre had at least one annual visit from a leading opera company and had begun to feature the musical comedies so much a novelty within the late Victorian musical environment.[303]

The West Riding was exceptional in the breadth of its provision, but most communities shared in the expansion to some degree. Thus in Newcastle-upon-Tyne, where in 1840 musical entertainment had consisted of a single piano recital and a series of financially unsuccessful promenade concerts plus one grand subscription concert, thirty years later major progress had been made. Not only was there a large concert hall offering weekly organ recitals and occasional oratorios, but there were at least half a dozen major concerts, as well as a four-week season of orchestral and choral performances arranged by William Rea, the borough organist, plus numerous amateur and charity events.[91]

An important contribution to the creation of choral societies was made by the singing of hymns, first in the Methodist churches, where they formed an important part of the services, and then among Anglicans. Many hymns became so popular that they virtually took on the status of folk-songs. They were sung at public meetings, political rallies and trade union gatherings, as well as at places of worship.[105] They were also included in the school curriculum and were performed by professional singers in concert halls and at recitals. Dame Clara Butt largely gained her reputation as a soloist during the 1890s through her renditions of 'Abide with me'.[105] But, most importantly, choirs formed by the churches to lead the congregation at weekly services became the basis of a wider choral tradition. In Wales, for example, the powerful religious revival of 1859, which boosted the congregations of many chapels, coincided with the introduction of the tonic sol-fa notation, which made the reading of music by non-experts easier, through the substitution of syllables for musical notes. As a result, singing festivals grew in popularity, particularly around Easter and Whitsun, with special sessions for children. In 1895 it was estimated that 280 such festivals were held in the principality by Nonconformist churches alone, and the established Church, too, had its choral events. In Swansea, out of 114 chapels giving evidence to a government commission in the early twentieth century 67 had a choir and 5 of them had 2. Many presented oratorios at Christmas and Easter, particularly in the major industrial centres.[261]

Elsewhere in Britain there were also strong links between church and chapel choirs and the development of a choral tradition. In Sussex the Sacred Harmonic Society of Brighton relied upon organists from local churches to act as its chorus masters, and many members were active church goers. Between 1846 and 1896 the society gave 228 concerts and put on oratorios, with a performance of *Messiah* given each Good Friday, from 1893.[234]

Sometimes the staging of ambitious works by Handel, Haydn and, later in the century, Mendelssohn, involved co-operation between amateur and professional musicians, with orchestras strengthened by experts brought in from elsewhere. Thus when Lancaster's new concert hall was opened in 1843 a selection from Handel's

Messiah was featured. Most of the leading families of the town and neighbourhood attended and one of the principal vocalists was a Miss Robinson from the Royal Academy. The sixty-strong choir came mainly from the Lancaster Choral Society, but the orchestra of thirty included members of the Lancaster, Liverpool, Preston and Manchester Gentlemen's Concerts.[96] Likewise at Brighton, where the celebrated Czech pianist Kuhe organized an annual festival between 1869 and 1883, leading composers were persuaded to attend. Gounod and Sullivan were among those who conducted their own works, although most of the performers were local.[234]

The upsurge of interest in choral singing encouraged a growth of competitive festivals, too, including the National Eisteddfod in Wales, where great prestige was gained by the victors. During the second half of the nineteenth century a multitude of *eisteddfodau* flourished in the principality. Their prime aim was to promote Welsh culture, language and literature, but music became increasingly important. The same was true of the national festival which began to be held alternately in north and south Wales from the 1860s. Choirs of several hundred voices, often drawn from the new industrial areas, competed not only within Wales but at festivals further afield, including the Crystal Palace in London, where in 1872 a choir of 456 members from south Wales won the trophy.

At local level the *eisteddfodau* encouraged a spirit of rivalry as well as communal pride. At a festival held in Bridgend at Easter 1872 the prize of £12 and a 'bardic chair' were awarded to a choir from Mountain Ash. On their return to their home community they were met by thousands of people and the choir leader was carried shoulder high through the streets, seated on the bardic chair. He was accompanied by the choristers, who sang 'See the Conquering Hero Comes'. According to the *Western Mail*, such a crowd of people had not been witnessed in the town since the last general election! A music festival held around the same time at Swansea likewise aroused much interest. 'It is needless to say that the gathering was large and tempestuous, as all Welsh musical gatherings are,' observed the *Western Mail*, adding that the hall was 'literally crammed to semi-suffocation'.

Choral performances became a popular feature of cultural life in the 1840s and 1850s, at a time when leisure opportunities were increasing. Equally there was a desire to ensure that they were conducted with due propriety. In 1872 the Huddersfield Choral Society rules included provisions to exclude the politically unorthodox: 'No person shall be a member of this society, who frequents the "Hall of Science" or any of the "Socialist Meetings", nor shall the Librarian be allowed to lend any copies of music (knowingly) belonging to this society, to any Socialist, upon a pain of expulsion'.[369]

Prestigious bodies like the Huddersfield and the Leeds Philharmonic drew their membership from across the class divides, including skilled workers and professional and business people. Competition to enter could be fierce. By the 1890s the élite Bradford Festival Choral Society was regularly turning down half of those who applied to join. Once a member, the singer had to be prepared for one lengthy rehearsal each week, and that increased if a concert or competition were looming.[303]

Even among humbler singers commitment could be considerable. Moses Heap, a cotton spinner from Rossendale, took his first singing lessons at the end of the 1830s when he was fifteen and was working over seventy hours a week in a mill. He and

Caernarfon orchestra taking part in the Eisteddfod *at Blaenau Ffestiniog, 1898. (Museum of Welsh Life, St Fagans, Cardiff)*

forty others attended a class in the tiny hamlet of Goodshaw. In addition he visited a nearby farmhouse in order to hear 'two pianos played at the same time and also one or two violins'. According to Heap, so intense was the love of Rossendale people for music-making that many houses 'were both workshops and music shops', in which hand-loom weavers sang as they laboured. He claimed to know one man who was so determined to give himself more time for music that he 'contrived to couple four looms together with strings, levers and pulleys so that he could produce four pieces of cloth at one time'. He also made a cello which he played in chapel on Sundays.[82]

For a few gifted performers involvement with a musical society offered a means of social advancement. Charles Knowles, a bookbinder who sang with the Leeds Philharmonic Society in the 1890s, eventually became an established opera singer in London, while Samuel Midgley, a miner's son from Bierley near Bradford, rose to become one of the most highly respected and prosperous music teachers in the town.[302]

The widespread interest in choral music found expression in the visits of travelling opera companies, especially to the north of England. During the early Victorian years, at a time when the theatre was held in low esteem, opera still commanded upper- and middle-class support, with two Italian opera companies performing in London by the end of the 1840s. In 1847 the Covent Garden Theatre was renamed the Royal Italian Opera, although the designation 'Italian' referred to the fact that performances were in that language rather than to the repertoire. This remained the case until 1884 when the Royal Italian was wound up. When regular

A fashionable audience enjoying a performance at the Royal Opera House, Covent Garden, c. 1900. (The author)

opera seasons were revived at Covent Garden four years later the policy of singing everything in Italian was abandoned: in future, works were to be performed in their original language. Meanwhile critics noted that for some of those attending, the main point of interest was not the ability of the singers or the merits of the work performed but the social position and fashionable attire of the audience.

In the provinces theatre managers sometimes put on operas to attract a more prestigious and well-to-do clientele. Touring companies made visits to various industrial towns from the 1840s and 1850s, with three companies going to Sheffield alone in 1856. At Newcastle-upon-Tyne, too, the manager of the Theatre Royal, in a quest for status, engaged London performers to stage ballet and grand opera in English, as well as arranging visits from the London-based Italian opera companies. In 1848 the famous Jenny Lind performed and two years later Mme Charton's French Opera Troupe came to the town. As an added incentive special party rates were offered to schools and large families anxious to improve their French.[91]

By the end of the century more than a dozen touring opera companies were on the road, the best-known of them being the Carl Rosa. This was set up by a German violinist, whose company performed frequently at Drury Lane in London. After his death in 1889 it became almost entirely a touring company, adding 'Royal' to its title after a recital at Balmoral in 1893.

There is little doubt about the popularity of these performances. Henry Coward, who became the conductor of at least five choirs in Yorkshire, recalled how as an apprentice cutler he visited the opera regularly in Sheffield during the 1860s: 'innumerable sixpences went into the pay-box of the local theatres when opera companies visited the town'.[303] Some of the smaller troupes appeared in quite humble venues, like J.W. Turner's English Opera Company which performed for three consecutive nights in 1890 in the Yorkshire textile centre of Yeadon. Even if allowance were made for the attendance of the major mill-owning families in the area, as Dave Russell comments, 'this would not have been economically viable without patronage from the "cheaper seats"'.[303] Through such companies opera became an important element in local culture. Neville Cardus, the illegitimate son of a Manchester laundress, spent his childhood in relative poverty. But he remembered his mother and aunt singing him to sleep with extracts from *Norma*, 'which is a fact significant of much of the general musical background of the period'.[303] Most of the popular operas were British and Italian, including the *Bohemian Girl*, *Il Trovatore* and, from the mid-1890s, Mascagni's *Cavalleria Rusticana*. From the middle of the century there was also an upsurge of interest in French and German works, with operas by Gounod and Meyerbeer becoming important features of the Covent Garden seasons. In 1852, out of a total of sixty-eight performances by the Royal Italian Opera Company, Meyerbeer's work occupied twenty-three, compared to Donizetti's sixteen.

In London Richard Wagner's early works were being performed by the 1870s, and during the next decade, as John Pemble comments, 'the cult of the Wagnerian music-drama' became established. During the 1898 season at Covent Garden thirty-two of the sixty-five performances were works by Wagner. Among the enthusiasts for this new trend was Jeannette Marshall. As a girl she had sometimes attended two concerts a day and in her thirties she took an interest in Berlioz, Brahms, Grieg and Wagner. After attending a concert of the latter's music in 1886 she wrote in her diary: 'I am a Wagnerian to the backbone.' Four years earlier, along with her parents and a sister she had gone to the *Ring* at Covent Garden, and in August 1889 they went to Bayreuth as part of a continental tour. Both the *Meistersinger* and *Parsifal* made a great impression, with Jeannette filling more than two pages of her diary with an account of *Parsifal*.[312]

Chamber music continued to appeal primarily to upper- and middle-class audiences, although on a broader basis there was an increasing emergence of professional orchestras. This was reflected in the growing number of musicians and music teachers in the population. According to the census returns they had increased from 11,200 in 1851 to 39,300 in 1901 in England and Wales alone.[155] In 1893 there were estimated to be around fifty concerts a week during the London Season and the Crystal Palace company, based in a South London suburb, was able to cover the costs of a full symphony orchestra by offering cheap seats which filled its vast arena. The Crystal Palace, with its triennial Handel festivals from 1857 and its pioneering Saturday concerts, played a major role in creating a Victorian orchestral tradition from the mid-1850s.[155]

In the provinces the growth of the railway network enabled concerts to be given by visiting soloists or by groups of musicians. However, there was a need to build up audiences, and this was only achieved in any substantial measure in Manchester and Liverpool. Both cities had 'prosperous middle-class communities and large halls with excellent acoustics' which had opened around the middle of the century.[155] Both also had a considerable number of German residents whose inherent love of music provided a core of regular concert-goers. In Manchester the moving spirit was the German-born Charles Hallé. He began modestly with a series of chamber-music concerts and with support provided by lady pupils and audiences drawn from the 'German colony'. Initially the concerts attracted sixty-seven subscribers but the list had trebled within a year. However, the most important boost to Manchester's orchestral development came in 1857 when the committee arranging the major Art Treasures Exhibition to be held in the city decided to enhance its general attraction by providing a daily performance of music, under the direction of Hallé. A large, well-balanced orchestra was recruited and symphonies by the finest classical composers were performed before large audiences. Around 1.5 million people attended the exhibition and according to Hallé it was the first time that many of them had heard a symphony. As the weeks passed interest grew and when the exhibition ended, rather than disband his new orchestra he moved into the city's Free Trade Hall.[305] There he began to give weekly public concerts, with tickets offered at 1s and 2s 6d. Support quickly grew and by 1860 the *Musical World* could claim that they had become 'the vogue with all classes, from the rich merchant and manufacturer to the middle-class tradesman and bourgeois . . . to the respectable and thrifty, albeit humbler, artisans'.[155] Hallé's son, writing in 1896, recalled the large working-class contingent who came, standing 'packed together in great discomfort as I have often seen them', listening 'for hours, and evidently with much appreciation' to his father's concerts.[303]

In Liverpool progress was slower and a greater degree of class rigidity survived. The city's Philharmonic Society carefully segregated its audiences, so that members of the general public were allowed access to the gallery only, where there was limited seating. Membership of the society was also restricted to those from a 'gentlemanly' background, and the rule governing this was frequently repeated in its programmes.[155]

While these developments were taking place within the choral and orchestral spheres, an equally significant innovation was occurring with the growth of the brass band movement. That applied particularly from the 1850s, with the adoption of the new saxhorns, and it was encouraged by employers, who saw it as an 'improving' pastime. However, like many 'sponsored' pleasures it was soon taken over by the men themselves. The movement spread rapidly and by 1887 there were reckoned to be forty thousand brass bands throughout the country, with one instrument maker alone having ten thousand on his books. The bands came from every conceivable institution in working-class life, including the workplace, the trade union, the church, the Sunday school, the co-operative society, the temperance organization and political bodies. As James Walvin notes, some of the new evangelical societies that sought to penetrate into working-class communities, like the Salvation Army, the Band of Hope, and the Boys' Brigade, 'often did so through the brass band. It was no accident that the sound of brass band music could be guaranteed to raise interest and support whenever it struck up.'[369]

The advantages of brass band instruments lay in the fact that they were relatively easy to master, not too expensive (with hire purchase agreements arranged between manufacturers and bands in some cases), and were ideal for playing out of doors, thereby overcoming the problem of securing suitable halls. Many groups started with second-hand instruments, and when Batley Old Band won a prize at the prestigious Belle Vue competition in 1896 it was said that the men had had to purchase a pound of soap beforehand so they could stop up places in their instruments that were 'losing wind'. One veteran claimed to have begun his musical career by practising upon a tenor horn so patched with string and sticking-plaster that it was in danger of falling to pieces in his hands. His parents had banished him to a lonely spot, well out of hearing, to carry out his practices.[304]

A major boost to the whole movement was given by the holding of competitions, each of which attracted crowds of supporters. For example, at a contest held in Bacup during August 1868 local factories were closed for the morning and special trains brought in hundreds of visitors to the town. 'Promptly at one o'clock to the cheers of 10,000 followers, the eight competing bands paraded up Market Street to the contest ground overlooking the town. There the instruments to be given as prizes were suspended from a cross beam and were much admired.'[82] Throughout the afternoon, until seven in the evening, the bands played selections from well-known operas, after which individual players competed for a four-valve euphonium, a tenor horn and a soprano cornet. The winning band, from Matlock, received £30 and a bass drum worth £14 14s. They ended the contest 'by playing their prize air amidst great cheering'.[82]

On occasion ill-feeling arose when decisions regarded as unfair were made or when supporters believed the judges had failed to recognize a particular band's artistic excellence. At a Sheffield contest in 1860 fights broke out between band members, and at Ilkley at the end of the 1890s a judge was thrown into a stream after an especially unpopular decision.[303] Fortunately such clashes were relatively rare.

Individual performers could play a major part in stimulating support for brass bands. One such pioneer was George Ellis in the Blackburn area. Although trained as a violinist, he became an enthusiastic supporter of the bands and in 1856 he was the leader of thirteen different ones in that district.[406]

The contests held at Belle Vue in Manchester from 1853 were the main focus of competitive interest. At the initial competition the first prize was won by Mossley Temperance Band and it was a sign of how seriously such events were taken that as competitions drew near the Mossley bandsmen would rise at 4 a.m. each morning in order to snatch an hour or two at rehearsal before they began their normal day's work.[82] By the 1860s support for 'banding' had become so strong that when Bacup Old Band competed at Belle Vue in 1864 the whole town was involved. According to the band's historian, for days beforehand the outcome of the competition was virtually the sole topic of conversation. 'The rehearsal in the yard of Broadclough Mill on the Sunday before the contest was attended by thousands. On the morning of the contest special excursion trains were run from Bacup.'[82] When the band's board was eventually hoisted as the winner of the prize, supporters were 'frantic with joy and could not tell how to express their feelings. It was after midnight when the band reached Bacup where the whole of the inhabitants were out waiting their arrival.' They marched along the road playing the rousing tune *John Brown's Body*, while the crowd, numbering thousands, joined in. The following year the band, backed by an even larger contingent of supporters, again won the Belle Vue championship. Meanwhile their 1864 victory had inspired six enthusiasts from the nearby village of Weir to form their own band. The first practice was held in a bedroom, with a bedstead serving as the bandstand.[82]

With the growth in popularity of the Belle Vue contests the crowds of supporters attending grew bigger. In 1888 no fewer than fifty excursion trains were reported to have brought in people from all over the north of England. Thirty-five bands began playing the test piece at 1 p.m.; it was a selection from Richard Wagner's *Flying Dutchman*.[304]

On a wider front the bands entertained visitors in public parks and performed at the tea parties of friendly societies and temperance organizations. They gave added gaiety to charity events, and 'the marches played . . . at union demonstrations and the hymns thundered at strike meetings must have given hope and inspiration'.[303]

By the 1890s well over two hundred brass band festivals were held throughout the country, and although the movement's main focus remained the Midlands and the north of England some support grew up in the southern counties. In 1900 the Crystal Palace brass band festival attracted twenty-nine bands; three years later one hundred and seventeen took part.[369]

Bands had their own publications, such as *Wright and Round's Brass Band News*, established in 1886, and *The British Bandsman*, inaugurated a year later. Outfitters, too, were 'kept busy designing and making the splendid uniforms which became so

A band concert in Hyde Park, c. *1900.* (*The author*)

important a part of a brass band occasion'. Band music began to find its own composers and, as James Walvin comments, 'a movement which had such plebeian roots had, by the early years of the twentieth century, become respectable, international, and attractive to all classes'.[369] Bands were a regular part of entertainments offered at the seaside, too, playing in parks, on piers and in pavilions and winter gardens.

THE MUSIC HALL

If many of the musical activities considered so far owed their inspiration to the religious or moral impulses present in much of Victorian society, the other popular phenomenon of the period – the music hall – had its origins in a far less elevated sphere. Music halls sprang, in the main, from the singing saloons attached to public houses and from the entertainments provided by pleasure gardens, saloon theatres (where the programmes normally comprised a mixture of opera, drama, farce and music), and the penny gaffs, or cheap theatres, that flourished in the poorer areas of major towns during the first half of the Victorian period. The latter were particularly popular among adolescents and, as such, were condemned as contaminators of the young. In 1858 James Grant castigated them as 'no better than so many nurseries for juvenile thieves'. He commented on the extreme youth of the audiences, most of them being between eight and sixteen years, and the fact that there were between eighty and a hundred gaffs in London alone, with an average attendance of 150 at each performance, and sometimes as many as nine houses a night.[137] Blanchard Jerrold, who visited one in the early 1870s, considered it a place where 'juvenile Poverty meets juvenile Crime'. After traversing narrow passages 'blocked by sharp-eyed young thieves', he and a companion entered the auditorium. Inside was a platform with a bedaubed proscenium that served as the stage, and watching the show were 'rows of brazen young faces . . . terrible to look upon'. On stage a trio sang a suggestive ditty, complete with 'searing words', mimes, gestures and 'hinted indecencies' which the young audience relished. 'The boys and girls nod to each other, and laugh aloud: and the comic ruffian in the tall hat has nothing to teach them.'[56]

When the gaffs were eventually superseded by music-hall entertainment their premises were turned to other uses, including the display of stereoscopic machines. These gave an illusion of pictures in three dimensions and were adapted to erotic purposes. Shops in working-class areas like Southwark were also gutted to provide rows of displays, offering an early form of moving picture. Most consisted of photographs of women undressing, showing their underclothing, sitting in suggestive poses and so forth. On many of the machines a placard would be placed with such titillating titles as 'How shocking!' and 'Naughty! Naughty!'. As Donald Thomas points out, some of the moving images may have been innocent, but most of them were not.

Nevertheless it was not so much from the penny gaffs as from singing rooms attached to public houses that music hall sprang during the 1830s and 1840s. One prototype was the Star at Bolton, which opened in 1832 in connection with the Millstone Inn. A few years later it moved to more extensive premises, where a menagerie, museum, photographic salon and promenade were established as well as the concert hall itself. Professional singers performed, together with clowns and acrobats, and there were spectacular displays, such as 'an illuminated tableau of the Great Fire of London', or 'Ethiopian Entertainments, in which the sports and pastimes of the coloured race are delineated in a masterly and chaste manner'.[274] By the early 1850s the Star could hold over a thousand people and at weekends it would be crowded out, with customers coming in from the surrounding towns and villages.

Other halls developed along similar lines, including the Canterbury which was opened in Lambeth by Charles Morton during the 1840s. It was probably the first of its kind in London and initially held about a hundred people, with entertainment offered between 7 p.m. and midnight. In 1851 a new hall was built at the rear of the premises, to accommodate four or five hundred people and this was licensed as a concert room. The entertainment included glees, madrigals, choruses, songs and comic renditions under the direction of a chairman-compère. Morton's aim was to create a respectable image, divorced from the seediness of the public house. He claimed that his audience included tradesmen, mechanics and their wives and children. However, evidence from music halls elsewhere suggests that, in practice, a large number of those attending were likely to be young people, particularly young men. A small admission charge was made, and as the Canterbury's reputation grew it became crowded every night. On the most popular evenings – Mondays and Saturdays – hundreds of people would wait at the doors for it to open, so that the street outside would be almost blocked. In 1854 yet another hall was opened, this time able to hold around 1,500 people. In order to promote a respectable 'educational' reputation, Morton provided a library, reading room and picture gallery as well.[85] He and the other leading music hall proprietors who appeared in his wake engaged first-class vocalists to whom they paid high wages. In these early days audiences would be seated at tables and chairs at right-angles to the stage, where they could enjoy drink, food and a smoke as well as the performances. Pease pudding, a dozen oysters with bread and butter (for 1s), and solid helpings of steak and kidney pie with baked potatoes were said to be favourite dishes among music-hall patrons.[151]

In 1861 Morton opened the first purpose-built music hall in London, the Oxford, with fixed seating facing the stage. He also introduced the turns system, which allowed him to fill his bill with artists already working at the Canterbury. They moved by cab between the two venues in Lambeth and Oxford Street. Soon it became customary for artists to do four or five turns a night in different halls. Hence when the twelve-year-old Vesta Tilley made her London debut as a male impersonator in 1875, she performed nightly at the Canterbury in Lambeth, Lusby's in Mile End, and the Marylebone, with wild dashes by hired brougham in between. She earned £3 a week at each and was by then virtually the family breadwinner. Vesta spent about three months in London every year, before touring provincial halls for a further six months and filling the remaining three months with engagements as a principal boy in pantomime.[238] Pantomime was recommended for young performers as a way of teaching them 'to shake hands with the audience', as one experienced stage-manager put it.[210]

Still more demanding was the nightly itinerary of the 'Great' MacDermott. MacDermott, a man of heavy build and loud voice who had once been a bricklayer, specialized in patriotic songs, including 'We Don't Want to Fight' in 1878, which added the word 'jingo' to the English language. The opening lines of its chorus ran:

> We don't want to fight, but by Jingo if we do
> We've got the ships, we've got the men, and got the money too . . .[308]

Subsequently a parody of the song by Herbert Campbell also won popularity in the music hall, beginning

> I don't want to fight, I'll be slaughtered if I do!
> I'll change my togs and sell my kit and pop my rifle too!

It exemplified what Hugh Cunningham has called the 'juxtaposition of heroism and comic cowardice' which was a well-established convention in popular entertainment.[138] Meanwhile the 'Great' MacDermott was pursuing his busy 1878 routine, appearing first at the Royal Aquarium at 8.15 p.m., followed by the Metropolitan at 9.10, the London Pavilion at 10, and Collins's at 10.50 p.m.[169]

By 1866 there were around thirty-three major music halls in London and that had increased to thirty-nine by the early 1890s, with about three hundred recognized halls in the United Kingdom as a whole at the later date. This number excludes the many public houses, coffee taverns, town halls, parish halls and assembly rooms in the capital and elsewhere which were also licensed for music or music and dancing.[22] By the turn of the century every major town had one or more music hall: Middlesbrough, with a population of 100,000, had ten while Birmingham had seven large halls with a seating capacity of over 16,500.[127] During the 1860s the number of premises outside London more than doubled, with the larger establishments in the Midlands and the north rivalling those in the capital in both size and popularity. By the end of the century music-hall architecture had also become increasingly exotic, featuring Moorish and Indian designs.[298] For example, the Empire Palace in Nottingham had pagoda domes with 'grinning idols representing Krishna at both sides of the stage and four vast elephant heads in gilt in each corner of the auditorium'. It was a strikingly incongruous setting for some of the turns. The famous 'cockney' star Albert Chevalier commented ruefully on the problem of singing 'Old Kent Road' in 'a scene representing a Moorish palace, or the Grand Staircase of a baronial hall'.[303] But for the audience, the lavish decor added to the glamour of their evening out.

In London one of the most spectacular of the early music halls was the Alhambra in Leicester Square. Converted from the former Panopticon of Science and Art, it opened in 1860 as a 3,500-capacity entertainment centre. Visitors were impressed by the scale of its productions and the wide range of its facilities. Although it retained the patronage of a solid core of working-class Londoners, it benefited increasingly from the capital's tourist trade and from the support of the more raffish young men-about-town.[85]

Music-hall proprietors in fact became increasingly conscious of the importance of rail connections in widening their potential audiences. From time to time Charles Morton tried to boost numbers at the Canterbury by including in his advertisements details of transport connections with central London.[86] To attract additional visitors some halls began to offer twice-nightly performances, an initiative facilitated by the introduction of fixed seating and programmes.

Another attraction was the wide variety of turns featured and the limited time allotted to each, so that there was always something new to anticipate. Meanwhile, audiences, particularly the younger people in the gallery, were ready to make their dissatisfaction clear to the performers. Charles Coborn complained of certain halls in Liverpool where 'the customers were as rough as the furniture'. Even well-known performers were not immune. Hostile Glaswegians drove the 'Great Vance' from the stage on one occasion by hurling handfuls of rivets at him.[85] But those who pleased the audience would be given generous applause and repeated encores. Often boys in the gallery would shout out the songs they wished to hear, and many performers would oblige. It was claimed that stars like Bessie Bellwood, who had once worked as a rabbit-skinner in London, and the incomparable Marie Lloyd owed a good deal of their popularity to their responsiveness and their skill in holding, and winning, cockney rhyming-slang matches with the gallery.[127]

Music-hall songs often reflected the social preoccupations of the day and in some cases, as in Newcastle-upon-Tyne, there was a genuine regional input. The city's famous Balmbra's music hall, set up in about 1848, for a long time relied on a varied bill which included local talent. Song writers and singers would express the humour and pathos of life around them. Among them was the former miner Geordie Ridley, who was the author of the well-known *Blaydon Races*.[91] But by the 1860s, as the major names from London music halls came north, this regional contribution declined in Newcastle and elsewhere, as the entertainment offered became increasingly 'national' in its content.

Nevertheless, it has been argued that music hall continued to appeal to the working and lower middle classes, its principal patrons, because it was 'both escapist *and yet* strongly rooted in the realities of . . . life'.[217] Marriage was presented as a comic disaster, while the 'problem of the lodger, the landlord and the pawnbroker shop' were other staple themes. Nor was the issue of destitution in old age evaded. 'The whole point' of Albert Chevalier's famous song 'My Old Dutch' was that it was sung in front of a 'back drop representing the workhouse with its separate entrances for men and women'.[217]

But some recent commentators have sounded a more sceptical note, pointing out that most of the songs were written by lower middle-class hacks who were poorly paid and followed recognized formulae in producing their lyrics.[127] Often they were instruments for propaganda rather than true reflections of the audience's emotions. Even the difficulties of rent day, food adulteration or the mother-in-law were dealt with in a way that transformed them into topics of humour rather than fear.[308] That distortion may have helped working people to come to terms with the problems of their lives, but when translated to the political sphere it could be less benign. That applied particularly around the time of the Boer War, when imperialistic sentiment was strong. Even in the late 1880s Vesta Tilley could observe, 'Nowadays, nothing goes down better than a good patriotic song.'[217] But during the Boer War many of the lyrics expressed a belief that 'combat duty could redeem even the most unregenerate lounge lizard or derelict'. In Vesta Tilley's West End hit, her man-about-town, Burlington Bertie (introduced in 1900), was portrayed in the first two verses as a philandering waster. But in verse three he was rehabilitated:

*Performers waiting nervously to go on stage at the Royal Music Hall in London, c. 1900.
(The author)*

When there are symptoms of warlike alarms,
And Burlington Bertie sees brothers in arms,
Altho' absent-minded he does not forget
That Englishmen always must pay off a debt.
He drops all his pleasure, the polo, the hunt,
And just like the rest he is off to the front;
Altho' he's a Johnny, he fights in the ruck,
He's wealthy and foolish, but if you want pluck . . .
He'll fight and he'll die like an Englishman,
Forgive all his folly we can.[308]

By the end of the Victorian era most music-hall managers were anxious to stress their patriotic and respectable credentials. Already in the 1880s the serving of alcohol had been banished from the auditorium to bars at the side, while encores were restricted, chorus singing was discouraged and uniformed commissionaires were employed to police the auditorium and ensure good behaviour.[85] Will Thorne claimed that proprietors in Birmingham refused to admit any man not wearing a collar, while the 'Order and Decorum which became the cliché of every music hall advertisement' were so strictly applied in Collins's Music Hall in Islington that it was known locally as 'the Chapel'.[85] Artists were strongly discouraged from using suggestive material, and typical of many was the appeal issued by the proprietor of the Middlesex Music Hall in Drury Lane in the early 1890s, asking members of the public to ensure that the entertainment offered was 'at all times absolutely free from any objectionable features'. Customers were invited to inform him 'of any suggestive or offensive word or action upon the stage that may have escaped the notice of the management'.[22] Elsewhere performers were warned that if they expressed vulgar words or actions on stage they would be dismissed instantly and would forfeit any salary owing to them for that week.[85]

Such efforts did not allay the fears of critics. The halls were condemned for selling strong drink, for the inanity of many of their songs and the extravagant wages paid to performers, which might encourage 'prodigality in the audience'. Sexual innuendoes were considered likely to 'corrupt working-class girls and make them easy prey for prowling roués', although evidence suggests that, in practice, most girls visited the halls with a group of friends of their own sex.[86] Some commentators labelled music halls 'anterooms to the brothels',[85] while to the Salvation Army they were 'Fortresses of Beelzebub'.[127] In London in 1889 promenades were forbidden in new music halls because they were thought to provide meeting points for prostitutes and their clients, and a year later the London County Council formed a committee of 'moral watchdogs' to examine performances and observe the conduct of the women. As it possessed power to revoke licences, the new body encouraged a 'voluntary' destruction of promenades at many older halls, and the move even spread to the provinces. Bradford and Leeds music halls lost their promenades in 1896.[127]

Of particular concern to moralists was the arrival of a new audience of 'sporting aristocrats' (including the Prince of Wales), Guards officers and medical and law students, as well as visitors from out of town who patronized certain of the halls in the West End. Although this audience began to appear in the 1860s its importance grew during the 1880s, as a number of lavish new West End premises were opened. Among these were the Empire, which earned a reputation for upper-class rowdyism and superior-grade prostitution, the Trocadero, the Tivoli and the Palace. In 1894 Mrs Ormiston Chant of the Social Purity League challenged the Empire's licence and with support from the Progressive and Labour Parties on the London County Council she succeeded in getting a screen erected between the auditorium and the bars, thereby cutting off the audience from the sale of drink and the solicitation of prostitutes who promenaded along the gallery looking for clients. But the young 'swells' who patronized the Empire objected strongly to this moral censorship. On the Saturday following the erection of the screen two or three hundred of them smashed it down with their walking sticks and paraded around Leicester Square brandishing its fragments. Their leader was Winston Churchill, then a young Sandhurst cadet.[217]

Yet attitudes were changing. Although strong drink continued to be sold, there must have been many like the young Joseph Stamper, who attended 'The People's Palace' music hall in St Helens with his father in the 1890s. During the intervals

*Dan Leno appearing as the Dame in the
pantomime* Mother Goose. *(The author)*

those who did not want alcohol could make purchases from youths circulating
with big, white wicker-baskets containing other refreshments: 'Eccles cakes full of
currants were one penny or a halfpenny according to size; pop was one penny a
bottle; and oranges were three a penny . . . Many a time, . . . when I smell an
orange, I am back in the People's Palace, a small boy seated next to father, sucking
an orange while he sipped his bottle of pop.'[326]

Still more significant was the intervention of the large Moss-Stoll syndicate, which
purchased a number of working-class halls with the aim of replacing their coarseness
and vulgarity with 'the gentility and decorum of the Palace of Variety', and thereby
extending their commercial success.[217] Respectability became the watchword.

It was from the mid-eighties that some of the greatest music-hall performers
came to the fore – Dan Leno, Marie Lloyd, Little Tich and many others. Most
sprang from humble backgrounds. Dan Leno, whose parents were on the stage,
started his theatrical career in the mid-1860s, aged three, as an acrobat. At five he
and his brother made their debut at a north London music hall as a dancing duo.
The stage on which they performed was ringed with mirrors and in their
excitement to get off at the end of their act, the two little boys ran into the
mirrors, knocking themselves down in the process. This pleased the audience,
who thought it was part of the show. They applauded so loudly that 'we had to go
and do it again'.[62] Dan Leno was destined to become one of the best known of the
music-hall stars and was a leading light in Christmas pantomimes, where he

played the dame.[391] Another, even more famous performer was Marie Lloyd. She saw the music hall as a rejection of Victorian moralizing, for all the attempts of proprietors to achieve respectability. In 1897 Marie told her critics bluntly:

> You take the pit on a Saturday night or a Bank Holiday. You don't suppose they want Sunday school stuff do you? They want lively stuff with music they can learn quickly. Why, if I was to try and sing highly moral songs they would fire ginger beer bottles and beer mugs at me. They don't pay their sixpences and shillings at a Music Hall to hear the Salvation Army.[217]

At the end of the Victorian era some of the halls, in their ceaseless quest for novelty, began to offer cinematograph performances as part of the programme. In 1896 the first moving picture was shown at the Empire, Leicester Square, and in March 1900, in the sixth month of the Boer War, the last act in the Alhambra's variety show at Brighton was advertised as 'the Edison-Thomas Royal Vitascope with an extensive selection of subjects connected with the present crisis, including Embarkation of the Troops . . . and the arrival of Lord Roberts at Cape Town'.[234] Ironically in taking this initiative the music halls were encouraging a rival which, in the twentieth century, was to play a major part in their downfall.

THEATRES AND PUBLIC ENTERTAINMENTS

The rise of the music hall in the second half of the nineteenth century was accompanied by an equally striking change in the status and reputation of the theatre itself. In the early Victorian years it was viewed with distaste by many upper- and middle-class people as a source of low morality and bohemian life styles. Increasingly its audiences were working class and in the 1840s the behaviour of some of them was disgraceful. Charles Dickens described an occasion in 1844 at the Sadler's Wells Theatre when conduct was 'ruffianly'. He called the proceedings 'a bear-garden, resounding with foul language, oaths, cat-calls, shrieks, yells, blasphemy, obscenity . . . Fights took place anywhere at any period of the performance.'[151] The presence of prostitutes was a further dubious aspect, while the uncomfortable seating, the lack of ventilation and the pervasive smell of oranges were other deterrents to well-to-do families. In addition there was widespread condemnation of the violent melodramas that were often staged. As late as 1866 a witness to the Select Committee on Theatrical Licences and Regulations agreed that the plays most popular among the lower orders were those 'founded on burglaries and robberies'.[102] The quality of acting was often poor, the main recommendation being a loud voice, and blood-curdling performances with realistic scenery and effects were the most popular. The importance of scenery in the early days is indicated by the fact that the names of scenic artists were often given on playbills. 'A blazing house that was seen to be ablaze was the reality sought after; a well-staged court scene with all the authentic legal trappings was irresistible.'[151]

Some theatre proprietors sought to counter this raffish image by emphasizing the respectability of their premises. In Lancaster the Theatre Royal was for a time renamed the Temperance Hall and when a 'Theatre of Arts' ran there for almost three weeks in February 1841, performances were advertised as 'totally different from those of a dramatic character'. Any whose religious scruples prevented their attending 'the regular drama' were encouraged to attend the new show, which was 'purely mechanical, and where nothing is introduced that can possibly offend the ear or eye of the most fastidious, but where nature, in the most perfect and interesting manner, is depicted in miniature'.[96] On display were mechanical models with views of Paris, Venice and the city and bay of Naples, including an eruption of Vesuvius, and a storm at sea.

Even in these years, however, there were exceptions to the low reputation of the stage to be found in the performances of the 'Eminent Tragedian', William Charles Macready, and of Charles Kean. The latter's seasons of 'Shakespeare, gentlemanly melodrama and refined comedy at the Princess's Theatre' during the 1850s not only won middle-class support but were boosted by the regular attendance of the queen. Her patronage of Kean also extended to giving him supervision of court theatricals at Windsor Castle.[102]

Yet these actors themselves had doubts about their calling. In 1840 Macready noted in his diary that he had tried to dissuade one aspiring actor 'from following so unprofitable and demoralizing a calling, and told him I had rather see one of my children dead than on the stage. He left me, very grateful for my advice.'[210] More than a quarter of a century later Charles Kean was anxious to safeguard his reputation, and income, by maintaining high prices for the seats at the theatres where he appeared. In May 1867 he wrote to the lessee of the Theatre Royal, Birmingham, who was arranging a tour of the Midlands for him, expressing concern about charging policy at a Nottingham theatre:

> Had I been aware that there would have been any opposition to the usual scale at which I play elsewhere, & more especially considering it will be my 'farewell', I would not have engaged to visit that city at all.
>
> I never have acted *successful* engagements anywhere to low prices . . . The lowest prices I will play to in Nottingham are 4s. Dress [Boxes], 2s. 6d. Upper [Circle?], Pit 1s. 6d., Gallery 1s.[210]

This hierarchical division of the auditorium into boxes, pit and gallery was reflected in the provision of separate entrances for each section of the house, so that box holders did not have to mix with lesser mortals who were heading for the cheaper seats.

Despite improvements in the status of the theatre during the second half of the nineteenth century, even in the early 1890s the famous actor-manager Henry Irving was vehemently opposed to music halls being allowed to stage plays. He gave as one of his reasons the belief that this would undermine the efforts made to achieve respectability within his profession:

> To-day the theatre holds a place in the esteem of all classes of the community . . .
> To give to places other than theatres . . . the right to perform stage plays would be a destructive innovation to stage art, unless proper theatre conditions be maintained. For we must not overlook the fact that the class of places whence

emanates the desire for the extension is that of the music hall, which is really a tavern which has obtained licences for music and dancing.[22]

By this date Irving's management of the Lyceum was regarded as 'so morally estimable that it was extensively patronised by the socially fearful and by clergymen'.[102] The award of a knighthood to him in 1895, the first to be received by an actor, was clear recognition of his contribution towards making the theatre acceptable to men and women who, a few years earlier, would have been 'shocked at the thought of being seen' in such a place.[102]

At the beginning of the Victorian era venues ranged from the London 'patent' theatres (Covent Garden, Drury Lane and the Haymarket), which alone were allowed to stage 'legitimate drama', and the Theatres Royal in leading provincial towns, to less prestigious premises where stock companies of varying quality were based, perhaps interspersing their appearances with tours around a local circuit. At the bottom of the scale were bands of travelling players. Not until 1843 was the monopoly of the patent theatres broken by Act of Parliament, with regard to the performance of farce, tragedy and comedy. Henceforward these could be staged legally in any licensed theatre. Under the previous dispensation, dramatic excerpts in non-patent premises had had to be interspersed with music, dancing and similar diversions.[102] Melodrama itself acquired its name because music accompanied its more dramatic moments.

Some of the travelling companies were of low calibre, perhaps performing in temporary buildings and with few props. But others offered audiences in small towns their sole opportunity to enjoy the theatre. One such was Henry Jackman's touring company which for a few weeks each spring staged a season of plays in Banbury. From 1805 until 1863 it travelled between various towns in a circuit stretching from the northern edges of London to Ludlow in Shropshire and Market Harborough in Leicestershire. The response of its audiences was variable. In 1838 one local newspaper lamented that this 'company of comedians have again come to waste their sweetness on the desert air of Banbury', with few watching their performances. But a decade later the respectable way in which Jackman conducted proceedings was praised. As was usual in those days performances were double or triple bills, so as to appeal to the widest possible tastes. They included anything from *King Lear* to displays by acrobatic dogs. In 1854 *Uncle Tom's Cabin* was featured and in 1861 *Garibaldi, the Hero of Italy*.[350] From the 1860s Jackman was succeeded by other travelling companies, including that of Sarah Thorne who in the 1870s came regularly to perform pantomimes. There were also dramatic readings, with Shakespeare proving particularly popular.

The staple of most of these humbler performers was melodrama, which appealed to their principal patrons, the working classes. Even at the end of the century Jack Jones, a miner's son, remembered visiting the two wooden theatres which stood in Merthyr Tydfil until 1894. There he saw *Sweeny Todd* and *Maria Marten or The Murder in the Red Barn*, as well as other favourites:

. . . the cheapest seats of that little theatre [were] nightly crowded *almost* entirely by nursing mothers . . . Those little travelling theatres were heaven upon earth for mam and us children, and to obtain admission to them she and us children would willingly go without food . . . we children preferred the plays with sword-fighting in them, such plays as 'The Corsican Brothers' and 'The Duke's Motto.' And we fought off oncoming sleep to stay awake for the farces which followed the plays, the nightcap of laughter which those little theatres so generously gave their audiences.[218]

Joseph Stamper in St Helens was another young patron of melodrama during the 1890s. He, too, went to the theatre with his mother. However, it was not just the play that interested him, but the surroundings. There was gas lighting and in the gallery the seating was ranged like giant steps: 'you sat on the forward edge, there was no back to lean on, and the people on the step higher kept kicking the base of your spinal column. In an exciting play the gallery patrons were said to go home with their lower back black and blue with the kicking'.[326]

During the second half of the century, however, melodrama's dominance of the stage steadily declined, as the more respectable classes were drawn back to the theatre. This process began with Macready's exclusion of prostitutes from Drury Lane in 1842 and was sustained by the provision of better seating and a reduction in the area devoted to the cheaper gallery and pit. Marie Wilton and her husband, Squire Bancroft, were pioneers of this reformation during the 1860s. In 1865 Marie took over management of the Queen's Theatre off Tottenham Court Road (which had the derogatory nickname of the 'Dusthole'). It was transformed into the well-appointed, attractive Prince of Wales, with 'rosebud chintz in the circle, and . . . carpet in the stalls'. Years later Clement Scott, the doyen of theatre critics, recalled that audiences were 'enchanted with the light, bright, joyous little playhouse, . . . where the very walls seemed to welcome you'.[210] These improvements were encouraged by the rising cost of staging plays, which made the attracting of an audience prepared to pay higher prices for comfortable seats a matter of importance. Significantly when the Bancrofts took over the Haymarket Theatre in 1880 they abolished the pit entirely, thereby giving rise to vociferous and prolonged protests from those who had formerly patronized those seats.[296] They also succeeded in reducing the bill to a single, well-rehearsed play which required the audience's full attention, instead of the lengthy, ill-assorted mixture of two or three different pieces which had been the theatre's traditional fare.[296]

It was in these circumstances that in 1892 William Fladgate, representing the views of London theatre managers, told an official committee that the capital was 'the home of dramatic art. Art has been cultivated there both in the form of amusement and in the form of instruction . . . You have both scenic art, and literary art.'[22] Henry Irving, too, argued that serious acting was 'the highest educational function of the stage'. At the Lyceum he gave dignity to the stage by completely darkening the auditorium during the performance, so that the audience concentrated on the actors.[296]

In deference to the taste of the new playgoers romantic works replaced melodrama at many West End theatres. At the same time there began the practice of long runs, rather than the old-style repertory system which had existed even in London. This was only possible because more people wanted to go to the theatre, not merely from within the capital but from the suburbs and even further afield. J.B. Buckstone, lessee of the Haymarket Theatre in the 1860s, claimed that this was because they appreciated the superior quality of the acting. 'I can always tell when a quantity of people have come from the surrounding districts; at a certain hour you can see them moving away to catch the trains to go home.' He noted, too, that many men who came to London on business from Manchester and Liverpool took the opportunity to visit the theatre as well.[23] There was a certain prestige in having been present at much-praised performances like those of Henry Irving and Ellen Terry in the Lyceum's 1879–80 revival of *The Merchant of Venice*. These two were to continue to appear together in various plays for almost a quarter of a century, their last joint performance being in a benefit matinée at Drury Lane in July 1903.[278]

It was the audience at a Victorian theatre which largely determined the 'nature of its drama and the extent of its repertoire'.[316] As theatre-going became fashionable among the social élite in the final decades of the century, so West End theatres produced a range of plays that reflected society's image of itself. T.H. Escott labelled these 'cup and saucer' domestic dramas and noted drily that in leading social circles it was 'considered as necessary to go to see the last new play as the last new opera'.[57]

Theatres like the St James's specialized in meeting the demand for stylish plays concerned with upper-class relationships. Many concentrated on the efforts of parvenus to penetrate high society by marriage or they focussed on 'the familiar

Sir Henry Irving, arguably the greatest of the Victorian actor-managers, c. 1900. Irving was knighted in 1895, the first actor to be so honoured. (The author)

figure of a "woman with a past" – a woman whose former sexual conduct disqualified her from polite society and whose secrets were (inevitably) revealed during the course of the play'.[316] The writings of Oscar Wilde, with their brittle wit and preoccupation with the controversial issues of adultery and divorce, proved popular with audiences in the mid-1890s, before his imprisonment for homosexual practices.[209]

Also on offer were Gilbert and Sullivan's comic operas at the Savoy Theatre, opened in 1881. The tasteful decor and comfort of the new premises were highly praised. It was the first theatre in the world to have electric light, and in another pioneering move space was reserved for orderly queues to enter the pit and gallery. They were served with tea and cakes while they waited. Audiences were also presented with free programmes, and a silk curtain replaced the traditional 'drop'. One critic quipped:

> And the Playhouse, no more the Play's the thing;
> We have crowned the upholsterer Lord and King.

The Gilbert and Sullivan operettas proved extremely popular, particularly among women, and their appeal was enhanced when in the 1880s the Savoy introduced matinée performances. Many females, both at this theatre and at others, shared the enjoyment of Marion Sambourne in watching interesting and famous fellow members of the audience as well. As her husband was a *Punch* artist, the Sambournes were able to take advantage of some of the complimentary tickets issued to the magazine's staff by theatre managers. Marion welcomed theatre-going as an opportunity to wear her best clothes and jewellery. But opera glasses were trained more often on the audience than on the actors, and to sit in a box meant being in full view of everybody else. According to her biographer, Marion often regarded it as more important to write 'Had stage box' in her diary than to give the name of the play or the performers, and her comments on the actual piece were always laconic: 'Sad piece', 'Capital performance', or 'Play bad', were typical entries, while 'Enjoyed it exceedingly' was her highest praise.[257]

Burlesque, originally a satirical parody of contemporary plays or events, underwent a major change, too, in the later Victorian years and became more like a revue, with sketches and songs. In the 1890s, under the management of George Edwardes, the Gaiety Theatre, once the home of burlesque, concentrated on light-hearted musical comedy. Plot was overshadowed by the glittering verve of the entertainment. In 1898 the drama critic of *Country Life Illustrated* enthused over 'that unique and wonderful thing, a Gaiety "show"'. He admitted that its plot might be defective and its repartee lacking in wit, but these were balanced by

> many little things, so graceful, so dainty, so clever; . . . Those who never go to the Gaiety have an idea that they would be shocked and insulted in speech and gesture and suggestion on the stage. Never was there a greater mistake. There is vulgarity, it is true, but it is quite of the innocuous kind; there is hardly anything 'French' – a word used as an euphemism – and what there is is less unpleasant than that of the majority of the farcical comedies to which materfamilias takes her daughters without a vestige of alarm.

Ellaline Terris, one of the Gaiety Girls, singing 'The Sly Cigarette' in A Runaway Girl *(1898). Women were beginning to smoke but it was still controversial – hence the lines in the chorus: 'Why did you teach me to love you so, When I have to pretend that I don't, you know?' (The author)*

He had equally lavish praise for Ellaline Terris, the star of the show he was reviewing. She was applauded for the sincerity of her performance, and for her personal magnetism and charm. Another leading 'Gaiety Girl' was Rosie Boote. This Irish-born actress first appeared at the Gaiety in the chorus line of *The Shop Girl* in 1895 but was catapulted to stardom in 1898 when she sang the main song in the *Messenger Boy*. She left the stage when she married the young Marquess of Headfort in 1901, but seems never to have forgotten the co-stars of her Gaiety days for she often arranged reunion tea parties.[267]

Not all theatregoers were satisfied with this diet of society drama and light-hearted musical entertainment. As the prestige of the theatre grew, a small but discriminating group of enthusiasts began to demand greater intellectual stimulus. By 1890 this had crystallized into an interest in the plays of Henrik Ibsen. It was in 1889 that *A Doll's House* and *The Pillars of Society* were first staged in England and over the next decade nine more of his works were produced in the West End. Many were shown only in matinée performances, while *Ghosts* was chosen by the newly established Independent Theatre as its first production, in 1891. Clement Scott of the *Daily Telegraph* condemned *Ghosts* as 'an open drain' and 'a loathsome sore unbandaged'.[296] Yet despite such savage criticism, Ibsen's work, with its harsh realism and depiction of the darker side of human experience, was destined to transform English drama. Jeannette Marshall, daughter of a leading London medical man, was apparently so impressed by Ibsen's work that she decided to learn Norwegian so that she could read his plays in the original. She and her sister tried to teach themselves but in 1890 engaged an instructor. Within a few months Jeannette had read eight Ibsen plays.[312]

However, as Michael Booth has pointed out, despite the influence of Ibsen's work and that of the other new social dramas of the 1890s, melodrama

> still held out in West End citadels like the Adelphi and Drury Lane, the latter specialising, as did the Standard in the East End, in huge, ponderous and spectacular melodramas of high society, sporting life, natural catastrophes and colonial wars. In the East End the Britannia successfully maintained its policy of melodrama and pantomime . . . The Elephant and Castle in Southwark and the Lyric, Hammersmith were local melodrama strongholds in the 1890s . . . [Melodrama's] decline in the metropolis did not occur until about 1905, when the popularity of the new cinema began to drain away audiences from theatres in working-class districts.[102]

Meanwhile the rising status of London theatres and general transport improvements were affecting provincial performances. Whereas audiences had once been satisfied with the traditional repertoire of a stock company or the occasional visit of a leading London actor or actress to appear with a theatre's usual cast, by the 1860s that was changing. Some people, as we have seen, preferred to travel to the capital to see performances in their original West End setting. But London companies increasingly found it profitable to go on tour, moving costumes, properties and performers from town to town. In 1893 the *Dramatic and Musical Directory* suggested four alternative itineraries for companies visiting thirty provincial towns, including Dublin, Belfast, Aberdeen and Plymouth, 'booked as close as possible'. Eighty-nine towns which boasted at least one theatre were placed in four different categories, judged according to their size rather than the taste of their potential audiences. Hence Hull and Glasgow appeared among the fourteen 'first class' towns, while genteel Torquay and Bournemouth appeared in the fourth category.[155] By 1900 more than 140 special trains ran every Sunday in England and Wales alone to convey touring companies of actors and musicians.[155]

These developments destroyed the profitability of the stock companies, while smart new theatres, built with touring companies in mind, were opened as major venues for the new regime. Sometimes a particularly popular play would be toured by three or four companies simultaneously, and in 1893 there were no fewer than seven of them touring the West End hit farce *Charley's Aunt* in the provinces. In 1871 about a dozen touring companies were estimated to be on the road, whereas on 28 March 1896 the theatrical newspaper, *Era* listed 158.[102] The emphasis on the London connection also appeared in newspaper advertisements of forthcoming provincial productions. Thus in September 1888 the *Western Mail* included a notice of the 'Enormously Successful Drama, in Five Acts', entitled *Shadows of a Great City*, to be staged at Cardiff's Theatre Royal. As an added attraction the 'Entire Scenery, Properties, and Effects from the Princess' Theatre, London' would be used. This was to be followed a few days later by Arthur

Roberts and the 'Entire London Avenue Theatre Company' in the *Old Guard*, a new opera comique. There are many similar examples in the late Victorian years.

On a broader basis pantomime became an increasing feature of the Christmas season, with Drury Lane productions in the 1880s and 1890s involving hundreds of dancers, supernumeraries and child performers, the latter being particularly welcomed both in the capital and elsewhere.[404] In January 1894 *The Stage* claimed that the pantomime *Bo-Peep*, now in its third week at the Theatre Royal, Bolton, had been 'received with great favour from crowded houses . . . The child actress, Little Luna, is a universal favourite, and is recalled nightly, her dancing being very clever.' Similarly *The Babes in the Wood* at the Avenue Theatre, Sunderland, owed much of its success to the 'Babes', described as 'two very clever children'. Their efforts were supplemented by various ballets, dances and marches also performed by children, 'whose . . . evolutions are among the most prominent things in the pantomime'. 'Special mention may be made of the umbrella song and dance in the opening scene by the Tiller Troupe, the ballet of *Reapers and Gleaners*, the old English dance by children.'[45]

One boy, taken to *Sinbad the Sailor*, his first pantomime, at the Grand Theatre, Fulham, in the early twentieth century, remembered it vividly more than fifty years later. 'I was thrilled to the core. Especially when Agrippa, the Old Man of the Sea, greenly glowing in a fearsome make-up, was seen at masthead, pulling down the ship to her doom. He looked (to me) so incredibly evil that I awoke crying out in the night. I wouldn't have missed it for worlds!'[292]

Indicative of the importance attached to child performers in both theatre and music hall was the fact that when the 1889 Prevention of Cruelty to Children bill sought to outlaw all child employment under the age of ten, this evoked such powerful opposition from theatre managers, the general public and members of both Houses of Parliament that it had to be amended. Instead of child performers under ten being banned, those over seven could be licensed by magistrates to appear, providing that proper arrangements were made to secure their 'health and kind treatment' – a conveniently imprecise phrase.[198] Not until 1903 did ten become the minimum licensing age for theatre children. As one critic put it, 'Society, alarmed at the possibility of a curtailment of its pleasures' pressed for the exemption of theatre children from regulation, and its wish was granted.[198]

The popularity of the commercial theatre in the second half of the nineteenth century was mirrored by the growing number of amateur performances. These could range from ambitious shows like those staged by Charles Dickens and his friends, with professional actresses taking part (since it was thought improper for middle-class women to go on stage for major performances), to plays put on for family and friends, perhaps at country house parties or for charity.[345] This was the case with Buxton Social and Dramatic Society in the 1890s. Their performances were designed to raise cash for the local cricket and football clubs and, in 1897, to support the Indian Famine Fund. Apart from such money-raising ventures the society's objects were defined as 'the cultivation of a taste for Dramatic Literature & Art together with the promotion of social intercourse among its members'. In order to ensure that the 'right' kind of people joined, all prospective members had to be acceptable to a majority of those attending the annual general meeting.

In Brighton, too, the well-to-do discovered the pleasures of amateur dramatics, with the Green Room Club of 'Aristocratic Amateurs' formed in 1887. Like its Buxton counterpart, it mainly performed light comedies, which in this case were presented at Hove Town Hall. Many dramatic clubs came to prominence in the 1890s as places where the unattached and leisured young could meet congenial companions in pleasant surroundings, as a winter alternative to the cycling and lawn tennis clubs which filled their summer hours.[234]

However, not all theatre-lovers welcomed this trend. In 1868 the *Saint Pauls* magazine, edited by Anthony Trollope, expressed distinct reservations. 'There are some surprising things in the social view of private theatricals,' it declared. 'Almost every human creature is ready to take a part; or, at least, thinks he is capable of taking one.' As a result it was

> being overdone . . . The difficulty is not to get actors but to get audiences. Above all, to hear plays which we have heard again and again done by good actors, mauled and mangled by inferior ones, is a dreary sort of entertainment. To sum up; if the amateur stage wishes to save itself from decay, and certainly contempt, it must first put forward what is new, so that if the acting be inferior, which it is not unlikely to be, we may have the surprise of novelty in the incident or dialogue set before us.[41]

But most would-be thespians were not deterred and at the end of the century the glamour of the stage even appealed to younger members of the landed aristocracy. Some became professionals, like the Earl of Rosslyn who made his stage debut in Arthur Pinero's hit *Trelawny of the 'Wells'* in 1898. Less acceptable was the extravagance of Henry Paget, 5th Marquess of Anglesey, who dissipated over £300,000 in three years around the turn of the century on private theatricals. Sometimes actresses and music-hall stars married into the peerage, as Rosie Boote of the Gaiety did in 1901. Belle Bilton, who performed in the music hall with her sister Florence, was another to make the transition. Belle married Viscount Dunlo in 1889, despite the energetic opposition of the groom's family. On the father's death in 1891 they became the Earl and Countess of Clancarty. Overall, between 1879 and 1914 twenty-one marriages took place between peers and players.[194]

At the humblest level, stage-struck amateurs could find an outlet for their talents by putting on 'penny readings' and recitals at church and chapel celebrations, or staging an 'improving' entertainment for the poor. Joseph Stamper attended some of these events at St Helens in the 1890s. They included 'instructive and educative' lantern lectures, complete with an appropriate story line, concerts by local artistes in schoolrooms or the parochial hall, and penny readings, usually in premises attached to a church or chapel.

> You paid a penny to go in and somebody gave readings from Scott, Dickens, Thackeray, or similar authors. I liked these, I would hang on to every word and for days after I would be making up stories in my mind just as good as, or even better than, those of Dickens or Scott.[326]

With few other amusements available, many of these simple entertainments were much appreciated and well attended. At Clyro in Radnor the curate, Francis Kilvert, noted that when the fourth penny reading of the season was held at the school early in February 1871, the room was crammed:

> people almost standing on each other's heads, some sitting up on the high window-seats. Many persons came from Hay, Bryngwyn and Painscastle. Numbers could not get into the room and hung and clustered round the windows outside trying to get in at the windows. The heat was fearful and the foul air gave me a crushing headache and almost stupefied me.[273]

But these events did not always run smoothly. In November of the same year, when about 167 people attended, Kilvert noted ruefully that his efforts to recite excerpts from Oliver Goldsmith's *Deserted Village* were less than successful. 'I . . . broke down several times, but I got through more than 100 lines with the help of Mr. Venables [the vicar] who had the book and prompted me.'[273]

The popularity of volumes of 'parlour poetry' in the Victorian years is confirmation of the enthusiasm felt by many for these impromptu recitals. One such volume, *The Thousand Best Poems in the World*, sold more than 100,000 copies in the 1890s alone.[352] It was one of many similar collections on offer and was a recognition of the improvements in literacy and general education which were taking place at that time. It is to the wider effects of these latter developments that we will now turn.

Additional Sources Used

Robert Bledsoe, 'Henry Fothergill Chorley and the Reception of Verdi's Early Operas in England' in *Victorian Studies*, Vol. 28, No. 4 (Summer 1985).

Michael R. Booth, 'The Metropolis on Stage' in H.J. Dyos and Michael Wolff, (eds), *The Victorian City*, Vol. 1 (London, 1973).

Buxton Social and Dramatic Society Minute Book, 1893–1900 at Derbyshire County Record Office, D.4404/8.

Country Life Illustrated, 22 January 1898.

Edward J. Dent, 'Early Victorian Music' in G.M. Young (ed.), *Early Victorian England*, Vol. II (London, 1934).

Theodor Fontane, *Ein Sommer in London* (Frankfurt am Main and Leipzig, 1995).

Stanley Jackson, *The Savoy. The Romance of a Great Hotel* (London, 1964).

John Pemble, *The Mediterranean Passion. Victorians and Edwardians in the South* (Oxford, 1988).

Playbills and information at the Theatre Museum, London.

Saint Pauls, Vol. II (1868).

The Stage, 4 and 18 January 1894.

Donald Thomas, *The Victorian Underworld* (London, 1998).

Western Mail, 2 and 4 April 1872 and 6 September 1888.

CHAPTER 9

Literature, Art and Architecture

The present is pre-eminently and avowedly the age of cheap literature. Cheap daily newspapers . . . are numerous, and cheap weekly ones are ditto . . . The cheap periodicals in extensive circulation are too numerous and of too diversified a character to be mentioned . . . Railway, Parlour, Shilling, Useful, and other cheap 'Libraries' have brought a great variety of books within the reach of readers of very humble means, and the books necessary for a complete course of self-education can be obtained for a few shillings.

[Thomas Wright], *The Great Unwashed*, by the Journeyman Engineer (London, 1868), 217

Too many of our own exponents of contemporary life express contemporary life without artistic power. In England, high taste and artistic sensibility, and the power to draw, and the power to colour, are too much ranged on the side of those who hold that modern life holds no themes for Art.

Frederick Wedmore, 'The Impressionists' in *Fortnightly Review*, Vol. XXXIII, New Series (January 1883), 76

LITERATURE

The quantity of books, magazines and newspapers available in the Victorian years grew with astonishing speed, stimulated by rising consumer incomes, greater leisure and improved literacy. By the end of the century around 97 per cent of males and females marrying could sign the register (the only crude measurement of literacy available), whereas half a century earlier just 69 per cent of males and 55 per cent of females had been able to do so.[198] Even transport changes played a part in the literature boom, as travellers spent the enforced idleness of a railway journey reading rather than merely staring out of the window. This trend intensified when, with the growth of suburbs around the major towns, commuting between home and business became part of the daily routine of many people. Newspaper sales benefited particularly from that development, partly because they provided suitable reading material and partly, perhaps, because families living in suburban villas would have lost face with neighbours if they had not taken the 'right' daily paper. Other journals, too, adjusted their format to meet the need for 'half-hour literature'. According to one correspondent, the

Ladies Gazette (1895), which kept its dimensions small, was 'the ideal size for reading in the train as so many of us like to do'.[380]

At the beginning of the Victorian period it was skilled workers, small shopkeepers, clerks and the higher grade of domestic servants who comprised the new reading public.[77] In helping to meet this demand, technological advances and taxation changes played a part by cutting costs. In 1855 the stamp duty of 1*d* imposed on every newspaper was finally repealed and in 1861 the paper duty was scrapped. The latter was particularly important in reducing the price of all publications. At the same time better communications and more retail outlets helped in distribution, as journals published in London could, by the 1860s, be sent by rail all over the country. In 1848 W.H. Smith began to build up a network of station bookstalls when he opened one at Euston, and within two decades the firm could get 5 a.m. editions of London-printed daily papers to subscribers in Bristol soon after 9 a.m. and to York by 10 a.m.[95] Travellers passing through railway stations were greeted by W.H. Smith stalls plastered with posters and offering a wide range of newspapers and books. It was very different from Nathaniel Hawthorne's experience at Leamington Spa in 1855 when he complained that 'we heard no news from week's end to week's end, and knew not where to find a newspaper'.[77] Often papers were handed round from one family to another, as the Revd J.C. Atkinson remembered of mid-century Danby in the North Riding of Yorkshire. He claimed that only about three newspapers were brought into the whole area. 'I myself remember the *Yorkshire Gazette* passing on from one farmer to another, and its circulation hardly ceasing until it was three or four weeks old.' As late as the 1860s an employee of W.H. Smith's in Birmingham was required to collect copies of *The Times* from hotels and restaurants which had hired them for the early part of the day, so that they could be posted to country customers. This was a legitimate commercial arrangement and not an informal private venture.[109]

By the 1850s numerous weekly periodicals and mass-circulation Sunday newspapers were already on the market, such as *Lloyd's Weekly Newspaper*, *Reynolds's Weekly News* and the *Illustrated Police News*, which concentrated on murders, sensational court cases and general scandal. In addition there were Sunday papers like the *Observer* and the *News of the World*, which hovered on the borderline of respectability.[95]

By 1864 the total circulation of London-published weekly newspapers was put at around 2.2 million (half of them in the cheap and sensational *Reynolds's News* category). This compared with 2.4 million other weeklies in circulation at that date, of which a third were mainly religious or educational in character, and 2.5 million monthlies – nearly 2 million of them religious. Sunday schools played a major part in the latter figure, distributing a wealth of reading material to the working-class young. Between 1805 and 1850 almost forty magazines aimed at Sunday school pupils began publication. Other literature ranged from books and pamphlets of a generally religious and 'improving' nature to the youth publications of temperance and religious tract societies, such as the *Juvenile Rechabite Magazine* and the *Gospel Tract Magazine*.[228] John Bunyan's *Pilgrim's Progress* was also widely read, while Milton's *Paradise Lost* gave many youngsters a taste for poetry. Thomas Burt, a Northumberland miner's son, claimed to have read Bunyan's great work in his childhood as 'solid literal history . . . I believed every word of it. Perhaps it was the only book I ever read with entire, unquestioning acceptance.'[77] Tens of millions of tracts, books, testaments and Bibles were distributed to instruct and entertain young people and to consolidate the communal bonds among those attending Sunday schools.

Similar motives applied to the promoters of temperance literature. In 1854 the prohibitionist United Kingdom Alliance founded the weekly *Alliance* journal. By 1859 its circulation (including copies distributed free of charge) had climbed to between 14,000 and 15,000 and it remained at that level a decade later. Brian Harrison considered this newspaper's role to be as vital to the health of the parent organization 'as the circulation of the blood of the individual'. However, he admitted that like the temperance meetings organized at the same time it probably appealed more to the already committed than to the sceptics and the indifferent whom it was seeking to win over.[179] The *Band of Hope Review*, with a distribution of over a quarter of a million copies, was the most widely circulated of the temperance journals. It was aimed at young abstainers and in 1872 the chairman of the Lancashire and Cheshire Band of Hope Union called on activists to 'strive to form such a hatred to the drink in the mind' of youngsters 'as will, in the next generation . . . be irresistible and sweep the whole traffic away'.[179]

Meanwhile daily newspapers were advancing, too, both in range and circulation.[77] *The Times*, selling at 4*d* after 1855 and 3*d* after 1861, mustered impressive sales of 60,000 copies or more per day during the 1860s and early 1870s, rising to 100,000 in the early 1880s.[77] That compared with a figure of 18,500 in 1840.[392] But by the 1870s its sales had been overtaken first by the *Daily News* and then the *Daily Telegraph*. The latter aimed initially at a new readership to whom it appealed by its informal style. It invented the 'Box' system by which replies to advertisements could be sent to the newspaper office rather than the advertiser's own address and it specialized in 'Apartments to Let', 'Situations Vacant', and similar popular selling points. Its success in attracting advertisements brought the *Daily Telegraph* to a permanent eight pages for 1*d* in 1857.[251] Circulation was also stimulated, reaching 200,000 copies a day in the early 1870s, compared to the *Daily News*'s sales of 150,000; a decade later it had reached 250,000. This was more than twice the circulation achieved by *The Times* in the early 1880s.[77]

Evening newspapers likewise proliferated, with London's first popular evening paper, *The Evening News*, appearing in 1881 and *The Star* following suit even more successfully in 1888. While not neglecting politics and other weighty matters, both gave primacy to sport rather than City news.[251]

In the provinces, too, advances were under way. In 1846 there were no daily newspapers published in Britain outside London, which then had fourteen. By 1880 there were (including evening papers) ninety-six in the English provinces and Monmouthshire, four in Wales and twenty-one in Scotland. Large cities might have several, like Newcastle-upon-Tyne which in 1874 had five dailies and five weeklies, and Cardiff, with two dailies and four weeklies. Even the London suburbs began to have their own newspapers to cover community matters, thereby helping to nurture communal links and a sense of civic pride.[95]

During the 1880s and 1890s a minority of newspapers developed a strong campaigning style designed to promote heated debate within their columns and thus boost circulation. This was particularly true of the London-based *Pall Mall Gazette*, under the editorship of W.T. Stead. The paper came out at tea-time and was widely read in the London gentlemen's clubs, where it could expect to provide a focus for discussion. In 1883 it became involved in efforts to expose the appalling living conditions in London slums. Two years later it published a series of sensational articles on prostitution among young girls in the capital and the need to raise the age of consent from thirteen to sixteen. The furore aroused led to the passage of the Criminal Law Amendment Act designed to achieve this, although Stead's own role resulted in his being sentenced to three months' imprisonment at the Old Bailey.[329] In the *Pall Mall Gazette* Stead made systematic use of interviews with prominent people, though to some critics this merely gave rise to 'cynical curiosity in readers and . . . dishonest ambivalence in interviewees'.[329] Expansion of the correspondence columns was a further ploy adopted by editors influenced by the 'New Journalism', since this not only encouraged reader participation in current debates but promoted loyalty towards the newspaper itself.

Even in the 1880s, however, few working-class or lower middle-class families purchased a daily newspaper. If they had enough spare cash for this they rarely had the time to peruse pages of closely argued text. It was in 1896, with the publication of Alfred Harmsworth's *Daily Mail*, that a change began. Harmsworth had already made a reputation as the founder of *Answers*, created in 1888. A weekly compilation of miscellaneous information, it was produced in response to George Newnes's highly successful *Tit-Bits*, a light-hearted penny paper containing a mixture of book extracts, snippets from periodicals and newspapers, and readers' correspondence. By the end of the century *Tit Bits*, *Answers*, and *Pearson's Weekly*, a similar journal, boasted weekly sales of 400,000–600,000, with circulation encouraged by the promotion of competitions. As a Salford newsagent declared sourly in 1906, although people bought papers, 'Reading don't matter that much. What does count is the chance of getting something for nothing.'[169] On one occasion a prize competition organized by *Pearson's* attracted more than a million respondents.[77]

The *Daily Mail* was designed to give such readers a paper which combined lively comment with a crisp style. It publicized itself as 'The Busy Man's Daily Journal' and as 'a Penny Newspaper for One Halfpenny', although Lord Salisbury unkindly called it a newspaper 'written by office-boys for office-boys'. It included a section to appeal to women readers, while whole pages were sold to advertising agencies, since Harmsworth appreciated the value of this as a source of newspaper revenue. For example, in 1900 Bovril took a full-page spread to explain its part 'in the South African War'.[169] The *Daily Mail*'s success in tapping the lower middle- and upper working-class market gave the paper the highest circulation hitherto reached by a daily. In the excitement over the Boer War, sales reached almost a million at the turn of the century. Meanwhile the *Daily Express*, started in 1900, was the first British daily to print news on its front page.[282]

Alongside these developments in the daily and weekly national and provincial press there grew up a wide range of specialist periodicals designed to stimulate the exchange of new ideas and techniques among innovators, as well as to entertain and inform a wider public. They ranged from consciously cultivated journals like the *Cornhill Magazine* to intellectual publications such as the *Fortnightly Review* and the *Nineteenth Century*, and medical works like *The Lancet* and the *British Medical Journal*. There was a multiplicity of family papers, women's magazines, sporting papers (reflecting the growing interest in sport and gambling), and humorous magazines like *Punch* (1840). Improvements in photography in the 1880s and 1890s made possible art magazines like *The Connoisseur*, as well as quality illustrated periodicals such as *The Army and Navy Gazette* and *Country Life Illustrated* (1897). The latter appealed especially to a new professional and business class anxious to acquire a place in the country and the status associated with that. Its nostalgic articles on English villages and rural crafts attracted those who lamented the passing of a traditional way of life. But above all, as Sir Roy Strong has put it, *Country Life Illustrated* became 'the manual of gentrification' for the late Victorian middle classes.[335] On a broader cultural basis the publishing revolution helped the Welsh language revival, by making available increasing numbers of newspapers, magazines, essays and books in that tongue at modest prices.

Also significant was the sharp rise in the number of magazines catering for women. Most of them, especially in the later years of the century, pandered to a Victorian 'vision of Womanhood, compounded of piety and domesticity',

Street boys reading one of the multitude of cheap newspapers outside the Customs House in Liverpool, c. 1890. (Liverpool Libraries and Information Service)

although a few, like *The Queen* and the *Englishwoman's Domestic Magazine*, covered feminine involvement in philanthropic work. Those which espoused the cause of female emancipation had little success. On the other hand, at a time of upward social mobility among successful business families, some magazines found a niche providing guidance for the insecure on the modes and manners of the upper and middle classes. Features on etiquette and answers to readers' queries concerning dress and taste became increasingly popular.[380] Advertisements, too, grew more important as firms realized the possibilities of female purchasing power. This was underlined by *The Gentlewoman*, which claimed a circulation of a quarter of a million among upper-class families. It advised 'astute advertisers' to note that the magazine was 'bought by women, read by women, and as women spend nine-tenths what men earn, the moral is obvious'.[380]

Magazines which concentrated on females lower down the social scale included features on domestic matters like nutrition, hygiene, health and child-care, as well as more light-hearted topics, including fashion. In response to the growing market for these, Alfred Harmsworth brought out *Home Chat* in 1895 as a penny weekly. By June 1895 it had achieved a circulation of just under 186,000 and its motto, at the magazine's head, was appropriately domestic: 'East, West, Home's Best.' A typical issue, dated 22 August 1896, included features on 'The Coronets of English Nobility', 'The Husband in the Household', 'How to Love your Husband', 'What a Girl Should *Not* Do', 'How to Get on the Stage', 'Behind the Footlights' and 'Outdoor Knowledge' competitions.[75]

By the end of the century the 'problem page' had emerged, with readers given guidance on personal difficulties. This seems to have been particularly appreciated by young married women living in suburbia. In 1900 a reader wrote to *Cartwright's Lady's Companion* to underline that wider role of the women's press: '. . . I am so very lonely, having no friend at all to talk to about household matters, and I do not care to worry my husband with them when he comes home tired from his day's work. Your columns form my only "chum" for such matters.'[380]

At the cheap end of the market 'penny dreadfuls' appealed to young and old alike, particularly in the early Victorian years. From the mid-1830s there was a thriving trade in scandalous and pornographic papers, and in periodicals devoted to London low life. In 1857 the *Daily Telegraph* complained of the 'disgusting nature of the prints and pictures' in the shop windows of Holywell Street and Wych Street, in the vicinity of Fleet Street:

> It is positively lamentable, passing down these streets, to see the young of either sex . . . and in many cases evidently appertaining to the respectable classes of society, furtively peeping in at these sin-crammed shop-windows, timorously gloating over suggestive title-pages, nervously conning insidious placards, guiltily bending over engravings as vile in execution as they are in subject.[288]

It was to curb this trade that in 1857 the Obscene Publications Act was passed, but the outcome was unsystematic in its application and, on occasion, unforeseen in its results. Often the works suppressed were translations of foreign authors, like Émile Zola. In 1889 the National Vigilance Association secured the conviction (and eventual imprisonment) of the English publisher of the novels of Zola and Maupassant. Prosecutors claimed in class-ridden terms that these were works which could be 'safely . . . allowed a gentleman in the original language in a private library but not an only recently literate mass audience in its own language'.[288] Meanwhile the old-style pornographic publications trade continued to operate discreetly, with a thriving mail-order business as part of its armoury. Some publishers specializing in pornography, such as Charles Carrington, moved to Paris in the wake of the 1889 prosecution. From there, as Donald Thomas points out, his books were smuggled into England, while 'gentlemen of rank, who should have known better, were having them sent to their West End clubs'. His novels appeared in plain covers, sometimes masquerading as 'Social Studies of the Century'. They 'slipped easily into the capacious pockets of late Victorian . . . overcoats or jackets and hence passed the scrutiny of Customs and Excise undetected'.

Far larger sales were achieved by penny dreadfuls targeted at the young. These were often serials issued in weekly parts, with the ones enjoying greatest popularity those condemned most harshly by middle-class critics. They included stories of the 'Newgate' type which invested 'with knightly qualities . . . highwaymen, jail-breakers, house-breakers'. In 1851 one such publication, concerned with the exploits of the highwayman Claude Duval, sold 550 copies a week in the Manchester area alone. The *Court of London*, concerned with scandalous goings-on at the Court of King George IV, sold 1,500 copies a week in the same area at that date. The latter proved particularly popular among girls and a certain kind of 'spreeing young men; young men who . . . go to taverns, and put cigars in their mouths in a flourishing way'.[10]

However, it was the appearance in 1866 of a periodical entitled *The Boys of England* that proved most significant in the battle for the youth market. It ran until 1899 and claimed to 'enthral' its readers by 'wild and wonderful but healthy fiction'. In the early 1870s it sold around 250,000 copies weekly, and middle-class parents forbade their sons to read it, although many managed to get hold of copies clandestinely. Its mixture of patriotism, violence, adventure and 'upwardly mobile heroes' soon brought competitors into the field, including Charles Fox's *Boys' Standard*, which ran for twenty years.[198] In 1874 the crusading journalist James Greenwood appealed to fellow writers to destroy 'the hideous dragon that, in the shape of "Boy Highwaymen" and "Knights of the Road", of late years has been nestling with our boys, growing every day more daring and pestilential'. The practice of blaming the 'dreadfuls' for juvenile crime emerged in press reports of court cases involving young people. Thus in May 1868 a fourteen-year-old lad charged with stealing two sacks from his employers was said to have had issues of the *Boys of England* and reprints of the weekly instalment series *Tales of Highwaymen, or, Life on the Road* (1865–6) with him when he was arrested. These were blamed for encouraging him in his life of crime and he was sent to prison for a fortnight with hard labour. In other cases young lawbreakers blamed an addiction to penny dreadfuls for their misdoings, although to a sceptical observer it would seem this was merely an attempt to mitigate the seriousness of their offence before a 'credulous policeman'.[323]

To counter the upsurge of penny dreadfuls, in 1879 the Religious Tract Society launched a new journal, the *Boy's Own Paper*. It, too, relied on tales of adventure and daring to entertain readers and often included a good deal of violence. But it avoided the glorification of criminality which so offended critics of the dreadfuls. Within a short time half a million copies of the *Boy's Own Paper* were being printed each week, including some distributed free of charge to pupils at London elementary schools in an effort to boost circulation and wean the youngsters from undesirable competitors.[198] In 1880 young females were catered for by the appearance of the *Girl's Own Paper*, one of the first magazines to penetrate that particular market.

Yet the penny shockers survived, with one firm claiming that between 1887 and May 1892 it had sold 18,250,000 copies of its 'Penny Stories for the People', which included *Mary, the Poacher's Wife* and *The Smuggler's Doom*.[77] In other cases, as at Flora Thompson's Oxfordshire hamlet, Juniper Hill, it was sentimental penny novelettes which were the main attraction for the womenfolk in the 1880s and 1890s. Several took in one of these each week, as they were published, and they were then handed round until 'the pages were thin and frayed with use'. Copies were exchanged with fellow addicts from nearby villages. As Flora noted, 'An ordinarily intelligent child of eight or nine found them cloying; but they did the women good, for, as they said, they took them out of themselves.'[342]

In the 1890s the penny dreadfuls came under strong pressure from another source, when Alfred Harmsworth published *Comic Cuts* (1890) at a halfpenny, to compete with the leading penny comic of the day, *Ally Sloper's Half-Holiday*. Harmsworth's cut-price alternative was an immediate success and it was followed by several similar publications. In producing *Halfpenny Marvel* in 1893 he made clear his determination to wage war on the dreadfuls. The 'healthy stories of mystery, adventure etc.' offered in the *Marvel* would prove too much for them.[198]

Comic papers also appealed to adults with limited reading ability, although the literate dismissed them as infantile. Robert Roberts remembered the superior smiles of customers in his mother's shop when the daughter of illiterate parents mentioned her next errand was to collect 'Father's weekly papers – *Chips, Comic Cuts, Merry and Bright* and *Lots o' Fun'*. Yet, as Roberts comments, 'such material must have played an important part in keeping the printed word at its simplest before the lowest social groups', as well as giving harmless pleasure.[290]

The Victorian era, therefore, saw an immense upsurge in the publication of newspapers, magazines and comics, designed to appeal to all classes and ages in society and to large numbers of special interest groups. They offered a pleasant way of acquiring information and pursuing hobbies, while serving as a binding force linking together people with similar interests or belonging to similar organizations, be they churches, trade unions, temperance organizations or learned societies.

However, this was the 'golden age' of novel writing, too, and by 1897 *Country Life Illustrated* could comment on the 'avalanche of books' then 'hanging over Society'. In bringing this about, changes in production methods played a part, as did better domestic lighting to enable people to read in comfort. (This included improvements in oil lamps and in gas-light technology from the 1870s, including the use of incandescent mantles.) Throughout the period there was a wide use of part issues or of serialization in magazines to promote novel sales. Charles Dickens revived the device of the part issue with *Pickwick Papers* in 1836–7. For people of modest means the payment of a shilling or so a month was an affordable way of acquiring the works of Dickens, Thackeray and Anthony Trollope. In about 1860 the part issue was superseded by the monthly shilling magazine, which not only serialized novels but included a range of other reading material as well. For example, *Macmillan's Magazine* ran Charles Kingsley's *Water Babies* and Thomas Hughes's *Tom Brown at Oxford*, while the *Cornhill* included George Eliot's *Romola* and Anthony Trollope's *Framley Parsonage*. Work of equal quality might appear in cheaper magazines, too, like Charles Dickens's *Household Words* (from 1850) and *All the Year Round* (from 1859–60), which sold at 2*d* a week and over time offered his own *Hard Times*, *Tale of Two Cities* and *Great Expectations*, as well as Wilkie Collins's *Woman in White* and Mrs Gaskell's *North and South*. There was much else besides, including articles of general interest.[95]

In order to maximize sales it was common for a novel to be published in book form shortly before its serialization was completed. This was true of Charles Dickens's *Great Expectations* (1861) which appeared first in *All the Year Round*. It then came out as a three-volume novel and within five months had gone through five editions in the trilogy form. A reprint in one volume was issued for 7*s* 6*d* in 1862 and another for 5*s* in 1863. By these means Dickens and other popular novelists could tap the widest possible market.[173]

The production of three-volume novels owed much to the influence of the circulating libraries. At a time when it was relatively expensive even for middle-class families to buy a book (with three-volume works costing 31*s* 6*d* each), most preferred to borrow new works through Mudie's circulating library, which was established in 1842, or that of W.H. Smith, which was set up in the 1860s and was based on the railway bookstalls the firm ran. For a guinea a year subscribers to Mudie's could borrow as many books as they could read, and for those living in the country brass-bound boxes of books were sent out from the London headquarters.

Mudie was selective in the works that he took. Those of doubtful morality were not permitted and the test was simple: 'Would you or would you not give that book to your daughter of sixteen to read?' Those which failed the test were not purchased, to the anger (and financial disadvantage) of the authors and publishers concerned, since Mudie would order several hundred copies of popular works. George Meredith, whose novel *The Ordeal of Richard Feverel* (1859) was withdrawn from the library on account of its frank treatment of sexual attitudes, vented his fury in a letter to a friend: 'I find I have offended Mudie and the British Matron . . . Because of the immoralities I depict! O canting Age! . . . Meantime I am tabooed from all drawing-room tables.'[173]

Mudie's borrowers were able to gain access to popular fiction soon after publication, although for some best-sellers there might be a waiting list. Mrs Humphry Ward, author of the controversial religious novel *Robert Elsmere*, received proof of its enormous success when she was in a train at Waterloo station. An excited fellow-passenger entered her compartment clutching a volume in its distinctive Mudie binding. She leaned out of the window to explain to a friend her delight at obtaining it: 'They told me no chance for weeks – not the slightest! Then – just as I was standing at the counter, who should come up but somebody bringing back the first volume. Of course it was promised . . . but I was *there*, I laid hands on it, and here it is!'[173]

Borrowers waiting to be served at Mudie's Library in London, c. 1900. *(The author)*

Jeannette Marshall was another Mudie borrower. Although little of her reading was intellectual she did occasionally choose works by Thomas Carlyle and Charles Darwin. English titles predominated but she was able to read in French and German, as well as in some of the Scandinavian languages by the end of the 1880s. Her parents made little effort to censor what she read and at the age of nineteen when her father lent her Pushkin's *The Captain's Daughter* she noted it was bound with Nathaniel Hawthorne's *Scarlet Letter*, 'wh. I am supposed not to read'. She ignored the prohibition. The lack of parental guidance also allowed her to obtain copies of works by authors considered unsuitable for unmarried young ladies, such as Ouida and Paul de Kock, although, according to her biographer, her own prudishness intervened after she had read one of the latter's works, 'so that she listed him in the diary by his initials alone'. Occasionally she experimented with new and less widely known novels, like Henry James's *Washington Square* and *Portrait of a Lady*, read in 1881 and 1882 respectively, shortly after their publication.[312]

From Mudie's point of view the three-volume book had the merit that three different readers could each borrow a volume at the same time, rather than one reader having the complete book, as was the case with a one-volume work. For authors, too, there was a certain prestige attached to having a novel published in three-volume form first of all, since that signified its suitability for the prestigious Mudie (or Smith) lending network. Sales were boosted since not only did the libraries take many hundreds of copies of popular items themselves but through their advertising they gave publicity to favoured works. Ironically, for much of the nineteenth century books published initially in single volumes were dismissed as 'railway reading', an indication that they were light-weight literature not to be taken seriously.

After the library edition of a three-decker novel had circulated for about a year, a one-volume reprint would usually be published at a much-reduced price. But for enthusiastic readers anxious to sample the latest best-sellers that was too long to wait.

Meanwhile at another level there began to emerge a market in cut-price reprints. In 1846 the Belfast firm of Simms and McIntyre issued the first monthly volumes of their Parlour Series at the previously unheard-of price of 2s in wrappers and 2s 6d in cloth. A year later prices were reduced further to 1s and 1s 6d respectively. But it was the appearance of George Routledge's 'Railway Library' in 1848, selling at 1s a volume, that transformed the cheap reprint market. By 1898 there were 1,300 titles in the Routledge series, and although most were novels some non-fiction was included, especially books on military events, like the Crimean War, the Indian Mutiny and the war of Italian independence. A few one-volume 'originals' were published as well, but they did not enjoy the success of the well-established reprint market.[77] What has been called the 'crowning refinement' of these cheap reprints occurred in 1896 when George Newnes introduced his 'Penny Library of Famous Books', comprising unabridged texts of well-known works by Goldsmith, Poe, Scott, Dickens and many more besides. 'Despite all the current activity in this cheapest of cheap-books fields,' notes Richard D. Altick, 'Newnes found that the market still was not saturated. The first forty-four weekly numbers of his series sold an average of 96,587 copies.'[77] Significantly, it was at about this time that the three-volume novel disappeared, with Mudie ceasing to purchase that format from 1894.

By such methods people of limited means could acquire their own libraries. The future Labour MP Will Crooks benefited in this way by purchasing cheap books from an old man who went round selling from door to door. 'From him I got some of Dickens's novels. I suddenly found myself in a new and delightful world. Having been in the workhouse myself, how I revelled in Oliver Twist!' After Dickens came Scott. 'It was an event in my life when, in an old Scotch magazine, I read a fascinating criticism of "Ivanhoe". Nothing would satisfy me until I had got the book; and then Scott took a front place among my favourite authors.'[182] Second-hand bookstalls offered still cheaper sources of such literature.[70]

For some readers, particularly women, novels offered an escape from the mundane realities of daily existence, especially once the impeccable piety of Charlotte Yonge's works had helped to make fiction respectable. Books written with the female market in mind were usually dominated by one person with whom the reader could identify. Often this meant a heroine who was involved in a complex emotional web of 'pain, suffering, and alienation' as the author recounted the way in which she overcame – or accepted – her lot in life.

Marion Sambourne was typical of many mid-Victorian female readers. She enjoyed romantic novels by women writers, although on occasion she read more controversial works, like those written by Zola, which she read in French. As we have seen, attempts to publish them in English in the 1880s had fallen foul of the Obscene Publications Act of 1857. Yet, although Marion wrote 'Read horrid book, Zola' in her diary, her reading list included most of his novels, as well as those of other French and Russian authors of a similarly 'advanced' type.[257] But more characteristic were such comments as 'Finished reading *The Shadow of Ashlydyat*, Mrs. Wood, most exciting.' She was much disappointed when she missed a party at which her husband was introduced to that writer. Mrs Henry Wood was one of the leading novelists of the day, and her second book, *East Lynne*, became a major best-seller. Of it, the literary critic of the *Observer* wrote enthusiastically: '*East Lynne* is so full of incident, so exciting in every page, and so admirably written, that one hardly knows how to go to bed without reading to the very last page.'[360] In 1898, eleven years after the author's death, Mrs Wood's publisher boasted that her books had collectively sold over 2,000,000 copies, with *East Lynne* by that date achieving sales of 460,000. Her next most famous book, *The Channings*, had sales of 180,000 copies, and out of a list of thirty-one novels, six (including those two) had reached sales of 100,000 or more.[403] One of her strengths was that while she produced an exciting story she was able to pander to Victorian moral sentiment by slipping in appropriate religious or 'improving' comments. Reviewing one of her books, *The Nonconformist* made clear her appeal in that regard:

> As he proceeds the reader wonders more and more at the manner in which the mystery, the criminality, the plotting and the murdering reconciles itself with a quiet sense of the justice of things; and a great moral lesson is, after all, found to lie in the heart of all the turmoil and exciting scene-shifting. It is this which has secured her admittance to homes from which the sensational novelists so-called are excluded.[360]

It was in the final quarter of the nineteenth century, as the market for mass literature burgeoned, that several quite separate reading publics became identifiable.[379] Whereas in the early Victorian years Charles Dickens and Charlotte Brontë, for example, had produced great popular novels read by the most literate people of the day, by the end of the century it was the 'sensational' writers like Mrs Henry Wood and Marie Corelli, rather than 'realists' like Thomas Hardy and George Gissing, who commanded the largest sales. Yet such authors were 'of no account with critical readers'. (Marie Corelli's *The Sorrows of Satan* (1895) sold more copies than any previous English novel.)[379] This, too, was the time when detective stories came to the fore, notably Sir Arthur Conan-Doyle's cult creation, Sherlock Holmes, whose exploits appeared in the *Strand Magazine* from 1891–92.[379]

On a broader basis the interest in imperialism and the 'scramble for Africa' inspired tales of mystery, romance and adventure in the 'dark continent', such as Rider Haggard's *King Solomon's Mines* (1885) and *Allan Quartermain* (1887). For

boys the works of G.A. Henty provided thrilling accounts of military missions
and adventures within the Empire, while reports of the explorations of David
Livingstone and H.M. Stanley attracted large readerships. Stanley's own book, *In
Darkest Africa*, was published in 1890. Seven years later came Mary Kingsley's
Travels in West Africa, Congo Français, and the Cameroons. Despite criticism of her
literary style the book was welcomed for the intelligent views it expressed on such
subjects as 'the civilisation of the African races' as affected by colonization, as
well as on 'rum and traders, and missionaries and polygamy'.[29]

The increasing popularity of foreign travel spawned its own literature,
including specialist guides like Murray's *Handbooks*, which appeared from 1836,
and Baedeker's publications; his Rhineland handbook, published in German in
1839, was translated into English in 1861, and was followed by many others.[390]
There were also travel books combining history, scenic descriptions and the
author's personal experiences. Among them was Amelia B. Edwards's *A Thousand
Miles up the Nile* (1877). Its evocative phrases compared her final weeks on the
Nile to 'one long, lazy, summer's day'.

Yet while many readers, like Marion Sambourne, read for pleasure –
'Afternoon read favourite novel' is a typical Sambourne diary entry – a substantial
minority had more elevated motives. For Margaret Gladstone, daughter of a
professor of chemistry, reading was a means of self-education and a way of
resolving personal religious and political doubts and difficulties. In 1887-8, while
in her teens, her reading list included ephemeral political tracts, *Darwin's Life and
Letters*, Drummond's *Natural Law in the Spiritual World* and a good deal of
poetry, including William Wordsworth's *The Excursion* and Elizabeth Barrett
Browning's *Aurora Leigh*. After her marriage in 1896 to J. Ramsay Macdonald,
who was destined to be the first Labour prime minister, Margaret and he spent
their evenings, when they could manage it, sitting in the lamplight while
Macdonald read aloud. As he recalled, his wife would be busy sewing and darning

> whilst I read from some book or other generally far removed in its thoughts
> from our everyday battles. In this way we read through most of Thackeray and
> Dickens, the best of Scott, Symonds' *Renaissance*, Carlyle, and Ruskin. The
> Sunday reading was always separate, because she did not like to have the week-
> day books read on Sunday as well.[235]

This custom of reading aloud was common in numerous middle- and upper
working-class homes. It was a means both of entertainment and of strengthening
family ties through a shared pleasure. Many households, too, had special books for
the Sabbath.

For other readers again, such as the political reformer William Lovett, access to
literature was a way of acquiring the knowledge needed for political progress.
Lovett, a Cornish-born cabinet-maker, moved as a young man to London in the
1820s. There he joined a small literary association entitled The Liberals, which
met at Newport Market. It was composed mainly of working men, who paid a
small weekly subscription towards the formation of a library to be circulated
among the members. Meetings were held on two evenings a week, on one of which

some topic of a literary, political or metaphysical character would be discussed. According to Lovett, this inspired him with a desire 'to read and treasure up' all he could find on the subject of Christianity. From this he turned to political issues and parliamentary debates, until his mind 'seemed to be awakened to a new mental existence; . . . and every spare moment was devoted to the acquisition of some kind of useful knowledge'.[233] He joined several other self-improvement societies and for a number of years rarely had a meal 'without a book of some description beside [him]'. In addition, he noted that by mid-century a number of London coffee houses had supplies of books and newspapers. In 1849 there were reckoned to be almost two thousand of them, offering reading and recreation to the 'temperate working classes'.[19] Some had libraries with as many as two thousand books.

But for many poorer people, forced to live in overcrowded, badly lit homes, there were few opportunities for study. John Passmore Edwards, the son of a Cornish carpenter, recalled the difficulty he experienced in reading by the light of a single candle in the middle of a talkative and active family. Often he had to press his thumbs firmly in his ears, in order to concentrate. Thomas Burt, too, grew up in a Northumbrian cottage that was 'virtually a neighbourhood crossroads'. He was repeatedly twitted by visitors for having his nose stuck in a book, but despite these discouragements he persisted and eventually became a trade union leader and member of parliament.

It was to cater for such working-class readers that publishers like William and Robert Chambers launched their 'cheap and wholesome' literature, including *Chambers's Journal* and *Chambers's Encyclopaedia*. They were soon followed by John Cassell, whose *Popular Educator*, first issued in 1852–4, was repeatedly reprinted. Its role in Victorian self-improvement is indicated by the number of successful men who learnt from it, including Thomas Hardy who taught himself German with its aid, and Thomas Burt who used it for English, French and Latin. Cassell also produced the *Illustrated Family Bible* in instalments, with sales of 350,000 copies in six years, and a multiplicity of other illustrated works on history, natural history, Shakespeare and many more topics. In 1862 Cassell's sales of penny publications were said to total 25–30,000,000 copies a year.[77]

However, for many working-class men the main source of reading material was provided by the libraries of mechanics' institutes, literary and philosophical societies, and similar voluntary adult educational organizations. At mid-century there were about seven hundred mechanics' institutes in Britain, including around thirty in Wales and fifty in Scotland. Their libraries concentrated on serious topics, although works of fiction, biography, travel and general subjects were to be found in most of them. Fiction was particularly popular. Unfortunately the books were very variable in quality, many having been obtained as gifts, 'turned out of people's shelves . . . never used, and old magazines of different kinds'.[359] In consequence, out of a thousand volumes less than half might be of use or interest to readers. This led George Dawson, a well-known public lecturer, to complain to the Select Committee on Public Libraries in 1849 that while people had been given an appetite to read they were unable to obtain suitable books.[19] Furthermore, in London even when libraries were available they were normally closed at the only hours working people could use them. For example, the prestigious British

Museum Library would close at 4 p.m. Hence 'in every case where the working men can form a society, they go and read there for hours of an evening'.[19]

It was in these circumstances that proposals were put forward for the provision of rate-aided public libraries. The first move in that direction came in 1847 when Canterbury corporation, using powers given under the Museums Act passed two years before, purchased for public use the museum and library of the town's Philosophical and Literary Institution. Warrington and Salford also set up public libraries under this Act, but in all three cases provision remained small. Even in 1870 Canterbury's public library had only about 2,600 books, some of them very old.[222]

In 1850 came the first Libraries Act, empowering towns with a population of ten thousand or more to levy a halfpenny rate to provide library premises. Five years later this was amended to raise the maximum permitted levy to 1d, while reducing the population limit for library districts to five thousand and authorizing money to be spent on books as well as accommodation. But from the start the initiative was controversial. Supporters argued that the libraries would make the working classes 'more sober, more industrious, and more prosperous' and would wean them from other, less desirable diversions. But critics claimed that they would be 'paying rates for the benefit of a lot of lazy people with nothing to do but lounge about reading'.[222] As late as 1891 an opponent of public libraries at Lowestoft asked what would happen to errand boys when they were sent out on messages if a free library were opened: 'They would loaf about the place and the people might wait for their meat and fish!'[224]

Even where public libraries were established – and as late as 1886 there were only 125 of them, covering a quarter of the total population – their readership was small. A survey of five towns, selected at random from returns published in the 1890s, showed that the number of active borrowers comprised only between 3 and 8 per cent of the population. This was partly because of the uninviting books stocked by the libraries, with many concentrating on serious non-fiction and regarding novels as no part of their remit, even though borrowing figures showed that fiction was what most people wanted to read after a hard day's labour. Only a few, like William Lovett and his friends, found their pleasure in instruction rather than light-hearted diversion. Among those taking this stricter approach was the librarian of Owens College, Manchester. In 1878 he argued that public institutions were not justified in making free provision of novels. From long experience of the Manchester Free Libraries, then among the largest in the country, he had found those young people who took to reading lightweight fiction never made much progress in life. 'Novel-reading has become a disease, a dissipation; and this dissipation, most librarians of circulating libraries will allow . . . is as enchanting and quite as hard to be rid of as other dissipations, and quite as weakening mentally.'[224]

But some took a more liberal view, as in Liverpool where there was a good provision of fiction in a public library provided in 1857 by the gift of William Brown, a wealthy local merchant and MP.[25] At Liverpool the attitude was that any kind of reading was better than none, and 'the reading of fiction might lead to better things'.[224]

Over the years this more enlightened approach gained ground, while the view that public libraries were only for the lower orders began to weaken. At Bristol, where the first library was opened in a poor part of the city in 1876, residents from the middle-class suburb of Redland appealed to the town council five years later for a similar provision; if libraries were a social asset in one area their suburb should benefit too. The council responded favourably and in 1885 the Redland Library was opened. Ironically it was in larger and more expensive premises than any other branch library in Bristol and its stock of ten thousand books was almost twice the total supplied to the town's first library.[245] Similarly, in Leeds it was estimated in 1876 that while 81 per cent of readers were working class, 19 per cent came from a professional or other better-off sector of society.[224] Sometimes, as at Dundee, the desire to cater for the middle classes and to gain extra funds, led to the running of a subscription library for the well-to-do alongside the normal free service. At Dundee from 1876 subscribers paid a guinea a year and this was used to purchase books which for the first year were issued to subscribers only. After that they passed into the general stock. Although this policy undermined the principle of equality of access which lay behind the public library service it did help to improve overall facilities.[222] But, in general, Scotland was not an enthusiastic supporter of public libraries in the nineteenth century. Even in 1890 only fourteen towns had them, and Edinburgh and Glasgow were still without any such facilities. In contrast, by then Manchester had a reference library of 92,000 books and a further 108,500 volumes in other branches. The average daily attendance in the city's reading rooms was 12,628, including visitors to the reference library, the newsroom and the boys' rooms.[21]

In some places would-be borrowers were discouraged by the brusque manner of library staff or the policy adopted by many authorities of excluding children from membership. Joseph Stamper recalled that when he first went to the St Helens Public Library he was told to leave as he was not yet sixteen. He only overcame the prohibition by getting his father to join, and then borrowing books on the parental ticket. Even then, open access was not allowed. 'They dare not trust working people among the books,' wrote Stamper bitterly, 'in case they swiped the lot and maybe took the shelves as well for firewood.'[326]

Part of the problem was perhaps that from the beginning publicly provided libraries seemed to some critics to attract the idler, the eccentric and the vagrant as well as the scholar. Even at the prestigious British Museum Library in Bloomsbury, then the sole reference centre for many people, such difficulties occurred. In 1854 *The Times* commented sarcastically that when three to four hundred readers were present the 'shabby genteel' predominated, with fifty or sixty of them employed in making extracts from encyclopaedias and books of reference, about two hundred and fifty occupied in reading novels and the rest engaged in looking at prints. 'Among the crowd are generally to be found a lunatic or two, sent there by his relatives to keep him out of mischief.'[122]

Elsewhere libraries were concerned to discourage racing enthusiasts who made their daily selections from newspapers on display in the reading rooms. To that end they obliterated the racing news from each paper as it arrived.[77]

Women were often reluctant to enter such a seedy environment, even though they might wish to read the books. To meet their needs a number of libraries set aside separate ladies' rooms or screened off part of the main reading room for exclusive female use. Some installed a separate women's entrance.[77]

Despite their faults, there is little doubt that public libraries made an important contribution to the Victorian reading revolution by enabling large sectors of the community to have access to books. Their value is exemplified by the experience of the historian E.L. Woodward, who came from a middle-class family in suburban London. He discovered the pleasures of English poetry through reading Scott, Gray and the ever-popular Tennyson. 'I might perhaps have stopped at this point,' he declared years later, 'if it had not been for the Reference Room in the Hampstead Public Library . . . Evening after evening, I used to sit in the pleasant Reference Room, reading one book after another, and walking home along the suburban roads in a ferment and turmoil of exaltation.'[77]

ART

The democratic impulse which had helped to boost the quality and quantity of literature available in the Victorian years had a more modest but nonetheless profound influence upon the fine arts. One effect was to encourage the belief that all social classes should be able to enjoy paintings and sculptures as part of their cultural heritage. Symptomatic of this was the way that the Summer Exhibitions held at the Royal Academy, the central institution in the Victorian art world, were reported in detail by many newspapers and journals. The exhibitions themselves were attended by more than a quarter of a million people each year, with a peak of 391,197 visitors recorded in 1879.[78] However, the levying of a shilling entrance charge (double if the catalogue were purchased) meant that the poorer classes were excluded.

In 1871 the Academy began holding a special Press Day and by the mid-1890s this was attracting around three hundred writers and critics. Illustrated catalogues started to appear as improvements in printing techniques made possible inexpensive photographic reproductions.[349]

The Royal Academy's importance lay not only in the status it conferred upon those who became academicians, but in the fact that acceptance at the Summer Exhibition could bring reputation and perhaps fortune to aspiring artists. By assembling a wide range of pictures it also gave artists freedom to paint a variety of subjects, beyond the portraits and landscapes which normally arose from commissions. At the same time it served as a conduit, to link the art world with potential purchasers and patrons.

It was in these circumstances that wealthy businessmen began to make their own collections of contemporary paintings, and the appreciation of art spread from a select group of aristocratic connoisseurs, with their galleries of Old Masters, to a broad spectrum of society. Such was the self-confidence of many Victorians that they did not think it 'impertinent or exaggerated' to rank leading modern painters with the giants of the past, such as Titian and Michelangelo.[349]

A more inclusive and moralistic approach to art was put forward in 1847 by Samuel Carter when he argued that 'a collection of pictures powerfully helps to thin our poor houses and prisons and men to whom public galleries are open will be seldom found in public-houses.'[236] Eight years earlier he had founded the monthly journal *Art Union* to serve as a vehicle for his views on the socially ameliorating potential of paintings. A further attempt to widen the appeal of art came in 1857 with the setting up of the Manchester Art Treasures Exhibition. It had the backing of Prince Albert and a million visitors admired not only the displays of Old Masters and contemporary works borrowed from private collectors, but a wide range of other high quality *objets d'art*. The *Art Treasures Examiner*, a weekly journal published during the exhibition, reinforced the notion of progress through cultural appreciation when it called on working men to be 'refined, – to be gentlemen in feelings and in manners . . . and they will speedily take their proper rank in the great human family'.[236]

Employers from the north of England and the Midlands arranged for their workers to take advantage of this opportunity for self-improvement, with special trains organized to bring them to Manchester. Among the largest groups were 2,500 workers brought by Titus Salt from his textile factory near Bradford. He paid all the expenses of the excursion, including dinner in a large refreshment tent.[236]

The opening of municipal galleries in cities like Liverpool (1877), Manchester (1882) and Leeds (1888) further helped to make art accessible to the general public. They were established as a result of local initiatives and benefactions plus the effects of the 1845 Museums Act, which permitted the levying of a small rate for the purpose. Many of the new galleries offered refreshment rooms, and in some cases profitable temporary displays funded the construction of a permanent gallery. This was true of the York City Art Gallery in 1892 or, more ambitiously, of the Kelvingrove Museum and Art Gallery in Glasgow, where the 1888 International Exhibition gave a necessary boost.[81] They were popular, too: in Leeds, with a population of around 367,000, visitors to the City Art Gallery totalled over 250,000 a year in the 1890s, reaching 420,000 in 1898.

In London provision was increased with the foundation of the National Portrait Gallery in 1856 and its removal from South Kensington to central London forty years later. In addition, the National Gallery of British Art was opened at Millbank in 1897 and the Wallace Collection in 1900, while the National Gallery itself was extended in 1887. The new National Portrait Gallery was constructed at the expense of a private donor, W.H. Alexander, and the National Gallery of British Art was funded by Sir Henry Tate, with the government merely providing the land. In 1899 Queen Victoria herself laid the foundation stone of what became the Victoria and Albert Museum.[157]

In the provinces and in some suburban areas of London, museums and galleries opened on Sundays, to provide 'rational recreation' for working people on their one day of leisure in the week. Hence in the first few months after the opening of the Mappin Art Gallery in Sheffield during July 1887 about six thousand visitors passed through its doors each Sabbath during the three hours it was open.[81] But attempts to have access to the national museums and galleries in London on that day were frustrated by the sabbatarians until 1896. Two years later the National Gallery alone was attracting over thirty thousand visitors a year on the thirty-one Sundays it was open, while the new National Gallery of British Art mustered almost forty-two thousand visitors over the same period.[24] The National Portrait Gallery attracted just under ten thousand people on Sundays in 1898, but its annual report indicated some of the problems that could arise, particularly on dark, foggy days in winter. Even during the week it had been necessary 'to close the Gallery for some hours on account of darkness, and one day in January, 1898, it was found impossible to open it at all'.[9] Securing proper lighting for works of art presented a difficulty for gallery directors even at the end of the century.

Awareness of the importance of art in national cultural life was raised by the proliferation of illustrated magazines, with the *Illustrated London News* (1842) achieving a circulation of 67,000 by 1850. In the 1850s and 1860s magazines like *Good Words* and *Once a Week* began using imaginative pictures to illustrate poetry and fiction. Such outlets gave profitable employment to artists and were a common way for young men to become established. For example, Luke Fildes first came to the fore as the illustrator of Dickens's last, incomplete novel, *Edwin Drood*.[390] Even leading painters like Frederic Leighton and John Everett Millais, both future presidents of the Royal Academy, boosted their income by accepting commissions for book illustrations. In Millais's case that included pictures for an illustrated edition of Tennyson's *Poems* in 1857 and for several Trollope novels. Both men were involved in Bible illustrations during the 1860s, working for the engraving firm of Dalziel Brothers. They followed these up with large-scale Old Testament paintings of their own.[313]

Improvements in the engraving process also enabled high-quality reproductions to be made of paintings, and in the 1850s and 1860s it was possible for an artist to sell the reproduction rights of a painting for more than the work itself. Almost all the leading art dealers of the day published prints, and in this way copies of famous paintings found their way into countless homes.[313]

Thomas Faed (1826–1900), My Ain Fireside. *Faed was born in Scotland but settled in London in 1852. He specialized in popular genre paintings of Scottish life, often choosing humble domestic themes or those likely to appeal to the religious sentiment of his native land. (From* Bright Hours. Popular Reading for the Home Circle, *n.d. [c.1910])*

Most Victorian artists were slow to find inspiration in the life and work of the major industrial cities, and continued to portray unchallenging rural topics. Some impetus towards depicting the harsher aspects of the contemporary scene was provided by the *Graphic*, a weekly news magazine first published in 1869. Even then, it was often literature rather than real life that provided the model for illustrations of social themes. The relatively common representations of starving sempstresses arose not from newspaper reports or direct observation, but from Thomas Hood's popular poem of the early 1840s, 'The Song of the Shirt'.[348] Sometimes *Graphic* engravings were associated with philanthropic appeals, with pictures of the mourning wives of fishermen lost at sea used to promote lifeboat appeals. The 'social realism' school was also stimulated by charity, when potential benefactors purchased pictures that depicted the problems they were seeking to alleviate.[348]

But social realism was not the only factor in the *Graphic*'s pictorial success. It included many general interest features as well, such as fancy-dress balls, royal visits and the opening of new town halls. Nonetheless some of the high-quality artists it commissioned to cover the grimmer aspects of working-class life, such as Luke Fildes and Hubert von Herkomer, went on to make a reputation with paintings on these themes.

Ultimately the cause of social realism was discouraged by the hostility of contemporary critics. In 1874 the *Art Journal* condemned Fildes's *Applicants for Admission to a Casual Ward*, with its miserable queue of destitutes, on the grounds that there was little in such a subject of 'grovelling misery to recommend it to a painter whose purpose is beauty'.[348] The work had first appeared as a *Graphic* engraving in 1869 entitled *Houseless and Hungry*. With attitudes like these it is not surprising that such art played only a small part in Victorian painting, or that many artists, perhaps unconsciously, edited out of their work features likely to upset potential purchasers. On the other hand some of the new municipal galleries in industrial cities did buy pictures on harsh themes considered relevant to the lives and experience of the public they wanted to attract.[348]

In general, however, patrons avoided works on disturbing subjects. As Julian Treuherz has put it, 'what was acceptable on the page of a magazine was less so hanging on a wall'. What they favoured instead were what Thackeray called 'a gentle sentiment, an agreeable, quiet incident, a tea-table tragedy or a bread-and-butter idyll', something that was reassuring and amusing.[349] So although there was a market for social realism, in the long run painters like Fildes abandoned this in favour of portraits, which were quicker, less demanding and more remunerative. 'I should probably make more money by portraits, which I have to entirely give up, after making a success, to go on with his commission', was Fildes's unenthusiastic reaction on being asked to paint *The Doctor*, showing a medical man watching at the bedside of a sick child. The commission was offered in 1890 by Sir Henry Tate, the sugar manufacturer and major patron, for his National Gallery of British Art.[348]

The growing interest in art among industrialists and professional men created an important outlet for contemporary painting. In the main they favoured works which reflected the middle-class values of respectability, hard work, sanctity of family life, self-improvement and moral rectitude. They liked pleasant 'genre' pictures, showing daily life in cottage interiors or within a peaceful rural landscape. Works which depicted 'the innocence of children or the virtues of obedience and charity' were very popular.[349] Many of the buyers were dependent on the advice of a new breed of specialist dealers, like Agnew's of Manchester, and some, like the Wigan cotton manufacturer Thomas Taylor, collected primarily for reasons of personal prestige. Others resembled the hard-headed Birmingham steel pen manufacturer, Joseph Gillott, who began collecting in earnest in the late 1850s. He favoured a mixture of idyllic landscapes and seascapes, heroic figurative compositions and highly detailed still-lifes. Yet, although he was interested in the brushwork, proportions and composition of the works he purchased, he also regarded them as commercial propositions. He even employed a restorer to touch up paintings before he resold them, and after nearly forty years of buying, bartering and selling, the '525 lots of oils and watercolors [*sic*] that brought almost £170,000 at Christie's in 1872', after Gillott's death, represented 'only a small portion of the pictures that passed through his hands'.[236] The businessman's respect for the work ethic can likewise be identified in the importance attached by some collectors to an artist's technical skills. John Gibbons, an Edgbaston ironmaster and enthusiastic early Victorian collector, made this clear in 1843 when he wrote: 'I love finish – even to the minutest details. I know the time it takes and that must be paid for but this I do not object to.'[349]

The Manchester engineer Thomas Fairbairn, who took a leading part in staging the 1857 exhibition in his city, favoured didactic art, believing it had a powerful redemptive influence. His collection included a wide range of moral subjects and he described 'the useful lessons of humility which gradually steals upon every one's thoughts, when he stands uncovered at the shrine of genius'. Yet this certainly did not lead him to treat the artists from whom he commissioned works as 'infallible paragons'. When he purchased *The Awakening Conscience* (1852) by William Holman Hunt he asked that the woman's anguished expression be replaced by one less tormented. Nevertheless, for him the value of the Manchester Art Treasures Exhibition lay in the fact that it introduced workers to an appreciation of art, which he saw as the basis for social integration and harmony.[236]

From a commercial stance these new-style patrons were also aware that if they purchased from living artists they were sure of getting a genuine article. A spate of forgeries and inferior copies had warned many off the market for Italian Old Masters. For contemporary artists this offered an opportunity of fame and fortune, exemplified in 1896 when Frederic Leighton, as President of the Royal Academy, was raised to the peerage.

Meanwhile the developments in the art market led to changes within painting itself. In early Victorian Britain it was genre pictures, history works depicting heroic events, landscapes and portraits which were most popular. The portraits might be of human sitters (as a mark of personal prestige) or of favourite animals. Edwin Landseer appealed to Victorian sentimentality with such works as *Dignity and Impudence* (1839), in which a 'magnificently impassive bloodhound' was contrasted with a 'cheeky little Scotch terrier'.[349] Both dogs belonged to Jacob Bell, a pharmaceutical chemist who was also the artist's friend and business manager. Nine years later the *Annual Register* enthused that at the Royal Academy's Summer Exhibition for 1848 nothing could exceed 'the fine and natural truth of Landseer's "Alexander and Diogenes;" all the characters are *dogs*, with a ludicrous humanity of expression; nothing more pathetic than his "Random Shot;" a hind laying [*sic*] dead in a snowy hill, with a fawn vainly seeking the maternal nutriment.' It was Landseer's Scottish pictures, such as *The Monarch of the Glen* and *The Stag at Bay*, which made him one of the most famous of Victorian artists, with enormous sales of engravings of both the latter works. He was also a great favourite with the royal family and provided many attractive pictures of them and their pets at Windsor, Osborne and Balmoral.[390]

John Frederick Herring senior was another prolific sporting and animal artist. He painted eighteen winners of the Derby and thirty-three successive winners of the St Leger, as well as a large number of other horses, stableyard scenes and farmyards. In 1848 Herring confessed to a friend his boredom with painting racehorses and hinted at the substantial income to be earned from engravings: 'I produced a painting a short time since in 15 hours which I refused 150 guineas for. I'll tell you why – I did not *chuse* [*sic*] to let the copyright go with it. It is now in the British Institution.'[321]

Leisure pursuits became popular themes for self-representation among the Victorians, with even formal portraits often showing sitters occupied in favourite hobbies.[78] Nostalgia for the peace and security of a lost rural world encouraged a depiction of rustic activities like haymaking, harvesting, or fishing in a picturesque landscape. These appealed to the newly urbanized middle classes, although it was a sanitized, sentimental view of country life they desired. Second-rank artists like John Linnell and George Vicat Cole made a comfortable living by specializing in harvest scenes. Farmsteads, too, were presented as picturesque and cheerful rather than the messy, muddy and smelly places that they were in reality. Miles Birket Foster was a particularly successful practitioner of this kind of subject. As Christopher Wood comments, his pictures 'give the impression that farm work was a perpetual holiday'.[390] But the ready market which his pictures found confirms that it was precisely this idealized, happy rusticity that many successful businessmen wanted to have on the walls of their suburban villas. Even when death was involved, as in paintings of grieving fishermen's widows, it was a stoical acceptance of loss that was depicted rather than the sharp anguish that such bereavement must have brought.

Some contemporaries, like the critic John Ruskin, railed bitterly against these superficial portrayals of daily life. They demanded a return to nature – to individual truth rather than general perceptions. 'Truth to Nature' lay at the heart of Ruskin's philosophy.[293] It found acceptance among a group of seven young men who in 1848 created the Pre-Raphaelite Brotherhood. Its aim was that the artist should define and express his own thoughts and that these were to be 'based upon a direct study of Nature, and harmonised with her manifestations'. Of the seven, three were to gain major reputations as painters. They were Dante Gabriel Rossetti, John Everett Millais and William Holman Hunt. Their avowed intention was to return to the clear-cut, uncluttered qualities of pre-Renaissance painting, which they saw as an antidote to the overblown sentimentality and triviality of contemporary artistic practice as promulgated by the Royal Academy. Yet, from the start, there was an ambiguity in their objectives. On the one hand they sought 'a hard detailing of natural data' and on the other they wished to shape 'historical and archaic materials' so as to give a romantic impression of the medieval past, rather than to represent its true character.[293]

Paintings depicting idealized rural scenes were very popular in Victorian England, as in this typical example of the work of Miles Birket Foster (1825–99), Lane Scene, Hambledon (c. 1862). *(The Tate Gallery, London)*

Initially these contradictions were obscured as the Pre-Raphaelites concentrated on themes of everyday life, including the poor, the dispossessed and the 'fallen woman'. For example, in *The Awakening Conscience* Holman Hunt tackled the thorny issue of prostitution by showing a kept woman in her St John's Wood love-nest. The newness of the furniture and the lounging attitude of the man underlined the vulgar details, and yet the theme of moral regeneration was also present, as the 'still small voice' of conscience spoke to the woman of her current plight. This mixture of accurate depiction of the furnishings and the people plus the conveying of a moral message conformed to principles that the Victorians expected to apply when interpreting works of art.[293]

The Pre-Raphaelite preoccupation with minute detail and accuracy was shown in landscapes, too, and photography was used as an aide-mémoire by some artists. When Holman Hunt visited Palestine in the 1850s he was accompanied by a photographer to help him secure complete accuracy in pictures which were finished later.[349] But many contemporary critics regarded this concern for meticulous detail as misplaced. In 1853 the *Annual Register*, in a typical comment, referred to the 'over-truthfulness' of the Pre-Raphaelite school.

Some of the harshest judgements, however, were levelled at John Millais for his painting of *Christ in the House of His Parents* (1849–50). There was condemnation

William Holman Hunt (1827–1910),
The Awakening Conscience *(1853)*
is an example of pre-Raphaelite
moralizing. It shows a caddish young
man-about-town with his mistress,
sharing a song at the piano, when she
suffers sudden pangs of guilt about her
situation. It was intended to portray
the first step on the road to salvation.
(The Tate Gallery, London)

of the way in which the Holy Family were shown as ordinary, not very attractive people, rather than as an idealized unit. Charles Dickens, in *Household Words*, attacked the representation of the child Jesus as 'a hideous, wry-necked, blubbering, red-haired boy in a nightgown', while Mary was 'so horrible in her ugliness . . . she would stand out from the rest of the company as a monster in the vilest cabaret in France or in the lowest gin-shop in England'.[186] However, some of the criticism appears to have arisen from a dislike of the presumption of these young artists in setting themselves up as a semi-secret 'brotherhood' to challenge the tenets of the art establishment. Even in 1851 the *Annual Register* described three pictures submitted by Millais to the Royal Academy's Summer Exhibition as 'talent strangely applied'. Yet it was precisely the naturalism of the Pre-Raphaelites that commended their work to Ruskin. He pointed out that they were attempting to return to 'archaic honesty' in painting not 'archaic art', and asserted that with experience they might lay the foundation 'of a school of art nobler than the world has seen for three hundred years'.[186]

The medieval aspects of the Pre-Raphaelite movement were emphasized by Rossetti and were to be taken up by William Morris and Edward Burne-Jones later in the century, as they sought to promote the values of craftsmanship in a world where the demeaning demands of industrialization had turned working people from artisans with individual skills into cogs in a mass-production machine.[166]

Nevertheless by 1853 the Pre-Raphaelite Brotherhood was breaking up, as Holman Hunt, Millais and Rossetti went their separate ways, each with a group of followers. Yet the movement's questioning of the superficiality of Victorian artistic methods continued to resonate. Even in 1899 Percy Bate claimed that 'the ripples of agitation started by the foundation of the Brotherhood are still sweeping on, and widening as they go'. Holman Hunt stuck most closely to the movement's original aims. As an evangelical he visited Palestine to search for authentic biblical backgrounds, believing that an accurate depiction of the landscape would supply evidence of the truth of the sacred writings. But over time his commitment to factual accuracy led to works that were sterile and unimaginative. Rossetti went in the opposite direction. His later canvases were filled with imaginative detail and lacked the sense of reality of his earliest paintings. Yet, as Anthea Rose comments, 'Alone among the Pre-Raphaelites he could penetrate . . . into the chivalric world of medieval romance and convey it with a remarkable sense of actuality.'[293] Later in the century Burne-Jones displayed some of those qualities both in his designs for stained glass and in his best paintings.

Millais after 1853 became increasingly conformist. In that year he was elected an Associate of the Royal Academy, thereby accepting the very institution which the Brotherhood had once condemned. Ten years later he became a full academician. And whereas in his Pre-Raphaelite days he had produced works in which the attention to detail was 'almost biological', as his reputation became firmly established he lost this concern for absolute truth. In 1863 he exhibited *My First Sermon*, the beginning of many sentimental studies of young children which, as engravings, were widely sold and brought him wealth and popularity. *Cherry Ripe* (1879), in particular, gained a large circulation through the application of mass-reproduction methods. It was issued both as a steel engraving and as a colour print with the *Graphic*, and sold around 600,000 copies.[349] In 1885 the queen made Millais a baronet, the first artist to be so honoured, and his financial success was such that at his peak he was earning £30,000 a year.[390]

On another level, William Powell Frith was a powerful portrayer of the contemporary scene, particularly in his three major panoramas, *Ramsgate Sands* (1854), *Derby Day* (1856–8) and *The Railway Station* (1862). He appears to have been more concerned with showing life in all its variety than in serving any didactic purpose or conveying a moral message. The spectacle of the Derby Day carnival, with its mixture of upper-class dissolutes, mountebanks, working-class crowds and ragged beggars attracted some of the largest crowds of any painting ever exhibited at the Royal Academy. For only the second time in the Academy's history a rail had to be erected to protect it. *The Railway Station*, showing passengers about to board a train at Paddington station, was sold to the dealer Flatou for the then large sum of £4,500, including the sketch and the lucrative engraving rights. Frith continued to paint modern life subjects for the next twenty years, sometimes using working photographs to assist him, and interspersing these with historical and literary subjects.[390] When his popularity waned in the late 1880s he turned to writing his autobiography and producing replicas of some of his earlier works.

Reverence for the cultural achievements of Ancient Greece and Rome was a central feature of upper-class education in Victorian Britain and this, too, had its influence on the world of art. In the second half of the century painters of classical scenes were inspired by two sources – Greek sculpture and the Italian Renaissance. Much antique sculpture (including the Elgin marbles) could be seen at the British Museum, although Frederic Leighton (later described as the 'Hercules of Victorian classicism') was converted by his experiences in Greece. He called the Parthenon 'the greatest architectural emotion of my life, by far' and kept a copy of its frieze upon his studio walls.[390] Edward Burne-Jones, too, was inspired by this romantic vision of a classical golden age, while Dutch-born Lawrence Alma-Tadema specialized in Greek and Roman genre works. He showed daily life as it would have been experienced by ordinary citizens and his success in making antiquity comprehensible to the middle classes was such that by the 1890s his work commanded some of the highest prices of the day. This growing affluence influenced his own lifestyle and not only did he reduce his output of pictures but he and his second wife, herself a very talented artist, moved to a large house in St John's Wood. There they entertained widely. In 1899 he received a knighthood.[162]

The new interest in foreign travel created a demand for paintings of exotic locations, with dealers despatching artists to various destinations abroad. Publishers, too, commissioned painters to undertake journeys in order to produce watercolours to illustrate travel and guide books. For example, David Roberts's tour of the Middle East resulted in a series of more than two hundred lithographs of Egypt, Syria and the Holy Land, published between 1842 and 1850. He subsequently used these sketches as the basis of studio oil paintings.[349]

The patriotic cause was served by military and battle scenes, with the Crimean War belatedly inspiring the most famous of all Victorian battle painters, Elizabeth Thompson (later Lady Butler). *The Roll Call*, showing guardsmen in the Russian winter, proved the sensation of the 1874 Royal Academy Summer Exhibition and made her famous overnight. It was subsequently purchased by Queen Victoria. Elizabeth also looked further afield, to Egypt and India, and the *Remnants of an Army*, which showed the sole survivor of the retreat from Kabul in the first Afghan War, was perhaps her most ambitious painting.[390]

During the 1870s and 1880s the influence of French art began to grow, culminating in the founding of the New English Art Club in 1886.[166] This was devoted to the propagation of French ideas in general and French Impressionism in particular, but its influence was limited. English Impressionism remained a diverse and complex movement, rather than a coherent school. Christopher Wood describes it as a 'loose association of individuals, united in their admiration for French art', and demonstrating very different responses to it.[390]

At a provincial level, lesser artists continued to make a livelihood supplying the local market with portraits, landscapes and comforting genre works, despite the increasing role of photographers in catering for many of these needs. Such practitioners included men like Joseph Sheppard, a farmer's son from the Weston-super-Mare region of Somerset. In 1866, at the age of thirty-two he was awarded a prize in Weston for a watercolour still-life of apples and this was followed in April 1867 by a certificate from the government's Council of Education for success in 'Freehand or Model Drawing'. With this qualification Sheppard undertook various commissions, mainly landscapes and portraits. The latter included a picture of Miss Bisdee, the daughter of a local gentry family.[84]

For many members of middle-class society, particularly the womenfolk, sketching and painting served as a pleasant pastime. This is confirmed by the large number of art classes and societies. Among them was the Halifax Art Society which began life as the Rembrandt Club in 1875. It held exhibitions of members' work, arranged meetings to promote special studies and sought to encourage 'active sympathy with everything relating to the progress of art generally'.[275] Some amateur artists, like Maud Sambourne, were able to turn their drawing skills to commercial advantage. With her mother's encouragement she submitted work to *Punch*, which employed her father, and to other journals. Several of the Sambournes' female friends were artists in their own right, having exhibited before marriage.[257]

For many, attendance at the Summer Exhibition of the Royal Academy and, from 1877, the annual exhibitions of the Grosvenor Gallery, which displayed avant-garde works, formed part of the London Season. On 'Picture Sunday', immediately prior to the submission date for the Royal Academy's annual exhibition, the Sambournes would tour the studios of artist friends, where pictures intended for display were on show. A month later they would go to see these same pictures on Private View Day at the Royal Academy itself. 'To Academy, met heaps of friends', wrote Marion Sambourne in a typical diary entry. She also visited the Grosvenor Gallery, then a focus of the Aesthetic movement, and the New Gallery, which took over its mantle in 1887 when the Grosvenor was forced to become more commercial. Although she noted that she had

Visitors admiring pictures at the National Gallery, London, c. 1900. (The author)

met 'shoals of people', she never mentioned the pictures she had seen at these events, nor did she give critical appraisals of the work done by her friends. Her personal preference was for Old Masters: 'Lovely pictures' was her judgement after seeing a collection of Rembrandts and Titians. At the annual exhibitions female visitors would wear the elegant clothes which were to establish the season's fashions, and Marion commented on these in her diary, as in 1892, when she reported: 'Many pretty dresses, striped all the fashion, long skirts, full sleeves & sashes to bottom of skirt.'[257]

ARCHITECTURE

The Victorian era saw no great stylistic developments in British architecture, and those changes which did occur were largely based on traditional designs. In the early and middle years of the queen's reign it was the Gothic Revival which was the predominant influence, promoted in particular by the young Augustus W.N. Pugin. Pugin was a convert to Roman Catholicism and designed a number of churches for his fellow Catholics. But he also received commissions for schools and country houses. His books, especially *Contrasts* (1836) and *The True Principles of Pointed or Christian Architecture* (1841), played a major part in promoting the Gothic cause. To Pugin the medieval ideals he espoused were a moral crusade, with Gothic the only mode of building possible for a Christian nation. Classical architecture he condemned as 'false' and 'pagan', whereas pointed arches and soaring spires bore the imprint of Christian faith and devotion.[152] Interestingly, even Nonconformists, who remained faithful to classicism for their church building in the early Victorian years, fell under the influence of the Gothic Revival in the 1850s.[144]

However, while Gothic gained steadily on the Grecian and Renaissance styles for churches and public buildings at the beginning of the queen's reign, different designs were applied to other structures. Italian-inspired campaniles were incorporated in the royal family's new Isle of Wight home, Osborne House, and in a number of other residences, while French influences could be detected in many of the hotels under construction. These included the luxurious Great Western Hotel at Paddington, whose style was described by the *Illustrated London News* in 1852 as 'French of Louis XIV or later'. Other hotels followed along similar lines. In railway building, too, there was a mingling of designs, with a classical portico constructed at Huddersfield station, Gothic used at Windsor and Tudor at Bristol Temple Meads, to name but three.[99]

Prior to the 1870s architects committed to the Gothic ideal were in the ascendancy, with Sir George Gilbert Scott the most prolific of them. He interpreted the medieval revival with great boldness, and ecclesiastical work (including church restorations) was the mainstay of his practice. But he also designed buildings of such varied types as the Albert Memorial (1864), Glasgow University (1864) and the hotel of the Midland Railway terminus of St Pancras, with its impressive skyline (1867).[97] Like the majority of his profession, he rejected the revolutionary challenge of the mid-century Crystal Palace, built of prefabricated iron and glass by Sir Joseph Paxton, in favour of the traditional.

In the final quarter of the Victorian era, however, there was a reaction against Gothic, with growing interest instead in English and French Renaissance. In the sphere of housebuilding, under the influence of the architect Norman Shaw the

Manchester Assize Courts built in the Gothic style (1859). The architect, Alfred Waterhouse, was chosen by competition from a field of over a hundred candidates. (From Charles L. Eastlake, A History of the Gothic Revival, *1872)*

Queen Anne style emerged. Its characteristic features were red brick, which had been unfashionable for a century, and the contrast of this with white wooden balconies and window sills.[152] But the most typical architect of these years was probably Alfred Waterhouse. Although his impressive Manchester Town Hall (1877) was on orthodox Gothic lines he subsequently displayed great stylistic variation, from 'Romanesque through Venetian Gothic to French Renaissance'.[152]

Growing national prosperity coupled with rising civic pride and a commitment to public works inevitably had an influence on the architectural profession. There was an enormous upsurge in commissions for town halls, museums, art galleries, banks, hospitals, workhouses and much else besides. Norman Shaw, for one, turned increasingly to official commissions for banks and insurance offices.[97] Church building, too, grew across all denominations, especially in urban areas. Kensington alone had forty-three churches and chapels erected over the twenty years prior to 1872.[144] Successful businessmen and professional people were able to afford to build or extend country houses on a major scale, with the 1870s described as the 'golden age' for construction.[168] Many were built in imitation Georgian or Tudor style, and as Sir John Betjeman has commented drily, a 'school of architects grew up versed in building in the style of the neighbouring country villages'.[97]

Even the world of entertainment contributed to the building boom, with the expansion of seaside resorts and a widening provision of theatres, opera houses and music halls. Some were inspired by Indian and Middle Eastern designs in accordance with the Victorian cult of imperialism.[298] For as R.C.K. Ensor has pointed out, the reaction against Gothic in the late nineteenth century merely led to an eclectic adoption of other fashions. Even versatile practitioners like Norman Shaw, who liked to make his buildings suit their purpose and setting, found it impossible to escape 'from the notion that to give a building architectural quality involved clothing it in some form of historical fancy-dress'.[157] Hence although the prevalent style was now called 'free classic', in reality it was largely derived from one of the many varieties of French Renaissance.

Additional Sources Used

Annual Register for 1848 (London, 1849), for 1851 (London, 1852), for 1853 (London, 1854), and for 1857 (London, 1858).

Country Life Illustrated, 13 and 27 February 1897.

T.J. Edelstein, 'They Sang "The Song of the Shirt": The Visual Iconology of the Seamstress' in *Victorian Studies*, Vol. 23, No. 2 (Winter 1980).

Hywel Teifi Edwards, *The Eisteddfod* (Cardiff, 1990).

E.D.H. Johnson, 'Victorian Artists and the Urban Milieu' in H.J. Dyos and Michael Wolff (eds), *The Victorian City*, Vol. 2 (London and Boston, 1973).

Sally Mitchell, 'Sentiment and Suffering: Women's Recreational Reading in the 1860s' in *Victorian Studies*, Vol. 21, No. 1 (Autumn 1977).

James Patrick, 'Newman, Pugin, and Gothic' in *Victorian Studies*, Vol. 24, No. 2 (Winter 1981).

Christiana Payne, *Toil and Plenty. Images of the Agricultural Landscape in England 1780–1890* (New Haven and London, 1993).

John Pemble, *The Mediterranean Passion. Victorians and Edwardians in the South* (Oxford, 1988).

Pre-Raphaelite Drawings: Exhibition Guide at Birmingham Museum and Art Gallery (Birmingham, 1989).

Charles Terrot, *The Maiden Tribute. A Study of the White Slave Traffic of the Nineteenth Century* (London, 1959).

Donald Thomas, *The Victorian Underworld* (London, 1998).

J. Don Vann and Rosemary T. Van Arsdel, *Victorian Periodicals. A Guide to Research* (New York, 1978).

Shearer West, 'Tom Taylor, William Powell Frith and the British School of Art' in *Victorian Studies*, Vol. 33, No. 2 (Winter 1990).

CHAPTER 10

Respectable Recreations and the Patriotic Spirit

The ideal Sunday school of the 1870s would have contained scholars from three to eighty . . . In addition to religious education it would have sponsored a Christian Endeavour Society, a Band of Hope, a branch of the International Bible Reading Association, recreational evening classes and lantern lectures, gym, cricket, swimming and cycling clubs, class teas, picnics, etc.

> Thomas Walter Laqueur, *Religion and Respectability. Sunday Schools and Working Class Culture 1780–1850* (New Haven and London, 1976), 249

This 23rd of June . . . for the Volunteer army and for the country, . . . proved how earnestly and efficiently the corps represented had devoted themselves to training and discipline . . . The authorities found that they would have to make arrangements for placing 20,000 men in review order. As the time approached, and it became evident how earnest the Volunteers were . . ., the review became a national spectacle, a 'general holiday' was arranged, London prepared to empty itself into Hyde Park, and the provinces to precipitate themselves into London.

> *Annual Register for 1860* (London, 1861), 87

RATIONAL RECREATION

Religion, respectability and rigorous morality were widely accepted watchwords in Victorian society and they applied as much to the world of recreation as to other aspects of national life. At the same time the number of voluntary associations formed rose sharply. In a complex and changing world many previously informal groupings established themselves as permanent bodies, with agreed membership rules. 'The present is pre-eminently an age of societies,' said a cutting among the records of St John's Church in Reading, 'and when some future historian takes pen in hand to narrate the characteristic features of the latter half of the nineteenth century, one of his chief duties will be to trace the rise and progress of the associated movements which have so largely developed in our midst during the past 50 years.'[394]

In their day-to-day application, however, these activities were more paradoxical than might appear at first sight. Those who followed apparently prudent pursuits like membership of a friendly society to provide sickness and funeral benefits could also, through their linked club celebrations, anniversary meetings, initiation ceremonies and use of regalia, engage in actions that were the reverse of rational. Thomas Wright, himself a member of a friendly society, was one who criticized the custom of holding meetings in public houses, arguing that the 'unrestricted drinking' encouraged at such gatherings was 'at all times detrimental to the business interests of the societies, and frequently leads to most unseemly proceedings'.[69] It was much easier to draw distinctions between 'thinkers and drinkers' or 'virtue and vice' in theory than in practice.[87]

Again, membership of a church or chapel could lead to a growth in personal faith but, in some circumstances, it could also encourage bitter denominational rivalries, as in Banbury, Oxfordshire, where despite the town's overall religious commitment the divisions between Anglicans and Dissenters deepened, at least up to the 1880s.[350] Elsewhere Protestants were ranged against Roman Catholics, and within the Church of England itself there was ill-feeling between High Church, with its commitment to ritual and colour in services, and evangelicals or Low Churchmen who favoured a ceremonial nearer to that of the Nonconformists. There were also struggles between religious believers and those advocating the right to free thought, which might include atheism. The writings of Charles Darwin, especially his *Origin of Species* (1859), proved particularly damaging to Christian orthodoxy. Such clashes between churches and creeds affected the formation of friendships and the broader rhythm of social life.[258]

In these circumstances, despite the self-consciously religious ethos of the age, a substantial number of people did not attend Sunday services at all. At the religious census conducted on 30 March 1851, perhaps 61 per cent of the population of England and Wales attended some place of worship (and this included a significant number who had been counted twice because they had attended twice). Furthermore, in large towns with populations of over ten thousand the proportion fell to only 49.7 per cent. The problem was particularly acute in the poorer districts of large towns, so that Bolton registered an average attendance of only 36.8 per cent, Sheffield 32.1 per cent and Lambeth and Tower Hamlets in London 31 per cent and 29.7 per cent respectively. As the census report concluded, 'the masses of our working population . . . are never or but seldom seen in our religious congregations'.[207]

Nor had the situation improved by the early 1880s when an unofficial census suggested that only around 38 per cent of the population in large towns attended a church or chapel. In Bolton and Sheffield the figures had fallen to 24.3 per cent and 23 per cent respectively.[123] Although the accuracy of such statistics was open to question, the trend they indicated was profoundly discouraging to churchmen. At the end of the century one eminent Anglican, a future bishop of London, commented gloomily that it was 'not that the Church of God had lost the great towns; it had never had them.'[393] A number of his contemporaries agreed, despite the resolute efforts made by all religious denominations to provide for the spiritual and social needs of urban dwellers. 'To most working-class people,' writes James Obelkevich the churches were alien, middle-class institutions where people like themselves, lacking good clothes and unable to afford pew rents, felt out of place. Church-goers they tended to regard as snobs and hypocrites; any working-class person going to church was liable to be condemned for putting on airs, setting himself above his neighbours. Social pressure did as much to deter church-going in the working class as it did to encourage it in the middle and upper classes.[258]

Yet he also admits that there was a solid core of working people, particularly in Wales and Scotland, who were deeply involved in church life. Likewise among Roman Catholics, priests all over Britain responded with almost missionary zeal to the needs of poor Irish immigrants. In many town parishes the Catholic Church became a focus for unskilled workers and their families, a place where it was considered no disgrace 'to be poor and stay poor'.[258] Primitive Methodism, too, appealed particularly to the working classes.[70]

Equally, not all middle-class people were zealous churchgoers, especially in London. At the end of the century in the wealthy suburbs and the West End little more than a third of the population went to church on Sundays. Partly this was owing to a general relaxation in sabbatarianism and partly to a growing secularism at the summit of society, with the Prince of Wales holding dinner parties at Marlborough House on Sundays. At Sandringham sermons were timed to last no longer than ten minutes when he was present.[192] Soon this influenced families lower down the scale. In the Sambourne household in Kensington, Linley never attended church and Marion worshipped intermittently. She rarely took the children to morning services, leaving that to the nurse or their grandmother, and often made excuses that she was 'too seedy' to attend on other occasions. In the 1880s for a time she was attracted to High Church rituals and even experimented with Roman Catholicism. The sermon was particularly important to her and she often commented on it in her diary. After one particularly stirring oration she wrote, 'Wish I could hear the like every Sunday.' But in the 1890s her interest waned, and when she and her husband stayed with friends or relatives she would note laconically: 'All to church except Lin & self.'[257]

Much the same situation applied to another London family, the Marshalls. According to one of the daughters, Jeannette, religion, prayers and spiritual matters seldom figured in her childhood, and by the 1870s she and her sister had become almost as slack as their parents about attending church. The threat of a shower of rain and even getting up late on Sunday morning were seized on as excuses for absence. 'Reading the order of service (aloud or to oneself) in the comfort of No. 10 [their home] became an adequate mark of allegiance to the Church,' comments Jeannette's biographer.[312]

Even among regular church- or chapel-goers friction might arise over the issue of social class and its associated relationships. In Wales, where Nonconformity was dominant, divisions between farmers and cottagers attending the same chapel could be painfully apparent. Thus when members of a south Cardiganshire chapel discussed building a manse for the minister, there was impatience when one of the cottagers spoke at length. After he had finished a farmer observed coldly, 'Now that you "wheelbarrow men" (every cottager had a wheelbarrow for use in his garden) have had your say, perhaps we "cart men" may have ours.'[212] The distinction was all too obvious. Again, in south-west Wales far more farmers became deacons than their number in the community would have suggested was equitable. In parts of north Pembrokeshire it was claimed that a man needed to own at least two horses before he could aspire to the diaconate. At the teas that accompanied church and chapel functions in rural Wales it was cottagers' wives and daughters who performed the menial tasks of tending the fire, boiling the water and washing up the dishes. Farmers' wives and daughters did the serving, with much rivalry as to who should attend to the ministers' table when several ministers were present. After more than half a century one woman recalled her embarrassment on realizing that she had inadvertently asked the daughter of a substantial farmer to help with the washing up.[212]

Yet these personal differences did not prevent a sense of solidarity from arising as well, with members anxious to uphold the prestige of their own place of worship as compared to that of others in the area. If one chapel recruited a well-known preacher for its annual festival, neighbouring congregations would strive

The congregation attending Sunday morning service at the Church of St Peter ad Vincula at the Tower of London, c. 1900. The church was only open to the public at the 11 a.m. Sunday service on special application. (The author)

to engage an equally prestigious minister for their own event, while the success of one chapel in a singing competition would soon arouse a spirit of emulation in the rest.[212] Such competitions were also important in bringing together people from a wide area, thereby broadening and strengthening social networks. In scattered rural communities this was welcomed, especially by young people who could meet suitable potential partners of the opposite sex.

In certain English country parishes people attended church in the morning out of a sense of duty towards their social superiors, and chapel in the evening from inclination. As Edward Steers, curate at Skegness, Lincolnshire, was told by one resident, 'We comes to church in the morning to please you, Sir, and goes to chapel at night to save our souls.'[259] Those who attended both church and chapel in this way were often nicknamed 'devil-dodgers', but for many it was a way of carrying out social obligations as well as securing spiritual sustenance. At Juniper Hill in Oxfordshire Flora Thompson remembered the Methodists meeting in a local cottage on Sunday evenings 'for prayer and praise'. 'Methodism, as known and practised there,' she wrote, 'was a poor people's religion, simple and crude; but its adherents brought to it more fervour than was shown by the church congregation, and appeared to obtain more comfort and support from it than the church could give.'[342] She noted drily that some of the churchgoers were inspired by less than praiseworthy motives, perhaps because they wanted to 'show off their best clothes and to see and criticize those of their neighbours', or because they liked to hear their own voices raised in the hymns, or because 'churchgoing qualified them for the Christmas blankets and coals'.[342]

But for large numbers of people attendance at a religious service was a genuine spiritual experience which gave meaning to their lives. In slum areas of London, for example, Roman Catholic churches were adorned with brightly coloured statues of the Virgin Mary, St Joseph and other saints. Priests believed that this was much appreciated by poorer worshippers, especially the Irish. In their miserable homes they saw nothing but 'wretchedness and desolation' and as a result they felt 'the greatest delight . . . in . . . all those objects of devotion which gladden the eyes and the hearts of Catholics . . . They, and they alone, really enjoy them.'

Sarah Thomas, the daughter of a Baptist minister from Fairford, Gloucestershire, similarly attached great importance to attendance at chapel. She prayed regularly to God for guidance in her personal life, and eventually refused the proposal of marriage of a young Baptist minister because of his apparent lack of commitment to his calling: 'I truly love him,' she wrote on one occasion, ' . . . but he never talks to me of religious affairs and I fear my own faith will suffer as a result, but he lays these things aside when I talk to him of them. I resorted to reading scripture after scripture and private prayer then went to chapel.'[230]

Good sermons were particularly appreciated and those preachers who combined a gift for words with an impressive pulpit presence attracted crowded congregations. The leading figures became household names, so that when some of A.L. Rowse's Cornish relatives visited London they put a high priority on going to hear the Baptist giant Charles Spurgeon preach at the Metropolitan Tabernacle. Spurgeon could 'fill chapels by his magnetic oratory'. Similarly the fiery Morley Punshon was able to 'lift all his hearers to their feet surging with the emotion roused by his eloquence and cheering wildly'.[108] G.M. Young even claimed that the 'form of preachers was canvassed like the form of public entertainers, and the circulation of some Victorian sermons is a thing to fill a modern writer with despair'.

In Wales during the outbursts of intense religious fervour which occurred during periodic 'revivals', as in 1859 or in the 1880s in parts of Cardiganshire and Carmarthenshire, there was sustained enthusiasm, passionate prayer, profound preoccupation with personal salvation and much rejoicing at the reception of the spirit.[148] Even those whose faith was expressed more discreetly might nonetheless devote much leisure to religious matters. One such was the Lincolnshire farmer and Methodist lay preacher Cornelius Stovin. Not only did Cornelius preach regularly but he chaired anniversary meetings over a wide area and helped to finance a number of chapels. 'My enjoyment of life and Christ intense. This is the key to human happiness . . . Christ is the charm of life', was typical of his diary entries.[334]

For some committed evangelicals a pilgrimage to the Holy Land was a means of justifying their belief in the literal truth of Scripture. In 1887 the Revd Bell of Cheltenham noted on his return from Palestine that all he had seen had confirmed 'the truth of God's Holy Word and given its wondrous story a reality for which I am most thankful'. A decade earlier an anonymous 'working man' joined one of Thomas Cook's tours of the Holy Land, after saving up for several years. According to *Cook's Excursionist*, no other member of the party gained so much from the visit. At Nazareth he seemed to pour out his soul in gratitude 'to God that He had permitted him to gratify his long-cherished hopes, and to behold the places so sacred with the memories of the Saviour whom he loved'.

For many less committed church- and chapel-goers, however, it was the subsidiary organizations which clustered around Victorian religious institutions that most attracted them. Although Sunday services were basic to the life and work of all denominations, an array of other activities grew up, particularly following the increase in leisure during the second half of the century. They included sports clubs, choirs, charitable societies, the running of libraries, the formation of special sections for men, women, and young people (like the Young Men's Christian Association for youths and the Mothers' Union for married women), the establishment of temperance societies, missionary guilds and the like, and the opening of halls and coffee taverns where meetings could be held. 'Visiting, sewing, discussing, listening, teaching, abstaining, selling, reading, collecting, singing . . . these and much else besides, became expected parts of church or chapel life,' comments Stephen Yeo. 'A total and interlocking system of participatory organisations, all of which ideally involved forms of *joining* or continuous *attending* had become part of the self-definition of religion.'[394]

Symptomatic of the trend was the report in 1900 from St John's parish, Reading, that the year's greatest event had been 'undoubtedly the Bazaar . . . a splendid success.' Not only had it raised a large sum of money but had required much voluntary effort. As a result 'the whole parish was united more closely together'.[394] Such initiatives particularly attracted middle-class women since they gave them an opportunity to display organizing skills which were little exercised in other areas of social life. For the younger ones they were also an occasion for mild flirtations, as many men attended bazaars and girls could widen acquaintanceships in that way without compromising their reputation.[279] It was in this context that *The Occasional Magazine* commented ironically: 'when we were told to see to it that the Gospel should be preached to the whole world, it was intended (though not so mentioned) that the money should be raised by a bazaar'.[394]

Yet, despite the mockery, for many involved these events were a means of demonstrating their respectability and their membership of a wide social network. Especially in the newly expanding suburbs middle- and upper working-class families found in these meetings and events a way of boosting self-esteem and widening their circle of acquaintances in what might seem a fast-changing and bewildering environment.[394] Reginald Underwood recalled of the Methodists of his youth that their social life was centred entirely around 'our chapel'. 'Every evening was occupied by a class-meeting, a guild-meeting, a prayer-meeting or choir practice. All very smug and self-centred to those outside, but, as I know, of real importance to those inside.'[353]

Yet such narrowness of outlook could mean that those who offended against the group mores would be excluded. In 1839 John Pearson lost his preaching credentials on the Retford Wesleyan circuit in Nottinghamshire because he had married 'a person not at all religious'. A year later the Mansfield Primitive Methodist circuit expelled Thomas Ward for 'improperly associating with Mrs. Wild and being with her in the fields and on the railway at a late hour'. These were not isolated cases.[202]

For the ambitious, churches and chapels might offer a way of advancing in the world. Well-to-do congregations conferred a certain lustre, as in Bristol where the leading congregations of the main denominations could be found in Clifton, an exclusive suburb. The Anglicans alone had five churches there.[245] Those wishing to be associated with community leaders would attend services in such places in the hope of being drawn into the magic circle. By contrast, sects like the Free Methodists, Bible Christians, Methodist New Connexion and the Salvation Army drew their support mainly from those lower down the scale and their influence was exerted by mass evangelical gatherings and 'conversion spectaculars' in the Moody and Sankey tradition rather than by social prestige. The Salvation Army, in particular, aroused initial hostility through its processions, street meetings and brass bands. In the 1870s and 1880s members were sometimes attacked by hooligans and pelted with stones and other missiles. One man beaten up in Liverpool in 1882 apparently returned from hospital with his head bandaged, 'leaping and praising God' and generally undaunted. Gradually police and magistrates recognized that the Army, for all its eccentricities, was an upholder of public order, while its officers, with their distinctive uniforms, moved more easily than most ordained ministers into public houses and the slums of large cities. Although their evangelical message was not as successful as their founder, William Booth, had once hoped, they never forgot that their aim was to 'win souls for Christ'. In the meantime with their bands they became a distinctive feature of urban street life, as they used music to announce meetings and to lead voices in singing 'simple, bouncing hymns'.[206]

The differing status of denominations was remarked upon by George Eliot, among others. In *Felix Holt* she described the surprise of Church people in her fictional community of Treby Magna that Esther Lyon, the daughter of a

Nonconformist minister, should be an expert teacher of French, a language 'so lively and altogether worldly'. For her part Esther felt some ambiguity towards her father's personal position. She

> knew that Dissenters were looked down upon by those whom she regarded as the most refined classes; her favourite companions, both in France and at an English school where she had been a junior teacher, had thought it quite ridiculous to have a father who was a Dissenting preacher . . .[399]

Even at the end of Queen Victoria's reign these distinctions survived. Although all the dissenting denominations included some rich business leaders among their members, it was believed that most such families would eventually transfer to the socially superior Church of England, on the basis that 'the carriage only stops for one generation at the chapel door'.[258] In Salford Robert Roberts remembered each denomination having its particular social cachet, with the Anglicans to the fore and the Primitive Methodists bringing up the rear, while the Roman Catholics 'didn't count' at all. It was symptomatic of their 'known low breeding' that while Sunday clothes were seen as an important status symbol, poverty-stricken Catholic mothers attended Sunday morning Mass wearing clogs and shawls, with their ill-clad children beside them.[290]

Of all the activities associated with church and chapel it was perhaps Sunday schools which played the major role in providing pleasures and pastimes, especially for children and adolescents. In Manchester in 1877 Canon Bardsley felt it necessary to reject a charge that they had become 'mere courting institutions', and there were claims that the social classes mixed more freely in Sunday school than anywhere else. Enrolment rose from 2.6 million or about 13 per cent of the population of Britain in 1851 to 5.9 million or 16 per cent of total population at the end of the century. By 1890 the Sunday School Union, the largest of the groupings, claimed that just over a fifth of its students were in the senior division, that is they were over the age of fifteen.[228]

The main aim of Sunday schools was to spread their religious message and inculcate the correct moral values, but they soon drew around themselves a network of leisure pursuits. These included special tea meetings, particularly at Christmas and Whitsuntide, outings, ancillary organizations like the Boys' Brigade and the Band of Hope, and the anniversary celebration, which was perhaps the most important event in a Sunday school's year. Preparations went on for months and it was an occasion for wearing new clothes, reciting specially learnt passages before parents and friends, listening to music and perhaps marching in procession through town or village. In the larger schools special hymns would be written and sometimes there was an excursion as well. Kate Edwards, who grew up in the Lotting Fen area of Huntingdonshire in the 1880s, remembered her mother saving up to take the whole family to the chapel anniversary tea ('6d. for grownups, 3d. apiece for the child'en'). Slabs of wood would be placed across the tops of the pews and brightly polished urns would be used to dispense tea to the assembled company. 'A lot of people 'ould come from villages all round . . . When the tea and the talk were over, the chapel 'ould be

Sunday school outing near the former Denbigh cock pit, c. 1900. (Museum of Welsh Life, St Fagans, Cardiff)

cleared, and some singers . . . 'ould come to "render" the Service of Song they'd been practising. The chapel 'ould be full . . . crowded to overflowing, and as soon as it got dark the oil lamps 'ould be lit and the doors and windows shut, and the preacher would go up to the pulpit.'[241] Lantern shows were appreciated, too, especially when they were presented by a missionary who described exciting adventures and hairbreadth escapes in distant parts of the world.[202]

Sunday school outings were also important events. They ranged from a village meeting where youngsters and their teachers would march out to have a picnic and play games in a nearby field, to elaborately organized visits to distant destinations. Longer trips became more popular with the growth in cheap mass transport, so that in 1849 over two thousand passengers went from Derby to Matlock in two trains with sixty gaily decorated carriages. Occasionally the outings would be arranged to counter an undesirable rival event, such as a fair or horse races. In 1846 the *Sunday School Magazine* reported with satisfaction a railway excursion for a thousand children during race week in Carlisle. They were 'regaled in teetotal style with two large plum cakes and abundance of rich new milk'.[228] Similarly the 'annual folly fair' on Easter Monday in Blackburn was counteracted by a day of sports in the country. In this way it was hoped to steer the young from the dangers of drinking, gambling and playing games on the

Sabbath, towards such 'rational' recreations as walks, railway excursions, teas and schemes for self-improvement.

But while Sunday schools enjoyed some short-term success, particularly among the offspring of better-off working-class families, their efforts to recruit the poorest children (who probably lacked suitable clothing to attend, even if they had wished to do so) and their attempts to boost adult church and chapel congregations were disappointing. In town and country alike working men, in particular, rarely attended a religious service and the women were little better.[258] Flora Thompson remembered that at Juniper Hill most adults stayed away from church, with the females occupied in cooking and nursing and the males undertaking 'an elaborate Sunday toilet' which including shaving and cutting one another's hair. They spent the rest of the day eating, sleeping, reading a newspaper and walking round to admire their neighbours' pigs and gardens.[342] In London Charles Booth reported a similar situation, with the men rising late and then 'sitting at breakfast half-dressed or lounging in the window reading *Lloyd's Weekly Newspaper*'. After they had washed and dressed they went to the public house, where they stayed until about 3 p.m. They then returned home to the dinner which the womenfolk had been preparing. 'After dinner the men, if they had drunk much, may go to bed, but the better sort take a stroll. In the evening the young people pair off for walking out, while the elders may perhaps go to a concert or Sunday League lecture', or perhaps would visit family and friends. According to Booth, Sunday was 'the great day for visiting'.[101] In some cases the children would be sent to afternoon Sunday school to give their parents rare privacy for sexual intercourse.

The inability of churches and chapels to attract and retain the bulk of the poorer working classes applied equally to youth organizations associated with them or with their Sunday schools. These included the Boys' Brigade and the Band of Hope. The Boys' Brigade was formed in Glasgow in 1883 to cater for lads between twelve and seventeen. It was non-denominational and its prime purpose was 'the advancement of Christ's Kingdom among Boys, and the promotion of habits of Reverence, Discipline, Self-Respect, and all that tends towards a true Christian Manliness'. Or as William Smith, its founder, put it, the brigade sought to associate 'Christianity with all that was most noble and manly in a boy's sight', so that he would lose the idea 'that there [was] anything effeminate or weak about Christianity'.[325] Within months of its inauguration the familiar uniform of pill-box cap, belt and haversack had been introduced, to be worn with a boy's ordinary clothes, and dummy rifles were issued. Discipline and drill were early features of the new organization and according to one of the original recruits, while hundreds wanted to join, 'many were rejected because they wouldn't attend Sabbath School'.[325]

The movement grew rapidly, with some companies formed by a single denomination and others by a combination of churches, as was the case in the small north Ayrshire town of Beith. There the Church of Scotland, Free Church, two United Presbyterian churches, the Evangelical Mission and Beith Mission School acted jointly. As a result three companies were formed in the first session, with 150 boys enrolled.[324] Elsewhere, as in Hawick and Perth, existing Working Boys' societies or boys' clubs formed companies under their own auspices.[324] In 1885 the first band was set up in Glasgow and by 1887 thirty-five bands were in existence, twenty-five of them drum and fife. As well as playing at parades and Sunday services the bands were soon in demand within the wider community, performing at flower shows, fêtes, bazaars and similar events.[324]

Within three years the movement had penetrated south of the border and by 1890 122 companies of the Boys' Brigade had been formed in England and Wales, with over five thousand members. Scotland at that date had 260 companies and a membership of 11,109. But in 1893 England and Wales overtook Scotland's lead and by 1899 there were 19,715 members in the former compared to 12,796 in the latter.[325] By 1899 some were calling the Boys' Brigade 'A juvenile Citizen Army', and similar denominational bodies followed in its wake. The Church Lads' Brigade was formed in 1891 by the Anglicans, while the Jewish Lads' Brigade was set up in 1895, and the Catholic Boys' Brigade, centred around a boys' club in London, appeared a year later.[324]

Most early recruits were the sons of skilled manual workers or those with white-collar occupations. Alongside the obligatory drill, Bible class and club-room activities there were athletic competitions and various concerts and field days. There was also the prestige of marching through one's own neighbourhood

Members of the Boys' Brigade wearing their distinctive uniform in London, c. 1900. (The author)

and having that event witnessed by others.[245] However, it was not all smooth sailing. At Enfield, where the first company was established in the late 1880s, one captain recounted that few drills passed without attacks from 'hooligans' and 'discontents' who resented the new organization's pretensions. Even the officers were 'pelted with bottles and other missiles as they went to drill, and the boys had to defend their uniform often with their fists'.[325]

For most lads the high spot of the year was the annual camp held at the seaside or in the country. It represented freedom from the restrictions of family life and from the noise, dirt and discomfort of many boys' home environment. Instead there was the chance of adventure in an unfamiliar setting. The first Jewish Lads' Brigade camp was held at Deal in 1896, on a site taken over from the West Kent Battalion of the Boys' Brigade. When the Jewish youngsters arrived at Deal station they were marched in formation, with the Norwood Band at their head, through the town to the camp. Once settled in, their daily routine began with reveille at 6 a.m., followed by prayers, a parade and coffee and biscuits. Then came bathing in the sea and physical drill, with breakfast at 8.30 a.m. and drill with rifles from 9 a.m. to 11 a.m. After 1 p.m. dinner there was 'play' – cricket, chess, rowing and similar activities – with tea at 5.30 p.m. and supper at 9 p.m. Prayers were held at 9.20 p.m. and lights out was at 10.15.[221] To boys accustomed to the squalor of much of working-class London it was a revelation, but for those who objected to the brigade's firm discipline or disliked its militaristic overtones the movement had little appeal. Hence total membership of the original Boys' Brigade in England, Wales and Scotland even in 1899 was under 33,000; and when the other denominational brigades were taken into account that was still a small minority only of the boys in the eligible age group who could have joined.

The temperance cause, likewise, was largely intertwined with religious institutions, relying on both churchmen and Nonconformists for the contacts it needed to achieve success. During the 1830s the movement drifted away from an acceptance of moderation in drinking towards teetotalism and subsequently to the prohibition of alcohol altogether. To keen reformers, conversion to the temperance cause was like a religious experience, with 'social aspiration' substituted for 'doctrinal commitment'.[179] But the movement's leaders rapidly realized that if people were to be persuaded of the merits of temperance their message must combine education with entertainment.[180] This included penny readings, concerts, lectures and weekly meetings in clubs and mission rooms. Many lectures were treated as recreational diversions by the local press, as in Banbury where persuasive speakers like the American John B. Gough visited the town more than once. The *Banbury Advertiser* in 1858 commented on Gough's histrionic skills and his ability to sway his audience 'till sighs and groans and tears begin to flow'. Then in an instant his manner would change 'and those eyes just filled with tears become full of laughter: seriousness has given place to ludicrousness, and the meeting is once more happy'.[350]

Other activities offered in Banbury included railway excursions, performances by teetotal concert parties and the setting up of a temperance choral society. Similar initiatives were taken in other towns and there was even a teetotal friendly society, the Independent Order of Rechabites, with a national membership in 1900 of

Dre-fach Felindre Rechabite Band, Carmarthenshire, playing in the temperance cause, c. 1900. Note the elaborate uniforms of the bandsmen. (Museum of Welsh Life, St Fagans, Cardiff)

137,316. In the same year a rival body, the Order of the Sons of Temperance, with American origins, had 49,287 members.[255] The social activities of the Rechabites largely centred around amateur sports meetings, fêtes, concerts and similar events.

The ability of the temperance cause to attract audiences to its entertainments even at the end of the century owed much to a national sub-culture of evangelical teetotalism and the 'institutionalizing' of the temperance year, with events carefully spaced so as to maintain interest among members and supporters.[245] This applied particularly to the movement's youth wing, the Band of Hope, set up in Leeds in 1847 and boasting around three million members at the end of the century, two million of them also being Sunday school pupils. Its formation was an indication of the promoters' belief that the best way to vanquish the evils of alcoholism was to equip the next generation to withstand the temptations of the 'demon drink'. To this end the Band of Hope assiduously combined recreation and instruction. In the winter there would be entertainments, punctuated by a Christmas tea; in the summer there would be street processions, games and nature walks with an annual outing as the highlight of the year.[245]

Walter Southgate joined the Band of Hope at Bethnal Green in 1900, when he was ten. He signed the pledge to abstain from all alcohol and was appointed a captain, with a blue sash as his badge of office. Each week there would be songs and recitations 'coached by a dramatic youth who had come all the way from Oxford University in need of experience in slumming in the East End'.[319] Meetings were held in a Church of England mission hall at the end of Walter's street and each year there was an outing to Epping Forest in a four-horse brake, with a free tea of bread, strawberry jam and 'seedy fruit cakes' provided. Those who behaved badly at the weekly meetings would be threatened with exclusion from this much-prized trip.

On a broader basis many local associations formed choirs or simple orchestras, with children often introduced to music through temperance songs and religious hymns. 'Was it not likely that a little girl singing a verse of some sweet melody in the hearing of her poor drunken father would melt his heart,' declared one Band of Hope worker optimistically.[310] From 1862 large annual concerts were staged in London for the massed choirs of the whole movement. At the first of them about a thousand singers took part, but by 1886 that total had climbed to fifteen thousand.[310]

Yet despite these efforts and the Band of Hope's impressive recruitment figures its long-term influence was limited. As with the other youth organizations most supporters were the children of the operative class rather than the offspring of the poorest families, who found difficulty in achieving the regularity, punctuality and cleanliness insisted upon and whose own life style often contradicted the movement's teetotal principles. When the children grew up they frequently forgot their temperance training and their abstinence pledges. So although consumption of wine, beer and spirits began to decline from its 1870s peak – as working-class leisure spending was diverted in other directions – even in 1900 drunkenness was still a serious problem. In the 1890s social reformers began to question the temperance movement's concentration on the alcohol problem, seeing this instead as part of a wider issue of working-class welfare. Symptomatic of the new mood was the comment of a labour leader that the cause was diverting working men from the real reasons for social evils 'to some of its minor effects'.[179] In such circumstances the importance of the temperance organizations in providing entertainment for their supporters and for the community at large inevitably diminished.

Friendly societies, by contrast, remained popular examples of working-class self-dependence and respectability. Through their rituals and initiation ceremonies, as well as through the benefits they provided and the rules they applied, they induced feelings of solidarity among their largely male membership. This was particularly true of the large affiliated societies, like the Manchester Unity of Oddfellows and the Ancient Order of Foresters whose membership grew respectively from 248,526 and 76,990 in 1845 to 736,181 and 663,232 by 1900.[255] Although the emblems, costumes, regalia, ceremonial, passwords and special kinds of handshake used by the main orders (and by Free Masons) were dismissed by outsiders as undesirable 'trumpery', they strengthened the loyalty and sense of comradeship of their members. The aim was to make an Oddfellow working in an Accrington cotton mill feel that he had more in common with an Oddfellow in the Portsmouth dockyard than with another cotton worker in Accrington who was not a member.[170] Although the ostensible purpose of the societies was to provide benefits during sickness and at death, this would have had little appeal without the social side. The deeper bonds of fellowship were indicated in a claim by the Oddfellows that the lodge where they met was 'always considered as sacred ground; and no sooner do those, who in any other place might meet together as enemies, enter into its precincts, than their bad feelings seem to vanish, . . . and in their stead, the desire to promote the well-being and happiness of all reigns predominant.'[170]

Those who wished to join not only had to satisfy regulations concerning residence, trade followed, age, health and character but they had to be acceptable to the existing members. For example, in Kentish London the William the Fourth Society, Deptford, decided to exclude all Irish people. Its own leaders were unskilled labourers. Likewise the Woolwich Foresters' courts differentiated between their members, so that some specialized in engineering craftsmen and others in shipbuilders while unskilled workers were channelled into courts that already had an unusually high proportion of such members.[134] Similar distinctions were made by many of the early trade unions.

During the second half of the century as the larger affiliated orders expanded they formed branches even in villages. However, here, too, there were class distinctions. One commentator noted in 1874 that in rural areas the members of the affiliated societies were mostly craftsmen. 'With few exceptions the lodges of a society like the Manchester Unity were practically closed against agricultural and other unskilled labourers by the high rate of contribution demanded,' he declared.[6]

But the most serious criticism levelled at the societies was that they met in public houses and in some cases publicans were the moving force behind their establishment, seeing it as a way of increasing their business. Often members, too, were reluctant to meet elsewhere. In Rochdale during the 1880s attempts by pro-temperance supporters to move a major society from its club room in a public house proved unsuccessful, despite much heated argument. In many of the smaller, unregistered societies it was common for publicans to make the club room available to members in return for their custom, with each expected to spend twopence or threepence on alcohol at every meeting 'for the good of the house'. Although registered societies were prevented by law from using club funds to pay for drink, some of the less scrupulous evaded the prohibition by falsely entering as rental the cash spent in this way. In Oldham out of twenty-four registered Oddfellows' lodges, with a total membership of over two thousand, only five complied with the law. The remaining nineteen even in the mid-1870s continued to pay for refreshments for the monthly meeting out of the funds and to show it in the accounts as rent.[170] So despite the meeting's business role as an occasion to collect members' benefit fund premiums, most clearly saw it as a pleasant social occasion as well.

In response to appeals to end the squandering of cash in public houses a few societies held meetings in school rooms or temperance halls or even in private houses. Thus the Loyal Brothers at Shepton Beauchamp in Somerset met at the New Inn until the 1850s when they decided to move to the local school room.[163] Yet, as Sir George Young remarked in 1874 in connection with the Royal Commission on Friendly and Benefit Building Societies, despite claims that public-house meetings were 'the great evil to be deprecated, and their removal . . . the great reform to be hoped', in practice there were few alternatives, especially in villages. 'A schoolroom is not a cheerful place for a benefit club to meet in, and an Athenaeum or Temperance Hall is not much better.'[6] Most members shared that view.

Hibernian Society Parade, complete with banner and regalia, in Cardiff, c. 1892. (Museum of Welsh Life, St Fagans, Cardiff)

Criticism was levelled, too, at the excesses associated with the annual feast held by many clubs. Members would parade through the streets, wearing sashes and carrying banners and staves, before attending a service at the church. They would then return to their club room for dinner. The feasts were blamed for encouraging drunkenness, and Thomas Wright was not alone in condemning the vulgar display associated with the street procession, with a band at the head followed by lodge officials wearing their badges of office and carrying the club regalia, while the members would bring up the rear. In Wright's view the only result was to afford amusement to the 'idle and juvenile portions of the population of the town', whose comments on the 'personal peculiarities and adornments of some of the processionists were much more pointed than pleasant'.[69]

In the final years of the century, as leisure time increased and railway excursions became popular some of the clubs (and most trade union branches) abandoned their yearly festival.[170] But in more remote areas the celebrations continued.[37] As one sympathetic commentator noted, many a member felt 'that a club from which, so long as he is in health, he gets absolutely nothing, "no beer, no feast, no fire," is too hard for human nature to bear'.[6] Furthermore, it was an opportunity for the men to demonstrate pride in their society to a wider audience. Several of the clubs laid down strict rules requiring members to take part in the annual celebrations and regulating their conduct. Fines would be imposed on those who became drunk or quarrelled on the feast day and in the most serious cases members would be expelled. But the controls were not always effective, as court reports make clear. For example, in June 1840 an inquest was held into the death of a shoemaker who had been killed in a fight after becoming drunk at the Oddfellows anniversary in Driffield. A decade later that town's petty sessions dealt with two men who were accused by a third of 'threatening his life'. It was noted that all of them had been drinking 'at the club feast'.[255] Yet perhaps the fault lay in expecting those who belonged to 'rational' organizations like friendly societies and trade unions to behave with due decorum at all times. As Peter Bailey points out, to friendly society members 'the concurrent pursuit of . . . "virtue and vice" represented not so much a conflict of value systems as a reconciliation'.[87]

A similar ambivalence was shared by working men's clubs as regards their avowed aims and practical conduct. Although a few clubs were formed in the 1850s under the influence of the temperance movement, it was in the following decade that they became firmly established. The prime mover was the Revd Henry Solly, a Unitarian minister, who formed the Working Men's Club and Institute Union in 1862, seeing in clubs a suitable milieu for the recreation and informal instruction of those who would otherwise spend their time in public houses. What 'working men wanted', Solly argued, 'was a place of amusement, a place of intercourse and fellowship. If a working man heard a good lecture or concert, played a game of cricket or chess . . . the great probability was he would make his home happy'. Once he had been weaned from the pubs to the clubs, recreation would offer a starting point 'for the "inclined plane"' up which 'many of the working men and youths should be rolled into the lecture and class room'.[277] It was quickly realized, however, that if these aims were to be achieved club promoters would have to play down the 'rational improvement' aspect in favour of more attractive pastimes. Hence St John's Working Men's Club, Brighton, began advertising the 'Largest Bagatelle Board' in the town, as well as a library of four hundred books 'to afford to members the means of social welfare, mutual helpfulness and moral improvement, industrial welfare and rational recreation'.[234]

But it was over the sale of beer that major difficulties arose. Originally Solly had wanted to exclude all strong drink, but under pressure from the members this was altered to a recommendation that clubs should seek to remain alcohol free where possible. Even then the situation was fraught with problems, especially where clubs were formed by middle-class patrons who wished to maintain a teetotal regime. During 1866–7 the 'beer question' dominated the club movement and it was soon obvious that by keeping out alcohol potential members were being discouraged.[277] As the pro-beer lobby pointed out, the men wanted to enjoy a pint in the company of their friends rather than having to go out to a public house. By the 1870s that argument was accepted, with clubs like St Luke's in Brighton selling bottled beer, although each member was limited to two half-pints in a single evening.[234] Against this background the number of clubs belonging to the Club and Institute Union rose from 245 in 1873 to 550 a decade later, and by 1904 had reached around 1,000.[277]

Once the sale of alcohol had been accepted there was pressure for other changes. Working men, particularly in London, chafed at the controlling influence exerted by middle-class founders and patrons and began to demand autonomy. They resented what was labelled 'the cup of tea and tract formula', with its censorship of the entertainment offered and a ban on all political discussions. Even in the early stages of the union some rank-and-file members had formed their own clubs, and bolstered by the proceeds from beer sales many more wanted to follow that example. Already by 1883 around three-quarters of the clubs were reckoned to be financially self-supporting.[85] The argument that middle-class guidance was needed for the achievement of moral and social improvement seemed to many members 'degrading nonsense' and pressure grew to exclude all outside subscribers and patrons. There was heated debate within the union before this became official policy, but by April 1884 the new system had been accepted. Despite the fears of the traditionalists the membership took over the movement without any disastrous consequences. The subscribers left and with their exodus the union became not only financially viable but a truly working-class organization.[277] Many clubs provided programmes of lectures, discussions, concerts, games, sports, excursions and picnics, but their real benefit to members was that they were free from commercial pressures, family problems and any encouragement to heavy drinking. They also offered opportunities to discuss politics in an atmosphere without harassment or official disapproval. Thus club members at Tower Hamlets Radical Club and Institute in London claimed that they were hounded from inn to inn by the police before they opened their own premises in 1874.[85]

However, none of these organizations had much to offer women. Even friendly societies and trade unions catered primarily for the menfolk. The most that wives and daughters could expect was perhaps an invitation to attend a special tea meeting on the occasion of a club anniversary or a share in the excursions which were arranged from time to time. Only in some of the bodies linked to the churches and chapels, such as mothers' meetings and sewing circles, were females widely involved. However, by the 1860s a few middle-class organizations like the Ladies' Discussion Society, formed in Kensington in 1865, and the Ladies' Edinburgh Debating Society were opening up opportunities for some of the more determined feminists. From 1883 the Women's Co-operative Guild offered poorer women the chance to meet each week to discuss mutual problems. As Virginia Woolf put it, the guild gave working-class wives

> the rarest of all possessions – a room where they could sit down and think remote from boiling saucepans and crying children; and then that room became not merely a sitting-room and a meeting place, but a workshop where, laying their heads together, they could . . . remodel their lives . . .

But, with all its merits the impact of the guild was limited. Even in 1930 when it had a network of nearly 1,400 branches its total membership was only about 67,000, concentrated mainly in the north of England and London.[199]

For men, and more rarely women, of a serious turn of mind, adult education offered opportunities to engage in rational pleasures and pastimes. Mechanics' Institutes were formed from the 1820s with the aim of giving artisans some technical instruction. But many of the potential students lacked the basic education needed to pursue complex courses and would, in any case, be too tired after a long day at work to follow intricate arguments. By the middle of the century, therefore, many of the seven hundred or so institutes were combining elementary instruction in reading, writing and arithmetic with short, popular lectures designed to appeal to a wide audience. For example, in the mid-1830s the Liverpool Mechanics' Institution was covering such topics as *Hamlet*, Stenography, Music of Ireland, The Middle Ages, Phrenology, Early and Home Training of Children, and German Customs.[291] Often, as was the case in Banbury, the institute maintained the only public library available during the mid-Victorian years, and it might sponsor additional entertainments like amateur dramatics, promenade concerts, a chess club and railway excursions to 'improving' destinations.[350] In some places, such as Warrington, discussion classes were formed and became virtually an exclusive 'club' within the institute. In Warrington the leading members were young middle-class men and the topics they studied and the level of debate engaged upon required a higher standard of education than would have been possessed by ordinary working men.[328] Yet despite the institutes' failure to supply the technical education for which they were set up – that came only in the final quarter of the century in most cases – they did widen educational provision through their lecture programmes and outings, and this benefited the lower orders as well as the more affluent. As the *Banbury Advertiser* commented in 1859, 'the working classes now enjoy opportunities of hearing lectures, amusing or instructive as the case may be, of which their grandfathers never dreamed'.[350]

Literary and Philosophical Societies performed a similar role in a number of towns. They sought to promote science and literature by the reading of papers to an audience of members and friends and by the formation of museums and libraries as well as, in some cases, the establishment of laboratories.[291] Many were aimed at the better-off members of society and it was symptomatic of the general attitude that in 1875 when a leading Banbury clergyman formed a Literary and Philosophical Society he argued tactlessly that this was needed because it was a disgrace that the town had 'nothing better than a Mechanics' Institute'.[350] A similar class consciousness has been found in respect of Bristol's Literary and Philosophical Society, which even in the 1860s and 1870s underpinned many of the cultural activities of the town's middle classes. Here membership of the city's principal intellectual associations was seen as a matter of social status.[245] Much the same was true of Warrington, with the town's leading business and political figures belonging to the Literary and Philosophical Society, the Phrenological Society and the Natural History Society among others. The Phrenological Society was particularly exclusive. Not only were the entrance fee and annual subscription kept relatively high, but membership was by election in a secret ballot. Three black balls were sufficient to exclude an application and in this way 'undesirables' could be kept at bay.[328]

In Bristol it was from the 'Lit. and Phil.' that those with a special interest in local history and antiquarianism formed the Clifton Antiquarian Club. To maintain its élite status membership was limited to fifty, with ten honorary members, and vacancies were filled by elective ballot at a general meeting, as with Warrington's Phrenological Society. An examination of members' backgrounds in the two Bristol organizations in the late 1880s shows a major overlap of support, with over three-fifths of the Antiquarian Club's members also belonging to the Literary and Philosophical Society. 'Ordinary citizens with an interest in local history had to pursue that interest in different, less exclusive institutions, particularly evening classes.'[245] Yet if class distinctions proved an impediment to study, for those within the 'magic circle' there was an opportunity to enjoy new experiences and interests.

In most provincial towns it was the Literary and Philosophical Societies which laid the foundation for the establishment of public museums. Sheffield's 'Lit. and Phil.' surrendered its museum to the town in 1875 and the society in Halifax did the same in 1897. Often the exhibits were collections of local curiosities assembled by antiquarians, or exotic specimens presented by returned travellers. Many museums concentrated on geology, botany and entomology. Yet despite their limitations (and the reluctance of local authorities to finance municipal museums), the collections were popular. At Ipswich, where a rate-aided museum was opened in 1847, attendance averaged six hundred for every day and evening it was open to the public, including free admissions on Wednesdays and on Friday evenings. In 1850 it was described by one visitor as a 'really noble and useful institution'. Its collections included stuffed birds and animals as well as geological specimens and a small library.[223] However, it is indicative of the limits of the self-improvement ethos in Victorian Britain that when attempts were made in Ipswich to organize classes for the study of natural history and other sciences they were a failure, with few working people attending to hear the lectures given by 'distinguished visiting scientists'.[223]

Even at the British Museum (which attracted over 2.5 million visitors during the Great Exhibition year of 1851), the popularity of the natural history collections did not always induce the solemn attitude some considered appropriate. In the 1860s there were complaints that children 'shouted and scampered about in a very improper manner, annoying their elders by eating oranges and throwing the peel about'.[122] Not until 1883 did the Zoological Department, with its 'stuffed tigers and medicated bird skins', leave Bloomsbury for the new Natural History Museum in South Kensington.

THE PATRIOTIC SPIRIT

Accompanying the urbanization of Britain during the later nineteenth century was a sharp upsurge in displays of patriotism and of pride in the Empire. Even the Sunday School Union produced a magazine entitled *Boys of Our Empire* during these years and the success of the Boys' Brigade and its imitators sprang in part from their appeal to national pride as well as their recreational provisions. Much the same was true of the Volunteer movement which developed in 1859, in response to anxiety about the territorial ambitions of the French emperor, Napoleon III.[140]

Initially it was intended that only 'reliable' members of the middle classes should become Volunteers and to this end recruits were expected to supply their own uniform and equipment. A number of prestigious people became involved, such as the painters John Everett Millais and Frederic Leighton, the arts and crafts reformer William Morris and leading political figures such as W.E. Forster and, later on, David Lloyd George. In 1868 at least ninety Members of Parliament held commissions in the Volunteer Force.[140] However, over time this changed, as government financial support enabled the less affluent to take part and as the Volunteers' prestige and credibility as a fighting force dwindled. Some of the well-to-do preferred to join the more highly thought-of yeomanry. It not only had a long history but was by tradition recruited from among the landed classes and the prosperous urban trades, with the larger landowners or their urban counterparts serving as officers. It, too, had its own ethos and leisure pursuits, in which horse racing, polo and tent pegging featured prominently.

Nevertheless almost every town soon had at least one Volunteer unit, and if its officers lacked the standing of those in the regular Army or the yeomanry, they did gain enhanced status from being members of the officer class. In September 1860 when a review was held at Knowsley Park, seat of the Earl of Derby, around 11,000 Lancashire Volunteers assembled. They were watched by between 150,000 and 200,000 spectators who, according to the *Annual Register*, cheered loudly as their respective local corps marched past. Christopher North, who witnessed the Knowsley parade, commented ironically upon the general enthusiasm: 'Melancholy indeed to think that all these fine, fierce, ferocious fire-eaters are doomed, but for some unlooked-for revolution in the affairs of Europe and the World, to die in their beds.'[110]

Doubtless many joined the Volunteers in a spirit of patriotic zeal. But in order to encourage the less committed, rifle shooting competitions were staged, with worthwhile prizes. These not only attracted contestants but large numbers of spectators. In other cases sporting facilities were offered. In 1872 officers in East Surrey were said to be keeping the men together 'by social gatherings, cricket clubs and quadrille parties', while at Kinross in Scotland during the 1870s it was social functions that 'kept the corps before the public eye, brought recruits to the ranks and made the force worth joining'.[140] Even at the turn of the century Major Liles, commander of the 26th Middlesex Volunteer Rifle Corps, claimed that recruits usually joined up in the spring, 'somewhere about Easter, just as a man is beginning to think he wants some outdoor amusement for the summer and if he does not come to me he goes and joins a cricket club or a yachting club'. He was sceptical about the patriotic aspect of this:

> I have a very poor opinion of patriotism as a factor in getting men either as soldiers or Volunteers. They call it patriotism, but I think it is principally a desire for sport. I think a man comes in as a soldier or offers to go to war from the same motive in which, if he was in better circumstances, he would go out big game shooting or exploring – a desire for excitement.[8]

Others were less cynical, and the amount of drill and rifle-shooting each recruit had to perform every year suggested at the very least a commitment to the principles of discipline and good order. The precise amount of time spent in this way varied according to the regulations. By 1881 a Volunteer had to do at least sixty drills during his first two years, although this could then be reduced to nine per annum. Each new recruit might thus spend around an hour or more drilling on twenty or thirty evenings or Saturday afternoons in a year. Rifle shooting was far more attractive: Lord Elcho, himself an enthusiastic supporter of the Volunteers, claimed in 1865 that this was what kept the men together, 'the shooting and the competition at the butts'. Almost two decades later another commentator argued that rifle shooting gave 'as much sport to the men as pheasant and rabbit shooting does to those who can afford it'.[140] The National Rifle Association, formed in 1860 with close links to the Volunteer movement, encouraged the activity. Its annual Wimbledon meeting became an important event in the social calendar, attracting large numbers of spectators. In 1889 the event was transferred to Bisley in Surrey but its prestige remained. Not only did prize-winners have the thrill of success but there were material rewards as well. When the association was launched under royal patronage in 1860 the queen herself presented an annual prize of £250 for Volunteers and the Prince Consort a prize of £100 for all comers of every nation entering the competition.[140] Even local events could offer worthwhile trophies. At Brigg in Lincolnshire in 1892 prizes ranged in value from £3 3s to 10s and included a marble clock, a liquor stand, a case of carvers, a fruit dish and various other domestic items. 'Rifle shooting,' concludes Hugh Cunningham, 'remained the staple attraction throughout the history of the Force.'[140]

But there were many non-military functions as well, including theatrical shows and bazaars to raise funds, or choral societies, like that connected with the Ramsgate Corps in East Kent. Bands were formed in many places and would be asked to play at charitable and civic events. At Banbury in the mid-1860s the local Rifle Corps Band led the Sunday School children on a picnic, serenaded members of the Foresters' friendly society on their club day and travelled on a Mechanics' Institute excursion train to Malvern. 'The volunteer movement was an integral part of the town community,' writes Barrie Trinder, 'and an important contributor to its culture.'[350]

Any substantial town without a flourishing corps would feel disadvantaged in comparison with its neighbours. Furthermore, if the future of a corps came under question because of inefficiency or wrongdoing this would be seen as a slur on the integrity of the whole town. When the War Office threatened to disband the Weston-super-Mare Volunteer Artillery a public meeting was held at the town hall to mobilize public opinion and prevent 'that disgrace falling on the town which must necessarily follow the disbandment of a Volunteer Corps'. Local magistrates were among those leading the protest. Similarly when the Airdrie Volunteers were disbanded as a result of irregularities in 1897, Members of Parliament in the area pressed for a reprieve. More than a thousand people attended a meeting to demand the rescinding of the order, to avoid 'a lasting stigma upon these men and upon the district from which they came'. They were unsuccessful.[140]

However, not all contemporaries approved of the militaristic approach of the Volunteers. As with the Boys' Brigade, members were subject to attacks from hooligans. The historian of a Middlesex corps claimed it was 'almost impossible for an officer to appear in the streets without being subjected to some form of insult by the more uneducated and less intelligent of his fellow countrymen'. At Canterbury, too, when they paraded on the cricket ground Volunteers were confronted by 'a motley crowd of roughs', who hurled turnips 'and missiles of a harder and more varied description'. It was with difficulty that the Volunteers were restrained from breaking ranks in order to retaliate. Even in 1897 it was reported to be one of the 'great difficulties of Metropolitan Corps to find accessible ground' in the capital 'where the mob will not interfere with the operations'.[140] In part at least this was probably because of suspicions about their role as associates of the wider forces of law and order.

Equally, though, there were those who claimed that by recruiting working-class men (and 70 per cent of the rank and file were working class in the early twentieth century), the Volunteers were achieving social improvement. A captain in the London Scottish maintained that in some places 'casinos, dancing saloons, skittle alleys, billiard rooms, and similar places have been closed by the absence of the custom of men who once frequented them, but who now give their days to shoot, and evenings to drill, and find pleasure in band music and chorus singing'.[140] A number of marches were even composed in their honour. These included 'The Rifleman's March', published in about 1861 for the 1st Wiltshire Rifle Volunteers

EH?

Street Boy (fortissimo). "WHO SHOT THE DOG!"

*Young cockneys making fun of a Volunteer. In 1860 an over-enthusiastic member of the new force had fired his rifle at a dog in Wandsworth Park. The incident was subsequently used to mock Volunteers all over the country. (*Punch, *28 April 1860)*

and 'The Artillery Volunteer Song', which appeared about four years later and was dedicated to the 2nd Hampshire Artillery Volunteers.

Field days and camps were also attractive to most of the men and to their admiring relatives. According to Metropolitan commanding officers, the Easter Monday Field Day at Brighton was 'unrivalled for recruiting purposes', with many participants making a long weekend of it. Some brought their families along to enjoy the sea air and the other amusements on offer. In 1870 around 26,000 Volunteers took part and on the days leading up to the event the beach was thronged with visitors, with boatmen and keepers of refreshment rooms doing brisk business, according to the *Annual Register*. The last Easter Monday review was held at Brighton in 1872, but even less attractive venues like Ashridge Park near Tring brought in thousands of spectators, as in April 1876. Then around seven thousand Volunteers from London and the Home Counties engaged in a review and a mock battle.[25]

Later, camps replaced field days as the high point in the Volunteer's year, with many of those attending regarding this as their holiday. As such they wanted to have a say in the choice of location, with seaside resorts particularly popular. Initially the camps were ad hoc affairs, sometimes organized and even funded by company officers, but by 1880 they were 'officially sanctioned, paid for, and even expected' by the district commanding officer and the War Office. Bolton Volunteers were among the first to hold regular 'encampments', going to Lytham each summer for over a decade before changing to Rhyl, when 'the well known attractions of Lytham had somewhat paled'.[110] At the turn of the century Sir John Colomb claimed that Volunteers from the Midlands and the north liked Yarmouth. 'They go into camp there in brigades, and the men give their whole time to military training, but their families are often there too, and they combine their holiday with the camp training.'[140]

Sometimes the drinking and conviviality would get out of hand. In July 1871 the Clyro curate, Francis Kilvert, noted disapprovingly that when the chaplain had attended an encampment on the common above Talgarth in order to conduct an open-air service and preach a sermon, he had found 'the Builth Volunteers were already well drunk. They were dismissed from the ranks but they fought about the common during the whole service. The officers and the other corps were bitterly ashamed and scandalized.'[273] In this context it is significant that a large number of public houses adopted the name 'Volunteer' or 'Volunteer Rifleman'. Colonel Fazan, writing of life in the Cinque Ports in the early twentieth century, certainly recalled the importance of beer in the force's social events. 'Field days, train journeys and prize shoots . . . were often occasions for copious libations of alcohol and light-hearted mischief.'[140] It was probably for these reasons that Colonel Haworth, commanding the 3rd Volunteer Battalion of the Lancashire Fusiliers, argued in 1904 that the camp was so popular that 'if I had no camp I should have no men. The men join for camp there is no doubt . . . I think the bulk of my men join because they like the show, the dress, and they like the camp. I do not think they join from very high patriotic motives.'[8] At that time around a quarter of a million men were enrolled nationally in the Volunteers, with about two-thirds of them aged between seventeen and twenty-five, and over half serving for three years or less.[140] Joining up was primarily done by young men. They might start when they were teenage apprentices and stay on for a relatively brief period only. Yet, as

Hugh Cunningham points out, despite the personal enjoyment that many may have derived from Volunteer activities the fact that 200,000 or more young men were prepared to spend their time in this way during each year from the 1860s to the end of the century, suggests 'that military values met with much less opposition in Victorian society than we have perhaps been accustomed to suppose. To join the Volunteers indicated a willingness to wear military uniform, to learn elementary military duties, and to both receive and obey orders.'[140]

Furthermore, whatever doubts may be expressed about the patriotic appeal of the Volunteer movement there were other powerful manifestations of the national spirit in the late Victorian period, not least at the time of Queen Victoria's Golden and Diamond Jubilees in 1887 and 1897 respectively. Military reviews were held, flags flown, celebratory parties arranged and thousands of beacon fires were lit from Cornwall to Caithness.[53] In Cambridge, as in many other places, in 1897 the local élite took a lead in organizing events, including a public concert, water carnival and firework display witnessed by an estimated forty thousand people. A 'monster public dinner' was arranged for a thousand elderly residents, with band music and entertainments, while five thousand school children received a tea and a commemorative card.[176] In Halifax, too, one eight-year-old boy remembered huge celebrations, with choral music and concerts of all kinds. He and the other elementary school pupils were taken to a local park, where they were given hot coffee and buns and took part in sports. At night a huge bonfire was lit at the top of Beacon Hill and people stole sleepers from the railway to use as fuel. The bonfire lasted for a week or two. 'Imperialism in the air,' wrote the Fabian social reformer Beatrice Webb, in disapproval at the 1897 junketings, 'all classes drunk with sightseeing and hysterical loyalty.'[176]

Far less attractive was the jingoistic spirit which surrounded the start of the Boer War in October 1899. Two days after war was declared the audience at the Crystal Palace broke out into enthusiastic cheers when the band of the Queen's Own Cameron Highlanders struck up 'Rule Britannia' in a selection of national airs. According to *The Times*, the tune was 'redemanded no less than six times, the large audience on each occasion singing the refrain with the utmost heartiness. At the conclusion the drummer was "chaired".' Around the same time in Hyde Park 'pro-Boer' speakers opposing the war were driven away by an angry crowd who then sang 'Rule Britannia' and other patriotic songs. Small wonder that Halévy, in his *History of the English People in the Nineteenth Century*, should write of the Boer War period, 'To attempt to analyse a fit of patriotic frenzy would be a thankless task.'[135] The British Army's early reverses and problems only intensified the frenetic sentiments. In 1900 Charles Masterman lamented the 'wave of imperialism' that had 'swept over the country'.[217] One of the uglier aspects of this was the hostility towards those identified as 'pro-Boers', with businesses and homes wrecked and people attacked. At Margate in March 1900 when one of the shopkeepers hung out a 'Dutch flag' and complained about the war and the royal family a crowd of youths and working men assembled and, egged on by a cheering crowd, they systematically attacked his premises. Despite appeals from the mayor for the people to go home and the arrival of the police, the unrest continued for three days. By the end all the windows were smashed, the window frames had been pulled out, the shop's stock was damaged, and it was with difficulty that the men were restrained from knocking down the house. Similar disturbances were reported as far apart as Scarborough and Stratford-upon-Avon, with cheering crowds singing patriotic songs in attendance.[46]

But it was the relief of the besieged British garrison at Mafeking which most seized the public imagination. When the news came through, London went wild, with special editions of the evening papers rushed out and information quickly passed on by word of mouth. In Richmond-on-Thames the young Rebecca West remembered her mother looking at her with tears of joy running down her cheeks, while out in the road a stream of shabby, happy men marched along in celebration:

> one I remember wearing hessian overalls, with trousers tied round the knee with twine, carrying a garden broom over his shoulder like a rifle, and smiling like a buck-toothed angel. He wore on his chest a huge placard that hung between his shoulders and his thighs to give all he passed the good news that the siege of Mafeking had been relieved after seven months.[377]

Late trains spread the message, too, with engine drivers 'making their feelings known', according to *The Times*, by setting their whistles blowing 'all the way down the line, arousing the villagers, who recognized the signal; and in more than one village the shops were reopened at midnight and the drapers cleared out their stocks of prints so far as they happened to be printed in red, white, or blue'. In retrospect the hysteria was difficult to understand. 'They are behaving as though they have beaten Napoleon,' commented Wilfrid Blunt of the rejoicing crowds.[262]

With the main squares and thoroughfares in London packed with crowds of cheering and singing people, traders did a good business selling Union Jacks, trumpets and peacock feathers. It was celebration on a scale never before seen in the capital and 'Mafficking' entered the British language as a word meaning to 'exult riotously'. The mood also spread to Lancashire and Yorkshire where even small villages were roused by the sounding of factory sirens. At Leeds the big bell of the town hall was unmuffled for the first time since the Diamond Jubilee celebrations and in Glasgow the rejoicings of residents were supplemented by large numbers coming in from nearby country districts to join in.[46] But it was London which remained the focus of excitement, with 'mafficking' continuing for several evenings.

In Bethnal Green Walter Southgate and his friends wore celluloid buttons in their lapels portraying their favourite generals, even though Walter's father disapproved of the war and was dubbed a pro-Boer by neighbours as a consequence. When news of the relief of Mafeking arrived there was dancing, singing in the streets, waving of flags and a good deal of drinking. 'Mafeking for all I and other children knew might have been in Timbuctoo. But on Mafeking night Joe Franklin, the landlord of the "Bakers Arms" public house, in our street, sold or gave away many barrels of beer. Nearly everyone was gloriously drunk. They let off a lot of fireworks and in their drunken frenzy tore down the wooden shutters from the cottages . . . to make a huge bonfire in the street.'[319] In the confusion the fire brigade had to be called out to save the cottages from going up in flames as well.

To alarmed liberals like Charles Masterman the exuberance seemed to exemplify the emergence of a 'new race . . . the city type . . . voluble, excitable, with little ballast, stamina or endurance – seeking stimulus in drink, in betting, in any unaccustomed conflicts at home or abroad'.[217] Yet closer examination shows that the predominant feeling on Mafeking night was not aggression but relief that the disgrace of military capitulation had been avoided. However, if the working classes did not initiate the jingoistic mood, they certainly shared in it and there were deplorable incidents where the property of alleged pro-Boers was attacked by mobs diverted from their celebrations. The victims included the journalist W.T. Stead, an outspoken opponent of the war, whose Wimbledon home was assailed by a crowd who broke windows, damaged flower beds and spent a 'considerable time hooting, yelling, ringing bells and generally making a great disturbance', according to *The Times*.

In January 1899 the hawkish Colonial Secretary, Joseph Chamberlain, had told a Birmingham audience, 'We are all Imperialists now', and there is little doubt that imperialist sentiment had percolated through many layers of British society by the time Queen Victoria's reign ended.[190]

Additional Sources Used

Annual Register for 1860 (London, 1861), for 1870 (London, 1871), for 1876 (London, 1876).

Cook's Excursionist and Tourist Advertiser, 3 February 1877.

East Kent Federation of Women's Institutes, *East Kent Within Living Memory* (Newbury, 1994).

Sheridan Galley, 'Catholic Faith of the Irish Slums. London 1840–70' in H.J. Dyos and Michael Wolff (eds), *The Victorian City*, Vol. 2 (London and Boston, 1973).

John Garrard, 'Friendly societies, the poor law and democratization in Britain', paper given at the Urban History Group Conference, 4 April 1997.

W.B. and G.D. Giles, *Yeoman Service* (Tunbridge Wells, 1985).

Labourers' Union Chronicle, 4 October 1873, for examples of trade union branch festivities.

Margaret Llewelyn Davies (ed.), *Life As We Have Known It* (London, 1931), for Virginia Woolf quotation.

R.J. Morris, 'Clubs, societies and associations' in F.M.L. Thompson (ed.), *The Cambridge Social History of Britain*, Vol. 3 (Cambridge, 1990).

David Newsome, *The Victorian World Picture* (London, 1998 edn).

John Pemble, *The Mediterranean Passion. Victorians and Edwardians in the South* (Oxford, 1988).

Fergus Read, *The Duke of Lancaster's Own Yeomanry* (Preston, 1992).

The Times, 16 October 1899, 13, 14 and 16 March and 21 and 22 May 1900.

David M. Thompson, 'The 1851 Religious Census: Problems and Possibilities' in *Victorian Studies*, Vol. XI, No. 1 (December 1967).

A.P. Wadsworth, 'The First Manchester Sunday Schools' in M.W. Flinn and T.C. Smout (eds), *Essays in Social History* (Oxford, 1974).

G.M. Young, *Victorian England. Portrait of an Age* (London, 1953 edn).

Conclusion

The period between 1837 and 1901 saw a transformation in the pleasures and pastimes available to all sections of the population. At the same time the concept of spare time itself became much valued. It was a 'matter of pride' to Victorians that they were living in a society 'sufficiently prosperous and well-organised to permit its individual members opportunities for relaxation and the sort of diverting social interaction which could only flourish outside a pattern of unremitting labour'.[78] Some of the new recreations, like the expansion of rail travel and the introduction of moving pictures, were the result of technological advances. Others, such as the opening of public libraries, art galleries and museums, were the outcome of a philosophical shift of mood in favour of a more inclusive approach to culture and self-improvement; and a number, like the rise of the music hall, the proliferation of cheap literature and the growth of mass sport (particularly association football), were the result of greater working-class affluence and more leisure time. For many urban dwellers, especially the menfolk, the success of the local football team became a matter of communal pride and helped to promote a sense of civic unity in a rapidly changing world. 'By supporting a club and assembling with thousands of others like himself a man could assert a kind of membership of the city,' comments Richard Holt.[386] There was satisfaction to be derived from this sense of belonging to a wider group and sharing in its triumphs and reverses.

By the end of the century recreational activities were more varied, more widespread and, in general, more 'respectable' than they had been at the commencement of the queen's reign. They also extended up and down the social scale, so that holidays at the seaside or the pleasures of a family Christmas spread from the middle to the working classes, while sports like rowing and pedestrianism, considered low pastimes of the people in the 1830s, had as sculling and athletics respectively, become acceptable to Oxford undergraduates half a century later. Music hall, too, although originally designed for working-class audiences was soon catering for clerks, shop assistants and other white-collar workers. In the West End of London, at the Empire and the Trocadero, it appealed to raffish young aristocrats as well.[169] This did not mean that class differences no longer existed or that contemporaries considered such a development desirable. 'In those days,' wrote a former stockbroker of life in London, 'East met West. And yet each "knew his place," the boast of the time.'[217] So even when pleasures were shared they would also be segregated. Seaside resorts catering for a wide range of visitors were normally divided into class-specific areas, and while a town might support its football team, 'the working men watched from the stand and the middle-class directors from their boxes'.[169]

On a broader basis Empire, aristocracy, established religion and capitalist ideology had become accepted by the majority of British people from all classes and this underpinned the pleasures and pastimes they pursued. Only in the twentieth century were those unifying values to be questioned and the recreations and social divisions associated with them subjected to critical scrutiny. At the same time new 'traditions' were being invented by the Victorians (as with the celebration of the Jubilees) which were to resonate well into the new century and thereby mould modern culture and experience.

Bibliography

(a) Parliamentary Papers (P.P.)

1. Agriculture, Royal Commission on the Employment of Children, Young Persons and Women in, P.P. 1868–69, Vol. XIII
2. Betting, Report of Select Committee of the House of Lords on, P.P. 1902, Vol. V
3. British Museum, Report of Select Committee on, P.P. 1860, Vol. XVI
4. Children's Employment Commission, Third Report of, P.P. 1864, Vol. XXII
5. Crofters and Cottars in the Highlands and Islands of Scotland, Royal Commission on the Conditions of, P.P. 1884, Vol. XXXII
6. Friendly and Benefit Building Societies, Royal Commission on, P.P. 1874, Vol. XXIII, Part II
7. Lands in Scotland used as Deer Forests, Report of the Departmental Committee on, P.P. 1922, Vol. VII
8. Militia and Volunteers, Report of Royal Commission on, P.P. 1904, Vols. XXX and XXXI
9. National Portrait Gallery, Forty-second Report of, P.P. 1899, Vol. XXIX
10. Newspaper Stamps, Report from Select Committee on, P.P. 1851, Vol. XVII
11. Paris Universal Exhibition, Report of H.M. Commissioners on, P.P. 1880, Vol. XXXII
12. Population Censuses: Reports for England, Wales and Scotland for 1851, P.P. 1852–53, Vol. LXXXVIII
13. Population Censuses: Report for England and Wales for 1871, P.P. 1873, Vol. LXXI, Pts. I and II
14. Population Censuses: Report for Scotland for 1871, P.P. 1873, Vol. LXXIII
15. Population Censuses: Report for England and Wales for 1901, P.P. 1903, Vol. LXXXIV
16. Population Censuses: Report for Scotland for 1901, P.P. 1904, Vol. CVIII
17. Public Houses, &c., Report of the Select Committee on, P.P. 1852–53, Vol. XXXVII
18. Public Institutions, Report of Select Committee on, P.P. 1860, Vol. XVI
19. Public Libraries, Report of Select Committee on, P.P. 1849, Vol. XVII
20. Public Walks, Report of Select Committee on, P.P. 1833, Vol. XV
21. Return under the Public Libraries Act, 1890, P.P. 1890–91, Vol. LXI
22. Theatres and Places of Entertainment, Report of Select Committee on, P.P. 1892, Vol. XVIII
23. Theatrical Licences and Regulations, Report of Select Committee on, P.P. 1866, Vol. XVI
24. Trustees and Director of the National Gallery, Reports of, for 1896, P.P. 1897, Vol. XXXIII and for 1898, P.P. 1899, Vol. XXIX

(b) Newspapers and Periodicals

25. *Annual Register*
26. *Bournemouth Guardian*
27. *Child's Guardian*
28. *Cook's Excursionist and Tourist Advertiser*
29. *Country Life Illustrated*
30. *Devon Weekly Times*
31. *Fortnightly Review*

32. *Halifax Guardian*
33. *Home Tidings* (in archives of the University of Westminster, London)
34. *Isle of Wight Times*
35. *Jackson's Oxford Journal*
36. *Keble's Margate and Ramsgate Gazette*
37. *Labourers' Union Chronicle*
38. *Pall Mall Gazette*
39. *Polytechnic Magazine* (in archives of the University of Westminster, London)
40. *Punch*
41. *Saint Pauls*
42. *The Animal World*
43. *The Field*
44. *The Rational Dress Society's Gazette*
45. *The Stage*
46. *The Times*
47. *Western Mail*
48. *Witney Gazette*

(c) Books and Articles published before 1900

49. [Anon.], 'Italian Vagrant Children' in *Chambers's Journal*, 15 September 1877.
50. [Anon.], *London and Fashionable Resorts. A Complete Guide to the Places of Amusement* (London, 1890)
51. Beaufort, His Grace the Duke of, *Hunting* (The Badminton Library) (London, 1894)
52. Mrs Isabella Beeton, *Beeton's Book of Household Management* (London, 1861)
53. *Cassell's History of England*, Vol. 8 (London, n.d. [*c.* 1898])
54. *Cook's Handbook to the Health Resorts of the South of France and Riviera* (London, 1893) (at the British Library 10174.aa.38)
55. Richard Harding Davis, 'Three English Race Meetings' in *Harper's Monthly Magazine* (European edition), Vol. 87 (July 1893)
56. Gustave Doré and Blanchard Jerrold, *London. A Pilgrimage* (London, 1872)
57. T.H.S. Escott, *England: Its People, Polity and Pursuits* (London, 1885 edn)
58. [T.H.S. Escott], A Foreign Resident, *Society in London* (London, 1885)
59. James A. Froude (ed.), *Letters and Memorials of Jane Welsh Carlyle*, 3 Vols. (London, 1883)
60. A.B. Granville, *The Spas of England and Principal Sea-Bathing Places*, 2 Vols. (London, 1841)
61. Lady Jeune, 'The Ethics of Shopping' in *The Fortnightly Review* (Jan. 1895)
62. Dan Leno, *Hys Book Written by Himself* (London, 1899)
63. Henry Mayhew, *London Labour and the London Poor*, 4 Vols. (London, 1861)
64. National Trust, *Annual Report of the Council for 1896–97* (London, 1897)
65. W. Fraser Rae, *The Business of Travel* (London, 1891)
66. George J. Romanes, 'Recreation' in *The Nineteenth Century*, Vol. VI, No. 31 (September 1879)
67. Anthony Trollope (ed.), *British Sports and Pastimes* (London, 1868)
68. John Verschoyle, 'Where to Spend a Holiday' in *The Fortnightly Review* (August 1894)
69. [Thomas Wright], *Some Habits and Customs of the Working Classes by a Journeyman Engineer* (London, 1867)
70. [Thomas Wright], *The Great Unwashed by the Journeyman Engineer* (London, 1868)

(d) Books and Articles published from 1900

71. Alison Adburgham, *Liberty's. A Biography of a Shop* (London, 1975)
72. Alison Adburgham, *Shops and Shopping 1800–1914* (London, 1989 edn)
73. Alison Adburgham, *Victorian Shopping. Harrod's Catalogue, 1895* (New York, 1972 edn)
74. Sally Alexander, 'St. Giles's Fair, 1830–1914' in R.J. Morris and Richard Rodger (eds), *The Victorian City* (London, 1993)

75. Jill Allbrooke (ed.), *Three Hundred Years of Women's Magazines 1693–1993* (London, British Library Newspaper Library Newsletter No. 16, 1993)
76. Richard D. Altick, *Paintings from Books* (Columbus, Ohio, 1985)
77. Richard D. Altick, *The English Common Reader* (Chicago, 1983 edn)
78. Gail-Nina Anderson and Joanne Wright, *The Pursuit of Leisure. Victorian Depictions of Pastimes* (Nottingham and London, 1997)
79. Gregory Anderson, *Victorian Clerks* (Manchester, 1976)
80. [Anon.], *Diamond Jubilee of the Halifax People's Park* (Halifax, 1917)
81. *Art Treasures of England. The Regional Collections. Catalogue for 1998 Exhibition* (London, 1998)
82. C. Aspin, *Lancashire. The First Industrial Society* (Helmshore, 1969)
83. C. Aspin (ed.), *Manchester and the Textile Districts in 1849* (Helmshore, 1972)
84. James Ayres, *English Naive Painting 1750–1900* (London, 1980)
85. Peter Bailey, *Leisure and Class in Victorian England* (London, 1987 edn)
86. Peter Bailey (ed.), *Music Hall. The Business of Pleasure* (Milton Keynes, 1986)
87. Peter Bailey, ' "Will the Real Bill Banks Please Stand Up?" Towards a Role Analysis of Mid-Victorian Working-class Respectability' in *Journal of Social History*, Vol. 12, No. 3 (Spring 1979)
88. William J. Baker, 'The Making of a Working-class Football Culture in Victorian England' in *Journal of Social History*, Vol. 13, No. 2 (Winter 1979)
89. Consuelo Vanderbilt Balsan, *The Glitter and the Gold* (Maidstone, 1973 edn)
90. Joanna Banham, Sally Macdonald and Julia Porter, *Victorian Interior Style* (London, 1995 edn)
91. Kathleen Barker, 'The performing arts in Newcastle upon Tyne 1840–70' in John K. Walton and James Walvin (eds), *Leisure in Britain 1780–1939* (Manchester, 1983)
92. Phyllida Barstow, *The English Country House Party* (Wellingborough, 1989)
93. Walter Baxter, *The Kent of Dickens (1812–70)* (London, 1924)
94. Alfred Rosling Bennett, *London and Londoners in the Eighteen-fifties and Sixties* (London, 1924)
95. Geoffrey Best, *Mid-Victorian Britain 1851–75* (London, 1971)
96. A.G. Betjemann, *The Grand Theatre, Lancaster* (Centre for North-West Regional Studies, University of Lancaster, Occasional Papers No. 11, 1982)
97. John Betjeman, *A Pictorial History of English Architecture* (London, 1972 edn)
98. Margaret Blunden, *The Countess of Warwick* (London, 1967)
99. T.S.R. Boase, *English Art, 1800–1870* (Oxford, 1959)
100. R.R. Bolland, *Victorians on the Thames* (Tunbridge Wells, 1994 edn)
101. Charles Booth, *Life and Labour of the People in London* (London, 1903)
102. Michael R. Booth, *Theatre in the Victorian Age* (Cambridge, 1995 edn)
103. E.W. Bovill, *The England of Nimrod and Surtees 1815–1854* (London, 1959)
104. Rhodes Boyson, *The Ashworth Cotton Enterprise* (Oxford, 1970)
105. Ian Bradley, *Abide with Me. The World of Victorian Hymns* (London, 1997)
106. Reginald A. Bray, 'The Boy and the Family' in E.J. Urwick (ed.), *Studies of Boy Life in our Cities* (London, 1904)
107. Piers Brendon, *Thomas Cook. 150 Years of Popular Tourism* (London, 1991)
108. Kenneth D. Brown, *A Social History of the Nonconformist Ministry in England and Wales 1800–1930* (Oxford, 1988)
109. Lucy Brown, *Victorian News and Newspapers* (Oxford, 1985)
110. Stephen Bull, *Volunteer! The Lancashire Rifle Volunteers, 1859–85* (Preston, 1993)
111. Mary Burgan, 'Heroines at the Piano: Women and Music in Nineteenth-Century Fiction' in *Victorian Studies*, Vol. 30, No. 1 (Autumn 1986)
112. John Burnett, *A Social History of Housing* (London, 1986 edn)
113. Anthony and Pip Burton, *The Green Bag Travellers* (London, 1978)
114. Penelope Byrde, *Nineteenth Century Fashion* (London, 1992)
115. Stephen Calloway (ed.), *Liberty of London* (London, 1992)
116. David Cannadine, *Lords and Landlords: the Aristocracy and the Towns 1774–1967* (Leicester, 1980)

117. David Cannadine, *The Decline and Fall of the British Aristocracy* (New Haven and London, 1990)
118. Raymond Carr, 'Country Sports' in G.E. Mingay (ed.), *The Victorian Countryside*, 2 Vols. (London, 1981)
119. Raymond Carr, *English Fox Hunting. A History* (London, 1976)
120. W.F. Cater (ed.), *Love among the Butterflies* (London, 1980)
121. Stephen Caunce, *Amongst Farm Horses* (Stroud, 1991)
122. Marjorie Caygill, *The Story of the British Museum* (London, 1992 edn)
123. Owen Chadwick, *The Victorian Church*, 2 Vols. (London, 1966)
124. Philip Chasmore, 'Shooting' in William Page (ed.), *Victoria History of the County of Sussex*, Vol. 2 (London, 1907)
125. Kellow Chesney, *The Victorian Underworld* (London, 1970)
126. Charles Chevenix-Trench, *The Poacher and the Squire* (London, 1967)
127. Michael J. Childs, *Labour's Apprentices* (London, 1992)
128. Garth Christian (ed.), *A Victorian Poacher. James Hawker's Journal* (London, 1978 edn)
129. D.C. Coleman, *Courtaulds. An Economic and Social History*, Vol. 1 (Oxford, 1969)
130. Howard Colvin, *Calke Abbey, Derbyshire* (London, 1985)
131. Stephen Constantine, 'Amateur Gardening and Popular Recreation in the 19th and 20th Centuries' in *Journal of Social History*, Vol. 14, No. 3 (Spring, 1981)
132. Cagliardo Coraggioso, *Wandering Minstrel* (London, 1938)
133. Mrs George Cornwallis-West, *The Reminiscences of Lady Randolph Churchill* (London, 1908)
134. Geoffrey Crossick, *An Artisan Elite in Victorian Society* (London, 1978)
135. Hugh Cunningham, 'Jingoism in 1877–78' in *Victorian Studies*, Vol. 14, No. 4 (June 1971)
136. Hugh Cunningham, 'Leisure and Culture' in F.M.L. Thompson (ed.), *The Cambridge Social History of Britain 1750–1950*, Vol. 2 (Cambridge, 1990)
137. Hugh Cunningham, *Leisure in the Industrial Revolution* c. *1780–c. 1880* (London, 1980)
138. Hugh Cunningham, 'The language of patriotism' in Raphael Samuel (ed.), *Patriotism: The Making and Unmaking of British National Identity*, Vol. I (London and New York, 1989)
139. Hugh Cunningham, 'The Metropolitan Fairs: A Case Study in the Social Control of Leisure' in A.P. Donajgrodski (ed.), *Social Control in Nineteenth Century Britain* (London, 1977)
140. Hugh Cunningham, *The Volunteer Force* (London, 1975)
141. C. Willett Cunnington, *English Women's Clothing in the Nineteenth Century* (London, 1937)
142. C. Willett and Phillis Cunnington, *The History of Underclothes* (New York, 1992 edn)
143. Phillis Cunnington and Alan Mansfield, *English Costume for Sports and Outdoor Recreations from the Sixteenth to the Nineteenth Centuries* (London, 1969)
144. James Stevens Curl, *Victorian Churches* (London, 1995)
145. Leonore Davidoff, *The Best Circles* (London, 1986 edn)
146. Leonore Davidoff, 'The family in Britain' in F.M.L. Thompson (ed.), *The Cambridge Social History of Britain 1750–1950*, Vol. 2 (Cambridge, 1990)
147. C. Stella Davies, *North Country Bred* (London, 1963)
148. Russell Davies, *Secret Sins. Sex, Violence and Society in Carmarthenshire 1870–1920* (Cardiff, 1996)
149. Dorothy Davis, *A History of Shopping* (London, 1966)
150. Alan Delgado, *The Annual Outing and other Excursions* (London, 1977)
151. Alan Delgado, *Victorian Entertainment* (Newton Abbot, 1972)
152. Roger Dixon and Stefan Muthesius, *Victorian Architecture* (London, 1995 edn)
153. Brian Dobbs, *Edwardians at Play. Sport 1890–1914* (London, 1973)
154. J.P.D. Dunbabin, *Rural Discontent in Nineteenth Century Britain* (London, 1974)
155. Cyril Ehrlich, *The Music Profession in Britain since the Eighteenth Century* (Oxford, 1985)
156. Cyril Ehrlich, *The Piano. A History* (London, 1976)
157. R.C.K. Ensor, *England 1870–1914* (London, 1964 edn)
158. Hilary and Mary Evans, *The Party That Lasted 100 Days* (London, 1976)
159. Alice Fairfax-Lucy (ed.), *Mistress of Charlecote. The Memoirs of Mary Elizabeth Lucy* (London, 1990 edn)
160. Elizabeth, Countess of Fingall, *Seventy Years Young. Memories told to Pamela Hinkson* (London, 1937)

161. Alice Foley, *A Bolton Childhood* (Manchester, 1973)
162. Burton B. Fredericksen, *Alma Tadema's Spring* (Malibu, California, 1978)
163. Margaret Fuller, *West Country Friendly Societies* (Reading, 1964)
164. Philip Gaskell, *Morvern Transformed. A Highland Parish in the Nineteenth Century* (Cambridge, 1968)
165. S. Martin Gaskell, 'Gardens for the Working Class: Victorian Practical Pleasure' in *Victorian Studies*, Vol. 23, No. 4 (Summer 1980)
166. William Gaunt, *English Painting* (London, 1991 edn)
167. Alison Gernsheim, *Fashion and Reality* (London, 1963)
168. Mark Girouard, *The Victorian Country House* (New Haven and London, 1979)
169. J.M. Golby and A.W. Purdue, *The Civilisation of the Crowd* (London, 1984)
170. P.H.J.H. Gosden, *The Friendly Societies in England 1815–1875* (Manchester, 1961)
171. R.Q. Gray, 'Styles of Life, the "Labour Aristocracy" and Class Relations in Later Nineteenth Century Edinburgh' in *International Review of Social History*, Vol. 18, Pt. 3 (1973)
172. Robert Q. Gray, *The Labour Aristocracy in Victorian Edinburgh* (Oxford, 1976)
173. Guinevere L. Griest, *Mudie's Circulating Library and the Victorian Novel* (Newton Abbot, 1970)
174. Lilias Rider Haggard, *I Walked by Night. Being the Life and History of the King of the Norfolk Poachers* (Ipswich, 1976 edn)
175. Eric Halladay, 'Of Pride and Prejudice: The Amateur Question in English Nineteenth Century Rowing' in *International Journal of the History of Sport*, Vol. 4, No. 1 (May 1987)
176. Elizabeth Hammerton and David Cannadine, 'Conflict and Consensus on a Ceremonial Occasion: The Diamond Jubilee in Cambridge in 1897' in *Historical Journal*, Vol. 24, No. 1 (1981)
177. Peter Hansen, 'Albert Smith, the Alpine Club, and the Invention of Mountaineering in Mid-Victorian Britain' in *Journal of British Studies*, Vol. 34, No. 3 (July 1995)
178. Brian Harrison and Barrie Trinder, *Drink and Society in an Early Victorian Country Town: Banbury 1830–1860*, English Historical Review Supplement 4 (London, 1969)
179. Brian Harrison, *Drink and the Victorians* (Keele, 1994 edn)
180. Brian Harrison, 'Religion and Recreation in Nineteenth-Century England' in *Past and Present*, No. 38 (December 1967)
181. James Haug, *Leisure and Urbanism in Nineteenth-Century Nice* (Lawrence, Kansas, 1982)
182. George Haw, *From Workhouse to Westminster. The Life Story of Will Crooks, MP* (London, 1911)
183. Erna Olafson Hellerstein, Leslie Parker Hume and Karen M. Offen (eds), *Victorian Women* (Brighton, 1981)
184. Christopher Hibbert, *The Grand Tour* (London, 1969)
185. Andrew Hignell, *A 'Favourit' Game. Cricket in South Wales before 1914* (Cardiff, 1992)
186. Timothy Hilton, *The Pre-Raphaelites* (London, 1985 edn)
187. P.C. Hoffman, *They Also Serve* (London, 1949)
188. Ethel M. Hogg, *Quintin Hogg. A Biography*, 2nd edn. (London, 1904)
189. Thea Holme, *The Carlyles at Home* (London, 1965)
190. Edgar Holt, *The Boer War* (London, 1958)
191. Richard Holt, *Sport and the British. A Modern History* (Oxford, 1990 edn)
192. Eric Hopkins, *Childhood Transformed* (Manchester, 1994)
193. Harry Hopkins, *The Long Affray* (London, 1985)
194. Pamela Horn, *High Society* (Stroud, 1992)
195. Pamela Horn, *Ladies of the Manor* (Stroud, 1997 edn)
196. Pamela Horn, *Labouring Life in the Victorian Countryside* (Stroud, 1995 edn)
197. Pamela Horn, *The Changing Countryside* (London, 1984)
198. Pamela Horn, *The Victorian Town Child* (Stroud, 1997)
199. Pamela Horn, *Women in the 1920s* (Stroud, 1995)
200. Patrick Howarth, *When the Riviera was Ours* (London, 1977)
201. George Howat, *Village Cricket* (Newton Abbot, 1975)
202. Alun Howkins, 'Dare to be a Daniel' in Raphael Samuel (ed.), *Patriotism, The Making and Unmaking of British National Identity*, Vol. II (London and New York, 1989)

203. Kenneth Hudson, *Patriotism with Profit* (London, 1972)
204. M. Huggins, ' "Mingled Pleasures and Speculation": The Survival of Enclosed Racecourses in Teesside, 1855–1902' in *British Journal of Sports History*, Vol. 3, No. 2 (September 1986)
205. Gervas Huxley, *Victorian Duke* (London, 1967)
206. K.S. Inglis, *Churches and the Working Classes in Victorian England* (London, 1963)
207. K.S. Inglis, 'Patterns of Religious Worship in 1851' in *Journal of Ecclesiastical History*, Vol. 11 (1960)
208. David C. Itkowitz, 'Victorian Bookmakers and their Customers' in *Victorian Studies*, Vol. 32, No. 1 (Autumn 1988)
209. Russell Jackson and Ian Small (eds), *Two Society Comedies* by Oscar Wilde (London, 1983 edn)
210. Russell Jackson, *Victorian Theatre* (London, 1989)
211. Gertrude Jekyll, *A Gardener's Testament*, ed. Francis Jekyll and G.C. Taylor (London, 1937)
212. David Jenkins, *The Agricultural Community in South-West Wales at the Turn of the Twentieth Century* (Cardiff, 1971)
213. Derek E. Johnson, *Victorian Shooting Days* (Woodbridge, Suffolk, 1981)
214. Nicola Johnson, 'Penny plain, tuppence coloured' in Raphael Samuel (ed.), *Patriotism: The Making and Unmaking of British National Identity*, Vol. III (London and New York, 1989)
215. David Jones, 'The Second Rebecca Riots: A Study of Poaching on the Upper Wye' in *Llafur*, Vol. 2, No. 1 (1976)
216. D.J.V. Jones, 'The Poacher: A Study in Victorian Crime and Protest' in *Historical Journal*, Vol. 22, No. 4 (1979)
217. Gareth Stedman Jones, 'Working-Class Culture and Working-Class Politics in London, 1870–1900; Notes on the Remaking of a Working Class' in *Journal of Social History*, Vol. 7 (Summer 1974)
218. Jack Jones, 'The Not so Good Old Days' in Noel Streatfeild (ed.), *The Day before Yesterday* (London, 1956)
219. Jon de Jonge, *A Tale of Three Piers* (Preston, 1993)
220. Mark Judd, ' "The oddest combination of town and country": popular culture and the London fairs, 1800–60' in John K. Walton and James Walvin (eds), *Leisure in Britain 1780–1939* (Manchester, 1983)
221. Sharman Kadish, *'A Good Jew and a Good Englishman'. The Jewish Lads' Brigade 1895–1995* (London, 1995)
222. Thomas Kelly, *Books for the People* (London, 1977)
223. Thomas Kelly, *A History of Adult Education in Great Britain* (Liverpool, 1962)
224. Thomas Kelly, *A History of Public Libraries in Great Britain* (London, 1977)
225. Fred Kitchen, *Brother to the Ox* (London, 1963 edn)
226. Richard S. Lambert, *The Universal Provider* (London, 1938)
227. Avril Lansdell, *Fashion à la Carte 1860–1900* (Princes Risborough, 1992 edn)
228. Thomas Walter Laqueur, *Religion and Respectability* (New Haven and London, 1976)
229. Anita Leslie, *Jennie. The Mother of Winston Churchill* (Maidstone, 1992 edn)
230. June Lewis (ed.), *The Secret Diary of Sarah Thomas 1860–1865* (Moreton-in-Marsh, 1994)
231. James Littlejohn, *Westrigg. The Sociology of a Cheviot Parish* (London, 1963)
232. Roger Longrigg, *The History of Foxhunting* (London, 1975)
233. William Lovett, *Life and Struggles* (London, 1967 Fitzroy edn)
234. John Lowerson and John Myerscough, *Time to Spare in Victorian England* (Hassocks, 1977)
235. J. Ramsay Macdonald, *Margaret Ethel Macdonald*, 6th edn. (London, 1929)
236. Dianne Sachko Macleod, *Art and the Victorian Middle Class* (Cambridge, 1996)
237. Philip Magnus, *King Edward the Seventh* (London, 1964)
238. Sara Maitland, *Vesta Tilley* (London, 1986)
239. H.L. Malchow, 'Public Gardens and Social Action in Late Victorian London' in *Victorian Studies*, Vol. 29, No. 1 (Autumn 1985)
240. Robert W. Malcolmson, *Popular Recreations in English Society 1700–1850* (Cambridge, 1973)
241. Sybil Marshall, *Fenland Chronicle* (Cambridge, 1980 edn)
242. Tony Mason, 'Football, Sport of the North?' in Jeff Hill and Jack Williams (eds), *Sport and Identity in the North of England* (Keele, 1996)

243. F.B. May, 'Victorian and Edwardian Ilfracombe' in John K. Walton and James Walvin (eds), *Leisure in Britain 1780–1939* (Manchester, 1983)
244. Ross McKibbin, 'Working-class Gambling in Britain 1880–1939' in *Past and Present*, No. 82 (February 1979)
245. H.E. Meller, *Leisure and the Changing City, 1870–1914* (London, 1976)
246. Alan Metcalfe, 'Football in the Mining Communities of East Northumberland, 1882–1914' in *International Journal of the History of Sport*, Vol. 5, No. 3 (December 1988)
247. Alan Metcalfe, 'Organized Sport in the Mining Communities of South Northumberland 1800–1889' in *Victorian Studies*, Vol. 25, No. 4 (Summer 1982)
248. Keith Middlemas, *The Life and Times of Edward VII* (London, 1993 edn)
249. H.F. Moorhouse, 'Scotland v. England: Football and Popular Culture' in *International Journal of the History of Sport*, Vol. 4, No. 2 (September 1987)
250. Joan Morgan and Alison Edwards, *A Paradise out of a Common Field* (New York, 1990 edn)
251. Stanley Morison, *The English Newspaper* (Cambridge, 1932)
252. R.J. Morris, 'Leeds and the Crystal Palace. A provincial-metropolitan link bringing education to industrial society' in *Victorian Studies*, Vol. 13, No. 3 (March 1970)
253. Lyn Murfin, *Popular Leisure in the Lake Counties* (Manchester, 1990)
254. Kenneth Neale (ed.), *Victorian Horsham. The Diary of Henry Michell 1809–1874* (Chichester, 1975)
255. David Neave, *Mutual Aid in the Victorian Countryside 1830–1914* (Hull, 1991)
256. Stana Nenadic, 'The Social Shaping of Business Behaviour in the Nineteenth-Century Women's Garment Trades' in *Journal of Social History*, Vol. 31, No. 3 (Spring 1998)
257. Shirley Nicholson, *A Victorian Household* (Stroud, 1994 edn)
258. James Obelkevich, 'Religion' in F.M.L. Thompson (ed.), *The Cambridge Social History of Britain 1750–1950*, Vol. 3 (Cambridge, 1990)
259. James Obelkevich, *Religion and Rural Society: South Lindsey 1825–1875* (Oxford, 1976)
260. Susan Oldacre, *The Blacksmith's Daughter* (Gloucester, 1985)
261. Trefor M. Owen, *Customs and Traditions of Wales* (Cardiff, 1991)
262. Thomas Pakenham, *The Boer War* (London, 1982 edn)
263. H. Pasdermadjian, *The Department Store* (London, 1954)
264. Sir John Paskin, 'Foxhunting' in Elizabeth Crittall (ed.), *Victoria History of the County of Wiltshire*, Vol. 4 (London, 1959)
265. Mrs C.S. Peel, 'Homes and Habits' in G.M. Young (ed.), *Early Victorian England*, Vol. 1 (London, 1934)
266. D.W. Peel, *A Garden in the Sky. The Story of Barkers of Kensington, 1870–1957* (London, 1960)
267. Terence Pepper, *High Society. Photographs 1897–1914* (London, 1998)
268. Harold Perkin, *The Rise of Professional Society* (London, 1989)
269. Harold J. Perkin, 'The "Social Tone" of Victorian Seaside Resorts in the North-West' in *Northern History*, Vol. II (1976 for 1975)
270. E. Benson Perkins, *Gambling in English Life* (London, 1950)
271. E. Royston Pike, *Human Documents of the Age of the Forsytes* (London, 1969)
272. J.A.R. Pimlott, *The Englishman's Holiday. A Social History* (London, 1947)
273. William Plomer (ed.), *Kilvert's Diary*, 3 Vols. (London, 1977 edn)
274. Robert Poole, *Popular Leisure and the Music Hall in Nineteenth Century Bolton* (Centre for North-West Regional Studies, University of Lancaster, Occasional Papers No. 12, 1982)
275. Arthur Porritt, '18th and 19th Century Clubs and Societies in Halifax' in *Transactions of the Halifax Antiquarian Society* (Halifax, 1964)
276. J.H. Porter, 'The Development of a Provincial Department Store 1870–1939' in *Business History*, Vol. 13, No. 1 (January 1971)
277. Richard N. Price, 'The Working Men's Club Movement and Victorian Social Reform Ideology' in *Victorian Studies*, Vol. 15, No. 2 (December 1971)
278. Tom Prideaux, *Love or Nothing* (New York, 1987 edn)

279. F.K. Prochaska, *Women and Philanthropy in Nineteenth-century England* (Oxford, 1980)
280. Eileen Quelch, *Perfect Darling. The Life and Times of George Cornwallis-West* (London, 1972)
281. P.E. Razzell and R.W. Wainwright (eds), *The Victorian Working Class* (London, 1973)
282. Donald Read, *Edwardian England 1901–15. Society and Politics* (London, 1972)
283. Barry Reay, *Microhistories: demography, society and culture in rural England, 1800–1930* (Cambridge, 1996)
284. Douglas A. Reid, 'The Decline of Saint Monday 1766–1876' in *Past and Present*, No. 71 (May 1976)
285. Douglas A. Reid, 'Interpreting the Festival Calendar: Wakes and Fairs as Carnivals' in Robert D. Storch (ed.), *Popular Culture and Custom in Nineteenth-century England* (London, 1983 edn)
286. Douglas A. Reid, 'Weddings, Weekdays, Work and Leisure in Urban England 1791–1911: The Decline of Saint Monday Revisited' in *Past and Present*, No. 153 (November 1996)
287. R.C. Riley and Philip Eley, *Public Houses and Beerhouses in Nineteenth Century Portsmouth* (Portsmouth Papers, No. 38, 1983)
288. M.J.D. Roberts, 'Morals, Art and the Law: The Passing of the Obscene Publications Act, 1857' in *Victorian Studies*, Vol. 28, No. 4 (Summer 1984)
289. Richard Roberts, 'The Corporation as impresario: the municipal provision of entertainment in Victorian and Edwardian Bournemouth' in John K. Walton and James Walvin (eds), *Leisure in Britain 1780–1939* (Manchester, 1983)
290. Robert Roberts, *The Classic Slum* (Manchester, 1971)
291. Gordon W. Roderick and Michael D. Stephens, *Education and Industry in the Nineteenth Century* (London, 1978)
292. F. Gordon Roe, *The Victorian Child* (London, 1959)
293. Anthea Rose, *The Pre-Raphaelites* (London, 1997 edn)
294. Lionel Rose, *The Erosion of Childhood* (London, 1991)
295. Walter Rose, *Good Neighbours* (London, 1969 edn)
296. George Rowell, *The Victorian Theatre 1792–1914*, 2nd edn. (Cambridge, 1978)
297. B. Seebohm Rowntree, *Poverty. A Study of Town Life*, 2nd edn. (London, 1903)
298. Royal Society of Arts 1997 History Study Group, 'The influence of Empire on Great Britain 1837–1901' in *RSA Journal*, Vol. CLXV (April 1998)
299. David Rubinstein, 'Cycling in the 1890s' in *Victorian Studies*, Vol. 21, No. 1 (1977)
300. David Rubinstein, 'The Buckman Papers: S.S. Buckman, Lady Harberton and Rational Dress' in *Notes and Queries*, Vol. CCXXII (January–February 1977)
301. Jonathan Garnier Ruffer, *The Big Shots* (London, 1984)
302. Dave Russell, 'Popular musical culture and popular politics in the Yorkshire textile districts, 1880–1914' in John K. Walton and James Walvin (eds), *Leisure in Britain 1780–1939* (Manchester, 1983)
303. Dave Russell, *Popular music in England 1840–1914* (Manchester, 1987)
304. John F. Russell and J.H. Elliot, *The Brass Band Movement* (London, 1936)
305. John F. Russell, *The Hallé Concerts.* (Timperley, Cheshire, 1938)
306. 'Lord' George Sanger, *Seventy Years a Showman* (London, 1966 Fitzroy edn)
307. W.S. Scott, *Bygone Pleasures of London* (London, 1948)
308. Laurence Senelick, 'Politics as Entertainment: Victorian Music-Hall Songs' in *Victorian Studies*, Vol. 19, No. 2 (December 1975)
309. Laurence Senelick (ed.), *Tavern Singing in Early Victorian London* (London, 1997)
310. Lillian Lewis Shiman, 'The Band of Hope Movement: Respectable Recreation for Working-class Children' in *Victorian Studies*, Vol. 17, No. 1 (September 1973)
311. Zuzanna Shonfield, 'Miss Marshall and the Cimabue Browns' in *Costume*, No. 13 (1979)
312. Zuzanna Shonfield, *The Precariously Privileged* (Oxford, 1987)
313. Robert Simon (ed.), *Lord Leighton 1830–1896 and Leighton House* (London, 1996)
314. George R. Sims (ed.), *Living London*, 3 Vols. (London, 1902 and 1903)
315. Michael Slater (ed.), *Dickens' Journalism. The Amusements of the People and other Papers* (London, 1997 edn)

316. Ian Small (ed.), *Lady Windermere's Fan* by Oscar Wilde (London, 1980 edn)
317. David Smith and Gareth Williams, *Fields of Praise* (Cardiff, 1980)
318. Joyce Stevens Smith, *Matilda* (Hong Kong, 1988) (In archives of Thos. Cook & Son)
319. Walter Southgate, *That's the Way it Was* (London, 1982)
320. Nancy Spain, *Mrs. Beeton and her Husband* (London, 1948)
321. Walter Shaw Sparrow, *British Sporting Artists from Barlow to Herring* (London, 1965 edn)
322. Lucio Sponza, *Italian Immigrants in Nineteenth-Century Britain* (Leicester, 1988)
323. John Springhall, ' "Corrupting the Young"? Popular Entertainment and "Moral Panics" in Britain and America since 1830' in V. Alan McClelland (ed.), *Children at Risk* (University of Hull: *Aspects of Education*, No. 50, 1994)
324. John Springhall, Brian Fraser and Michael Hoare, *Sure and Stedfast. A History of the Boys Brigade 1883 to 1983* (London and Glasgow, 1983)
325. John Springhall, *Youth, Empire and Society* (London, 1977)
326. Joseph Stamper, *So Long Ago* (London, 1960)
327. Peter Stearns, *Lives of Labour* (New York, 1975)
328. W.B. Stephens, *Adult Education and Society in an Industrial Town: Warrington 1800–1900* (Exeter, 1980)
329. John Stokes, *In the Nineties* (Hemel Hempstead, 1989)
330. Robert D. Storch, 'Introduction: Persistence and Change in Nineteenth-Century Popular Culture' in Robert D. Storch (ed.), *Popular Culture and Custom in Nineteenth-Century England* (London, 1983 edn)
331. Robert D. Storch, ' "Please to Remember the Fifth of November": Conflict, Solidarity and Public Order in Southern England, 1815–1900' in Robert D. Storch (ed.), *Popular Culture and Custom in Nineteenth-Century England* (London, 1983 edn)
332. Robert D. Storch, 'The Policeman as Domestic Missionary: Urban Discipline and Popular Culture in Northern England, 1850–80' in R.J. Morris and Richard Rodger (eds), *The Victorian City* (London, 1993)
333. Robert D. Storch, 'The Problem of Working-class Leisure. Some Roots of Middle-class Moral Reform in the Industrial North: 1825–50' in A.P. Donajgrodski (ed.), *Social Control in Nineteenth Century Britain* (London, 1977)
334. Jean Stovin (ed.), *Journals of a Methodist Farmer 1871–1875* (London, 1982)
335. Roy Strong, *Country Life 1897–1997. The English Arcadia* (London, 1996)
336. Douglas Sutherland, *The Yellow Earl* (London, 1965)
337. Christopher Simon Sykes, *Country House Camera* (London, 1980)
338. Richard Tames, *William Morris. An Illustrated Life* (Princes Risborough, 1996 edn)
339. Judy Taylor, *Beatrix Potter, Artist, Storyteller and Countrywoman* (London, 1996 edn)
340. Melanie Tebbutt, *Women's Talk* (Aldershot, 1995)
341. F.M.L. Thompson, *English Landed Society in the Nineteenth Century* (London, 1963)
342. Flora Thompson, *Lark Rise to Candleford* (London, 1963 edn)
343. Thea Thompson, *Edwardian Childhoods* (London, 1981)
344. S. Minwel Tibbott, 'Liberality and Hospitality. Food as Communication in Wales' in *Folk Life*, Vol. 24 (1985–6)
345. Claire Tomalin, *The Invisible Woman* (London, 1991 edn)
346. Neil Tranter, *Sport, economy and society in Britain 1750–1914* (Cambridge, 1998)
347. John F. Travis, *The Rise of the Devon Seaside Resorts 1750–1900* (Exeter, 1993)
348. Julian Treuherz, *Hard Times. Social realism in Victorian Art* (London, 1992 edn)
349. Julian Treuherz, *Victorian Painting* (London, 1996 edn)
350. Barrie Trinder, *Victorian Banbury*, Banbury Historical Society, Vol. 19 (Chichester, 1982)
351. Louis Turner and John Ash, *The Golden Hordes* (London, 1975)
352. Michael R. Turner (ed.), *Parlour Poetry* (London, 1967)
353. Reginald Underwood, *Hidden Lights* (London, 1937)
354. Mariana Valverde, 'The Love of Finery: Fashion and the Fallen Woman in Nineteenth-Century Social Discourse' in *Victorian Studies*, Vol. 32, No. 2 (Winter 1989)
355. Wray Vamplew, *Pay up and play the game* (Cambridge, 1988)
356. Wray Vamplew, *The Turf* (London, 1976)

357. David Verey (ed.), *The Diary of a Victorian Squire* (Gloucester, 1989)
358. Richard Greville Verney, Lord Willoughby de Broke, *The Passing Years* (London, 1924)
359. David Vincent, *Bread, Knowledge and Freedom* (London, 1982 edn)
360. F. Alan Walbank, *Queens of the Circulating Library* (London, 1950)
361. Richard Walker, *Savile Row. An Illustrated History* (New York, 1989 edn)
362. John K. Walton, 'Mad Dogs and Englishmen: The Conflict over Rabies in Late Victorian England' in *Journal of Social History*, Vol. 13, No. 2 (Winter 1979)
363. John K. Walton, *The Blackpool Landlady* (Manchester, 1978)
364. John K. Walton, 'The Demand for Working-Class Seaside Holidays in Victorian England' in *Economic History Review*, 2nd Series, Vol. 34, No. 2 (May 1981)
365. John K. Walton, *The English Seaside Resort* (Leicester, 1983)
366. John K. Walton and Robert Poole, 'The Lancashire Wakes in the Nineteenth Century' in Robert D. Storch (ed.), *Popular Culture and Custom in Nineteenth-Century England* (London, 1983 edn)
367. John K. Walton, *Wonderlands by the Waves* (Preston, 1992)
368. James Walvin, *Beside the Seaside* (London, 1978)
369. James Walvin, *Leisure and Society 1830–1950* (London, 1978)
370. James Walvin, *The People's Game. A Social History of British Football* (London, 1975)
371. Frances, Countess of Warwick, *Afterthoughts* (London, 1931)
372. Frances, Countess of Warwick, *Life's Ebb and Flow* (New York, 1929 edn)
373. Merlin Waterson (ed.), *The Country House Remembered* (London, 1985)
374. Sidney and Beatrice Webb, *Industrial Democracy* (London, 1902 edn)
375. E. Webster, 'Leisure and Pleasure in 19th Century Halifax' in *Transactions of the Halifax Antiquarian Society for 1989* (Halifax, 1990)
376. Heike Wernz-Kaiser et al., *Museum der Stadt Bad Neuenahr-Ahrweiler: Museumsführer* (Bad Neuenahr-Ahrweiler, Germany, 1993)
377. Rebecca West, *1900* (London, 1996 edn)
378. Oliver M. Westall (ed.), *Windermere in the Nineteenth Century* (Centre for North-West Regional Studies, University of Lancaster, Occasional Paper No. 1, 1976)
379. Michael Wheeler, *English Fiction of the Victorian Period* (London, 1994 edn)
380. Cynthia White, *Women's Magazines 1693–1968* (London, 1970)
381. Neil Wigglesworth, *The Evolution of English Sport* (London, 1996)
382. H.D. Willcock (ed.), *Browns and Chester. Portrait of a Shop 1780–1946* by Mass Observation (London, n.d. [1947])
383. Alfred Williams, *Life in a Railway Factory* (London, 1915)
384. Gareth Williams, 'How Amateur was my Valley: Professional Sport and National Identity in Wales 1890–1914' in *British Journal of Sports History*, Vol. 2, No. 3 (December 1985)
385. H. Williams, *A Short History of the Commons, Open Spaces and Footpaths Preservation Society 1865–1965* (London, 1965)
386. Jack Williams, ' "One Could Literally Have Walked on the Heads of the People Congregated There". Sport, The Town and Identity' in Keith Laybourn (ed.), *Social Conditions, Status and Community 1860–1920* (Stroud, 1997)
387. James Wilson (ed.), *The Victoria History of the County of Cumberland*, Vol. 2 (London, 1905)
388. Sophia Wilson, 'Away with the Corsets, on with the Shifts' in *Simply Stunning. The Pre-Raphaelite Art of Dressing* (Cheltenham, 1996)
389. Lynne Withey, *Grand Tours and Cook's Tours. A History of Leisure Travel 1750 to 1915* (London, 1997)
390. Christopher Wood, *Victorian Painting in Oils and Watercolours* (Woodbridge, 1996)
391. J. Hickory Wood, *Dan Leno* (London, 1905)
392. Sir Llewellyn Woodward, *The Age of Reform 1815–1870* (London, 1964 edn)
393. Nigel Yates, *The Anglican Revival in Victorian Portsmouth* (Portsmouth Papers, No. 37, 1983)
394. Stephen Yeo, *Religion and Voluntary Organisations in Crisis* (London, 1976)
395. Philip Ziegler and Desmond Seward (eds), *Brooks's. A Social History* (London, 1991)
396. John E. Zucchi, *The Little Slaves of the Harp. Italian Child Street Musicians in Nineteenth-Century Paris, London, and New York* (Montreal, Canada, 1992)

(e) Novels and Short Stories

397. Charles Dickens, *Our Mutual Friend* (London, 1864–5)
398. Charles Dickens, *Sketches by Boz* (London, 1833–6, published in parts)
399. George Eliot, *Felix Holt. The Radical* (Edinburgh and London, 1901, Warwick edn)
400. George and Weedon Grossmith, *The Diary of a Nobody* (Harmondsworth, 1965 edn)
401. George Moore, *Esther Waters* (London, Everyman edn 1994)
402. R.S. Surtees, *Mr. Sponge's Sporting Tour* (London, 1958 edn)
403. Mrs Henry Wood, *The Master of Greylands* (London, 1898 edn)

(f) Theses

404. Brian A.M. Crozier, *Notions of Childhood in London Theatre, 1880–1905* (University of Cambridge PhD thesis, 1981)
405. M.R. Oakley, *The Holiday Industry of Dorset and Somerset* (University of Oxford, BLitt thesis, 1964)
406. M. Brooke Smith, *The Growth and Development of Popular Entertainment and Pastimes in the Lancashire Cotton Towns 1830–1870* (University of Lancaster, MLitt thesis, 1970)

Index